PATRIOT-IMPROVERS

BIOGRAPHICAL SKETCHES OF MEMBERS OF
THE AMERICAN PHILOSOPHICAL SOCIETY

VOLUME ONE ❧ 1743–1768

PATRIOT-IMPROVERS

BIOGRAPHICAL SKETCHES OF MEMBERS OF THE AMERICAN PHILOSOPHICAL SOCIETY

VOLUME ONE ❧ 1743–1768

WHITFIELD J. BELL, JR.

AMERICAN PHILOSOPHICAL SOCIETY
Philadelphia 1997

Memoirs of the American Philosophical Society
Held at Philadelphia
For Promoting Useful Knowledge
Volume 226

Copyright © 1997 by the American Philosophical Society for its *Memoirs* series, volume 226. First of three volumes. All rights reserved. Publication of this volume has been made possible in part through the generosity of the McLean Contributionship. DESIGN: Adrianne Onderdonk Dudden

ISBN: 0-87169-226-0
US ISSN: 0065-9738

Library of Congress Cataloging-in-Publication Data

Bell, Whitfield J., Jr. (Whitfield Jenks)
    Patriot-improvers : biographical sketches of members of the American Philosophical Society / Whitfield J. Bell, Jr.
        p.   cm. — (Memoirs of the American Philosophical Society Held at Philadelphia for Promoting Useful Knowledge, ISSN 0065-9738 ; v. 226)
    Includes index.
    Contents: v. 1. 1743–1768.
    ISBN 0-87169-226-0 (v. 1. : cloth)
    1. American Philosophical Society—Biography.   2. United States—Intellectual life—18th century.   I. Title.   II. Series: Memoirs of the American Philosophical Society ; v. 226.
Q11.P612   vol. 226
[AS36.P52]
191—dc21
[B]   97-44313
                                                                                                            CIP

To the memory of
RICHARD HARRISON SHRYOCK
Historian of Science and Medicine
Librarian, American Philosophical Society, 1959–1965

CONTENTS

Portrait List ix
Preface xiii
Acknowledgments xviii
Short Titles and Abbreviations xx
Alphabetical List of Members, 1743–1768 530

AMERICAN PHILOSOPHICAL SOCIETY
1743–1746

HISTORY OF THE SOCIETY 3
SKETCHES OF MEMBERS 9

Thomas Hopkinson 10
William Coleman 15
Benjamin Franklin 19
Thomas Bond 37
John Bartram 48
Thomas Godfrey 62
Samuel Rhoads 67
William Parsons 72
Phineas Bond 79
  1744
James Alexander 86
Robert Hunter Morris 94
Archibald Home 101

John Coxe 103
David Martin 105
Richard Nicholls 107
Cadwallader Colden 110
James DeLancey 120
Daniel Horsmanden 125
Joseph Murray 130
William Smith 134
John Mitchell 138
"Mr. Faries" 148
Francis Alison 149
John Tennent 158
John Clayton 166

"YOUNG JUNTO" 1750–1766

HISTORY OF THE SOCIETY 175
SKETCHES OF MEMBERS 181

  before 22 September 1758
Charles Thomson 183
George Bryan 197
Francis Rawle 203
Stephen Woolley 205
Peter Chevalier 207
Joseph Mather 209

Philip Syng 210
Isaac Paschall 212
Edmund Physick 214
William Franklin 219
Joshua Howell 229
William Hopkins 232
Paul Jackson 233

9 February 1759
George Clymer *236*
Isaac Bartram *247*
James Pearson *251*
7 March 1760
Samuel Powel *257*
2 October 1761
Thomas Wharton *270*
16 October 1761
Daniel Wister *275*
Before 3 September 1762
George Roberts *277*
Before 25 April 1766
Moses Bartram *280*

Isaac Zane *286*
Joseph Paschall *290*
Owen Biddle *292*
19 September 1766
William Bettle *303*
Samuel Eldridge *304*
Benjamin Davis/Davies, "Mercht." *306*
Nicholas Waln *308*
3 October 1766
John Lukens *314*
Clement Biddle *321*
5 December 1766
John Morgan *327*

AMERICAN SOCIETY FOR PROMOTING AND PROPAGATING USEFUL KNOWLEDGE ~ 1766–1768

HISTORY OF THE SOCIETY 339

SKETCHES OF MEMBERS 347

27 March 1767
William Henry *348*
William Johnson *361*
Charles Mason *366*
Samuel Bard *373*
19 January 1768
John Dickinson *383*
Cadwalader Evans *391*
David Evans *396*
Thomas Mifflin *400*
12 February 1768
John Morris, Jr. *411*
19 February 1768
William Bartram *414*
John Chapman *424*
26 February 1768
Isaac Jamineau *427*
Jonathan Odell *429*

Richard Wells *440*
Hugh Mercer *447*
Benjamin Rush *452*
Oswell Eve *465*
Samuel Eliot *468*
4 March 1768
James Alexander "gardiner" *476*
1 April 1768
Samuel Robinson *480*
Stephen Hopkins *481*
Joseph Harrison *488*
Peter Harrison *492*
Charles Bensel *497*
John Sellers *500*
Pierre E. DuSimitiere *504*
Andrew Oliver "of Salem" *514*
Jonathan Belcher *519*
Jeremiah Dixon *525*

PORTRAIT LIST

THOMAS HOPKINSON. By Robert Feke. *National Museum of American Art, Smithsonian Institution. George Buchanan Coale Collection.* 10

BENJAMIN FRANKLIN. By Robert Feke. *Harvard University Art Museums. Bequest of Dr. John Collins Warren*, 1856. 20

THOMAS BOND. Miniature by an unidentified artist. *Mütter Museum, College of Physicians of Philadelphia.* 37

PHINEAS BOND. By Robert Feke. *Philadelphia Museum of Art. Gift of Phyllis Cochran Derby.* 78

JAMES ALEXANDER. By John Wollaston. *Museum of the City of New York.* 86

CADWALLADER COLDEN. Attributed to Matthew Pratt. *New York State Office of Parks, Recreation and Historic Preservation, Schuyler Mansion State Historic Site.* 110

WILLIAM SMITH (1697–1769). By John Wollaston. *Historic Hudson Valley, Tarrytown, N.Y. Gift of J. Dennis Delafield.* 134

CHARLES THOMSON. By Charles Willson Peale. *Independence National Historical Park Collection.* 183

GEORGE BRYAN. By J. Augustus Beck after the unlocated original. *Historical Society of Pennsylvania.* 197

PHILIP SYNG. Silhouette by an unidentified artist. Reproduced from a photograph. *Courtesy of the American Philosophical Society.* 211

EDMUND PHYSICK. By Charles Willson Peale. Reproduced from a phototype by Frederick Gutekunst of the unlocated painting. *Courtesy of the American Philosophical Society.* 214

WILLIAM FRANKLIN. By Mather Brown. *Collection of Mrs. Jackson C. Boswell. Photograph courtesy of Frick Art Reference Library.* ❧ 220

JOSHUA HOWELL. Silhouette by an unidentified artist. *Historical Society of Pennsylvania.* ❧ 229

GEORGE CLYMER. By Charles Willson Peale. *Pennsylvania Academy of the Fine Arts. Gift of the artist.* ❧ 236

SAMUEL POWEL. By Angelica Kauffmann. *Courtesy of the private owner.* ❧ 258

THOMAS WHARTON. By Charles Willson Peale. *Philadelphia Museum of Art. Given in memory of Marianna Lippincott O'Neill by her children.* ❧ 270

ISAAC ZANE. By Joseph Sansom. *Historical Society of Pennsylvania.* ❧ 286

NICHOLAS WALN. By an unidentified artist. *Friends Historical Library, Swarthmore College.* ❧ 308

CLEMENT BIDDLE. By Charles Willson Peale. *Courtesy of the owner, a descendant.* Photograph by Carol Aiken. ❧ 321

JOHN MORGAN. By Angelica Kauffmann. *National Portrait Gallery, Smithsonian Institution.* ❧ 328

WILLIAM HENRY. By Benjamin West. *Historical Society of Pennsylvania.* ❧ 348

SAMUEL BARD. By James Sharpless. *Museum of the City of New York.* ❧ 374

JOHN DICKINSON. By Charles Willson Peale. *Historical Society of Pennsylvania.* ❧ 384

THOMAS MIFFLIN. By Charles Willson Peale. *Independence National Historical Park Collection.* ❧ 401

WILLIAM BARTRAM. By Charles Willson Peale. *Independence National Historical Park Collection.* ❧ 414

HUGH MERCER. By John Trumbull. *Fordham University Library, Charles A. Munn Collection.* Photograph courtesy of Frick Art Reference Library. ❧ 448

BENJAMIN RUSH. By Charles Willson Peale. *Henry Francis du Pont Winterthur Museum. Gift of Mrs. Julia B. Henry.* 453

SAMUEL ELIOT. By Jane Stuart after Gilbert Stuart. *Harvard University Art Museums.* 470

PETER HARRISON. By Louis Sands after Nathaniel Smibert. *Redwood Library and Athenaeum, Newport, R.I.* 492

ANDREW OLIVER. By John Singleton Copley. *National Portrait Gallery, Smithsonian Institution.* 514

JONATHAN BELCHER. By John Singleton Copley. *Beaverbrook Art Gallery, Fredericton, New Brunswick, Canada. Gift of the Canadian International Paper Company.* 520

❧ PREFACE

THIS IS THE FIRST of several volumes of biographical sketches of members of the American Philosophical Society elected between 1743, when Franklin proposed it, and 1769, when it was established on its present foundation by the union of several earlier institutions. It is the first such collection of biographies and, indeed, the only systematic attempt to collect and preserve data on the lives of the members. During most of its history the Society kept no biographical records. Occasionally in the nineteenth century biographical memoirs were printed in the *Proceedings*, and one or two attempts were made to issue a volume of memoirs like the *Biographical Memoirs* of the National Academy of Sciences. Since 1937, however, obituary notices (when potential authors responded to requests for them) have been printed in the Society's *Year Book*; since 1991 they have appeared in the *Proceedings*.

Obviously no biographical dictionary is needed for Franklin, Rittenhouse, John Dickinson, and some ten or a dozen other great and famous characters whom most persons have in mind when they think of the eighteenth-century Society. But the great majority of the early members were not men of Franklin's caliber and reputation. They were merchants, shopkeepers, mechanics, artisans, and small farmers, with a leaven of physicians, lawyers, and clergymen—persons like Isaac Bartram, Clement and Owen Biddle, Benjamin Davis (or Davies), Joseph Paschall, and James Pearson, about whom little if anything has been written and published. Yet these lesser-known persons are the ones who attended meetings, paid their dues, served on committees, and promoted the Society's objects in many ways over many years. It seems that before historians describe the Society confidently, as they often do, as dignified, venerable, august, eminent, or elitist, they should understand, as Brooke Hindle does in *The Pursuit of Science in Revolutionary America*, just who the philosophers were and how often—or even whether—they showed any interest in the Society's activities. That is a reason why this work was begun. To the degree that these sketches are more than a contribution to an institution's history they may also add something to the general history of eighteenth-century America.

❧ PATRIOT-IMPROVERS. Readers of these biographies will appreciate the appropriateness of this general title for members of Franklin's American Philosophical Society. Almost without exception they were men who, in addition to their private concerns and ambitions, made disinterested exertions for the prosperity of their country and the well-being of their fellow-citizens. "A patriot," Bishop Berkeley wrote in 1750, "is one who heartily wisheth the public prosperity, and doth . . . also study and endeavour to promote it." Such men undertook to improve trade, navigation, and commerce by better roads, canals, bridges, and sailing vessels; they introduced new methods of agriculture and new crops, like silk and mangel wurzel; they designed better tools and machines; they built schools, colleges, and hospitals; they reformed the laws and attempted to rationalize morals and social customs.

Not every effort succeeded then or later, but each was made in the confidence that it would improve the lot of America and Americans. Long before the term acquired its narrower political connotation, patriots were understood to be lovers of their country in the best and broadest sense; and those who made improvements, whether in plows, pumps, or barnyards, were applauded for their patriotic services. Patriots were improvers, and improvers were their country's patriots.

The identity or at least interchangeability of the terms, implicit in the purposes and labors of eighteenth-century societies of arts, was explicit in the name of one such European society (of which Franklin was elected a corresponding member in 1786)—Societa Patriotica di Milano diretta all' Avanzamento dell' Agricolture, delle Arti, e delle Manifatture. Its members were encouraged to investigate every kind of subject; they were rewarded for their improvements in stoves and furnaces, the quality of potatoes and olives, the construction of apiaries and of a machine for making pasta. Americans had the same ideas. In *The Picture of Philadelphia* (Philadelphia, 1811) Dr. James Mease listed the Agricultural Society, the Cattle Society (both of which held their meetings in Philosophical Hall), and the Domestic Society "for the encouragement of domestic manufactures," under the heading "Patriotic Societies." ("Every city and populous town," Mease advised, "should establish a similar society, as it is only in this way, that the permanent, the real independence of the country, can be established. . . .") The philosophers of Philadelphia and Lombardy were alike improvers and patriots.

Research for this dictionary had not been long under way when it was realized that the Society and its secretaries did not always make and keep full and accurate records. Thus several persons in the eighteenth century were actually elected twice, while "Professor Famitz" of Naples, whom the minutes and publications of the Society record as a member, has defied all efforts to identify him. Nor can the biographer be certain that the members always knew whom they were voting for, as is illustrated by the case of Andrew Oliver, lieutenant governor of Massachusetts, and his son Andrew Oliver, Jr., a scientist and astronomer, who sent the Society copies of several of his publications just before his father (or he?) was elected a member. Add to such questions those posed by insufficient identification—five Philadelphians named David Evans all alive at the time when the Society elected one of them; "Dr. Brooke of Maryland," whom the members knew but who required a year's research to identify; Benjamin Davis or Davies, whose name appears both ways in the Society's records.

In addition to identifying members of the Society accurately, this biographical dictionary should provide a balanced view of the membership. As members of the Society, Sir William Johnson, General Thomas Gage, and Governor James Hamilton of Pennsylvania might be thought to have been recognized for "philosophical" interests and to have conferred prestige upon it. But Johnson and Gage never attended a meeting and Hamilton did not come again after he was defeated in the first election for president. On the other hand, the schoolmaster William Johnson took a lively interest in the Society, and his widow gave his books and instruments to its library and cabinet. Similarly, a biographer or historian might claim that William Bartram found congenial company among the philosophers; but Bartram never attended a single meeting in the more than forty-five years he was a member.

Such facts as these justify different standards of treatment. For the great and famous, especially those with long and distinguished public careers, it is not necessary or desirable to give even a reasonably adequate account. Full and authoritative biographies of such persons are widely available, and more appear each year. But for the minor figures a sketch as reasonably full as could be written—sometimes only two or three pages—is presented. Thus Franklin and Lewis Nicola here receive about the same amount of space, and the schoolmaster Johnson has more pages than Britain's proconsul to the Iroquois. (This wise principle, it must be admitted, has not always been observed.)

MEMBERSHIP. The by-laws of the several societies that ultimately formed the present American Philosophical Society specified the terms and conditions of election. No requirements were spelled out, and at most the minutes note only a candidate's profession or institutional connection, if he had one. In general, persons were proposed at one meeting and elected at the next. Sometimes, in cases of persons of prominence, a committee was appointed to report the Society's action to the newly elected member and to request his assent. Not every committee performed its duty, and in consequence readers of the Society's minutes remain uncertain whether the election was accepted. This uncertainty is increased where minutes that might have recorded the committee's report were lost or never recorded.

The minutes do not record why any person was nominated and elected, and in only a handful of instances does a letter or some other reference offer a reason. In most cases this can be inferred; but in others the biographer can only surmise. Obviously, genuine achievement and interest in "philosophy" might lead to election; thus Professor John Winthrop of Harvard College and the Reverend Mr. Ebenezer Kinnersley, Franklin's associate in electrical experiments, were early members. Public position was a likely reason for election, especially in the societies' early years, when they were aggressively seeking rank and prestige. Thus the governor and other officers of the Pennsylvania Proprietary government were elected, although, as the event proved, they contributed little but their names, and soon stopped attending. Many members were wealthy, but wealth alone gave no assurance of nomination and election. Having said all this, it should be added that in the eighteenth century, as in the twentieth, personal associations and friendships were understandably sometimes the reason a particular name was put forward. Membership in the American Philosophical Society, like an honorary degree or a seat on the board of a college, museum, or orchestra, offered a respectable distinction and was only rarely declined. Robert Morris was one of the rare few, explaining simply and honestly that his interests and achievements did not warrant election. Too much significance, therefore, should not be attached in every case to the mere fact of election and membership.

Those members who were most frequent in attendance and most interested in the Society's work were not the great and famous figures whom twentieth-century historians and publicists usually have in mind when they speak of it. The most regular attendants at meetings of the American Society in 1767, members present at more than half the meetings that year, were Isaac Bartram, Clement Biddle, Owen Biddle, Benjamin Davis, David Evans, Lewis Nicola, Joseph Paschall, James Pearson, Edmund Physick, Charles Thomson, and Nicholas Waln. Of these only Thomson, later secretary of Congress throughout the period of the Revolution and Confederation, is likely to be known to any but genealogists and local historians.

SOURCES. The principal sources of information for each sketch are indicated in the footnotes, with two exceptions. Citations to the societies' minutes, which are usually self-evident, are not given. (*Early Proceedings of the American Philosophical Society, 1769–1837*, American Philosophical Society, *Proceedings*, XXII, pt. 3 [1884] is a useful, though not complete, abstract of the minutes.) Information of another sort is taken from such obvious records as the *Memoirs* of the Philadelphia Society for Promoting Agriculture and Robert B. Beath's *Historical Catalogue of the St. Andrew's Society*, from lists of contributors like those in Morton and Woodbury's *History of the Pennsylvania Hospital* and the *Collection Books of Provost Smith*; and from lists of subscribers to publications like William Cullen's *First Lines in the Practice of Physick* (such lists, incidentally, being a potential source of information about readers, "the book," and personal libraries). Research for these volumes was done over a long period of time; some sketches were prepared some years ago, and the bibliographical references do not always include the latest publications.

🕭 ORGANIZATION. The sketches are arranged chronologically by date of election. Where two or more men were elected at the same meeting, their names appear as they are listed in the manuscript minutes. This probably indicates nothing but the order in which their sponsors attracted the secretary's attention, but it is kept here because there seems to be no good reason to alter it (and because someone may some day discover significance in it).

🕭 INDEXES. Although these volumes, for practical financial reasons, are issued separately at different times, they should be regarded as a single work. Because there is no easy way to locate even roughly a particular sketch in the chronological arrangement adopted here, an alphabetical list, with page references, is included in this volume; and in each subsequent volume all the sketches in that and the volumes preceding it will be listed in alphabetical order. Thus a reader can open any volume and quickly learn where to find the sketch he or she requires.

A cumulative name and subject index will be printed in the last volume of the work. Reflections and observations on the entire membership may also be included in the final volume.

ACKNOWLEDGMENTS

FEW WORKS OF SCHOLARSHIP can be undertaken or completed without the assistance, cooperation, and even guidance of other scholars and knowledgeable persons. A biographical dictionary, which contains hundreds of subjects, each with its own various sources of information, owes much of its authority to many kinds of help from many individuals, some of whom may not even know that they contributed to the work.

It is no exaggeration to state that this work might not have been undertaken, and certainly could not have achieved whatever usefulness it may have, without the collections of the American Philosophical Society, the Historical Society of Pennsylvania, and the Genealogical Society of Pennsylvania. The Philosophical Society's manuscript collections and its complete runs of learned society publications were, of course, indispensable; and it is no less true that without the manuscripts and printed books of the Historical and Genealogical Societies many of the early Philadelphia members—little-known and unknown shopkeepers, artisans, and farmers—could not have been identified, much less provided with even the shortest life history. And here I must also express my warmest thanks to particular members of the staffs of those institutions, who have catalogued and indexed the staggering masses of their holdings. In my own time at the Philosophical Society much of this work was done by Murphy D. Smith, for many years its manuscripts librarian, and to his successors, J. Stephen Catlett and Beth Carroll-Horrocks. I remember also the late J. Harcourt Givens and the late Catharine H. Miller at the Historical Society, who first extended their friendly helpfulness to me when I was a graduate student and continued to give and offer assistance into the early researches for these volumes; this acknowledgment to Harry Givens and Miss Miller should be understood to include thanks to all their assistants and successors, notably Linda M. Stanley, who have come and gone in the Manuscripts Department of that institution. Much of the Genealogical Society's collections has been indexed for researchers by devoted and unwearying volunteers from that organization. In this connection, too, I gratefully acknowledge, as every historian of colonial America must, Eugene E. Doll's incomparable *Index* to the *Pennsylvania Magazine of History and Biography*, which unlocks the first 75 volumes (1877–1951) of that journal, so rich in the sorts of information that this biographical dictionary required; without Doll's *Index* the *Pennsylvania Magazine* could not have been used with efficiency or confidence. A similar tribute of thanks is due the anonymous workers of the Work

Projects Administration in the 1930s who indexed the Eighth Series of the *Pennsylvania Archives*.

I also express my thanks to, among others, the librarians and staffs of the Pennsylvania State Archives, Harrisburg; the New York Public Library; the New-York Historical Society; the Massachusetts Historical Society; the Virginia Historical Society; the South Carolina Historical Society; the University of Pennsylvania; the Library Company of Philadelphia; the Royal Society; the British Library; the Public Record Office, London; the National Archives, Washington; and the Library of Congress. The citation of a document in any institution, however small or remote, includes an unspoken expression of thanks to its librarian or other member of its staff who provided me with what I asked for.

Silvio A. Bedini, Joseph Ewan, Charles C. Gillispie, Roy E. Goodman, Brooke Hindle, Randolph S. Klein, John C. Van Horne, and the late Edwin Wolf 2d read some of these biographical sketches in draft form, and made helpful suggestions. As head of the reading room and reference librarian of the American Philosophical Society, Mr. Goodman, as I have had reason almost every day to know, can find in the Society's collections—or elsewhere—anything a researcher may need. James E. Mooney read about two-thirds of the sketches, and offered corrections and suggestions, most of which have been gratefully inserted in revised drafts.

During two summers Randolph S. Klein, then a graduate student in history at Brown University, assisted me in research, and wrote several sketches on his own, which were published, and are cited in these volumes.

One of many pleasant accompaniments of the research for this volume was that it brought me into correspondence with descendants of some of the subjects. Their interest was mainly genealogical; by tireless inquiry they had learned much about their ancestors' family history, and this information is just what is so hard to come at. Sometimes we exchanged information—as was the case with Clifford Lewis III of Philadelphia, who had collected a vast stock of data on Lewis Nicola; and with Mrs. Harold E. Hall of Charles Town, West Virginia, who shared with me and the late Elizabeth H. Thomson of New Haven, Connecticut, her considerable knowledge of the elder Thomas Bond. Several persons, who prefer to remain anonymous, graciously allowed family portraits to be reproduced here.

The first—and often second and third—drafts of many of these sketches were flawlessly typed by Mrs. Jean T. Williams; and after technology overtook us, many of these and some other sketches were put into a word-processor by Thomas Hladczuk.

The physical design of this volume is the work of the Society's Editor Carole LeFaivre-Rochester and of Adrianne Onderdonk Dudden. When errors and changes appeared unsought just before type-setting, Ms. LeFaivre-Rochester and Associate Editor Susan M. Babbitt brought the computers to heel with expertise and patience. In the last stages of preparation Mary Alice Hines read much of the text of this volume with care and intelligence.

W. J. B., Jr.

SHORT TITLES AND ABBREVIATIONS

APS: American Philosophical Society.

Butterfield, *Rush Letters*: Lyman H. Butterfield, ed., *Letters of Benjamin Rush* (2 v., Princeton, 1951).

Col. Recs. Pa.: *Colonial Records of Pennsylvania*.

DAB: *Dictionary of American Biography*.

DNB: *Dictionary of National Biography*.

DSB: *Dictionary of Scientific Biography*.

Darlington, *Memorials*: William Darlington, *Memorials of John Bartram and Humphry Marshall* (Phila., 1849).

Franklin, *Autobiography*: Leonard W. Labaree and others, *The Autobiography of Benjamin Franklin* (New Haven, [1964]).

Franklin Mss.: Franklin Manuscript Collection in American Philosophical Society.

Franklin Papers: Leonard W. Labaree and others, eds., *The Papers of Benjamin Franklin* (New Haven, 1959–).

HSP: Historical Society of Pennsylvania.

Hindle, *Pursuit of Science*: Brooke Hindle, *The Pursuit of Science in Revolutionary America, 1735–1789* (Chapel Hill, 1956).

Hinshaw, *Amer. Quaker Genealogy*: William W. Hinshaw, *Encyclopedia of American Quaker Genealogy* (Ann Arbor, Mich., 1936–).

Jour. Cont. Cong.: Worthington C. Ford and others, eds., *Journals of the Continental Congress* (Washington, 1904–37).

Lib. Co. Phila.: Library Company of Philadelphia.

Montgomery, *University of Pennsylvania*: Thomas H. Montgomery, *History of the University of Pennsylvania . . . to 1771* (Phila., 1900).

Morton, *Pennsylvania Hospital*: Thomas H. Morton and Frank Woodbury, *History of the Pennsylvania Hospital* (Phila., 1897).

PMHB: *Pennsylvania Magazine of History and Biography*.

Pa. Arch.: *Pennsylvania Archives*, series 1–9.

Pa. Gaz.: *Pennsylvania Gazette*.

Phil. Trans.: *Philosophical Transactions of the Royal Society*.

Scharf and Westcott, *Philadelphia*: J. Thomas Scharf and Thompson Westcott, *History of Philadelphia, 1609–1884* (Phila., 1884).

Watson, *Annals*: John F. Watson, *Annals of Philadelphia, and Pennsylvania, in the Olden Time* (Phila., 1881).

AMERICAN PHILOSOPHICAL SOCIETY

≥ 1743—1746

HISTORY OF THE SOCIETY

JOHN BARTRAM, farmer, seedsman, and botanical traveller, whose wide correspondence won him an international reputation, seems to have been the first in Philadelphia to propose a society for promoting natural history.[1] The idea may have been planted and grown in his mind after Cadwallader Colden and Benjamin Franklin each told him in the 1730s about the Boston Medical Society.[2] In 1739 Bartram broached his proposal in a letter to Peter Collinson, his London correspondent, who was also the agent of the Library Company of Philadelphia and the patron of several American naturalists. The letter to Collinson survives only in a draft, fragmented, torn, faded, illegible, and undated. In it Bartram suggested that an academy or society of the "most ingenious & Curious men" be established for the study of "naturale secrets[,] arts & scyances," that this society should have "A House for to Meet in to Communicate all [?] discoveries freely," and possibly also that lectures should be given regularly under its auspices.[3] Collinson's response was not encouraging:

> As to the Society that thee Hints att, Had you a Sett of Learned Well Quallified Members to Sett out with it might Draw your Neighbours to Correspond with you. . . . but to Draw Learned Strangers to you, to teach Sciences requires Salaries & good Encouragement and this will require the publick as well as proprietary assistance—which can't be att present complyed with Considering the Infancy of your Colony.

Meanwhile, Collinson suggested, the Library Company was "an Essay towards such a Society."[4]

---

[1] For the origin and early history of APS see Brooke Hindle, *The Pursuit of Science in Revolutionary America, 1735–1789* (Chapel Hill, 1956), 64–74. Many of the pertinent documents are quoted or cited in Peter S. Du Ponceau, *Historical Account of the Origin and Formation of the American Philosophical Society* (Phila., 1914). An appendix by J. Francis Fisher, 1841, argues convincingly against Du Ponceau's opinion that APS was a continuation of Franklin's Junto of 1727.
[2] Bartram Papers, I, 38 (HSP).
[3] Ibid.; Francis D. West, "John Bartram and the American Philosophical Society," *Pa. Hist.*, XXIII (1956), 463–66, was the first to identify this letter as relating to the origins of APS. Dr. West dated the letter 1739; Edmund and Dorothy Berkeley, *The Life and Travels of John Bartram* (Tallahassee, Fla., [1982]), 112, give it the date of 1738.
[4] Collinson to Bartram, 10 July 1739, Bartram Papers, III, 9.

Here the matter rested for several years. Bartram continued to make his botanical excursions and to extend his ties with American and European naturalists. By 1740 he was perhaps the most widely known American man of science. In 1742 his friend Benjamin Franklin undertook to raise a fund to support him in regular botanical expeditions. Although the Proprietor Thomas Penn seems to have been prepared to contribute to the fund, nothing came of this proposal either, partly because in Philadelphia James Logan offered it no support.[5] But in 1743 Franklin and Bartram refined and developed the latter's proposal of a learned society, reducing it to practicable dimensions. Franklin printed a proposal, and he and Bartram circulated it among their friends and to likely correspondents.

A PROPOSAL for Promoting USEFUL KNOWLEDGE among the British Plantations in America.

The English are possess'd of a long Tract of Continent, from Nova Scotia to Georgia, extending North and South thro' different Climates, having different Soils, producing different Plants, Mines and Minerals, and capable of different Improvements, Manufactures, &c.

The first Drudgery of Settling new Colonies, which confines the Attention of People to mere Necessaries, is now pretty well over; and there are many in every Province in Circumstances that set them at Ease, and afford Leisure to cultivate the finer Arts, and improve the common Stock of Knowledge. To such of these who are Men of Speculation, many Hints must from time to time arise, many Observations occur, which if well-examined, pursued and improved, might produce Discoveries to the Advantage of some or all of the British Plantations, or to the Benefit of Mankind in general.

But as from the Extent of the Country such Persons are widely separated, and seldom can see and converse or be acquainted with each other, so that many useful Particulars remain uncommunicated, die with the Discoverers, and are lost to Mankind; it is, to remedy this Inconvenience for the future, proposed.

That One Society be formed of Virtuosi or ingenious Men residing in the several Colonies, to be called *The American Philosophical Society* [,] who are to maintain a constant Correspondence.

That Philadelphia being the City nearest the Centre of the Continent-Colonies, communicating with all of them northward and southward by Post, and with all the Islands by Sea, and having the Advantage of a good growing Library, be the Centre of the Society.

That at Philadelphia there be always at least seven Members, viz. a Physician, a Botanist, a Mathematician, a Chemist, a Mechanician, a Geographer, and a general Natural Philosopher, besides a President, Treasurer and Secretary.

That these Members meet once a Month, or oftner, at their own Expence, to communicate to each other their Observations, Experiments, &c. to receive, read and consider such Letters, Communications, or Queries as shall be sent from distant Mem-

---

[5] Bartram to Collinson, 11 June 1743, Darlington, *Memorials*, 164.

bers; to direct the Dispersing of Copies of such Communications as are valuable, to other distant Members, in order to procure their Sentiments thereupon, &c.

That the Subjects of the Correspondence be, All new-discovered Plants, Herbs, Trees, Roots, &c. their Virtues, Uses, &c.; Methods of Propagating them, and making such as are useful, but particular to some Plantations, more general. Improvements of vegetable Juices, as Cyders, Wines, &c.; New Methods of Curing or Preventing Diseases; All new-discovered Fossils in different Countries, as Mines, Minerals, Quarries, &c. New and useful Improvements in any Branch of Mathematicks; New Discoveries in Chemistry, such as Improvements in Distillation, Brewing, Assaying of Ores, &c. New Mechanical Inventions for saving Labour; as Mills, Carriages, &c. and for Raising and Conveying of Water, Draining of Meadows, &c.; All new Arts, Trades, Manufactures, &c. that may be proposed or thought of. Surveys, Maps and Charts of particular Parts of the Sea-coasts, or Inland Countries; Course and Junction of Rivers and great Roads, Situation of Lakes and Mountains, Nature of the Soil and Productions; &c. New Methods of Improving the Breed of useful Animals; Introducing other Sorts from Foreign Countries. New Improvements in Planting, Gardening, Clearing Land, &c.; And all philosophical Experiments that let Light into the Nature of Things, tend to increase the Power of Man over Matter, and multiply the Conveniencies or Pleasures of Life.

That a Correspondence already begun by some intended Members, shall be kept up by the Society with the Royal Society of London, and with the Dublin Society.

That every Member shall have Abstracts sent him Quarterly, of every Thing valuable communicated to the Society's Secretary at Philadelphia; free of all Charge except the Yearly Payment hereafter mentioned.

That, by Permission of the Postmaster-General, such Communications pass between the Secretary of the Society and the Members, Postage-free.

That, for defraying the Expence of such Experiments as the Society shall judge proper to cause to be made, and other contingent Charges for the common Good, every Member send a Piece of Eight *per Annum* to the Treasurer, at Philadelphia, to form a Common Stock, to be disburs'd by Order of the President with the Consent of the Majority of the Members that can conveniently be consulted thereupon, to such Persons and Places where and by whom the Experiments are to be made, and otherwise as there shall be Occasion; of which Disbursements an exact Account shall be kept, and communicated yearly to every Member.

That at the first Meetings of the Members at Philadelphia, such Rules be formed for Regulating their Meetings and Transactions for the General Benefit, as shall be convenient and necessary; to be afterwards changed and improv'd as there shall be Occasion, wherein due Regard is to be had to the Advice of distant Members.

That at the End of every Year, Collections be made and printed, of such Experiments, Discoveries, Improvements, &c. as may be thought of public Advantage: And that every Member have a Copy sent him.

That the Business and Duty of the Secretary be, To receive all Letters intended for the Society, and lay them before the President and Members at their Meetings; to abstract, correct and methodize such Papers, &c. as require it, and as he shall be directed to do by the President, after they have been considered, debated, and digested in the Society; to enter Copies thereof in the Society's Books, and make out Copies for distant Members; to answer their Letters by Direction of the President, and keep Records of all material Transactions of the Society, &c.

> Benjamin Franklin, the Writer of this Proposal, offers himself to serve the Society as their Secretary, 'till they shall be provided with one more capable.
> Philadelphia, May 14, 1743.[6]

Among those who encouraged the idea from the first was Cadwallader Colden. A native of Scotland who had practiced medicine in Philadelphia before moving to New York and entering upon a political career, Colden was deeply interested in botany and was currently writing an extension of Newton's theories. More than a dozen years before, Colden had suggested to Dr. William Douglass of Boston that "a Voluntary Society for the advancing of Knowledge" should be established with its headquarters in that city; but Douglass had pointed out that Boston in 1728 had too few persons qualified to support such an organization.[7] Colden warmly endorsed Franklin's proposal.

During the winter of 1743–44 Franklin pressed forward with his scheme. Before 27 March an organization was effected, three meetings were held, and the members looked forward to growth. On 5 April Franklin, then in New York, informed Colden of their progress. Nine Philadelphians constituted the core of the Society and would be responsible for correspondence in their particular fields: Dr. Thomas Bond in medicine, Bartram in botany, Thomas Godfrey in mathematics, Samuel Rhoads in mechanics, William Parsons in geography, and Dr. Phineas Bond, whose field was "general natural philosophy"; and in addition there were three officers: Thomas Hopkinson, president, William Coleman, treasurer, and Franklin, secretary. "To whom," Franklin continued, "the following Members have since been added": James Alexander of New York, Chief Justice Robert Hunter Morris of New Jersey, Archibald Home, secretary of the New Jersey Council, and John Coxe and David Martin, both of Trenton, New Jersey. Franklin had also been informed by Richard Nicholls, lawyer and postmaster of New York, that "several other Gentlemen" of that city "incline to encourage the Thing." And still others in Virginia, Maryland, Carolina, and New England were expected soon to join.[8]

"Our Philosophick Society increaseth finely," Bartram wrote confidently to Colden on 29 April. "I think we had 7 members initiated last meeting of which thee was one by unanimous consent." Dr. Archibald Spencer, the itinerant lecturer on electricity, promised to attend a meeting and to carry the Society's proposals to the southern colonies and West Indies.[9] Colden in his turn expressed his satisfaction to Collinson. "We have in America for some time past made great progress in

---

[6] *Franklin Papers*, II, 378–83. An original copy is in Yale University Library; it has been facsimiled in APS *Year Book*, 1947.
[7] *Colden Papers*, I (N.-Y. Hist. Soc., *Colls.*, 1917), 271–73; VIII (1934), 190–91.
[8] *Franklin Papers*, II, 387–88, 406–07.
[9] Bartram to Colden, 29 April 1744, Gratz Coll., Case 7, Box 21 (HSP). The letter was franked to New York by Franklin as postmaster.

Aping the Luxury of our Mother Country. I am glad that some now indeavour to imitate some of its Excellencies."[10] Collinson was no less pleased with this latest American achievement.

> I can't enough commend the Authors & promoters of a Society for Improvemt of Natural knowledge Because it will be a Means of uniteing [sic] Ingenious Men of all Societies together and a Mutual Harmony be got which will be Dayly produceing Acts of Love & Friendship and will ware [sic] away by Degrees any Harsh opinions, parties may have Conceived of Each other, the Fruits of Wisdome & knowledge are Excellent, besides the Mind being Enlarged the Understanding Improved, the Wonders of the Creation Explored, and Ingenious & Good people will know one another & Rejoice in the Friendship of those Like minded as themselves, and as there will be a Laudable Emulation to Excell [sic] in the Several Branches of Science the Same good Desposition [sic] will Influence them to Benevolence & Good will to Each other in Every Capacity.

He would await "with Some Impatience" the Society's first publication. "I expect Something New from your New World, our Old World as it were Exhausted. . . ."[11]

In New York James Alexander also encouraged Franklin's project and sent along the names of several persons interested in promoting it: Chief Justice De Lancey, Daniel Horsmanden, Joseph Murray, William Smith, "& Several others sent their names as members of the Society."[12] Just what Alexander meant by "sending their names" is not clear. Certainly not everyone proposed for election was admitted. Colden nominated several persons in a letter to Bartram, but the latter rejected some as "persons of little Curiosity & I believe was never aquainted [sic] with our proposals or not till very lately."[13] Among those accepted in 1744 were Dr. John Mitchell of Urbanna, Virginia, Dr. John Tennent of Caroline County in that colony, and the Reverend Mr. Francis Alison, who conducted a school in Chester County, Pennsylvania.

By 1745 notice of the Society had been sent or carried to naturalists in Europe. "I find the [sic] mentioned to Collinson," Bartram wrote Colden, "hee to Catesby, & hee to Gronovius, which was to him from Claton [Clayton]."[14] Writing from Leiden, Gronovius several times made inquiries about the Society and its work.[15]

But even as word of its existence extended into Europe, the Society in Philadelphia was not flourishing as Bartram and Franklin had expected. John Mitchell in London heard "their laudable design is in a manner entirely dropt." "The Mem-

---

[10] *Colden Papers*, III (N.-Y. Hist. Soc., *Colls.*, 1919), 60–61.
[11] Ibid., 69.
[12] Ibid., 82–83.
[13] Bartram to Colden, 29 April 1744, Gratz Coll., Case 7, Box 21 (HSP).
[14] *Colden Papers*, III (1919), 160.
[15] Darlington, *Memorials*, 357.

bers of our Society here are very idle Gentlemen," Franklin complained to Colden in August 1745; "they will take no Pains."[16] Six weeks later, so Bartram told Colden, he, Franklin, and Dr. Bond talked of "carrying it on with more dilligence [sic] then [sic] ever which we may very easily do," he continued in an aside, "if we could but exchange the time that is spent in the Club, Chess & Coffee House for the Curious amusements of natural observations."[17]

It had been expected that the Society, once established, would publish a journal. In an effort to revive the Society as well as to achieve one of its purposes, Colden again raised the question.[18] Several essays were already on hand—on yellow fever by Dr. Mitchell, on rattlesnake bite by Dr. Evan Jones of New York, and an essay on ocean currents that Franklin had written.[19] As a printer Franklin was drawn to the idea of a periodical, and as postmaster he was in a position to expedite its circulation. If a philosophical society could not succeed, perhaps a philosophical journal could. "I am now determin'd to publish an American Philosophical Miscellany, Monthly or Quarterly," Franklin wrote Colden on 28 November 1745. "I shall begin with next January, and proceed as I find Encouragement and Assistance." Neither encouragement nor assistance was forthcoming, however. Several times Franklin assured correspondents that the "American Philosophical Miscellany" was about to appear, but each time publication was inexplicably postponed.[20] After 1747 there is no further mention of the "Miscellany" in the *Pennsylvania Gazette* or in Franklin's correspondence. For whatever reason—doubtless an insufficient number of subscriptions—the magazine never appeared. The Society was now dead—Franklin later preferred the term "dormant"—and nothing more was heard of it publicly for more than twenty years.

---

[16] *Colden Papers*, VIII (1934), 321; *Franklin Papers*, III, 36.
[17] *Colden Papers*, III (1919), 160.
[18] *Franklin Papers*, II, 447–48.
[19] *Colden Papers*, III (1919), 65–66, 187; VIII (1934), 314–28.
[20] *Franklin Papers*, III, 47–48, 92.

SKETCHES OF MEMBERS

THOMAS HOPKINSON

By Robert Feke. *National Museum of American Art, Smithsonian Institution. George Buchanan Coale Collection*

THOMAS HOPKINSON (1709–1751)
AMERICAN PHILOSOPHICAL SOCIETY: 1743

THOMAS HOPKINSON, first president of the American Philosophical Society, was a merchant, lawyer, and judge, who was also a natural philosopher—one of the small group led by Benjamin Franklin who made the earliest experiments and observations on electrical phenomena in Philadelphia. His accounts with Franklin's printing shop for the purchase of books reveal the variety of his interests—a dictionary, "Shepherd's Com. Aff.," James Anderson's *Constitutions of the Free-Masons,* "2 Tune books," a gazetteer, Cicero's *Cato Major,* Rapin's *History of England,* and *A Collection of all the Laws of the Province of Pennsylvania.*[1]

Hopkinson had come to Philadelphia in 1730 or 1731 and, though a reserved man, had quickly won the respect of the mechanics, tradesmen, and shopkeepers who composed the Junto. He was made a member of St. John's Masonic Lodge in Philadelphia in 1733. The following year Franklin, who had become Grand Master of Pennsylvania Masons, appointed him one of the Junior Grand Wardens; in 1735 Hopkinson was Deputy Grand Master, and in 1736 he presided over the Provincial Grand Lodge as its Grand Master.[2]

Hopkinson was born in the parish of St. James's Westminster, London, on 6 April 1709, the son of Thomas and Mary (Nicholls) Hopkinson. The elder Hopkinson, a scrivener and "gentleman of the Middle Temple," died in 1710; but his son appears to have been generously provided for by the will of an uncle.[3] Though he did not matriculate at Oxford, as some nineteenth-century descendants liked to believe, young Hopkinson had a good education, as his penmanship reveals. In Philadelphia Franklin and Franklin's public-spirited friends drew him into their circle. He was one of the original directors of the Library Company in 1731, and, returning to England in the spring of 1732, he carried a list of 45 books wanted by the new institution and a bill of exchange to pay for them. He discharged the commission to general satisfaction, only substituting for titles he could not find or which were too expensive, books of equal usefulness, which he chose in collaboration with his fellow director Dr. Thomas Cadwalader, who was in London at the same time. Hopkinson remained a director of the Library Company until 1745, attending board meetings faithfully and performing cheerfully a variety of services, among them compiling with William Coleman, Hugh Roberts, and Franklin the

---

[1] Franklin, Ledger A & B, 114; Ledger D, 53 (APS).
[2] Julius F. Sachse, *Old Masonic Lodges of Pennsylvania* (Phila., 1912), I, 37.
[3] George E. Hastings, *The Life and Works of Francis Hopkinson* (Chicago, 1926), 9–11; Charles P. Keith, *The Provincial Councillors of Pennsylvania* (Phila., 1883), 265–67. See also Hopkinson Papers in HSP.

first printed catalogue of the collection.[4] Although Hopkinson shared Franklin's skepticism about George Whitefield's plans for an orphan asylum in Georgia, he, like Franklin, came under the spell of the evangelist's eloquence, but with one difference: whereas Franklin emptied his pockets into Whitefield's collection baskets—first the coppers, then the silver, finally the gold—Hopkinson tried to borrow money from a neighbor to make his contribution.[5]

The Library was a focus of intellectual interests in Philadelphia, and its appeal broadened as it added scientific inquiries to literary study. In 1738 John Penn gave an air pump "and other curious Instruments of great Use in the Study of Natural Knowledge," and a few years later he added a microscope and camera obscura. Peter Collinson sent glass tubes for experiments in static electricity, and the Proprietor Thomas Penn presented a complete electrical apparatus.[6]

Franklin described one of their experiments in a report to Collinson on 25 May 1747:

> Place an Iron Shot of three or four Inches Diameter on the Mouth of a clean dry Glass Bottle. By a fine silken Thread from the Ceiling, right over the Mouth of the Bottle, suspend a small Cork Ball, about the Bigness of a Marble: the Thread of such a Length, as that the Cork Ball may rest against the Side of the Shot. Electrify the Shot, and the Ball will be repelled to the Distance of 4 or 5 Inches, more or less according to the Quantity of Electricity. When in this State, if you present to the Shot the Point of a long, slender, sharp Bodkin at 6 or 8 Inches Distance, the Repellency is instantly destroy'd, and the Cork flies to it. . . .
>
> To shew that Points will *throw* off, as well as *draw* off the Electrical Fire: Lay a long sharp Needle upon the Shot, and you can not electrise the Shot, so as to make it repel the Cork Ball. Fix a Needle to the End of a suspended Gun Barrel, so as to point beyond it like a little Bayonet, and while it remains there, the Gun Barrel can not be electrised (by the Tube applied to the other End) so as to give a Spark; . . .[7]

The last experiment and its demonstration were Hopkinson's. In his own copy of the earliest edition of *Experiments and Observations* Franklin penned a note to that effect; and in the 1769 and 1774 editions, the only ones Franklin supervised, he included a footnote acknowledging his friend's discovery:

> This power of points to *throw off* the electrical fire, was first communicated to me by my ingenious friend Mr. Thomas Hopkinson, since deceased, whose virtue and in-

---

[4] Edwin Wolf 2nd, "The First Books and Printed Catalogue of the Library Company of Philadelphia," *PMHB*, LXXVIII (1954), 45–70; *Franklin Papers*, I, 209; II, 205–06.
[5] Franklin, *Autobiography*, 177–78.
[6] *Franklin Papers*, II, 207, 312.
[7] Ibid., III, 127–28.

tegrity, in every station of life, public and private, will ever make his Memory dear to those who knew him, and who knew how to value him.[8]

Meanwhile Hopkinson had been prospering in Philadelphia as both a merchant and a lawyer. He acted as agent for several London firms and, in partnership with William Coleman, imported and sold the usual variety of goods from linens, lawns, and oznabrigs to hardware, gunpowder, spices, writing paper, and "bar Iron of all Sizes."[9] On the death in the winter of 1736–7 of Charles Read, clerk of the Orphans Court, whose deputy he had been, Hopkinson petitioned the Provincial Council for the office, and received it. After 1740, when his reputation and financial situation were firmly established, he sought and received other appointments of a public and semi-public character. He was master of the rolls and recorder of Philadelphia from 1736 to 1741, when he was elected a member of the Philadelphia Common Council. In this last-named body he often served on committees to draft loyal and other formal addresses to the king, proprietor, or governor. He was commissioned judge of the Court of Vice-Admiralty on 17 January 1744/5. In 1747 the Governor gave him a seat in the Provincial Council. As a councillor he attended the Treaty of Lancaster in 1748, and two years later was in the Pennsylvania delegation that met with one from Maryland to agree on surveying the boundary between the two provinces. He was commissioned prothonotary of Philadelphia County on 24 November 1748, and a justice of the peace in 1749.[10] Hopkinson held most of these offices at the time of his death, for plural office-holding was as common in colonial Pennsylvania as in England at that time. He was, in short, Thomas Penn wrote, "a very honest Man, had a good understanding, & was of great use in his Country."[11]

Hopkinson was one of those who first gave warning of Spanish incursions into Delaware Bay, and vigorously supported the defensive Association of 1747. Franklin consulted him as well as Tench Francis and Coleman about strategy and the drafting of *Plain Truth*. When the Council directed Hopkinson and Abraham Taylor to draft the proclamation of a general fast, Hopkinson turned to Franklin, who, as a New Englander, was acquainted with the style and content of such instruments. Hopkinson also served as a manager of the lotteries that raised money for the defense of the city in 1747 and 1748.[12] In 1749 he joined Franklin and other citizens in founding the Academy of Philadelphia, served as one of the origi-

---

[8] Ibid., 128n.
[9] *Pa. Gaz.*, 30 June 1743; Hastings, *Francis Hopkinson*, 16.
[10] *Col. Recs. Pa.*, IV, 151; 2 *Pa. Arch.*, IX, 628, 632, 698, 699; 3 *Pa. Arch.*, VIII, 643; Thomas and Richard Penn to John Kinsey, William Allen, Thomas Hopkinson and others, 30 June 1750, Penn Letter Books, III, 1 (HSP); Allen, Hopkinson, Richard Peters and others to Proprietors, 22 Sept. 1750, Penn Mss., Off. Corres., V, 51; also a report, ca. fall 1750, ibid., 197 (HSP).
[11] Penn to Lynford Lardner, 23 March 1752, Penn Letter Books, III, 133 (HSP).
[12] *Franklin Papers*, III, 215, 223, 227, 296; Stauffer Coll., IV, 324 (HSP).

nal 24 trustees, subscribed £10 to the institution, and was one of a committee to lay out £100 "in Latin and Greek Authors, Maps, Drafts and Instruments for the use of the Academy."[13]

Thomas Hopkinson was married at Christ Church, Philadelphia, on 9 September 1736 to Mary Johnson, daughter of Baldwin Johnson of Philadelphia by his wife Mary, widow of Colonel William Dyer of Appoquinimink Hundred, New Castle County, Delaware.[14] They had eight children, of whom six survived to maturity. Their son Francis, a lawyer, essayist, and musician, was a principal figure in the American Philosophical Society for forty years. One daughter married the Reverend Mr. Jacob Duché, another became the wife of Dr. John Morgan; these sons-in-law, too, were active in both the cultural life of the city and the affairs of the Society.

Thomas Hopkinson died on 5 November 1751 after an illness of several weeks. "His benevolence was as extensive as the Object of it, the whole human Race," declared the author of his obituary, possibly Franklin, in the *Pennsylvania Gazette;*

> but his great Modesty, and his not seeking to be known, caused the Number of his intimate Friends to be but small: Among these, in the Hours of Recreation, he had the particular Faculty of tempering the *Facetious* with the *Grave*, in so agreeable a Manner, as made his Conversation both delightful and instructive.[15]

Though not rich, Hopkinson left his family in reasonably comfortable circumstances. His will mentioned particularly a small farm of 21 acres at Moyamensing called "Rowington," a 537–acre plantation on Blackbird Creek, New Castle County, and a one-eighth interest in Pool Forge in Berks County; and there were bequests of £900 to both sons and £700 to each of his four daughters.[16] Mrs. Hopkinson survived her husband more than half a century, dying in 1804. Franklin remained her friend, even to searching out her genealogy in England. "The marks of Regard you are continually Shewing to the Family of a deceased Friend," she wrote him gratefully in 1765,

> is to me a convincing proof of the Goodness of your Heart and I must declare that among all my Husband's former Friends I know of but one Gentleman besides your-

---

[13] *Franklin Papers*, III, 422, 429; IV, 3n.
[14] 2 *Pa. Arch.*, VIII, 138.
[15] *Pa. Gaz.*, 14 Nov. 1751. He had visited South Carolina for his health's sake in the winter of 1749–50. James Hamilton to Thomas Penn, 26 Nov. 1749, Hamilton, Letter Book, 1749–1783 (HSP).
[16] Hopkinson, Will, dated 11 Sept. 1751 (Register of Wills, Phila.). The Blackbird Creek property was offered for sale in 1753. *Pa. Gaz.*, 5 April 1753.

self who has been good enough to extend any of their Regard to his Wife and Children. . . .¹⁷

WILLIAM COLEMAN (1705?–1769)
AMERICAN PHILOSOPHICAL SOCIETY: 1743

WILLIAM COLEMAN, merchant, was one of the founders of the American Philosophical Society in 1743, and its first treasurer. As a clerk in a mercantile firm more than fifteen years before, he had been a member of the Junto of 1727, and ever since had been a good friend of Franklin's, who judged he "had the coolest, clearest Head, the best Heart, and exactest Morals, of almost any Man" he had ever known. It was Coleman, already prospering, who, simultaneously with, but independently of, Robert Grace, another member of the Junto, offered Franklin the money he needed to buy Hugh Meredith's share in the printing office and make himself sole proprietor of the *Pennsylvania Gazette*. Franklin took half from each; the newspaper thus became in a sense one of the Junto's earliest undertakings.¹ When Franklin prepared his will in 1750 and again in 1757 he asked that his friend Coleman advise the executors, who were Mrs. Franklin and William.²

Born of Quaker parents in 1704 or 1705, he was the son of William Coleman, a carpenter, and of Rebecca, his wife, who was one of the first Pennsylvanians, for she had been brought to Philadelphia as a child in 1683 and could remember, she used to say, when the city had but three houses and all the rest of the inhabitants lived in caves cut into the high river bank. When she died in 1770 at the age of 92, men marveled that she had witnessed "such a rapid Progress" in the city's growth "as perhaps no other Instance in the known World has fully equalled."³

Coleman appears to have taken a lively interest in the Junto's projects, especially in the Library Company, which its members sponsored. With a head for figures and commercial ties abroad, he made a good treasurer for the Company from 1731, when it was established, to 1734, and again from 1742 to 1757; in the intervals until 1763 his colleagues, unwilling to lose his counsel and his service, elected him each year one of the Library directors. Coleman was usually put on committees to draft resolutions, addresses, petitions and letters of thanks to the

¹⁷ Franklin, *Autobiography,* 118.

1 Franklin, *Autobiography,* 118.
2 *Franklin Papers,* III, 481–82; VII, 204.
3 Hinshaw, *Amer. Quaker Genealogy,* II, 348, 442; *Pa. Gaz.*, 20 Sept. 1770.

Proprietors and other personages; and though he must usually have given satisfaction, at least once he produced the draft of an address of welcome to John Penn which the Company could not approve and returned to another committee to amend. Not a few of the letters of thanks Coleman wrote were for pieces of philosophical apparatus, which must have gratified him. In 1741 he was one of a committee with Franklin, Philip Syng, and Hugh Roberts to prepare a catalogue of the Library.[4] In the Common Council, to which he was elected in 1739 and whose meetings he attended with rare faithfulness, Coleman was also frequently asked to draft messages to the governor, testimonials of loyalty and affection, resolutions, and other formal papers; and these clerkly functions he performed so willingly and well that in 1747 he was chosen town clerk and clerk of the Common Council in succession to Andrew Hamilton. He held the appointment until 1758, when he resigned. In 1750 he signed a petition of the Council to the Assembly for a night watch and for measures to pave and clean the streets of Philadelphia.[5]

Of Coleman's activities in the American Philosophical Society nothing is known. He had more than common understanding of mathematics, and could readily participate in most philosophical discussions that took place; but like James Logan, Thomas Hopkinson, and some others, he could make nothing out of an early draft of Cadwallader Colden's "Explication of the First Causes of Action in Matter," which the New Yorker sent to Franklin and his friends for criticism. This, Franklin explained gently, was not because Colden had written unintelligibly, but because the subject was abstruse, and they were not competent to it.[6] Some years later Coleman looked forward eagerly to the transit of Venus in 1761, which he hoped, for the town's glory, might be observable in Philadelphia.[7]

Meanwhile Coleman was prospering in his mercantile ventures, and by 1750 was firmly established as one of the leading merchants. He was one of the first directors of the Philadelphia Contributionship in 1752, and in the same year was treasurer of a committee of Philadelphia merchants which, protesting a scheme of the British Parliament to give a London company a monopoly of trading rights in Labrador, organized an expedition of their own to go to Labrador and find a northwest passage.[8] He was ready to extend and defend the trade of Philadelphia whenever occasion arose—too ready, as the event proved, in the eyes of some of his fellow Quakers. When French and Spanish privateers entered Delaware Bay in the spring of 1747, actually carried off slaves and other property, offered violence to the citizens, and raised the prospect of heavier incursions closer to Philadelphia, a number of the city's merchants, including Coleman, fitted out the *Warren* privateer

[4] *Franklin Papers,* II, 33–34, 207, 312, 347; III, 164, 351; *PMHB,* LXXVIII (1954), 49.
[5] Philadelphia Common Council, *Minutes, 1704–1776* (Phila., 1847), 384, 479–80, 628.
[6] *Franklin Papers,* III, 90.
[7] Ibid., IX, 369.
[8] Ibid., IV, 384.

to defend the bay and river and draw off the invaders. The Friends Meeting called such warlike conduct into question at once; Coleman defended his conduct and was disowned on 29 Eleventh Mo. 1747/8. Unrepentant, he, Franklin, and others consulted about how best to rally sentiment in favor of military preparations; he offered Franklin suggestions for *Plain Truth*, and agreed to serve as one of the managers of the lottery conducted in the winter of 1748 to raise £3,000 for expenses of the volunteer Association.[9] Nevertheless, as with so many disowned Friends, Coleman did not entirely abandon the principles and manners of his rearing. To young James Pemberton, then in England, Coleman observed in characteristically Friendly tones: "As far as my Experience goes the greatest Happiness arises, not so much from new Scenes & Entertainments, as from a Steady quiet Mind & the Consciousness of doing right, and this Sort of Happiness a Man may find at Home; and yet," he added, as though he might have damped the younger man's excitement at being abroad, "I believe it proper that a young Man should see the World to be better convinced of the little it affords."[10]

Though he might think the world afforded very little, Coleman tried to increase its stock. He was one of the original trustees of the Academy of Philadelphia in 1749, and served as their clerk; in 1753 he was named a trustee in the charter of the College, and held the post of treasurer until his death. He took such responsibilities seriously, helping select and order books, maps and instruments abroad, consulting Franklin on the most suitable philosophical apparatus to get for the college.[11] Similarly he supported the Pennsylvania Hospital from 1751, when he signed a petition to the Assembly for a small lunatic hospital, until his death, when he bequeathed the institution £50.[12] For some years he kept a hospital charity box in his house. He was equally prompt with small, unobtrusive, but no less welcome gifts. To Trinity Church in Oxford township he gave £1 towards rebuilding the glebe house destroyed by fire in 1760; and he subscribed to John Beveridge's *Familiar Epistles, and other Miscellaneous Pieces* (Philadelphia, 1765).

Coleman was unquestionably one of the most influential men in town, and was often mentioned as a candidate who would strengthen the ticket. None other than William Allen in 1756 importuned him to run.[13] But Coleman seems to have had little taste for the usual kinds of politics, none at all for the Assembly. He did, however, accept appointment in 1757 as one of the justices of the Provincial Supreme Court, and in 1766 he moved up from third to second justice on the bench.[14] Franklin, who used to send him books from London, thought a copy of

---

[9] Ibid., III, 215; *Pa. Gaz.*, 12 Dec. 1747; Hinshaw, *Amer. Quaker Genealogy,* II, 491; Albert C. Myers, ed., *Hannah Logan's Courtship* (Phila., 1904), 126, 130–31.
[10] Coleman to James Pemberton, 18 Nov. 1748, Pemberton Papers, IV, 159 (HSP).
[11] *Franklin Papers,* III, 423, 428, 429; IV, 3; V, 8–9.
[12] Ibid., V, 285; 8 *Pa. Arch.*, VI, 5448; VII, 6485.
[13] *PMHB,* XXXI (1907), 246.
[14] 3 *Pa. Arch.*, IX, 189–90, 269, 304, 352.

Lord Kames' *Principles of Equity* (Edinburgh, 1760) an especially appropriate gift at this time.[15]

Less because of his judicial eminence than because of his mathematical knowledge, in 1761 the Proprietor put Coleman on a commission to adjust the Pennsylvania-Maryland boundary. He performed the task with difficulty, for he was suffering from the stone, could not ride horseback, and did not wish to be away from home long. He got to New Castle by boat and, though he could not go on all the journeys of inspection, he did attend the important meetings. The Commission's reports of November 1761 and May and October 1762 are in his hand.[16]

Coleman's health did not improve; indeed some other trouble attacked him; and in March 1768, desperate to find relief, he sailed to England for an operation. What it was we are not sure—probably a cancer. The surgeon who he hoped would operate was abroad; the best doctors he consulted advised him "to have the diseased part cut out"; and this was accordingly done in June. He appears to have recovered rapidly under the "Care & good Nursing" of Mrs. Stevenson, Franklin's landlady in Craven Street, Strand, where Coleman took a room. The friends even talked of returning home together in July; as it was, Coleman returned alone in the fall, his arrival being noticed in the *Pennsylvania Gazette* of 20 October.[17]

Within a month, on 15 November, Coleman lost his wife, Hannah Fitzwater, whom he had married in Philadelphia Monthly Meeting in 1738; she was buried in Friends ground.[18] Mrs. Coleman's death was a blow, and soon afterwards a "fresh Disorder" attacked Judge Coleman.[19] On 11 January 1769 he too died. Old Edward Shippen of Lancaster heard that Coleman left £15,000, of which £6000 was to go to George Clymer, Coleman's nephew, whom he had adopted, being childless. Personal property was inventoried at £7066 18s. 8d., including a library of 315 volumes, valued at £120, a pair of globes, and a case of mathematical instruments.[20] In addition, Coleman owned a handsome house and large garden at Second and Pine Streets, and on the Wissahickon Road four miles from Philadelphia a 12–acre country seat called "Woodford," which he had acquired and improved in 1756; a stone house, three rooms to a floor, outbuildings, and a handsome garden and thriving orchard of good apple and other fruit trees. (Woodford was bought by Alexander Barclay, who did not long enjoy it, for he died in 1771,

---

[15] *Franklin Papers,* IX, 281.
[16] Coleman et al. to Thomas Penn, 14 Nov. 1761, Penn Papers, Private Corr., V, 39; same to same, 10 May, 9 Oct. 1762, Penn Papers, Official Corr., IX, 170, 174 (HSP).
[17] *Pa. Gaz.*, 31 March, 20 Oct. 1768; *Franklin Papers,* XV, 139.
[18] Philadelphia Monthly Meeting, Minutes, 27 Eleventh Mo. 1737/38 (Arch Street); *Pa. Chronicle,* 21 Nov. 1768.
[19] *Franklin Papers,* XVI, 57.
[20] Lewis B. Walker, *The Burd Papers* (n.p., 1899), 33; Coleman Inventory, 10 Feb. 1769 (Phila. Register of Wills).

when the property was sold by his son Robert.)[21] The *Pennsylvania Gazette* wrote with unusual warmth of his death:

> He was always esteemed a valuable and useful Citizen, and a Gentleman of great good Sense, and unblemished Virtue. Tho' much pleased with Study and Retirement, he possessed many social Virtues, and was ever fond of those Subjects, which were most likely to render him serviceable to his Neighbour. He was an able and upright Judge, and in that Character gave the greatest Satisfaction to his Country. And we may say, with much Reason, that this Province has few such Men, and that few Men will be so much missed as Mr. Coleman.[22]

BENJAMIN FRANKLIN (1706–1790)
AMERICAN PHILOSOPHICAL SOCIETY: 1743

BENJAMIN FRANKLIN, a printer of Philadelphia, was the principal founder of the American Philosophical Society, its first secretary, and its president after 1769, when it was reorganized. One of the first philosophers of the age, during his lifetime and for more than a generation after his death he gave it reputation throughout America and Europe. During most of the 21 years of his presidency Franklin was in England or France; of that period he spent only six years in Philadelphia. Although in those years he attended meetings of the Society only when it was possible and convenient, during the whole of his connection he assisted the Society in many ways—offering suggestions and advice, presenting books, serving as a conduit between it and its European members, even making it a generous loan of money.

The idea of a scientific learned society was not unknown to Americans in 1743. The Royal Society of London, founded in 1662, enjoyed great prestige in the colonies; 18 men, resident in or closely connected with the mainland colonies, were or had been Fellows; and its *Philosophical Transactions* were in institutional libraries and some private collections as well. In Dublin a Society of Gentlemen began to publish in 1733 papers on agriculture, mechanics, trade, and such practical arts as raising flax and hops, making cider and brewing beer, building roads, and the manufacture of linen.[1] Following these British examples, Cadwallader Colden in New York in 1729 proposed that a philosophical society be established in that

---

[21] *Pa. Gaz.*, 27 April 1769; H. D. Eberlein and Cortlandt Van Dyke Hubbard, *Portrait of a Colonial City: Philadelphia, 1670–1838* (Phila., 1939), 313–23; Watson, *Annals*, I, 444.
[22] *Pa. Gaz.*, 19 Jan. 1769.

[1] Society of Gentlemen in Dublin, *Essays and Observations* (London, 1740).

BENJAMIN FRANKLIN
By Robert Feke. *Harvard University Art Museums. Bequest of Dr. John Collins Warren,* 1856

town, and in 1736 Boston doctors formed a medical society. In 1738 or 1739 John Bartram, a Quaker farmer and seedsman of Philadelphia, in a letter to his patron Peter Collinson of London, suggested that a society for the promotion of the "syances" be formed in America. Collinson discouraged the idea, but Bartram clung to it, and in 1743 his friend Franklin issued a proposal for an American society to be patterned on the societies in London and Dublin.

Franklin was slow to organize the society, but by April of 1744 he had enlisted six Philadelphians to form the nucleus of the organization. Visiting New York in the spring of that year, he revealed his plan to Colden, who responded enthusiastically. The result was that some eight or ten citizens of that province and New Jersey expressed a desire to join. Most were prominent office-holders in New York. One was James Alexander, a Scotsman, surveyor-general of the colony, who had a considerable knowledge of mathematics and astronomy; another was Lieutenant Governor James De Lancey of New York; and a third was Archibald Home, also a Scotsman, secretary of the Council of New Jersey, who had a flair for verse. One or two Virginians also became members of the Society at this time, possibly invited at times when they were in Philadelphia. In the ensuing two years the Philadelphians appear to have met with some regularity; Colden and others corresponded with them, sending them scientific observations and speculations; and Franklin in 1745 looked forward to the imminent publication of an "American Philosophical Miscellany."[2]

But the Society soon languished. The members were but "very idle gentlemen," Franklin complained in a letter to Colden in 1745; "they will take no Pains." Even his vision and energy could not keep the Society alive. By 1747 it was dead—although Franklin later preferred to say it was only "dormant."

No steps were taken to revive it or to establish another, although about 1750 Charles Thomson consulted Franklin about establishing a society—known here as the "Young Junto"—patterned on Franklin's famous club of 1727. The young Junto, however, was in no sense a philosophical society and its history is part of the history of the American Philosophical Society only because in 1766 it transformed itself into the American Society for Promoting Useful Knowledge, which soon became a philosophical society and in 1769 united with the revived American Philosophical Society of 1743 to form the society whose president Franklin was chosen to be. Thus for 20 years, from the demise of the first American Philosophical Society in 1747 to the creation and re-creation of the American and American Philosophical societies in 1766–68, there was no learned society in Philadelphia; and Franklin, engaged in electrical experiments, Pennsylvania politics, and his agency in London, seems to have given no thought to founding once more a learned society in the American colonies.

---

[2] *Franklin Papers,* III, 47.

In London, however, they had heard of the American Philosophical Society. A copy of Franklin's proposal of 1743 was sent by Dr. Alexander Garden of Charleston to William Shipley in London, and on 21 May 1755 was read in the newly formed Society for the Encouragement of Arts, Manufactures and Commerce. Learning of this, Franklin wrote on 27 November 1755 asking to be admitted a corresponding member and enclosing 20 guineas for its premium fund. He took an interest in this Society thereafter and was eventually elected a perpetual member.[3] (In 1956 it was discovered that the Philosophical Society owned a copy of the Society of Arts' first printed constitution, and that the Society of Arts owned the manuscript copy of Franklin's proposals for an American Philosophical Society that Dr. Garden had sent to them in 1755. An exchange was amicably effected.)[4]

But by 1767 conditions in Philadelphia and the American colonies had changed. Dr. John Morgan, freshly home from medical studies in Edinburgh and London and from travels in France and Italy, where he had met learned men of distinction and been elected to the Royal Society of London and to other learned bodies, organized a medical society in Philadelphia in 1766. Professing high standards for the profession, the Medical Society elected principally younger men with university degrees, and quickly achieved a certain éclat by including on its rolls some British and Irish physicians as well. But, either thoughtlessly or on purpose, Morgan had not invited several of the older Philadelphia doctors to be among the initial members of his society. Understandably regarding this as a calculated snub, some of these, led by Dr. Thomas Bond, who had been a member of Franklin's society of 1743, revived that long-dormant institution and proceeded to elect members. Thus at the end of 1767 there were three organizations in Philadelphia—the American Society, the Medical Society, and the revived American Philosophical Society—with similar or related programs and drawing members from the same group of philosophers and physicians. (In fact, several men belonged to two or even all three societies.)

Although he had no part in these developments, Franklin in London was apprised of them by his friends at home, notably Dr. Cadwalader Evans. Evans was aware of the political considerations behind these two principal groups, and deplored them. The revived American Philosophical Society had a high proportion of members of the Proprietary Party, who were Anglicans and wealthy Presbyterians. American Society members were more likely to be of the anti-Proprietary party, like Franklin, Quakers, dissenters of various sorts, artisans, and shopkeepers rather than rich merchants. When Bond's group claimed to be the legitimate successor to Franklin's society of 1743 and planned to elect Franklin's son William to membership, thus garnering whatever reputation this might give them, Dr. Evans

---

[3] Ibid., VI, 187, 275–76; Society of Arts, *Trans.*, I (1783), 292.
[4] "Report of the Committee on Library," APS *Year Book* (1956), 417–18.

warned Governor Franklin. William Franklin replied that he would have nothing to do with this scheme and would advise his father against it. The members of the American Society successfully thwarted their rivals' plan by electing the elder Franklin their president on 19 February 1768. In November 1768 the American Society took advantage of the Philosophical Society by electing into their number the entire membership of the Medical Society.

Philadelphia was obviously too small to support two learned societies, as wiser heads knew. Much of the year 1768 was spent in negotiating a plan of union, and on 2 January 1769 the two societies united on terms of perfect equality. There were three vice-presidents, three secretaries, and three curators. These offices could be evenly apportioned among members of the two societies; but there could be only one president. Franklin was proposed by members of the American Society; Governor James Hamilton by the Philosophical Society. The election was carefully canvassed. A count made by a member of the American Philosophical Society survives. It identifies the members by their politics—"Old Ticket" or "New Ticket"—and by other distinctions. This tally shows that of 43 members whose political affiliation was given, 29 were attached to the Proprietary party, 14 to the anti-Proprietary; and another classification shows there were 20 "Esquires," eight "Doctors of one sort or other," and ten "Common Characters."[5] Franklin was elected president; the governor and many of his party never came to another meeting, the governor even refusing to accept the honorary title of Patron. "The philosophical Society have done me great honour in electing me their president," Franklin acknowledged his election in what seems a cool and impersonal note. "Be so good," he wrote Bond, "as to present them my thankful acknowledgments, and best wishes of success to their undertaking."[6] Although defeated in election for the presidency of the united society, the Proprietary party could take some solace from the fact that Dr. Bond, as senior vice-president, presided over meetings for the next few years and carried out the business of the Society in the place of its absent president in London.

During the next six years, until he returned to Philadelphia, Franklin served the Society principally as a conduit for correspondence, gifts of books and apparatus, and notices of nominations and elections. The committee appointed "to draw up such an Account of the Transits of Venus & Mercury as they may think proper to be communicated to the Astronomers in Europe," was directed to send a copy to Franklin. When the first volume of the Society's *Transactions* was printed in 1771, copies were sent to Franklin for distribution among the learned societies of Europe and to certain individuals, namely Buffon, Professor James Ferguson, Dr. John Fothergill, Linnaeus, Professor Johann-David Hahn of Leiden, Nevil Maskelyne,

---

[5] APS, "List of Members," 1743–2 Feb. 1768 (Ms. Coll., APS).
[6] Ms. Minutes, 20 May 1769 (APS).

the Astronomer Royal, Richard Penn, Sir George Savile, and Benjamin West.[7] The European societies in turn sent copies of their transactions and memoirs to Franklin to be forwarded to Philadelphia, where they formed the basis of the Society's library. On his travels through England and the Continent Franklin met men of science who he thought should be made members of the American Philosophical Society. One of these was the Baron de Klingstedt of St. Petersburg,

> who has lately travelled thro' England to collect Improvements in Husbandry &c. Being acquainted with him I took the Liberty of requesting his Care of our Book [*Transactions*] directed to the Academy of Sciences at Petersburg & I gave it to him open as he expressed a Curiosity to read it. He was so pleased with it & conceived so high an Opinion of the Society that he desired the Honor, as he politely expressed it, of being a Member, offered to correspond with the Society & send them from Time to Time any Information, Seeds or other things they might want from Russia.[8]

On this recommendation the baron was promptly elected on the same night on which Franklin's letter was read.

During most of 1774 the meetings of the Society were suspended as the attention of the members was drawn away to the tremendous political issues under debate. On 17 December, the first meeting after the resumption of business, the Society received 15 books from Franklin—Buffon's *Histoire naturelle des Oiseaux* (Paris, 1771–72), the Abbé François Rozier's *Observations sur la Physique, sur l'Histoire naturelle, et sur les Arts et Métiers* (Paris, 1773), Nevil Maskelyne's *Astronomical Observations, made at Greenwich in 1765–69* (London, 1774), Samuel Dunn's *New Atlas of the Mundane System* (London, 1774), Lavoisier's *Opuscules physiques et chimiques* (Paris, 1774), Sir John Pringle's *Discourse on the Different Kinds of Air* (London, 1774), and Pierre LeRoy's *Précis des recherches . . . pour la détermination des longitudes en mer* (Amsterdam, 1773), all gifts to the Society from their authors. At the same meeting Dr. Franklin on his own behalf presented copies of Jacob von Storcksburg Staelin's *Account of the New Northern Archipelago* (London, 1774), to which Franklin had subscribed, and of John Walsh's paper *Of the Electric Property of the Torpedo* (London, 1774), which had been read to the Royal Society. Also included in this parcel of books was a copy of *Experimental Inquiries* (London, 1774), dedicated to Franklin by the author, the anatomist William Hewson, a recently deceased member, a gift to the Society from his widow, through Franklin, who was a close friend of the Hewson family.

On 30 December the Society received several communications from Franklin enclosing requests from French savants for information. The Abbé Raynal inquired about the population, commerce, and wealth of the American colonies. In reply

---

[7] Ibid., 15 Jan. 1773.
[8] Ibid., 15 Jan. 1773.

the Society concluded that Raynal's inquiries lay outside its proper field, and so notified Franklin. In another letter to Franklin, Louis-Jean-Marie Daubenton, keeper of the Cabinet du Roi and a collaborator of Buffon, requested for the King's Cabinet specimens of the natural productions of Pennsylvania, especially birds, "which are the Objects that are the most necessary for M. de Buffon to complete his ornithological work." Yet another set of queries, sent by the Marquis de Condorcet to his "dear & illustrious Brother" Franklin, dated 2 December 1773, received a warm response.

> 1st. Do the calcarious stones and the Soils contain Marine productions, or impressions of Shells, or Fishes, or Vegetables? Do they belong to known species, to be found in the Seas in the neighbourhood of Philadelphia, or in remote Seas? (The living analogies of the fossils found in France, exist often no where else, than the Seas near the Equator.) To what elevation on the Mountains and in what depth of the Earth, are those productions found? Are they to be found alike in the Mountains of a pyramidal form, and in those that are hemispherical? Are any fossil bones to be found, and to what species do they belong?
>
> 2nd. Are there any observations made in Philadelphia, or in the neighbouring Colonies, on the direction of the Magnetic needle, so that accounts may be obtained what variations it has undergone every year, in the same place? The observations made in Paris seem to denote, that the needle describes great oscillations, insomuch that its greatest swiftness has corresponded with the year 1684, and to near four degrees to the West, and the duration of the oscillation should be betwixt a century & a half, & two centuries. If there are any good observations made yearly in Philadelphia, I should like to have a table of them.
>
> 3rd. Has the height of the Mercury in the barometer the same conformity, with the change of weather as in our Continent. This must be the case generally speaking. But there may be some singularity, capable of throwing a great light upon the Meteorological Science—a science still in its infancy, since we do not know what part in the alterations in the weight of the atmosphere, is owing to the effect of the Celestial bodies, and what part is owing to local causes, and since we have only conjectures on the formation of most of the meteors.
>
> 4th. I should be glad to know if there are in the English Colonies, Negroes who having obtained their liberty, have lived without mixing with the white people? If their black Children born free and educated as such, have retained the genius and character of the Negroes, or have contracted the Character of Europeans? If Men of genius & parts have been observed among them?
>
> 5th. Whether you find in the plains, or on the Mountains of America, Stones which like the Basaltes & Pumice appear to owe their origin to Volcanoes? If coals, inflamable [sic] or non inflamable fossils have been found? and whether these productions lie above or below some banks of Shells.[9]

Provost William Smith, John Lukens, David Rittenhouse, and Owen Biddle were appointed to answer the questions on meteorology; Dr. Thomas Bond,

---

[9] Ibid., 30 Dec. 1774.

Richard Wells, Pierre E. Du Simitière, and Dr. Benjamin Rush undertook to prepare replies to the questions on natural history. The committees were slow in performing their assigned tasks; and on 30 May 1775 specific assignments were made: Du Simitière to answer queries one and five; Rittenhouse two and three; and Dr. Bond four. Whether these men completed their replies is unknown. It is, however, a significant indication of how and why persons were elected to the Society that on 28 January 1775, a month after their queries and gifts of books were brought to the attention of the Society, Condorcet, Daubenton, Raynal, Lavoisier, and Rozier were all elected foreign members.

Franklin returned to Philadelphia from London in the spring of 1775. He presided at several meetings, bringing to the Society gifts of books from the Abbé Jacques François Dicquemare, the Abbé Rozier, and Sir John Pringle, and communicating a letter from Sir John that contained an abstract of Captain Cook's last voyage that had not yet been published in London.

The Society's meetings were suspended in 1776 because of the war; in the late summer of that year Franklin went to France as Congress' agent and minister; not until March 1779 were meetings resumed. Franklin was promptly reelected president on 19 March, and he was reelected, apparently unanimously, every year thereafter until his death. Despite the hazards of wartime communication, Franklin and the Society continued to correspond, although intermittently. They soon had an additional resource, however: they could sometimes make use of the mails of the French ministers. Thanking Buffon on 10 December 1779 for the gift several years before of his natural history of birds, the Society assured the great naturalist that if it could be of any use to him, M. Conrad Gérard, who had been elected a member, "or our learned and truly respectable president, Doctor Franklin, while he continues at Paris, will furnish you with opportunities of conveying to us your commands."[10] In 1783 Franklin sent the Society, through Dr. Bond, six volumes of the Abbé Jean-Louis-Giraud Soulavie's work *Histoire naturelle de la France méridionale* (Paris, 1780–84); and a few months later he sent to Dr. Rush for the Society a letter and pamphlet about the French experiments with air balloons.[11]

Franklin returned home to Philadelphia on 14 September 1785. A few days later the Society directed a committee of three prestigious members, Chief Justice Thomas McKean, the Reverend Dr. William White, and Dr. Samuel Magaw, to invite Franklin "to take his Seat as *President* of this Society, and . . . [to] prepare an *address,* to be presented to him in that Character, at their next meeting, if it may be convenient for him to be present."[12] Franklin named 27 September; a special meeting was called for that day; and 19 members attended. Chief Justice McKean delivered the Society's address.

[10] Ibid., 10 Dec. 1779.
[11] Ibid., 26 Sept. 1783; 19 March 1784.
[12] Ibid., 16 Sept. 1785.

Sir,

It is with peculiar pleasure, that the American Philosophical Society address you on this occasion.

The high consideration and esteem in which we hold your character, so intimately combine with our regard for the public welfare, that we participate eminently in the general satisfaction which your return to America produces.

We bid you welcome to your native country, for which you have done the most essential services: And we welcome you to this Chair, your occupying of which, as *President,* adds to our institution much lustre in the eyes of the world.

Sir, it reflects honor on *Philosophy,* when one, distinguished by his deep investigations and many valuable improvements in it, is known to be equally distinguished for his philanthropy, patriotism, and liberal attachment to the rights of human nature.

We know the favourable influences that freedom has upon the growth of sciences and arts. We derive encouragment and extraordinary felicity from an assemblage of recent memorable events.

And, while we boast in a most pleasing equality permanently ascertained; and that independence which you had so great a share in establishing; we have reason to expect, that this society will proceed with an increasing success, to conduct the important business for which they originally associated.

To this Dr. Franklin responded.

Gentlemen,

The great honor done me by this society, in choosing me so many years successively their President, notwithstanding my absence in Europe, and the very kind welcome they are pleased to give me on my return, demand my most grateful acknowledgments; which I beg they would be pleased to accept, with my warmest wishes of success to their laudable endeavours for the promoting of useful knowledge among us; to which I shall be happy if I can in any degree contribute.[13]

These agreeable formalities concluded, the Society turned to its regular business. Francis Hopkinson presented a specimen of the East Indies method of writing on long strips of cocoanut leaves; and John Fitch laid before the Society "a Drawing and Description of a Machine for working a Boat against the Stream, by means of a Steam Engine."

Hopkinson was especially close to Franklin at this time, and was often asked to carry the older man's letters and essays to meetings of the Society. On 21 October he read "a full and particular Dissertation" by Franklin "upon the various defects in the construction of Chimneys"; on 2 December he presented Franklin's paper of curious and useful observations and discoveries relative to voyages and marine matters; and in the first months of 1786 Franklin presented, through Hopkinson, papers on the hygrometer, an urn stove, smoky chimneys, and a letter from Louis

---

[13] *Pa. Gaz.*, 5 Oct. 1785. This is a cleaner copy, with unimportant changes in wording and punctuation, than is recorded in APS Ms. Minutes, 27 Sept. 1785.

Otto, chargé d'affaires of France at New York, with a paper relating to the first discovery of America. Other books were on such subjects as ancient shorthand and Chinese paper-making; and there was a copperplate engraving of the Duc de Chaulnes' improvements on Franklin's electrical kite.

In February of 1786 Franklin attended the Society's annual oration, delivered by Dr. Benjamin Rush on "the influence of physical causes upon the moral faculty." By midsummer he had unpacked from his voyage home, collected the books that had been entrusted to him for the Society, and delivered them on behalf of the authors. They included, among other volumes, Father Joseph Etienne Berthier's *Histoire des premiers temps du monde* (Paris, 1778), Count Gian Rinaldo Carli's *Le Lettere Americane* (Cremona, 1781–83), six copies of Mesmer's *Précis historique des faits relatifs au magnétisme-animal* (London, 1781), Giovanni Battista Beccaria's *Della elettricità terrestre atmosferica a cielo sereno* ([Rome?], 1775), the Abbé Sans' *Guérison de la paralysie par l'électricité* (Paris, 1772), and several publications of Franklin's friend and correspondent Dr. Jan Ingenhousz of Vienna.

On 21 July 1786 the Society voted 34 persons into membership, the largest number ever chosen at a single meeting. One of the Americans was Franklin's grandson William Temple Franklin, and 22 were foreigners, mostly French. A few, like Dr. Noël, had served with the French army or navy in America; some were known by reputation to the Philadelphia members; but most of the rest were associates, correspondents, or friends of the President, by whom, it seems fair to believe, they were recommended.

> Louis-Alexandre, duc de La Rochefoucauld d'Enville, president of the Royal Academy of Sciences
> Marie-Jean-Antoine-Nicolas Caritat, marquis de Condorcet, perpetual secretary of the Academy[14]
> Jean-Baptiste LeRoy, member of the Academy
> Abbé Jean-Louis-Giraud Soulavie, "littérateur"
> Jan Ingenhousz, physician to the Emperor of Austria
> René-Georges Gastellier, physician, of Montargis
> Guillaume Grivel, writer and author of *Théorie de l'Éducation*
> Jacques-Alexandre-César Charles, aeronaut
> Pierre-Jean-Georges Cabanis, physician, of Auteuil

---

[14] Condorcet was already a member. He had been elected on 18 January 1775, and his name appeared among those of new members in *Pa. Evening Post*, 23 Feb. 1775. He identified himself as a member of the Society on the title page of one of his publications in 1785; but his name does not appear in APS *Trans.*, II (1786) among those elected since 1771. The explanation is doubtless human error or negligence. This is not the only instance in the eighteenth century of a person's being elected twice—or in the twentieth century either. In the 1970s the name of a distinguished scientist was printed on a preliminary ballot although he had been a member for some fifteen years. He took it with good humor and remarked that he was pleased that his colleagues thought him still worthy of election.

Louis-Guillaume Le Veillard, mayor of Passy
   Thibert Gerbier, Physician to the King's Brother
   Aimé-Ambroise-Joseph Feutry, engineer and author
   Lorenz Crell, physician, of Helmsted in Brunswick
   Count Luigi Castiglioni, botanist and traveller in America
   Nicolas Noël, military surgeon of Paris
   Guillaume-Jacques-Constant de Liberge, chevalier de Granchain, naval officer, astronomer and hydrographer
   Richard Kirwan, F.R.S., chemist and physician
   John Whitehurst, F.R.S., instrument-maker
   Benjamin Vaughan, physician and editor, of London
   James Beattie, professor of moral philosophy, Aberdeen
   Thomas Percival, F.R.S., physician, of Manchester
   Thomas Henry, F.R.S., chemist, of Manchester

Twenty-one men were elected at the next intake of members on 19 January 1787. Louis Otto, the French chargé at New York; Antoine-Alexis-François Cadet de Vaux and Louis-Claude Cadet de Gassicourt, both chemists of Paris; Sir Edward Newenham, Bart.; Dr. John Coakley Lettsom and Robert Barclay, merchant, both of London; the Duke of Richmond; and the others were all friends or correspondents of Franklin. Many of the new members acknowledged their election with copies of their recent publications.

As the Society's principal member with international contacts, Franklin not only received gifts for the Society, but was consulted about European learned societies and "particular persons" to whom copies of the second volume of its *Transactions* should be sent. The list grew so long that the Society's original limit of 20 complimentary copies was quickly raised to thirty.[15] One of the academies receiving a copy of the *Transactions* was that at St. Petersburg. Its president, the Princess Dashkova, acknowledged the gift in a letter to Franklin, who proposed her for election, which was accomplished on 17 April 1789.

When John Hyacinth Magellan offered 200 guineas to the Society to endow a prize for the best improvement in navigation, Franklin and Francis Hopkinson were directed to consider the offer and to suggest terms and conditions of the award. On their recommendation the Society prudently invested the money in Philadelphia ground rents, which they purchased from John Dickinson, that yielded £33 12*s.* annually.[16]

On 18 September 1787, the day after the adjournment of the Federal Convention, the Society's scheduled meeting was held at Franklin's house. In the following months Franklin attended with considerable regularity. On these occasions he often brought along letters and books that had been addressed to him as presi-

[15] Ms. Minutes, 21 July, 18 Aug. 1786.
[16] Ibid., 2 March, 20 April 1787.

dent—Patrick Wilson's description of Herschel's 40–foot telescope, Earl Stanhope's *Principles of Electricity* (London, 1779), written as Lord Mahon before succeeding to the title, *Memoirs* of the Royal Academy of Sciences of Turin, three papers on medical subjects by Dr. Gastellier, *Institutes of Physics* by John Anderson, professor of natural philosophy at Glasgow University, and John Adams' *A Defense of the Constitutions of Government of the United States of America* (London, 1787–88). Gifts of artifacts came in as well, laying the basis for the Society's museum. On 5 October 1787, with Franklin presiding, Timothy Matlack and young Dr. Caspar Wistar exhibited "an exceedingly large Thigh-bone of some unknown Species of animal" found near Woodbury Creek in Gloucester County, New Jersey, and they were requested to search for the remaining parts of the skeleton.[17] The Reverend Mr. Beeson in 1789 gave to the Society, through Franklin, petrified shells from the Ringwood iron works in New Jersey. Edward Nairne, the London instrument-maker, presented two improved hygrometers; the Society promptly lent one to Peter LeGaux at Spring Mill on the Schuylkill, who was making observations on the weather, which he sent to the *Columbian Magazine* for publication.[18] Franklin gave to the Society some charts and drawings, including a description and drawing of the chevaux de frise given him by its designer Robert Erskine in 1776, the drawing of an iceboat of the kind used in northern Europe, and drawings of the lighthouse at Plymouth by Edmonstone.

Meanwhile, led and encouraged by Samuel Vaughan and Francis Hopkinson, the Society had begun to make plans to erect a meeting hall. Franklin promptly gave £100 for the purpose. Some time was spent in finding a location; other institutions, notably the Library Company of Philadelphia, were approached with schemes for sharing the space and, of course, the costs; and the Grand Lodge of Masons approached the Society about renting room in the building. Eventually a portion of the State House Yard facing Fifth Street was deeded by the Assembly to the Society; subscriptions at £5 a share were solicited; and construction began in 1785. Charles Willson Peale, wishing to contribute "in that manner which accords best with his own Habits & Line of business," presented his copy of David Martin's portrait of Franklin to grace the hall.[19] Unwilling to go into debt, the Society allowed the building to proceed only as money was in hand to pay for it, and in 1787 it was still unfinished. In this situation Franklin made another gift of £100, "provided the Society carry on the Building so as to be cover'd in," and offered a loan of £500.

> Whereas the President of this Society, his Excellency Benjn. Franklin, Esq., to enable this Body to complete the building begun for their use, in the State-House Square,

---

[17] Ibid., 5 Oct. 1787; 4 Jan. 1788.
[18] Ibid., 15 Aug. 1788.
[19] Lillian B. Miller, ed., *Selected Papers of Charles Willson Peale and his Family* (New Haven, 1983–), I, 438.

and which was lately at a stand, for want of sufficient Funds to prosecute the intentions of the Society,—has subscribed a second Hundred pounds in addition to his former Donation; and has also offered a Loan of what Money may be requisite to raise & cover the Building, upon legal Interest; it is therefore,

Resolved, That the Thanks of the Society be returned to his Excellency Benjn. Franklin, Esq., President of this Society, for his generous additional contribution of One Hundred pounds, to be laid out in raising & covering the Building; & for his offer of a Loan of what Money may be wanted to finish the raising & covering the same, upon legal Interest; it is therefore, farther

Resolved By this Society, that the said offer be accepted; and that the Society do appoint Dr. White & Samuel Vaughan, Esq; as a Committee to wait upon the President, in order to confer wth. him upon the proper Mode of giving Security for his Advances; the result of which, they are to report to the Society.

After the interview wth. the President, and a Report brought in by the Committee, Resolved That the Society give to his Excellency Benjn. Franklin, esq; a Bond for the money he may advance for carrying on, and covering their Building in the State-house Square,—not exceeding Five hundred Pounds,—so soon as the sum can be ascertained; payable in one year, together with legal Interest on the same; as also a Mortgage on the lot of land bought by the Society of Fra. Hopkinson, Esq;—as also of the Rent of the Cellars, and such part of the Building as may be let by the Society; until the said Advance & Interest be fully paid; And that, in the mean time, a copy of these Resolutions signed by the Vice-Presidents and Secretaries, and having the Society's Seal affixed thereto, be delivered to the President.[20]

Franklin's participation in the Society's work extended to some smallest details. The Society's archives contain several bills dated 1787, 1788, and 1789 and endorsed variously "Pass'd by the Society" or "Allow'd. B. Franklin. Presidt." One such bill is for "a Conductor measuring 129 feet."[21]

The hall was completed in the summer of 1789, at least to the extent that meetings could be held in it. On 21 August the Society resolved, "That the future meetings of the Society shall be in the Philosophical Hall, unless on occasions, when the President's health may allow him to be present; then, they shall be held in his house."

Anticipating completion of the Hall and wishing both to decorate it and to honor their president, the Society on 17 July 1789 voted "That a Portrait of Dr. Franklin, the President of this Society, shall, as speedily as is convenient, be executed, in the best manner,—to be perpetually kept in one of their Appartments [sic]." David Rittenhouse and Dr. John Jones were directed to apply to Charles Willson Peale for this purpose. Finding the old man too ill to sit, Peale copied a painting he had made several years before. Apparently at the time the Society commissioned this portrait in 1789, no one remembered that four years before Peale had presented it with "an elegant Portrait" of Franklin, copied from "a much ad-

---

[20] Ms. Minutes, 2 Nov. 1787.
[21] APS *Year Book* (1979), 159.

mired Painting of [David] Martin." At that time the Society had voted Peale their thanks and asked him to retain the painting until the Society had an appropriate place for it. The result was that in 1789 there were two portraits of Franklin which the Society owned or had a claim to. It chose Peale's copy of the Martin portrait, and ordered it framed "in the best manner" for a price not exceeding £6. (This painting has occupied the place of honor in the Society's meeting room for more than two centuries.) The other painting, kept by Peale for some years, eventually passed into the Historical Society of Pennsylvania.[22]

Though not in good health and often in pain, Franklin continued to attend meetings during the fall and early winter of 1789–90 and to take part in the Society's work. On 12 September, at a meeting at his house, Franklin read an extract from a history of the Royal Society that indicated that that Society exercised a right to sue members for unpaid dues; the philosophers' treasurer was given a copy of the extract and authorized to pursue delinquent members. At the next meeting Franklin presented specimens of coal, slate, nitre, and other minerals from David Reddick; specimens of papyrus from Syracuse; and a letter from Samuel Mather of London accompanying a copy of *An Essay on the Powers and Mechanism of Nature* by Robert Young (London, 1788). On 6 November a member—the minutes do not give his name—read a paper "containing a number of observations on ventilation, chiefly collected from conversations with Dr. Franklin."

Franklin was reelected president on 15 January 1790 and on the same night presented a letter from James Bowdoin "containing sundry curious queries relating to magnetism and the theory of the Earth." Two weeks later he sent to the Society the *Memoirs* of the Royal Academy of Sciences of Turin and the two-volume *Nouvelles Expériences et Observations sur divers Objets de Physique* (Paris, 1785–89) by his friend Jan Ingenhousz, who had dedicated the work to him. This is the last reference to Franklin in the minutes of the Society before his death on 17 April.

Among the first to receive news of Franklin's death that day was Governor Thomas Mifflin, a member of the Society. It came during a great thunderstorm while he was entertaining Chief Justice Thomas McKean, Henry Hill, Thomas Willing, David Rittenhouse, and Provost William Smith at his house at the Falls of Schuylkill. On the impulse of the moment, without leaving the table, Smith wrote a few lines.

> Cease! cease, ye clouds, your elemental strife,
> Why rage ye thus, as if to threaten life?
> Seek, seek no more to shake our souls with dread,
> What busy mortal told you "Franklin's dead"?

---

[22] Ibid., 16 Dec. 1785; 2 Dec. 1791; Charles Coleman Sellers, *Benjamin Franklin in Portraiture* (New Haven, [1962]), 335–36, 349–51.

> What, though he yields to Jove's imperious nod,
> With Rittenhouse he left his magic rod.

To which Willing responded,

> What means that flash, the thunder's awful roar—
> The blazing sky—unseen, unheard before?
> Sage Smith replies, "Our Franklin is no more."
> The clouds, long subject to his magic chain,
> Exulting now their liberty regain.[23]

Twenty thousand people were estimated to have marched in Franklin's funeral procession or lined the streets through which it passed.[24] Only Philadelphia's Grand Federal Procession of 4 July 1788, marking the anniversary of independence and the ratification of the Constitution, had exceeded it in this respect. The Society ordered 200 notices printed and sent out, and on 21 April the members, 23 in number, assembled at a special meeting in Philosophical Hall, from which they "went in Procession to the Funeral of their late illustrious President, Dr. Benjamin Franklin." Two days later, at another special meeting, the members voted unanimously "that an Eulogium shall be prepared by one of their Numbers, to be pronounced before this Body, as soon as may be convenient." Their votes on who should be the orator were divided equally between David Rittenhouse and Provost William Smith. The Society agreed that the two should determine between them who should speak.

Unaccountably no further action was taken in Philadelphia for nearly a year. Meanwhile in Paris an *éloge civique* was delivered before the French National Assembly by the Abbé Fauchet, and copies of his oration reached America. Congress, however, disputed whether to honor Franklin, and President Washington declined for reasons of republican protocol to order a national period of mourning. For months no national memorial service for Franklin was mounted. The neglect was not only an embarrassment, but something of a scandal as well as a political issue.[25] On 4 February 1791 the Philosophical Society appointed Dr. Rush, Dr. Benjamin Smith Barton, and John Vaughan to find out from Smith and Rittenhouse which of them would deliver the eulogium the Society had called for the year before. Smith agreed to undertake the task, and on 21 February a special meeting of the Society was called to make the necessary arrangements. Invitations were extended in the Society's name to "public Characters and public Bodies."

---

[23] Horace W. Smith, *Life and Correspondence of the Rev. William Smith, D.D.* (Phila., 1879), II, 324–25.
[24] Benjamin Rush, *Autobiography,* George W. Corner, ed. (Princeton, 1948), 183.
[25] "The Politics of Mourning in France and the United States," in Julian P. Boyd, ed., *The Papers of Thomas Jefferson* (Princeton, 1950–), XIX, 78–106.

1. The President of the United States
2. The Vice President, and Senate of the United States
3. The Speaker, and House of Representatives of do.
4. The Governor of this State
5. The Speaker, and Senate of do.
6. The Speaker and House of Representatives of do.
7. Ministers of the United States, for the departments of State, Treasury, and War
8. Ministers, and Consuls of Foreign Nations
9. The Family of the Deceased
10. The Judges of the Supreme Federal Court; and the District Courts
11. Attorney General of the U. states
12. The Judges of the Supreme Court of Pennsylvania
13. The Mayor and Corporation of the city
14. The Trustees and Faculty of the University
15. The Trustees and Faculty of the college
16. The Printers of the city of Philadelphia
17. The College of Physicians
18. The Clergy—individually
19. The Directors of the Library Company
20. The Managers and Physicians of the Pennsylvania Hospital
21. The President and Officers of the Abolition Society
22. The Corporation of the German Lutheran Church
23. Citizens, by a general notification in the public papers [26]

The selection of Provost Smith as memorial orator was in many respects puzzling and inappropriate. Though he had come to Philadelphia nearly forty years earlier through Franklin's influence, the two men had soon fallen out over both the conduct of the Academy and College of Philadelphia and provincial politics. Smith was the Proprietors' man, defender, and apologist; and Franklin the leader of the anti-Proprietary party. Each had spoken harsh words of the other, and there was no evidence that their early friendship had been restored. On the other hand, Smith had been one of the ablest and most active members of the Philosophical Society after 1768 and, as he had demonstrated by his eulogy of General Montgomery and other public sermons, he was a speaker of power and grace. He could be counted on to produce something that would be an honor to its subject, the Society, and the nation.

Smith fell to work collecting historical and biographical material. He asked Rittenhouse for data on Franklin's scientific career. From Rush he obtained some general remarks on Franklin's character, and from Jefferson a long, thoughtful estimate of Franklin's reputation in France (with the engaging story of how, when

---

[26] Ms. Minutes, 21 Feb. 1791.

asked, "It is you, Sir, who replace Doctor Franklin?" Jefferson would usually modestly reply, "No one can replace him, Sir; I am only his successor").[27] Smith consulted the minutes of the Young Junto and of the American Society, and included in his eulogy generous extracts from the queries their members discussed. He made use of Joseph Priestley's *History of Electricity,* Benjamin Vaughan's edition of Franklin's writings, and Henry Stuber's continuation of Franklin's autobiography in the *Columbian Magazine.* Smith noted that Franklin's last public act was to sign the petition of the Pennsylvania Abolition Society, of which he was president; and he quoted Franklin's letter of condolence to his niece on the death of her father, with its comforting words on immortality. He quoted from the public eulogies in France by Fauchet and La Rochefoucauld.

"Citizens of Pennsylvania! Luminaries of Science! Assembled Fathers of America!" Smith began. He referred to Franklin's achievements—the Library Company, the Academy and College, the Pennsylvania Hospital; he alluded to *The Way to Wealth;* he mentioned the fire company, the insurance company, the night watch, and the Pennsylvania fireplace; and in speaking of Franklin's public career did not conceal the fact that bitterness had sometimes marked the politics of the day. He saluted Franklin as "*a Citizen of the World*—successfully labouring for the benefit of the whole human race, by the diffusion of liberal science and the invention of useful arts."[28] Franklin's "vast and comprehensive mind," Smith declared, "was cast in a mould, which Nature seems rarely to have used before. . . ."

> His original and universal genius was capable of the *greatest* things, but disdained not the *smallest,* provided they were useful. With equal ease and abilities, he could conduct the affairs of a Printing-Press, and of a great Nation; and discharge the duties of a public Minister of State, or the private Executor of a Will. Those talents, which have separately entered into the composition of other eminent characters in the various departments of life, were in *Him* united to form one great and splendid character. . . . Franklin . . . might have become a Newton . . . [or] a Lycurgus: But he was greater than either of them, by uniting the talents of both, in the practical Philosophy of doing good; compared to which all the palms of speculative wisdom and science wither on the sight.[29]

This high-flown rhetoric must have sounded better than it reads two hundred years later, and indeed the surviving printed version may in fact have been written afterwards from the preacher's notes.

---

[27] Boyd, ed., *Jefferson Papers,* XIX, 112–14. Jefferson's letter to Smith, 19 Feb. 1791, is ibid., 112–13.
[28] William Smith, *Eulogium on Benjamin Franklin, L.L.D.* (Phila., 1792), 19.
[29] Ibid., 7.

The eulogy was delivered in the German Lutheran Church on the afternoon of 1 March. Forty-five members of the Society attended, including Jefferson, Rittenhouse, Alexander Hamilton, Bishop White, and Dr. Caspar Wistar. A copy of the address was requested for publication—perhaps no completed manuscript was then available, for it was not printed at last until 1792.

There is an unpleasant story about Smith's eulogium that was long cherished by his descendants, who carried into the late nineteenth century a family enmity towards Franklin. Having returned home after the memorial service, Provost Smith asked his little daughter Rebecca whether she liked the address. "I don't think you believed more than one-tenth part of what you said of old Ben Lightning-rod, did you?" was her reply. And Smith, without affirming or denying the charge, laughed heartily.[30]

For many years thereafter the Society had occasions to remember Franklin. A few months after his death his bequest of 91 volumes of the *Histoire* of the Royal Academy of Sciences of Paris was delivered. In 1792 his son-in-law Richard Bache gave them the chair in which Franklin "used to sit when the Meetings of the Society were held at his House."[31] (All succeeding presidents of the Society used it until 1931, when the presiding officer collapsed and died in it.) On 19 February 1796 Charles Willson Peale, the Society's curator and proprietor of Peale's Museum, which occupied rooms in Philosophical Hall,

> presented to the Society a young son of four Months and four days old, being the first child born in the Philosophical Hall, and requested that the Society would give him a name— On which the Society unanimously agreed that after the name of the chief founder and late President of the Society he should be called *Franklin.*

And in 1797, accepting election as president of the Society, Thomas Jefferson made reference, as most of his successors in that post were to do, to "our Patriarch, whom Philosophy & Philanthropy announced the first of men, and whose name will be like a star of the first magnitude in the firmament of heaven, when the memory of those who have surrounded & obscured him, will be lost in the abyss of time."[32]

In 1798, after being threatened with a suit for its recovery, the Society at last repaid Franklin's loan of £500 to his heirs.[33]

---

[30] Smith, *Life and Correspondence of Rev. William Smith,* II, 344.
[31] Ms. Minutes, 3 Feb. 1792.
[32] Ibid., 17 Feb. 1797.
[33] Ibid., 17 Nov. 1797; 20 April 1798.

THOMAS BOND
Miniature by an unidentified artist.
Mütter Museum, College of Physicians of Philadelphia

THOMAS BOND (1713–1784)
AMERICAN PHILOSOPHICAL SOCIETY: 1743

THOMAS BOND, physician and surgeon of Philadelphia, was an original member of the American Philosophical Society in 1743, a principal figure in reviving the long "dormant" institution in 1767–68, and vice-president of the united Society in 1769. Reelected to this post annually until his death, he was, during Franklin's long absences abroad, in effect the president, presiding at most meetings, serving on many committees, receiving and answering the Society's correspondence. From time to time he exhibited specimens of natural history or read a paper; and on 21 May 1782 he delivered the Society's annual oration—on "the Rank and Dignity of Man in the Scale of Being."

Born on 2 Third Month [May] 1713 in Calvert County, Maryland, he was the third of five sons of Richard and Elizabeth (Benson) Chew Bond, members of Herring Creek Monthly Meeting of Friends.[1] Mrs. Bond was the widow of Benjamin Chew, who had died in 1700, and the mother of Dr. Samuel Chew "of Maidstone," who later moved to Philadelphia; she thus linked Bond to the influential Chew connection in Maryland, Delaware, and Pennsylvania. Young Thomas began the study of medicine with Dr. John Hamilton of Calvert County, and continued his studies in Philadelphia with his half-brother Samuel. In 1734 Chew and Bond had a shop in Market Street, where they offered for sale "fresh Drugs, just imported from London," and "most kinds of Chymical and Galenical Medecines duely [sic] and honestly prepared." A few years later Bond was one of seven physi-

---

[1] The principal modern biographical account is Elizabeth H. Thomson, "Thomas Bond, 1713–84: First Professor of Clinical Medicine in the American Colonies," *Jour. Med. Education,* XXXIII (1958), 614–24. I am indebted to Miss Thomson for additional biographical data in the present sketch. It may be useful to call attention to several corrections made here in accounts of Bond in *DAB,* Howard A. Kelly and Walter L. Burrage, eds., *Dictionary of American Medical Biography* (N.Y., 1928), J. Alison Scott, "A Sketch of the Life of Thomas Bond, Clinician and Surgeon," *Univ. Penna. Med. Bull.,* XVIII (1905–06), 306–18, and other places:

Miss Thomson has established the correct year of Bond's birth (formerly always given as 1712) by an examination of the Herring Creek Monthly Meeting records.

Bond's preceptor was not the famous Dr. Alexander Hamilton of Annapolis, but probably Dr. John Hamilton (d. 1768) of Calvert County. Dr. Alexander was two years *younger* than Bond and, on his famous journey from Annapolis to Boston in 1744, carried an *introduction to* Bond—of which he certainly would have had no need had he once been Bond's preceptor. Carl Bridenbaugh, ed., *Gentleman's Progress: The Itinerarium of Dr. Alexander Hamilton, 1744* (Chapel Hill, N.C., 1948), 19; Eugene F. Cordell, *Medical Annals of Maryland, 1799–1899* (Baltimore, 1903), 655.

There is an unresolved question about Mrs. Bond's family. Her name is sometimes given as Sarah Venables. However, the register of New Jersey marriage licenses records that a license was granted 31 October 1742 "unto Doctor Thomas Bond of the City of Philada. . . . and Sarah Weyman Spinster Daughter of the Revd. Robert Weyman deced. . . ." (Archives and History Bureau, N.J. State Library; 1 *N.J. Arch.,* XXII, 452). Weyman, an Anglican missionary sent to America by the S.P.G. in 1719, served Trinity Church, Oxford, Philadelphia, and congregations in Radnor and Whitemarsh, and moved to Burlington, N.J., in 1731 (*PMHB,* XXVII [1903], 289–90). The name Venables appears in both Philadelphia and Burlington in the eighteenth century. A modern family genealogist identfied Sarah Weyman as "of the Venables family of Philadelphia" (chart in Thomas Bond house, South Second Street, Philadelphia).

Rebecca Venables, widow of Thomas Venables (who died 26 January 1731: Edward L. Clark, *A Record of Inscriptions . . . in the Burial-Ground of Christ Church, Philadelphia* [Phila., 1864], 26), by her will dated 1781 and probated 1784, made bequests to "my worthy Friend Dr. Thomas Bond," to his wife Sarah Bond, and to their children—the youngest of whom was named Venables—and grandchildren; but Mrs. Venables does not identify any beneficiary as son-in-law, daughter, or grandchild.

It is possible that Sarah Weyman, after the death of her father (and mother?), was reared and in effect adopted by Mrs. Venables (who may have been a family friend or relative), who thereafter took an interest in, and accepted some responsibility for, Sarah (understandably though inaccurately thought of as Sarah Venables) and for Sarah's children, although none was of her (Rebecca's) blood.

cians who publicly recommended inoculation for smallpox, pointing out that of 129 cases under their care the preceding winter only one proved fatal.[2]

With fair prospects in his profession Bond married 11 September 1735 at Philadelphia Monthly Meeting Susannah, daughter of Edward Roberts, who was soon to be elected mayor of the city. She died in 1737 of complications following the birth of their second child.[3] The next year Bond went abroad. He bore an introduction from the seedsman John Bartram to the London Quaker merchant and horticulturist Peter Collinson, as well as turtle eggs, insects, a jar of papaw fruit and flowers, and some roots "packed up carefully."[4] He spent several months attending lectures and observing hospital practice in London (where he met young John Fothergill), and then crossed to France. In Paris he enrolled in lectures at the Hôtel-Dieu (whose professors—Astruc, Winslow, Le Cat, and others—he would later call his "friends")[5] and at the Jardin du Roi, where Bernard de Jussieu, to whom he brought a letter from Collinson, was in charge of the teaching of botany. In Paris Bond studied

> the most diligently I ever did in my life, and, I fear, to the prejudice of my tender constitution; but if I was almost sure 'twould kill me, I could not avoid tending the curious courses of Anatomy, Surgery, Physiology, &c. And, in short, 'tis impossible there can be better, if so good schools in the world.[6]

Bond gave Jussieu specimens of Seneca snakeroot from America. The French botanists tried it frequently with "surprizing Success" and pronounced it highly efficacious in cases of pleurisy. This judgment, communicated by Bond to his brother Phineas in Philadelphia, given by Phineas to the *Pennsylvania Gazette,* and reprinted widely through the colonies thereafter, gave support to John Tennent's claims for his discovery.[7] Bond returned home in 1739. He had neither received nor sought a medical degree, but he was a "doctor," and so "Dr. Bond" he ever was.

In 1742 Bond was married again, to Sarah Weyman, daughter of Robert Weyman, rector of the Episcopal Church at Burlington, New Jersey. Such a marriage "out of meeting" would have brought the Quakers' censure upon him, but Bond had already drifted away from his early faith and was out of favor with the Friends, the Philadelphia Monthly Meeting having but recently "dealt with him for taking

---

[2] *Pa. Gaz.,* 27 June 1734; *Am. Weekly Mercury,* 8 Sept. 1737.
[3] Hinshaw, *Amer. Quaker Genealogy,* II, 636; Frank Willing Leach Coll., Le61, 4,6 (Geneal. Soc. Pa.).
[4] Darlington, *Memorials,* 121.
[5] *Franklin Papers,* XVIII, 164–67.
[6] Darlington, *Memorials,* 316–17.
[7] *Pa. Gaz.,* 26 July 1739; *Boston Evening Post,* 6 Aug. 1739; *Va. Gaz.* (Parks), 17 Aug. 1739.

the oath."⁸ The couple had seven children, of whom five survived to maturity. Of these Thomas, Jr. became a physician and a member of the American Philosophical Society; Richard also studied medicine and was about to go to London and Edinburgh for further study when he died in 1772; and Venables, to whom his father bequeathed his medical books, apparatus, and drugs, began the study of medicine but soon gave it up. The Bonds lived on the east side of Second Street between Chestnut and Walnut Streets at the Sign of the Golden Mortar. As early as 1750 Bond had a country place in the Northern Liberties overlooking the Schuylkill River. John Adams, who visited there in 1775, described it as a "little Box," one small room with a chamber above; but the farm contained 120 acres, the gardens were "very spacious," the orchard "noble," and the fruit trees "very numerous and of great Variety." The tax roll of 1772 showed there were seven horses, ten cows, twenty sheep, and two negro slaves on the place. In town Bond kept a carriage in which to make his calls.⁹

In partnership with his younger brother Phineas, who had also studied medicine in Europe and had a degree from the University of Rheims, Bond soon acquired a large and profitable practice. The brothers' "Co-partnership Ledgers" for September 1765 (a date arbitrarily selected) show that they saw or prescribed for fifteen to twenty patients a day. One of these was the wife of Thomas' good friend Benjamin Franklin; he attended her in her final illness in 1774. Bond took apprentices, among others Cadwalader Evans, Gerardus Clarkson, Samuel Stringer, James Wilkinson (later General Wilkinson), and Thomas Smith, son of the provost of the College of Philadelphia. His nephew John Bond was apothecary of the Pennsylvania Hospital in 1756–58.¹⁰ To instruct his pupils and for his own use Bond acquired in addition to medical texts "some pritty good anatomical preparations of the muscles and blood vessels injected with wax," which he was proud to show visitors.¹¹ In 1741 Bond was named one of the Port Physicians in conjunction with Dr. Thomas Graeme.

Bond's mature views on medicine are suggested in opinions he expressed in a letter to Franklin in 1771.

> The School of Edingburgh [sic] seems at this Time to be better calculated to please the Fancy, than to form the Judgement; and indeed the many extraordinary Novelties in-

---

⁸ Phila. Mo. Meeting, Minutes, 30 Fifth Month 1742.
⁹ *Pa. Gaz.,* 27 Sept. 1750; L. H. Butterfield, ed., *Adams Family Correspondence* (Cambridge, Mass., 1963), I, 251; "List of the Families that kept Equipages in Philadelphia . . . in . . . 1772" (Du Simitière Papers, Lib. Co. Phila.).
¹⁰ 8 *Pa. Arch.,* VI, 5016.
¹¹ Bridenbaugh, *Gentleman's Progress,* 19. "Mrs. Bond and I air old acquintans," said Deborah Franklin in 1767. *Franklin Papers,* XIV, 282; XXI, 401. Franklin gave Bond a portrait of himself painted in London. Ibid., XVIII, 204; Charles C. Sellers, *Benjamin Franklin in Portraiture* (New Haven, 1962), 410–12.

cullcated [sic] there, would be a Barr to public Confidence in this Part of the World. As far as We can judge from the public Exhibitions, Surgery in London is a mere *mechanic Art,* well executed. The Accademy of Surgery in Paris, aims at uniting Science to their Profession and have done thereby Honour to it.

He thought well of Gaubius but had heard that the medical school at Leyden was "neglected," while Vienna under Van Swieten had misled the world "by Absurdities and Falsehoods."[12]

No thoughtless follower of a system, Bond's treatments were in general moderate, directed more by observation and experience than by theory. In many cases he recommended warm or cold baths, although these were little used in private practice; and in the Hospital he prescribed warm air and vapor baths. He bled patients, himself included, when bleeding was indicated, and at least once relieved a victim of hypochondriasis by this means. On another occasion, as Benjamin Rush told it, Bond inadvertently cured a mental patient of one of his symptoms by inducing anger. After long confinement the patient had stopped talking and nothing could induce him to speak. Dr. Bond made an attempt. Approaching the man, who was drawing a flower, Bond observed, "A very pretty cabbage." "You are a fool and a liar," came the reply; "it is a flower," and with that the patient resumed speaking as usual.[13]

As a surgeon Bond achieved a wide reputation. Patients came to him from considerable distances—Robert Treat Paine from Boston in 1751 to be inoculated against smallpox, Caesar Rodney from Delaware in 1768 and Richard Stockton from Princeton in 1779 for removal of cancerous growths in face and jaw.[14] He performed several lithotomies at the Pennsylvania Hospital as early as 1756, and did many thereafter, including a successful operation on a child of four. Several of these operations were witnessed by laymen, who reported their observations and reactions to the newspapers, thus spreading Bond's reputation still farther.[15] At the

---

[12] *Franklin Papers,* XVIII, 165.
[13] Rush, "An Inquiry into the Comparative State of Medicine, in Philadelphia, between the Years 1760 and 1766, and the Year 1805," *Medical Inquiries and Observations* (2nd ed., Phila., 1805), IV, 379; Rush, *Medical Inquiries and Observations upon the Diseases of the Mind* (Phila., 1812), 99, 222, 231.
[14] John Jones, "State of Mr. Stockdon's Case," Dec. 1779, Carson Coll., V (Coll. Phys. Phila.); Paine to Joseph Palmer and Richard Cranch, 26 Sept. 1751, Paine Diary, Paine Papers (Mass. Hist. Soc.); George H. Ryden, ed., *Letters to and from Caesar Rodney* (Phila., 1933), 30–31; *PMHB,* XLVIII (1924), 246–47.
[15] *Md. Gaz.,* 24 Oct. 1765; *Pa. Gaz.,* 7 Oct. 1772; David Ramsay, *History of South-Carolina . . . to the Year 1808* (2v., Charleston, 1809), II, 94, says Bond performed 17 lithotomies, that John Jones in New York and Philadelphia performed 60, and that Philip Turner performed 200 in Connecticut. This last figure seems improbably high and may be a copyist's or printer's error. Thacher (*Am. Med. Biography,* II, 153) gives Turner's number as 20, all but two being "perfectly successful." See also Thomas G. Morton and William Hunt, *Surgery in the Pennsylvania Hospital* (Phila., 1880), 135, and Scott, "A Sketch of the Life of Thomas Bond," loc. cit., 306–18.

end of his life Bond described himself in his will, not as "Physician," but as "Thomas Bond, Surgeon."

The discovery of mineral springs in Virginia in the early 1740s attracted patients with various ailments. Appreciating that claims for the springs' curative powers were often exaggerated and inaccurate, the Bond brothers in 1746 called for detailed reports from any who had had personal experience with the waters—the age and manner of life of the patient, his disease, the method of taking the waters, their effects. "This Exactness," they explained, "is absolutely necessary to assist us in distinguishing between those Cures which have been really performed by the Springs, and such as are only Effects of Time, Exercise, a Change of Air, Diet, or some other Accident."[16] What response they received does not appear; at least the Bonds seem not to have published anything on the subject.

Thomas Bond did, however, communicate observations on two unusual cases in his practice to London friends in this period. One, on a worm found in the liver, was sent to Dr. John Clephane of St. George's Hospital; the other, on the use of bark in cases of scrofula, went to Dr. Fothergill. Both letters were published in the London *Medical Inquiries and Observations*.[17]

Bond played a primary role in founding the Pennsylvania Hospital. Thanks to the full account Franklin's memoirs, the story is well known:

> In 1751, Dr. Thomas Bond, a particular Friend of mine, conceiv'd the Idea of establishing a Hospital in Philadelphia, for the Reception and Cure of poor sick Persons, whether Inhabitants of the Province or Strangers. A very beneficent Design, which has been ascrib'd to me, but was originally his. He was zealous and active in endeavouring to procure subscriptions for it; but the Proposal being a Novelty in America, and at first not well understood, he met with small Success. At length he came to me, with the Compliment that he found there was no such thing as carrying a public Spirited Project through, without my being concern'd in it; "for, says he, I am often ask'd by those to whom I propose Subscribing, Have you consulted Franklin upon this Business? and what does he think of it? And when I tell them that I have not, (supposing it rather out of your Line) they do not subscribe, but say they will consider of it." I enquir'd into the Nature, and probable Utility of his Scheme, and receiving from him a very satisfactory Explanation, I not only subscrib'd to it myself, but engag'd heartily in the Design of Procuring Subscriptions from others. Previous however to the Solicitation, I endeavoured to prepare the Minds of the People by writing on the Subject in the Newspapers, which was my usual Custom in such Cases, but which he had omitted.[18]

Bond was an early and generous contributor to the Hospital and served briefly as one of the first managers, but resigned upon being appointed to the medical staff

---

[16] *Pa. Gaz.,* 6 Jan. 1746/7.
[17] "An Account of a Worm bred in the Liver," 1754; "On the Use of the Bark in Scrophulous Cases," 1759, London *Med. Obs. & Inq.,* I (1757), 67–80, II (1762), 265–68; *Franklin Papers,* VI, 10–12.
[18] Franklin, *Autobiography,* 199–200.

when the Hospital opened in 1752. As physicians of the Hospital, Bond and his colleagues had a rare opportunity to instruct their pupils in the wards. So obvious was the benefit from such instruction that, when the Medical Department of the College of Philadelphia was created in 1765, Bond proposed that he should deliver a formal course of clinical lectures each year. The Managers of the Hospital assented and the trustees of the College decreed that Bond's course should be required for the M.D. degree. First presented to the Managers privately at Bond's house on 26 November 1766, the proposal was made publicly to the Managers, the medical professors, some thirty students, "and most of the Physicians of the Place" on 3 December.[19]

> . . . the Clinical professor comes into the Aid of Speculation and demonstrates the Truth of Theory by Facts: he meets his Pupils at stated times in the Hospital, and when a case presents adapted to his purpose, he asks all those Questions which lead to a certain knowledge of the Disease, and parts affected; this he does in the most exact and particular manner, to convince the Students how many, and what minute circumstances are often necessary to form a judgment of the curative indications, on which, the safety and Life of the Patient depend, from all which Circumstances and the present Symptoms, he pronounces what the Disease is, whether it is curable or Incurable, in what manner it ought to be treated, and gives his reasons from the Authority or Experience for all he says on the occasion; and if the Disease baffles the power of Art, and the Patient falls a sacrifice to it, he then brings his knowledge to the Test, and fixes Honour or discredit on his Reputation by exposing all the Morbid parts to view, and Demonstrates by what means it produced Death; and if perchance he finds something unsuspected, which betrays an Error in Judgment, he like a great and good Man, immediately acknowledges the mistake, and for the benefit of survivors points out other methods by which it might have been more hapily [sic] Treated. The latter part of this field of Tuition is the surest method of obtaining just Ideas of Diseases. The great Booerhave [sic] was so attentive to it, that he was not only present at the opening of Human Bodies, but frequently attended the Slaughter Houses in Leyden, to examine the Carcases of Beasts; and being asked by a learn'd Friend, by what means he had acquired such uncommon certainty in the Diagnostic's and Prognostic's of Diseases, answered by examining dead Bodies, studying Sydenhams observations, and Bonetus's *Sepulchretum Anatomicum,* both which he had read ten times, and each with greater pleasure, and improvement.
>
> * * *
>
> I am now to inform you, Gentlemen, that the Managers and Physicians of the Pennsylvania Hospital, on seeing the great number of you attending the School of Physic in this City, are of opinion, this excellent institution likewise affords a favourable opportunity of farther improvement to you in the practical part of your Profession, and . . . have allotted to me the Task of giving a course of Clinical, and Meteriological [sic] Observations in it, which I chearfully undertake (though the season of my

---

[19] Carl Bridenbaugh, ed., "Dr. Bond's Essay on the Utility of Clinical Lectures," *Jour. Hist. Med.,* II (1947), 10–19. The essay is also printed in Morton and Woodbury, *Pennsylvania Hospital,* 462–67. An account of the lecture was published in *Pa. Gaz.,* 11 Dec. 1766.

Life points out relaxation and retirement, rather than new Incumbrances.) in hopes, that remarks on the many curious Cases that must daily occurr, amongst an Hundred and thirty Sick persons, collected together at one time, may be very instructive to You. I therefore purpose to meet you at stated times here, and give you the best information in my Power of the nature and treatment of Chronical Diseases, and of the proper management of Ulcers, Wounds and Fractures. I shall shew you all the Opperations [sic] of Surgery, and endeavour, from the Experience of Thirty Years, to introduce you to a Familiar acquaintance with the acute Diseases of your own Country, in order to which, I shall put up a compleat Meteriological Apparatus, and endeavour to inform you of all the known Properties of the atmosphere which surrounds us, and the effects it's frequent variations produce on Animal Bodies, and confirm the Doctrine, by an Exact register of the Weather, and of the prevailing Diseases, both here, and in the Neighbouring Provinces, to which I shall add, all the interesting observations which may occurr in private practice, and sincerely wish it may be in my power to do them to your Satisfaction.

A few years later Bond and his former pupil Cadwalader Evans, both physicians to the Almshouse, began to offer lectures there on obstetrics. Linking practical observation and work in the Hospital and the Almshouse with the formal instruction in the Medical School, Bond's lectures made medical training in Philadelphia superior to anything that could be had elsewhere in the colonies and states for more than half a century, and brought students to the city by the scores and hundreds each year, even from New England.

Meanwhile Bond was participating in many other activities of the city's life. He was made a member of St. John's Masonic Lodge in 1734, was Deputy Grand Master for a short time under Franklin in 1749, subscribed £15 towards the building of Freemasons' Hall in 1754, and was elected Senior Grand Warden of the Pennsylvania Grand Lodge in 1755.[20] He became a subscriber to the Library Company in 1741. He was elected a member of the Philadelphia Common Council in 1745, and was captain of one of the companies of Associators in 1747. He belonged to the Fishing Company of Fort St. David's and was an original member of the Society of the Sons of St. George, established in 1772. In 1774 he was one of the physicians of the Society for Inoculating the Poor Gratis.[21] More important, he was one of the original trustees of the Academy and College of Philadelphia, to which he contributed money and sent his sons. He served as trustee without interruption from 1749 until 1779, when the trustees were ousted by the Revolutionary government; but, as an informed and prominent citizen, he was appointed to the board of the successor institution, the University of the State of Pennsylvania.

---

[20] Julius F. Sachse, *Old Masonic Lodges of Pennsylvania* (Phila., 1912–13), I, 32; 2 *Pa. Arch.,* II, 503.
[21] *Pa. Packet,* 7 Feb. 1774. The Society was formed in response to a sharp rise in deaths from smallpox. In the previous year, according to the bills of mortality, 1,344 persons had died, about 300 of them, mostly children, from smallpox received in the natural way. The necessary funds were raised by charitable citizens, and eight physicians—all members of the APS—agreed to inoculate and to provide medicines and attendance at no expense to the patients.

In this capacity he was especially active in reviving medical instruction, and at the Board's request added lectures on theory and practice to his clinical lectures at the Hospital.

In the years before the Revolution Bond had a major part in reviving the American Philosophical Society. The revival was partly a response to the formation of the Philadelphia Medical Society. John Morgan had founded the medical group with a number of younger physicians early in 1766, then sent invitations to the older men to join. Some did so, but others were offended by the unwarranted slight. Accordingly Bond rallied the survivors of the old Philosophical Society of 1743, and they elected new members and officers, wrote by-laws, and held regular meetings. In this organization Bond was a member of the Committees for Medicine, Anatomy, and Chemistry and for Natural Philosophy, Mathematics, Optics, and Astronomy. Thus in 1767 there were two groups in the city, perceptibly distinguished by purpose and by the political and religious character of their members, yet essentially more alike than different. Sensibly, the leaders of the two groups moved towards union. That goal was finally achieved in 1769, not without frustrating delays and eager efforts by each society to take advantage of the other. Franklin, a founder of the old Society but now the hero of the flourishing new American Society for Promoting Useful Knowledge, was president, and Thomas Bond, also a member of the original Society, was vice-president of the united society. In this Bond was a member of the Committees on Medicine and Anatomy and on Husbandry and American Improvements. In 1770 he subscribed £3 to the Silk Society, in which the Society and many of its members were much interested.

Bond was past 60 years of age when the American Revolution commenced. Although he had signed the Non-Importation Agreement in 1765 and was properly reckoned a supporter of the Proprietary party, he played little part in politics and was no partisan. He was therefore, perhaps understandably, suspected of mild Loyalism (his nephew Phineas, a lawyer, was strongly of that persuasion), but his son Dr. Thomas Bond, Jr. was active in the rebel cause. Bond could not, however, withhold his professional skill. "When I see so many friends and valuable citizens exposing themselves to the horrors of war," he wrote the Council of Safety on 4 December 1776, "I think it my duty to make them a tender of the best services in my power. . . . As I am told many of the sick are near the city, the sooner the matter is concluded on the better." One of his wartime patients in 1776–77 was a British prisoner, the indomitable Lieutenant Alan Cameron (later Lieutenant General Sir Alan Cameron of Erracht), who badly injured himself when he fell from the rope by which he attempted to escape from the Walnut Street jail.[22]

---

[22] Frederick P. Henry, ed., *Standard History of the Medical Profession of Philadelphia* (Chicago, 1897), 82; Lorraine Maclean of Dochgarroch, *Indomitable Colonel* ([London], 1986), 33–36; Bond to Board of War, 19 April [1777], Stauffer Coll., XXVIII, 2204 (HSP); Alan Cameron to Bond, 21 June 1777, Gratz Coll., European Military and Naval Forces (HSP).

War and the British occupation of Philadelphia seriously curtailed medical instruction. Because the Hospital was almost empty, he told Franklin in 1779, he could scarcely conduct his clinical lectures "without hiring the Sick to go into it," and he feared that he would have to give up his demonstrations in midwifery at the Almshouse for want of patients in the lying-in ward.[23]

The war also disrupted the American Philosophical Society. Meetings were suspended during and after the occupation and were not resumed until 1779. Bond did what he could to restore normal activities. On 10 December 1779 he read an essay on inoculation, and was requested to prepare a copy for publication. (This was probably the treatise, or part of the treatise, that he wrote earlier in the year, possibly at the request of the French Minister Gérard, to overcome continuing objections to the procedure, "especially in France, a Country I love";[24] it was published in French at Strasbourg in 1784 and in a German translation at Nuremberg three years later.) In 1780 Bond gave the Society $20, presumably to defray current expenses. In 1781 he exhibited an "uncommon kidney of a human body" which he proposed to dissect, wanting the Society to see it first. He continued to take an interest in American improvements, urging a young Philadelphian going to France to learn all he could, for the benefit of America, about natural history and new methods of agriculture, mining, manufacture, and transportation.[25] This concern found expression in a theme of his annual oration before the Society on 21 May 1782: "The Conveniencies [sic] and Advantages he [Man] derives from the Arts and Sciences, and a Prognostic of the increasing Grandeur and Glory of America, founded on the Nature of its Climate."

"Point out the Nation which has not Science, or that which has abandoned it," Bond declared, "and I will point out to you Savages or Slaves." Military fame, he continued, may be won or lost in an hour, but the reputation for science, that is, knowledge, "is the Child of a thousand Years—approaches slowly to Maturity, and is long in dying." Noting that Russia had recently entered the world of the Enlightenment, he urged the Philosophical Society to promote acquaintance with Russian scholars and learned societies. "Science is the Nurse of universal Friendship. . . . She is at War with none—she is at Peace with all,—and the Line of Communication which she opens, is open to all Mankind." Then, addressing America and Americans in particular, he voiced a lofty aspiration for it and them:

> The European World will soon make a closer Enquiry into our Disposition and Conduct, than merely whether we are Patriots and Soldiers. The Fame of America must rest on a broader Basis than that of Arms alone. Is she just, mild, generous, grateful and

---

[23] Franklin Mss., XV, 216.
[24] Ibid.
[25] Ibid., XVIII, 49.

learned, as well as brave, will soon be the Enquiry of the World. Curiosity, which leads Mankind to know every minute Circumstance of a new Character, will naturally excite these Questions, and we cannot too seriously reflect,—that our Consequence abroad, depends on our preserving a noble, generous and *unspotted Character* at Home.[26]

In September 1782 Bond was elected president of the Humane Society for the rescue of persons from death by drowning and similar accidents; he was reelected in 1783 and held the office until his death.[27]

The revival of the Philosophical Society put it and its members once more in a position to provide European scholars and amateurs with information and specimens of American natural history. The French minister Gérard asked Bond to get him American seeds and plants; Bond turned to Humphry Marshall for a selection. Although Gérard was slow to acknowledge the shipment, Bond urged Marshall to keep up the correspondence and hope for an exchange. Meanwhile M. Barbé-Marbois proposed an exchange with the Jardin du Roi. "They do not desire botanical curiosities," Bond explained to Marshall; "but such things as would enrich France,—such as Pines, Oaks, Hickories, Poplars, Persimmons, Magnolias, &c. . . ."[28]

Never physically robust, probably suffering from pulmonary consumption—he had gone to Barbados for his health in 1748–49—Bond cared for himself throughout life by proper diet, avoidance of cold and damp, and occasional bleeding. At 70, according to a German physician who met him, he displayed "great cheerfulness and activity of mind." He died at Philadelphia on 26 March 1784 at the age of 71, and was buried in Christ Church cemetery two days later. "32 Drs. & 22 medical pupils attended the funeral & a *vast* number of citizens."[29] He was survived by his wife and three children. By the terms of his will his two slaves were freed upon Mrs. Bond's death, which occurred in September following her husband's.[30]

---

[26] Bond, *Anniversary Oration, delivered May 21st, before the American Philosophical Society . . . for the Year 1782* (Phila., [1782]), 8, 30–34.
[27] Minutes and other papers of the Humane Society are in Pennsylvania Hospital archives.
[28] Darlington, *Memorials,* 536–41.
[29] William Shippen, Jr. to Thomas Lee Shippen, 29 March 1784, Shippen Family Papers (Lib. Cong.)
[30] Thacher, *Am. Med. Biography,* I, 178; Johann D. Schoepf, *Travels in the Confederation* (Phila., 1911), I, 79–81; *PMHB,* XIII (1889), 382; *Pa. Gaz.,* 3 April 1784; Will Book Q, 413 (Register of Wills, Phila.).

botanist daughter Jane. Impressed by Bartram's far-ranging knowledge of American botany, Colden suggested that he publish a monthly report on the subject.[12]

Bartram's earliest journeys were to Delaware and the Eastern Shore in 1737 and to western Pennsylvania in 1738. In the ensuing years he visited New York, the Catskill Mountains, and the Mohawk Valley. He travelled to New England in 1755, to South Carolina in 1760 and 1762, and to Fort Pitt in 1760.

In the summer of 1743 Bartram made a journey of six weeks to Onondago in western New York with the surveyor Lewis Evans and the Province Interpreter Conrad Weiser.[13] While Weiser attended a conference between representatives of the colony of Virginia and of the Five Nations, Bartram continued on to Oswego and Lake Erie. He visited Indian towns, found a great mountain magnolia, made salt from salt springs, and noted that fossils were found even on mountain tops. The Indians received the travellers hospitably, making them welcome with meals of "Indian soop," corn dumplings, cold boiled squash, boiled bread, and dried eels. One night Bartram was awakened by "the Musical howling of a wolf," and he could not conceal his alarm when, as often happened, he came upon a rattlesnake.

The journal Bartram kept on that trip was published at last, after many vicissitudes, in London in 1751. The printer was "scandalously" careless and Collinson did not read the proofs, but, in the words of the author of the preface, it contained valuable information and displayed "evident marks of much good sense, penetration, and sincerity, join'd to a commendable curiosity." The book was filled with descriptions of the natives, their customs and ceremonies, their towns and dwellings, and their country with its beasts, trees, and flowers. Everywhere Bartram noted with precision the character and pitch of the terrain, the quality of the soil, and especially the forest growth. The picture Bartram presented of the Indians was neither condescending nor uncritical. Of the Mohawks, who had many close contacts with the English, he wrote,

> I am very sorry to say their morals are little if at all mended by their frequent intercourse with us Christians, tho' I am persuaded it is not the fault of our religion but its professors. Perhaps this may be esteemed a principal cause why they are become less numerous than any of their confederates.

The journal concluded with interesting speculations on the origin of the native inhabitants, who Bartram thought might be descended from Egyptian, Phoenician, or Carthaginian traders blown westward from the Guinea coast across the South Atlantic to Brazil and the Antilles. Yet, for all the information it contained, the account of the journey to Onondago did not contain, Peter Kalm complained,

---

[12] *Colden Papers*, II (N.-Y. Hist. Soc., *Colls.*, [1918]), 208, 247.

[13] Bartram, *Observations on the Inhabitants, Climate oil, Rivers, Productions, Animals, and other matters . . . from Pensilvania to Onondago, Oswego, and the Lake Ontario, in Canada* (London, 1751).

"a thousandth part of the great knowledge which he [Bartram] has acquired in natural philosophy and history, especially in regard to North America."[14]

A reader of the journal was likely to share the sense of awe and wonder that Bartram felt in the presence of natural phenomena and growths, of the natural world dwarfing men by its power and immensity. There are swift glimpses of the wilderness that Bartram, Weiser, and Evans travelled through—of streams "tumbling down the mountains in glistening cascades," creeks "so clear one might have seen a pin at the bottom," crystals at a salt spring glittering "like flashes of Ice or Snow in a Sunshiny day." And readers might also admire the courage, trust, and perseverance that Bartram and his companions displayed as they "crawled over many deep wrinkles on the face of our antient mother earth."

> Our way . . . lay over fine rich level land as before, but when we left it, we enter'd a miserable thicket of spruce, opulus, and dwarf yew, then over a branch of Susquehanah, big enough to turn a mill, came to ground as good as that on the other side the thicket; well cloathed with tall timber of sugar birch, sugar maple, and elm. In the afternoon it thunder'd hard pretty near us, but rained little: We observed the tops of the trees to be so close to one another for many miles together that there is no seeing which way the clouds drive nor which way the wind sets; and it seems almost as if the sun had never shone on the ground, since the Creation. About sunset it cleared up, and we encamped on the east branch of Susquehanah. The night following, it thundered and rained very fast, and took us at a disadvantage for we had made no shelter to keep off the rain, neither could we see it till just over our heads and it began to fall.[15]

The preface to Bartram's journal—possibly written by Richard Jackson or Dr. Fothergill—expressed thoughts on the importance of the western country to Great Britain.

> But when it is consider'd, of how great importance an intimate acquaintance with the natural state of this wild vast wilderness, and its capacity of further improvement is to Great Britain, and how little the endeavours of our countrymen have yet advanced this work, while we are indebted to our most dangerous rivals for the little we do know, who will, if possible, repay themselves by excluding us from all we do not actually cultivate, and leave us *that only* while they want power to take it from us: I cannot but think this plain yet sensible piece merits attention. It is by pursuing the discovery of the interior state of this great continent, that we can scarcely fail attaining an end, the most worthy the aim of a great maritime power, honoured as well as strengthened by a fair progeny of the most flourishing colonies in the world, and of which a good Englishman with peculiar pleasure will find P. Charlevoix confessing (however unwilling to own any thing inconsistent with the glory of his country) that France cannot behold them without Terror.[16]

---

[14] Peter Kalm, *Travels in North America* (A. B. Benson, ed., N.Y., 1937), I, 61–62.
[15] Bartram, *Observations,* 37; Berkeley and Berkeley, *Bartram Correspondence,* 336.
[16] Bartram, *Observations*, ii–iii.

Journeys such as this to Onondago excited the admiration of Bartram's fellow-citizens, for they linked him to an unknown country, at once fearsome and romantic, filled with marvels, risks, and dangers. With this in mind his friend Joseph Breintnall paid him a poetical tribute in imitation of Horace's *Integer Vitae*.

> Whose life is upright, innocent and harmless,
> Needs not, O Bartram, arm himself with Weapons;
> Useless to him, the Sword, the venomed Shaft, or
>   Murdering Musket.
> Thus when thou'rt journeying tow'rds wild Onondago,
> O'er pathless Mountains, Nature's Works exploring,
> Or thro' vast Plains where rowls his mighty Waters
>   Fam'd Missisipi;
> Should the fierce She-Bear, or the famish' Wildcat,
> Or yet more fierce and wild the Savage Indian,
> Meet thee, God praising, and his Works admiring,
>   Instant they'd fly thee.
> Tho' now to piercing Frosts, now scorching Sunbeams,
> Now to unwholesome Fogs, tho' thou'rt exposed,
> Thy Guardian Angel, Innocence, shall keep thee
>   Safe from all Danger.[17]

Each of these journeys was arduous. They were made in cold, rain, and all weathers, often amid clouds of mosquitoes, gnats, flies, and other winged pests. Almost everywhere there was danger from rattlesnakes and sometimes from hostile Indians. Food was often bad and sometimes insufficient. Bartram contracted diarrhea and malaria and other fevers. He fell, stumbled, and suffered bruised limbs and other accidents, but displayed remarkable resilience, recovering after a day or two to be on his way again. Through it all Bartram persevered with single-minded devotion to his mission.

Eventually Bartram systematized his seed business. For those who wanted only a representative selection he made up parcels of 100 species of trees and shrubs, for which he charged five guineas. The most generous and consistent of his customers in the years after 1735 was Baron Petre, whose garden at Thorndon in Essex soon contained so many specimens from America that Collinson, walking through it, could not help thinking he was "in North American thickets—there are such Quantities."[18]

Bartram soon came to realize that if he could be assured of a steady income, he could devote all his time to botanizing and leave the care of his farm and family to

---

[17] [Joseph Breitnall], "Tribute to John Bartram in Imitation of Horace's Integer Vitae," *PMHB*, LXXXIII (1959), 446–51.

[18] Berkeley and Berkeley, *Bartram Correspondence*, 167. A list of the seeds Bartram sent abroad in his boxes is in R. Hingston Fox, *Dr. John Fothergill and his Friends* (London, 1919), 163–65.

others. Accordingly he proposed that a number of persons should each subscribe £10 towards his support, and receive plants and seeds in return. Collinson encouraged him in this purpose. Annual subscriptions were secured from Lord Petre, the Duke of Richmond, Philip Miller, and some other principal customers, but the total was insufficient. Even this small patronage suffered loss in 1742, when young Lord Petre died suddenly of smallpox. "All our Schemes are broke," Collinson lamented, "all is att an End."[19] If support could not be found in Britain, Bartram thought, perhaps American gardeners might seize their opportunity. He explained the benefits of such steady support to Franklin, who endorsed the proposal that an annual fund be raised in the colonies to enable Bartram "wholly to spend his Time and exert himself" in discovering and collecting plants, trees, flowers, and other productions of nature in Pennsylvania, New York, New Jersey, and Maryland. In return, Bartram would communicate each year the results of his findings.[20] This scheme, too, failed to materialize. The next year Franklin proposed the American Philosophical Society. Perhaps Bartram hoped that, like the organization he had suggested to Collinson five years before, it would send out botanical and geological expeditions with himself as leader.

How to free Bartram for uninterrupted botanical excursions and study remained a concern of his friends. Dr. John Mitchell, who settled in London in 1746 and was intimate with the Duke of Argyll and Lord Bute, offered to use his interest to get Bartram a suitable post, with an income that would relieve him of the cares of his farm.

Without such support Bartram remained bound to his farm and could make botanical tours only as time and funds permitted. His customers in Britain were often demanding, wanting some different species in every new shipment. "Do they think I can make new ones?" he demanded querulously. Not even Collinson, sympathetic and understanding in so many ways, appreciated the physical efforts it took to find even common plants. "You are not sensible of the fourth part of the pains I take to oblige you," Bartram reminded him. In general, Bartram travelled in the fall, when the harvest was in and gathering seeds was likely to be easier and most productive.

Bartram and his garden were soon famous. The Swedish botanist Peter Kalm visited it in 1748. Bartram showed his visitor wasps' nests, pieces of Indian pottery, and hummingbirds that he had captured, caged, and kept alive on a diet of sugar water. They discussed geology—"thee cant bang me out of the notion that limestone & marble were originally mud," Bartram later insisted to Collinson, defend-

---

[19] Ibid., 198. Lady Petre sent Bartram seeds of a pear tree; they matured after about twenty years and the tree lived and bore fruit until 1931. Francis D. West, "The Lady Petre Pear Tree," *Garden Jour.*, Jan.–Feb. 1958, 6, 21; Robert Carr to J. S. Skinner, 9 Oct. 1829, Hazard's *Register of Pennsylvania,* IV (1829), 302.
[20] *Pa. Gaz.*, 17 March 1742; *Franklin Papers,* II, 356–57.

ing the theory of Thomas Burnet.[21] He offered reasons for the extinction of the mastodon. Had Bartram noticed, Kalm asked, that trees and plants decreased in size in proportion as they were carried north, as Catesby contended. "He answered that the question should be more limited and then his opinion would prove more worth while"—some trees grew better in the South, Bartram responded sensibly; others in the North. Kalm conceived a warm admiration for his host, and departed much indebted to him, "for he possessed that great quality of communicating everything he knew."[22]

Bartram was essentially a lover of nature, its plants and animals and fossil remains; he was not a systematic scholar. He was a practical farmer, with a bent for experiment and the talent of acute observation. He was a gatherer and a distributor of the botanical wealth of America, with which he helped to stock the gardens and herbaria of Europe; but, unable to use some botanical treatises of the time, he left it to Linnaeus, Dillenius, Gronovius, and others to describe, identify, and give names to his discoveries. In this respect he was quite unlike his correspondent Alexander Garden of Charleston, South Carolina, for example.

Garden had several occasions to observe Bartram closely and to describe him, his enthusiasm, and his garden. To Cadwallader Colden he wrote in 1754:

> Since my leaving that place [New York] I have met wt very Little new in the Botanic way unless Your acquaintance Bartram, who is what he is & whose acquaintance alone makes amends for other disappointments in that way. I first waited of [on] him with Govr Tinker & Dr Bond whom he received wt so much ease, Gaiety & happy Alacrity, and invited to dine with so much rural vivacity, that every one were [sic] agreably pleased & surprised. . . . One Day he Dragged me out of town & Entertain'd me so agreably with some Elevated Botanicall thoughts, on oaks, Firns, Rocks &c that I forgot I was hungry till we Landed in his house about four Miles from Town. There was no parting with him for two Days, During which time I breakfasted, Dined & Supped [&] Sleep't & was regaled on Botany & Minerology [sic], in which he has some excellent Notions & grand thoughts.
>
> His garden is a perfect portraiture of himself, here you meet wt a row of rare plants almost covered over wt weeds, here with a Beautifull Shrub, even Luxuriant Amongst Briars, and in another corner an Elegant & Lofty tree lost in common thicket—on our way from town to his house he carried me to severall rocks & Dens where he shewed me some of his rare plants, which he had brought from the Mountains &c. In a word he disdains to have a garden less than Pensylvania & Every den is an Arbour, Every run of water, a Canal, & every small level Spot a Parterre, where he nurses up some of his Idol Flowers & cultivates his darling productions. He had many plants whose names he did not know, most or all of which I had seen & knew them—On the other hand he had several I had not seen & some I never heard of.[23]

[21] Berkeley and Berkeley, *Bartram Correspondence,* 407.
[22] Kalm, *Travels,* I, 71–76, 114, 172–73, 281.
[23] *Colden Papers,* IV (N.-Y. Hist. Soc., *Colls.*, 1920), 471–72.

Some ten years later Garden described Bartram more fully and critically in a letter to John Ellis. Bartram had spent nine days in July 1765 with Dr. Garden at Charleston prior to setting out for East Florida.

> I have had many conversations with him, and have endeavoured to give him all the light and assistance I could, into the nature of the hot southern climates, and their productions. I have been several times into the country, and places adjacent to town, with him, and have told him the classes, genera, and species of all the plants that occurred, which I knew. I did this in order to facilitate his enquiries, as I find he knows nothing of the generic characters of plants, and can neither class them nor describe them; but I see that, from great natural strength of mind and long practice, he has much acquaintance with the specific characters; though this knowledge is rude, inaccurate, indistinct, and confused, seldom determining well between species and varieties. He is however alert, active, industrious, and indefatigable in his pursuits, and will collect many rare specimens, which, from their being sent home, will give you a good idea of the country productions. He is well acquainted with soils and timber, and will be able to give you much light on these heads. He appears to me not very credulous, which is one great matter. His collections and specimens all go to Mr. Collinson, where you will have an opportunity to see and examine them. I have given him many specimens here, and made him well acquainted with the appearance and common habit of most of our *plantes qui naissent aux environs de Charlestown.*[24]

Bartram's correspondence with Americans was almost as large as with English and European botanists. Through Franklin he sent ginseng root to Boston in 1744. He corresponded with Jared Eliot of Connecticut on agricultural matters in 1752, answering queries about fertilizers and tillage, advising him how to increase the productivity of salt marshes, and instructing him how to split rocks.[25] He exchanged seeds and bulbs with Mrs. Martha Logan, who kept a famous garden in Charleston, South Carolina; she "spares no pains or cost to oblige me," Bartram told Collinson.[26] He enriched the garden of Mrs. Colden on the Hudson River with "fine Tulips Snow drops &c &c &c" that would produce a "Gaudy show" the next summer.[27]

Like other botanists before and since his time, Bartram saw the mind of God in the order and beauty of the productions of nature all around him. "My head runs all upon the works of God in nature. It is through that telescope I see god in his glory."[28] Without rejecting the essential principles of the Quaker faith he had

---

[24] James E. Smith, ed., *A Selection of the Correspondence of Linnaeus, and Other Naturalists* (London, 1821), 1, 537. Berkeley and Berkeley, *Bartram Correspondence,* 527.
[25] Jared Eliot, *Essays upon Field-Husbandry in New England* (Rexford G. Tugwell and Harry J. Carman, eds., N.Y., 1934), 191–206.
[26] Martha B. Prior, ed., "Letters of Martha Logan to John Bartram, 1760–1763," *So. Carolina Hist. Mag.*, LIX (1958), 38–46.
[27] *Colden Papers,* IX (N.-Y. Hist. Soc., *Colls.*, 1935), 142.
[28] Berkeley and Berkeley, *Bartram Correspondence,* 579; *Colden Papers,* VII (N.-Y. Hist. Soc., *Colls.*, 1923), 339–42.

been brought up in, he came to question some of the corollary tenets of the Christian faith that his co-religionists held. "Often where there is the greatest talk & pretence," he observed to Colden, "religion & the mind is taken up with a zeal in the Performance of the Ceremonial part & the substantial part which is Love Resignation & humility to the Eternal Power is often Neglected." He had "little respect," he wrote on another occasion, for "disputes about the ceremonial parts of religion which often introduced animosities confusion & disorders in the mind & sometimes body too."[29] For disbelieving in the divinity of Jesus Bartram was disowned by the Darby Friends Meeting on 1 Second Month 1758. He and his family continued, however, to attend Quaker meetings for worship. (In 1993 the Darby Monthly Meeting of Friends, acting "to right a wrong we made some time back," rescinded its act of disownment and voted "to count John Bartram among its members," as heretofore.)[30]

John Bartram received many gifts and honors in appreciation of his personal services and his contributions to science. Sir Hans Sloane, president of the Royal Society, sent him a Bible, a copy of his *Voyage to the Islands* (London, 1707–25), and five guineas, with which Bartram bought a silver cann or cup that he had handsomely engraved: "The Gift of S[r] Hans Sloane Bart. to his Frd John Bartram. Anno 1742."[31] Collinson sent him botanical and other books, a microscope, and various gifts. On recommendation of Peter Bergius, Bartram was elected a foreign member of the Royal Swedish Academy of Science on 26 April 1769 (news of his election was sent him by Carl Magnus Wrangel, and Bartram acknowledged the honor in a letter to Linnaeus).[32] A Society of Gentlemen at Edinburgh, for the Advancement and Propagation of Arts and Sciences, in 1773 voted him a gold medal "in testimony of the great respect they bear to the many ingenious and useful discoveries he has favoured them with, in the course of a long correspondence." (The gold medal was also payment of a charge of £7 10s. for seeds!)[33] In 1764 Bartram asked Collinson to collect funds to send him on another, more ambitious botanical exploration; in response Collinson got him named Botanist to the King, with an annual stipend of £50, to explore and collect in the region of the St. John's River in Florida. Characteristically, for he often grumbled that he was unappreciated, Bartram complained that the allowance was not enough. Nor was the appointment

---

[29] Berkeley and Berkeley, *Bartram Correspondence,* 222, 381, 552; and advice to his children, 442–51, 772–75.
[30] *Phila. Inquirer,* 28 June 1993.
[31] The cup is illustrated in Darlington, *Memorials,* 305. The copy of the *Voyage to Jamaica* that was the gift of Sir Hans Sloane is in the Boston Public Library.
[32] E. W. Dahlgren, *Kungl. Svenska Vetenskapsakademien. Personforteekningar, 1739–1915* (Stockholm, 1915), 122; Francis D. West, "Sweden Honors John Bartram," *PMHB,* LXXXI (1957), 88–90; Berkeley and Berkeley, *Bartram Correspondence,* 712–13, 719.
[33] *Franklin Papers,* XVIII, 62; XIX, 40, 316–17; *Pa. Packet,* 26 April 1773. The medal is illustrated in Darlington, *Memorials,* 405.

universally applauded. "Is it really so?" Dr. Garden asked his friend John Ellis in disbelief.

> Surely John is a worthy man; but to give the title of King's Botanist to a man who can scarcely spell, much less make out the characters of any one genus of plants, appears rather hyperbolical. Pray how is this matter? Is he not rather appointed or sent, and paid, for searching out the plants of East and West Florida, and for that service only to have a reward and his expences?[34]

The journey to Florida was the last major expedition Bartram made. He set out from Philadelphia for Charleston on 1 July 1765, and was joined by his son William. After several weeks of exploring and collecting, he and his little party left St. Augustine for St. John's River on 19 December. Bartram filled his journal with observations on the geography, meteorology, natural history, and productions of the region. He crossed plains and travelled through swamps, taking note of the native plants, flowers, shrubs, and trees. "Monstrous grape-vines 8 inches in diameter, running up the oaks 6 foot in diameter" astonished him, as did swamp magnolias 70 feet tall. The party passed through woods full of "bitter-sweet oranges, next in goodness to the China," and along streams in which fish were "jumping continually." Near Lake Beresford Bartram saw alligators that were "very numerous either on the shore or swimming on the surface of the water, and some on the bottom, so tame, or rather bold, as to allow us to row very near them." The party's hunter killed one, whose jaws Bartram then examined, and Bartram himself killed a 400–pound bear, whose meat Bartram found mild and sweet. Yet Bartram was not the first European or American to visit this country. The travellers frequently saw evidences of Florida's Indian and Spanish history. Two or three days before returning to St. Augustine, Bartram visited a Mr. Hazard, "one of the best planters in Florida," at his plantation on Fort George Island. Because of high winds they

> could not venture on the river, so walked all over the island; observing his improvements; and the curiosities, both natural and artificial, of the Indians and Spaniards; of the former, were several middling tumulus's or sepulchres of the Florida Indians, with numerous heaps of oyster-shells, which one may reasonably suppose were many hundred years in collecting by as many thousands of Indians, also variety of old broken Indian pots. 'Tis very demonstrable that the Spaniards had a fine settlement here, as there still remain their cedar posts on each side their fine straight avenues, pieces of hewn live-oaks, and great trees girdled round to kill them, which are now very sound, though above 60 years since they were cut. This rich island, though it appears sandy on the surface, yet hath a clay bottom, above which in some places there is a dark-coloured strata of indurated sand-rock.[35]

---

[34] Smith, *Correspondence of Linnaeus*, I, 538.
[35] William Stork, *A Description of East-Florida, with a Journal kept by John Bartram of Philadelphia* (London, 1769), app. 32.

Bartram made "A fine Collection of strange florida plants," 259 specimens in all, which he sent to Collinson and the King's herbarium. One of the plants was the rare and beautiful flowering shrub that he named for his old friend *Franklinia alatamaha;* it no longer grows in the southern Appalachian mountains, but survives only in scions of the specimens Bartram brought home to his garden. All this collecting, Bartram told Collinson as he sent the Florida plants and seeds to London,

> hath cost thy friend many score pounds pains & sickness which held me constantly near or quite two months in florida. The fever & Jaundice & A looseness thro No & So Carolina & georgia yet some how or other I lost not an hours time of travailing thro those provinces & when at Augustine with the fever & Jaundice I traveled both by water & land all round the town for many miles & at Picolata to the congress [of Indians] altho so weak as hard set to get up to small bed chamber & during the meeting of the governor & indians in the Pavilion I was forced to sit or ly down upon the ground, close by its side that I might observe what passed.[36]

Edited and rewritten from his diary, the part of Bartram's account that related his travels in Florida, was printed as an appendix to Dr. William Stork's *Description of East-Florida* (London, 1769).[37]

Bartram was now approaching 70 years of age. His health began to fail. Peter Collinson, his correspondent, agent, patron, and friend of thirty-five years, died in 1768. "I wish you would now decline your long and dangerous peregrinations, in search of your plants," his "good ould Friend" Benjamin Franklin urged in 1769,

> and remain safe and quiet at home, employing your leisure hours in a work that is much wanted, and which no one besides is so capable of performing—I mean the writing a Natural History of our country. I imagine it would prove profitable to you, and I am sure it would do you honour.[38]

Even ordinary correspondence was now difficult. "My eyes is so dim," he told his son William in 1771, "that I cant know my own children [at] 3 foot distance & I write with trouble & must hould my face within 2 or 3 inches of the paper." That

---

[36] Berkeley and Berkeley, *Bartram Correspondence,* 668–69.
[37] Bartram's diary of the entire trip, July 1765 to April 1766, with the Florida weeks reprinted from Stork, was edited by Francis Harper, ed., "Diary of a Journey through the Carolinas, Georgia, and Florida," APS *Trans.*, XXXIII (1942), 1–120.
[38] *Franklin Papers,* XVI, 9. Franklin sent Bartram a copy of Fothergill's memoir of Collinson, which was prefaced by an engraved portrait. "The pamphlet & espetially the picture of my dear Peter was very acceptable," Bartram replied in acknowledgment, "& now I am furnished with four of our worthies Lineus, Franklin, [George] Edwards and Collinson (but I want Dr. Fothergill,) to adorn my new stove and lodging room which I have made very Convenient for thair reception alltho I am no picture Enthusiast, Yet I love to looke at the representation of men of inocency integrity ingenuity & Humanity." Ibid., XVII, 290.

year Franklin sent him from London a set of lenses with instructions how to use them.[39] In 1772 Bartram wrote his will.

He continued, however, to cultivate the garden. He was as interested as ever in new seeds and plants, and he filled his customers' orders. He corresponded with Franklin in the early 1770s about rhubarb and turnip seeds, and "a few Seeds of what is called the Cabbage Turnip" (kohlrabi), used for forage for cattle. Even after the Revolution broke out and put a stop to communication between England and the former colonies, English gardeners were eager for American seeds. Franklin, now settled in France as agent of the American States, offered a way around the difficulty. He suggested that Bartram send to his care in Paris "the same Number of Boxes . . . that you used to send to England, because England will then send here for what it wants in that Way."[40]

Three months after receiving this suggestion Bartram died, after a short illness, on 22 September 1777. To his eldest son Isaac he left Sir Hans Sloane's silver cup.[41] The farm went to John, who provided there a home for his mother and brother William, who tended the garden and its precious plants and trees. There were bequests of land, lots, or cash to each of his children and grandchildren. Ann Bartram survived her husband by seven years, and died in 1784.

William Bartram described his father as "a man of modest and gentle manners, frank, cheerful, and of great good nature; a lover of justice, truth, and charity," a man of "humanity, gentleness, and compassion," who was never "at enmity with any man" or ever engaged "in a litigious contest with any of his neighbours, or others."[42] So indeed he was. But he could also be impatient, complaining, and tart. And there is more than a touch of Quaker humor in his comment on an ardent evangelist who assured his congregation that he (the preacher) would sit at the right hand of God the Father to judge the multitudes—"but surely first he must heave the sun [son: Christ] out of his seat." When Collinson warned Bartram against buying and reading too many books, citing Solomon—"in Reading of Books there is no End"—Bartram replied, "I take thy advice about books very kindly—altho I love reading such dearly and I believe if Solomon had loved women less & books more he would have been a wiser & happier man than he was."[43]

Two years after Bartram's death in 1777 his friend Isaac Gray, fearing that his name was already being forgotten, urged Benjamin Rush to write their friend's biography; it was something that would "give an additional lustre to American reputation," Gray assured him.

---

[39] Ibid., XVIII, 89–90, 180–81; Bartram to William Bartram, 21 July 1771, Gilbert Coll. of Ms. Letters, I, 159 (Coll. Phys. Phila.).
[40] *Franklin Papers,* XIX, 268, 316–17, 367–68; XX, 40; XXIV, 89.
[41] Bartram, Will, dated 17 Jan. 1772, Will Book R, 277 (Register of Wills, Phila.).
[42] William Bartram, "Some account of the late Mr. John Bartram," loc. cit., 121.
[43] Berkeley and Berkeley, *Bartram Correspondence,* 89.

> He who more particularly excels in any useful or laudable Science may with propriety be deemed great. I cannot therefore well refrain ranking under this Character our late worthy & ingenious friend & Countryman John Bartram, dec'd, and having often admired & lamented that no friend to Science hath yet taken to public Notice of such a signal Character, which I apprehend if adequately described would do credit to the Biography of America.[44]

Rush did not respond to this invitation, but with the publication of William Darlington's edition of letters of Bartram and Humphry Marshall in 1849, sufficient historical materials became available to insure Bartram a firm place in "the Biography of America." His house and garden survived industrial encroachment in the nineteenth century and "development" in the twentieth, and now, cared for by the John Bartram Association, are today a part of Philadelphia's park system.

THOMAS GODFREY (1704–1749)
AMERICAN PHILOSOPHICAL SOCIETY: 1743

THOMAS GODFREY, glazier, almanac-maker, inventor of the reflecting quadrant, was designated "Mathematician" on the roll of original members of the American Philosophical Society. He had known Franklin at least since the latter returned from England in 1726; he was a member of the Junto of 1727, but he was not a congenial associate. Franklin remembered him as

> a self-taught Mathematician, great in his Way, and afterwards Inventor of what is now call'd Hadley's Quadrant. But he knew little out of his way, and was not a pleasing Companion, as like most Great Mathematicians I have met with, he expected unusual Precision in every thing he said, or was forever denying or distinguishing upon Trifles, to the Disturbance of all Conversation. He soon left us.[1]

Born in 1704 in Bristol Township near Germantown, on a farm adjoining Lukens' Mill, he was the son of Joseph and Catharine Godfrey and grandson of Thomas Godfrey, who had bought the farm in 1697.[2] Joseph Godfrey, who farmed the land and was a maltster as well, died when his son was only a year old; Mrs. God-

---

[44] Isaac Gray to Benjamin Rush, 9 Eighth Mo. 1779, Rush Mss., VI, 67 (Lib. Co. Phila. in HSP).

[1] Franklin, *Autobiography,* 117.
[2] The principal biographical sketch is in Watson, *Annals,* I, 528–31; but see also Nathan Spencer, "Account of Thomas Godfrey," 1809 (Ms., APS), and a modern evaluation by Brooke Hindle in *DSB*.

frey remarried; and Thomas, after some formal schooling, was apprenticed to learn the glazier's trade in Philadelphia. Glaziers in those days, his biographer was at pains to explain, were not mere house-painters, but "soldered the glasses into leaden frames," which they made themselves. Though some persons, relating the facts of his career, have seemed to want to magnify Godfrey's achievement by minimizing his background and education, the fact is that he was neither poor nor uneducated. He wrote a good hand and spelled correctly; he worked on the State-House, at Andrew Hamilton's house Bush Hill, at James Logan's Stenton, and on Thomas Penn's house Springettsbury; and he was a measurer of buildings.[3]

By 1726 Godfrey, his wife Ann, and their family were settled in Philadelphia, where they rented rooms from Benjamin Franklin, who boarded with them. In 1727 Godfrey commissioned Franklin and his partner Hugh Meredith to print an edition of Isaac Watts' *Psalms of David,* but the book did not sell.[4] Mrs. Godfrey, concerned for the welfare of her bachelor landlord and boarder, tried to arrange a marriage between Franklin and one of her relations; but the project foundered on the practical conditions Franklin imposed; the Godfreys were resentful; there were words, and in late 1729 or 1730 they moved out, leaving Franklin in sole possession of his house.[5] This falling out, however, did not last, or keep the men from business: in 1730, 1731, and 1732 Franklin printed Godfrey's *Pennsylvania Almanac*. In the fall of 1732 Godfrey took his copy to Andrew Bradford, who printed the almanac through 1737, when it was dropped. Meanwhile Franklin hurriedly put together an almanac of his own.[6] *Poor Richard's Almanac* began publication with the issue for 1733.

By this time Godfrey had made considerable progress in mathematics. James Logan recounted the young man's history, not without some embellishment, to Edmund Halley, the Astronomer Royal, relating how he first encountered him.

> Thomas Godfrey . . . having in his apprenticeship . . . accidentally met with a mathematical book, took such a fancy to the study, that by the natural strength of his genius, without any instruction, he soon made himself master of that, and of every other of the kind, he could borrow or procure in English: And finding, there was more to be had in Latin books, under all imaginable discouragements, applied himself, to the study of that language, till he could pretty well understand an author on these subjects, after which, the first time I ever saw or heard of him, to my knowledge, he came to

---

[3] Watson, "Note on Thomas Godfrey," 12 Dec. 1836, in Supplemental Annals of Philadelphia, 8 (Ms., HSP); Godfrey and Ebenezer Tomlinson, Certificate, 29 Sept. 1738, Dreer Coll., Inventors (HSP), printed in *PMHB,* XLII (1918), 75; Godfrey to Thomas Penn, 15 April 1737, 10 Oct. 1738 (Friends Library, London, photocopies in HSP).
[4] C. William Miller, *Benjamin Franklin's Philadelphia Printing* (Phila., 1974), no. 2.
[5] Franklin, *Autobiography,* 115, 127–28.
[6] *Franklin Papers,* I, 188, 190–1.

borrow Sir Isaac Newton's Principia of me. Inquiring of him hereupon who he was, I was indeed astonished at his request, but after a little discourse, he soon became welcome to that or any other book I had.[7]

A similar story, with all the homely particulars of an apocryphal tale, is related of the origin of his invention of the quadrant. Speaking at the dedication of a memorial stone in 1843, Dr. Gouverneur Emerson told how Godfrey

was one day engaged in replacing a pane of glass in the window of a house on the North side of Mulberry street. A girl who had filled a pail with water, at a pump that stood opposite, placed it on the side walk, and Godfrey on turning towards it, saw the sun which had been first reflected from the window on which he had been at work, into the bucket of water, and a second time from the surface of the water to his eye. His philosophic mind seized at once upon the observation, and the principle was thus applied to the construction of an instrument with which he could draw the sun down to the horizon by means of a contrivance incomparably superior to any that had even been used for the purpose of ascertaining angular measurements.[8]

How to find longitude at sea was a problem for all mariners, especially after transoceanic voyages became common. This required an instrument capable of measuring effectively on tossing ships the altitude of known celestial bodies above the horizon or of their position in relation to neighboring stars. Neither the cross-staff nor back-staff, commonly in use, was efficient or accurate. Various attempts at improvement were made, but they did not meet success until 1730. In the summer of that year Godfrey conceived the idea of a double refracting quadrant. He had perfected the instrument by November, when he showed it to James Logan, and then gave it to ship captains to test in Delaware Bay and on voyages to Newfoundland and Jamaica. Meanwhile in England John Hadley, working on the same problem, invented a quadrant in May 1730 and described the instrument to the Royal Society on 13 May 1731.[9] Learning of Hadley's invention from the pages of the *Philo-*

---

[7] Logan to Halley, 25 May 1732, *American Magazine and Monthly Chronicle,* I (1757–58), 476–80. Deborah Norris Logan almost a century later related the story with improvements: intrigued by the reflection of light from panes he was fitting at Stenton, Godfrey "left his scaffold & going into the Library took down a Volume of Newton. James Logan entering at this moment and seeing the Book in his hand, enquired into the Motive of the search; he was exceedingly pleased with Godfrey's ingenuity, and from that period became his zealous Friend." "Memoir of James Logan," 1814, Logan Papers, II, 102 (HSP).
[8] Gouverneur Emerson, *An Address delivered at Laurel-Hill Cemetery, on the Completion of a Monument erected to the Memory of Thomas Godfrey, June 1st, 1843* (Phila., 1843), 2.
[9] *Phil. Trans.*, XXXVII (1731–32), 147–57; Abraham Wolf, *History of Science, Technology and Philosophy in the Eighteenth Century* (N.Y., 1939), 149–52.

sophical Transactions, Logan on 25 May 1732 sent Edmund Halley a full account of Godfrey and his invention, and recommended the inventor to Halley's notice. He followed this letter with others to scientific friends, especially the astronomer William Jones, vice-president of the Royal Society.[10] At the same time Godfrey wrote a brief description of the quadrant, which was printed in the *American Weekly Mercury* of 8 June 1732. On 9 November 1732 Godfrey sent the Royal Society an account and appeal for recognition.[11]

Halley made no response to Logan's letters; on the contrary he disparaged Logan's report and questioned its veracity. Properly offended by this "unhandsome" behavior, Logan on 28 June 1734 sent a further account of Godfrey and his quadrant; this was addressed to Peter Collinson; and Collinson presented it to the Royal Society, which received it on 16 January 1735 and ordered it printed.[12] Meanwhile, however, in the summer of 1732 the Admiralty had tested and proved Hadley's design,[13] and thus in effect acknowledged him as the inventor.

Unquestionably Hadley had priority of both invention and publication; but Americans, like other men in the eighteenth century, unacquainted with the possibility and fact of independent simultaneous discoveries, inclined to believe that the British had cheated Godfrey out of his invention, charging that Hadley had learned of it from a nephew who had it from one of Godfrey's seamen friends in Jamaica. The suspicion is groundless. In any event Godfrey soon became a symbol of what untaught native genius may achieve, and thus a welcome, if little known, figure in the American pantheon.

Godfrey continued his mathematical work, sometimes sending puzzles and problems or astronomical calculations to the press. In November 1740 he opened a school, announcing he would teach navigation, astronomy, and other parts of mathematics at his house on Second Street during the winter season.[14] His observations of the occultations of Jupiter were used by Lewis Evans to determine longitudes on his maps of the Middle Colonies of North America in 1749 and 1755.[15]

Godfrey was one of the original members and directors of the Library Company of Philadelphia, serving on the board from the founding of the institution in

---

[10] Logan to Halley, 25 May 1732, loc. cit.; Logan to Jones, 8, 12 Nov. 1732, in Stephen P. Rigaud, *Correspondence of Scientific Men of the Seventeenth Century* (reprint, Hildesheim, Germany, 1965), I, 282–88.
[11] So dated in Royal Society; but 1734 in *American Magazine,* 528–29.
[12] *Phil. Trans.,* XXXVIII (1733–34), 441–50.
[13] Ibid., XXXVII (1731–32), 341–56.
[14] *Pa. Gaz.,* 30 Oct. 1740, 5 March 1745, 7 July 1748. Note the astronomical calculations signed "T.G." ibid., 26 Feb. 1756.
[15] Lawrence H. Gipson, *Lewis Evans* (Phila., 1939), 146; Evans, *Map of Pensilvania, New-Jersey, New-York, and the three Delaware Counties* (Phila., 1749).

1731 until 1735. Of his reading little is known. That he read books of mathematics in English and Latin is clear. He once advertised for the return of books and papers he had lent and misplaced—s'Gravesande's *Mathematical Elements,* Newton's *Optics,* "a Quarto blue paper book, containing about two sheets, having in one end of it Doctor Hally's Numbers and Radixes of the Planets; at the other end, a collection of about 100 observations of the Moon from Flamsted."[16] The books he bought of Franklin in 1741–43 reflected his religious views—he appears eventually to have joined the Moravians: Wesley's *Sermons,* two copies of Whitefield's *Account of the Orphan House in Georgia,* John Shower's *Serious Reflexions on Time and Eternity,* Isaac Watts' *Divine Songs,* John Flavell's *A Saint Indeed,* and Jonathan Edwards' *Sermons.*[17]

When the American Philosophical Society was formed in 1743 Godfrey's reputation had spread beyond Philadelphia. Cadwallader Colden in New York asked him, through Franklin, for observations and calculations. But as the years passed Godfrey's passion for astronomy appears to have cooled. "I have no Observations of Jupiter's Satellites to send you, as I expected I should have," Franklin informed Colden on 13 February 1749/50.

> Being myself otherwise engag'd, and not very skilful in those Matters, I depended on our Astronomer Mr. Godfrey, and put the Telescope into his Hands for that purpose: He had a fine Summer for it, but I am inform'd he was so continually muddled with Drink, that our Surveyor General, Mr. Scull, who was his Neighbour, could never get him to assist in making the Meridian Line. He is now dead. . . .[18]

Godfrey died in the fall of 1749. Letters of administration were issued to his widow on 16 November,[19] but notice of his death appeared in the *Pennsylvania Gazette* only on 19 December: "Last Week [sic] died here Mr. Thomas Godfrey, who had an uncommon Genius for all kinds *of Mathematical Learning,* with which he was extreamly well acquainted. He invented the *New Reflecting Quadrant,* used in Navigation." He was survived by his wife, Ann, who died in 1752, and by two sons. The eldest, Joseph, became a glazier like his father, and Thomas Jr., though taught the trade of watchmaking, is best known as a poet and author of the first

---

[16] *Pa. Gaz.,* 5 Nov. 1747.
[17] Franklin, Ledger D, 15 (Ms., APS); *PMHB,* XV (1891), 361.
[18] *Franklin Papers,* III, 462–63. Logan may have had Godfrey's fondness for drink in mind when he wrote William Jones on 25 July 1737, "T.G. has indeed a fine natural genius for the mathematics, and it would, for the sake of his birthplace, the same with that of my own children here, be a great pleasure to me, if I could say that he wants no other interior qualification necessary in the composition of true merit." Rigaud, *Correspondence of Scientific Men,* I, 316–17.
[19] Admin. No. 36, 1749 (Register of Wills, Philadelphia).

American drama, *The Prince of Parthia*.[20] Godfrey's personal property was valued at £50 12*s*.; it included clock tools, 14 old books, and 42 gallons of rum.[21]

SAMUEL RHOADS (1711–1784)
AMERICAN PHILOSOPHICAL SOCIETY: 1743

SAMUEL RHOADS, carpenter, was one of the original members of the American Philosophical Society, in which he was described as a "mechanician." He supported Dr. Thomas Bond in the revival of the Society after its long "dormancy," attended as a member on 19 January 1768, and was active in the Society's affairs from that time until the Revolution.

He was the fifth son of John and Hannah (Willcox) Rhoads, born in 1711 in Whitemarsh Township, Philadelphia County, where his father was a farmer.[1] With whom he served his apprenticeship is not known, but he was admitted a member of the Carpenters' Company of Philadelphia before 1736. By that time he was already engaged in speculative building, but was content for many years to call himself simply "carpenter in Philadelphia." Before he was 30 years old Rhoads received

---

[20] The inventory of the inventor's widow lists a "Sign" and "shop Window"; whether these were the glazier's or indicate that Mrs. Godfrey opened some sort of small retail store after Thomas' death does not appear. Admin. No. 30, 1752 (Register of Wills, Philadelphia).

[21] Godfrey, Inventory, 8 Dec. 1749. Administrations, No. 36, 1749 (Register of Wills, Phila.). In 1737 the Godfreys had an indentured servant maid, who ran away. *Pa. Gaz.*, 19 May 1737.

Godfrey was said to have been buried in the family lot on the farm near Germantown, but no stone was placed on his grave. In 1836 a committee of citizens headed by Dr. Charles D. Meigs proposed that the bodies of David Rittenhouse, Thomas Godfrey, Alexander Wilson, and Thomas Say be removed to Laurel Hill Cemetery, and a monument placed over the common grave copied after the pyramid of Caius Cestius in Rome. Though this ambitious plan failed, the annalist John Fanning Watson in 1838 removed the remains of the Godfrey family to Laurel Hill, and erected a suitable stone. In 1843, under the auspices of the Mercantile Library Company, with members of the APS in attendance, a monument was raised over the grave. *Proposals for Erecting a Monument, by subscription, in the Laurel Hill Cemetery, commemorative of Native Genius and Worth, as exemplified in the Life and Writings of the Late David Rittenhouse, Thomas Godfrey, Alexander Wilson, and Thomas Say, Citizens of Philadelphia* ([Phila., 1836]). The tribute Meigs' committee proposed to inscribe read: "Thomas Godfrey, the unpretending genius, the self-taught philosopher, who, as the undoubted original inventor of the quadrant, has conferred on commercial and nautical science an invaluable boon, and elevated the intellectual reputation of his native country."

[1] Sandra L. Tatman and Roger W. Moss, *Biographical Dictionary of Philadelphia Architects: 1700–1930* (Boston, 1985), 656–58; Henry D. Biddle, "Colonial Mayors of Philadelphia. Samuel Rhoads, 1774," *PMHB*, XIX (1895), 64–71; S. Castner, Jr., *The Rhoads Family of Pennsylvania* (Phila., 1901), 7–13.

the first of a number of public commissions related to his trade and experience. In 1740/1 he was asked, with Joseph Fox, Samuel Powell, and John Nicholas, to measure Edmund Woolley's work on the State House.[2] In 1751 he was on a committee that recommended to the Assembly that a bridge be built across the Schuylkill River at Market Street. He was engaged with William Parsons in 1755 to lay out new streets in the expanding town. In 1757/8 he was on a committee to advise the town authorities on "the best Method of improving the . . . Swamp" between Budd's Buildings and Society Hill "for the general Use and Benefit of the City."[3] In the latter year the Philadelphia Monthly Meeting of Friends, of which he was a member, asked him to check the strength of the roof of the Great Meeting House in Market Street.[4] Perhaps his most impressive and lasting achievement as a builder was the Pennsylvania Hospital.

Rhoads was one of the twelve original Hospital Managers in 1751. Promptly after organizing, the board rented a private house, converted it to temporary hospital uses, and, in 1754, having acquired a piece of land at the edge of town, asked Rhoads and Joseph Fox to draft a plan for a permanent structure. The two men consulted the Managers, physicians, and Contributors; they reviewed the plans of British hospitals, especially of the Royal Infirmary of Edinburgh, and presented their own design to the board in January 1755. What share each man had in the plan is not known and cannot be determined; but it seems reasonable to believe that Rhoads made the greater contribution. In any event, when construction began and the cornerstone was put in place in May the Managers publicly stated that Rhoads had "Oversight of the Building." Thereafter he was sometimes called on to perform or oversee finishing work; and in 1762 was in charge of erecting a small additional "Elaboratory" building.[5]

Rhoads' increasing reputation as a builder brought him commissions to build larger houses for private clients. He built a house for Alexander Barclay on Delancey Street in 1758 and one for William Coleman on Second Street in 1766. In 1760 John Cadwalader purchased a house in Second Street that Rhoads had built a few years before. Benjamin Franklin engaged him to build a house on a court off Market Street between Third and Fourth streets. Plain, substantial, and comfortable, the house was not only to serve his family's needs, Franklin explained, but should also be "considered as a kind of Pattern House by future Builders, within the Power of Tradesmen & People of moderate circumstances to imitate and fol-

[2] Samuel Hazard, ed., *Register of Pennsylvania,* II (1828), 376.
[3] *Franklin Papers,* III, 276–78; IV, 180–81; 8 *Pa. Arch.*, IV, 3418, 3440.
[4] Phila. Monthly Meeting, Minutes, 26 Second Mo., 26 Fourth Mo. 1758.
[5] *Pa. Gaz.*, 21 May 1755; *Franklin Papers,* VI, 62; William H. Williams, *America's First Hospital: The Pennsylvania Hospital, 1751–1841* (Wayne, Pa., [1976]), 21–23; Morton, *Pennsylvania Hospital,* 36–37.

low."[6] Because the house was completed while Franklin was in London, there was much correspondence between the owner, his wife, and the builder, especially about interior decoration and furnishings, like brass locks, hinges, and other hardware not available in Philadelphia.[7]

Franklin and Rhoads were good friends during more than fifty years. They served together as directors or managers of the same institutions. Rhoads witnessed Franklin's will of 1750.[8] There are references to visits by Rhoads to Franklin's house. On one occasion, when Rhoads brought his daughter and son-in-law to tea, Deborah Franklin served them "the beste Buckwheat Kakes that ever I maid."[9] On the night the mob threatened Franklin's house because he had supported the Stamp Act, Rhoads offered to stay the night there to protect Deborah and her family.[10] From London Franklin sent Rhoads political pamphlets "to distribute among the Committee [of Correspondence] and others as you may think proper." Mutual friends conveyed greetings and good wishes. "Mr. Rhoades continues to enjoy a good share of health and vivacity," young Thomas Coombe wrote Franklin in 1774, "and has but few marks of Age about him." At dinner Rhoads toasted his absent friend "and wished, with a sigh of friendship, that you were at home again."[11]

Not only was Rhoads a Hospital Manager for thirty years, he encouraged and served other institutions as well. He was a founding director of the Union Fire Company in 1736 and a director of the Philadelphia Contributionship for the Insurance of Houses from Loss by Fire from its founding in 1752 until 1763. He was a director of the Library Company from 1739 to 1769 and again from 1772 to 1774, corresponding with Franklin in London about book orders.[12] He was a partner in a company formed to carry on the manufacture of linen,[13] and was a vice-president of the Silk Society, to which he contributed £3.

Meanwhile Rhoads had been elected a member of the Philadelphia Common Council in 1741; he was chosen an alderman in 1761. In this body he was appointed to a score or more committees to inspect, oversee, and regulate a wide variety of civic activities, structures, and improvements—roads and pavements, boundary lines, ferries, market houses and sheds, fire engines, hay scales, and the town watch. Many appointments related to the wharves, whose condition, often deteriorating, seems to have been an object of constant concern to the Council and

---

[6] Quoted in Tatman and Moss, *Biographical Dictionary,* 657; Nicholas B. Wainwright, *Colonial Grandeur in Philadelphia: The House and Furniture of General John Cadwalader* (Phila., 1964), 3–10.
[7] *Franklin Papers,* X, 291.
[8] Ibid., III, 482.
[9] Ibid., XII, 351.
[10] Ibid., 274.
[11] Ibid., XXI, 237, 316.
[12] Ibid., 187–88, 256–57.
[13] Ibid., XI, 314–16.

citizens. When it was reported that the town's standard copper measure for grain was bulging out of shape and so held more than it should, Rhoads was put on a committee instructed to have a new one cast that would contain the exact and legal amount.[14]

Rhoads was elected to the Assembly in January 1761 in the place of William Masters, who had died. Here, as in the Common Council, he quickly won attention and respect—and an endless succession of committee assignments. "Without the talent of speaking in public," wrote one who knew him, "he possessed much acuteness of mind, his judgment was sound, and his practical information extensive."[15] He was reelected in October 1761 and again in 1762 and 1763. He was on the committees of correspondence and of grievances. He was often appointed to inspect accounts and audit the Loan Office. He introduced bills to regulate taverns, dram shops, and "tippling houses," to regulate the night watch, to improve lighting in the city, and to prohibit the importation of slaves. In 1762 he went to Lancaster as one of the delegates of the Assembly to treat with the Indians.[16] In 1764, along with Franklin and others, he lost his seat in the defeat of the "Quaker party," and retired to his country place. Writing from London, Franklin congratulated him on now "being able to divert yourself with farming; 'tis an inexhaustible Source of perpetual Amusement. Your Country *Seat* is of a more secure kind than *that* in the Assembly: and I hope not so much in the Power of the Mob to jostle you out of."[17]

But Rhoads did not stay long in "retirement." He was put on the Board of Managers of the Almshouse, when that institution was established in 1766.[18] He was returned to the Assembly in 1770, and there interested himself especially in the survey and construction of canals. The reason he explained in a letter to Franklin on 3 May 1771.

> The growing *Trade* of Baltimore Town in Maryland drawn principally from our Province west of Susquehanna begins to alarm us with serious Apprehensions of such a Rival as may reduce us to the Situation of Burlington and New Castle on Delaware and we can devise no Means of saving our selves but by a Canal, from the Susquehanna to Schullkil [sic] and amending the Navigation of all our Rivers so far as they lead towards our Capital City.[19]

---

[14] *Minutes of the Common Council . . . 1704 to 1776* (Phila., 1847), 522, 566, 618, 626, 656, et passim.
[15] Biddle, "Colonial Mayors," loc. cit., 68.
[16] 8 *Pa. Arch.*, VI, 5366, 5405, 5420, 5472, and following volumes, passim.
[17] *Franklin Papers,* XII, 204–05.
[18] Charles Lawrence, *History of the Philadelphia Almshouses and Hospitals* ([Phila.], 1905), 22; *Pa. Gaz.,* 21 May 1767. Other managers included Joseph Fox, Abel James, Philip Syng, and Hugh Roberts.
[19] *Franklin Papers,* XVIII, 93–94.

Franklin sent his friend several "Canal Papers and Pamphlets," especially reports by John Smeaton and James Brindley on the Caledonian Canal. They provided, Rhoads wrote in acknowledging them, "a great deal of Instruction to us unexperienced Americans." Canalling, which was at first regarded "as a wild Chemerical Project which all the Strength of America could never execute," was now growing "more into Credit among us." In 1772 the Assembly appointed Rhoads and David Rittenhouse to make a survey of a route from the Schuylkill to the Susquehanna River. Franklin continued to send Rhoads practical advice and warnings about canal construction.[20]

At the same time, the two men exchanged information about fire-resistant roofing. Rhoads used a mixture of sand and paint. Franklin replied with a copy of John Wooler's pamphlet on copper roofing and a description of the stone-built houses of Paris. Rhoads promised to experiment with roofing of crushed limestone.[21]

Meanwhile Rhoads had helped Thomas Bond to revive the American Philosophical Society. He was a member of its committee to arrange union with the American Society for Promoting Useful Knowledge, and in 1769 he was on the committee that drafted by-laws for the united Society. A member of the standing Committees on Mechanics and Architecture and on Husbandry and American Improvements, he was also a member of the committee that appealed to the Assembly for funds to observe the Transit of Venus and also of the committee that supervised the construction of the observatory in the State-House Yard from which the observations were made on 3 June 1769. He was on the committee that prepared the first volume of the Society's *Transactions* in 1771. Among proposals for inquiry and improvements made to the Society was one to restore worn-out lands with marl and other fertilizers; Rhoads was one of those appointed to consider the idea. It was he who informed the Society about Arthur Donaldson's "machine for cleaning the Docks," and was put on the committee to investigate it.[22] Rhoads was elected one of the vice-presidents of the Philosophical Society in 1770 and was re-elected annually through 1776.

Though not a fiery rebel—Rhoads had thought John Dickinson's *Farmer's Letters* inflammatory[23]—he participated, as far as his Quaker principles permitted, in some of the movements towards independence. In the Assembly he drafted a statement favoring the citizens of Boston and on American grievances.[24] He was elected to the Provincial Convention in 1774 and was chosen its Speaker. He was elected a delegate to the First Continental Congress on 22 July, but attended for only a

---

[20] Ibid., XIX, 157–58; 8 *Pa. Arch.,* VIII, 6748, 6931–34.
[21] *Franklin Papers,* XVII, 181–83; XVIII, 33–34, 93–94.
[22] 8 *Pa. Arch.*, VIII, 7143, *Pa. Mag.*, May 1775, 206.
[23] *PMHB,* LIV (1930), 358–59.
[24] 8 *Pa. Arch.*, VIII, 7098.

short period, for on 4 October he was elected mayor of Philadelphia, and it was felt he should not and could not hold both posts simultaneously. One of the projects he cherished as mayor in the late winter of 1775 was to erect a city hall and court house on the State-House Yard, as had been long contemplated;[25] but the outbreak of war postponed the matter more than a dozen years. In September 1775 Mayor Rhoads ordered out the militia to disperse the mob that had taken Dr. John Kearsley, Jr. from his house, held him in the London Coffee House, and threatened him with tar and feathers.[26] In 1778, out of office but still active in Hospital affairs, Rhoads carried a strong protest to the Inspector General of British Army Hospitals against "the Loss of Blankets, Medicines and Hay that the Institution had sustained by the admission of the sick and wounded Soldiers of their Army, and the detention of the Instruments. . . ."[27] He was, Dr. Bond assured Franklin in 1779, "a Good Whig."[28]

The next year Rhoads was elected president of the Managers of the Pennsylvania Hospital, but resigned from the board after little more than a year. Also in 1780 Rhoads was elected master of the Carpenters' Company, succeeding Joseph Fox, his longtime friend and associate in Philadelphia endeavors; he held that position until his death, which occurred in Philadelphia on 7 April 1784. He was survived by his wife Elizabeth (Chandler) Rhoads, whom he had married at Philadelphia Monthly Meeting on 12 May 1737, and by a son and two daughters.

WILLIAM PARSONS (1701–1757)
AMERICAN PHILOSOPHICAL SOCIETY: 1743

WILLIAM PARSONS, Surveyor-General of Pennsylvania, was an original member of the American Philosophical Society, in which he was designated as "Geographer." As a young man Parsons "acquir'd a considerable Share of Mathematics, which he first studied with a View to Astrology that he afterwards laught at."[1] A member of the Junto of 1727, he owed his advance in life both to his own abilities and industry and to the influence and encouragement of fellow-members of that club. He was a founder of two of the Junto's projects—the Library Company of Philadelphia in 1731 (which he served as a director for three years and as librarian

---

[25] *Minutes of the Common Council*, 804.
[26] Christopher Marshall, *Passages from the Diary* (Phila., 1839–49), 47.
[27] Morton, *Pennsylvania Hospital*, 59.
[28] Franklin Mss., XV, 216.

---

[1] Franklin, *Autobiography*, 117.

for twelve) and the Union Fire Company in 1736. He appears to have been brought to the notice of James Logan.

Born in England on 6 May 1701, the oldest child and only son of Robert and Grace Parsons, he was brought to Philadelphia as a baby.[2] Robert Parsons, who was a weaver, died in 1708, leaving a wife and four children and, among other things, "a hawse and Loote," a "weaving Lume," "2 Iorn potts," and "thre bras kettles." Young William was apprenticed to a shoemaker. Once out of his apprenticeship, he rose rapidly: by 1726 he had taken on two apprentices, in 1727 he became owner of a tavern with Nicholas Scull, and in the 1730s he was engaged in trade as a merchant. All the while he was teaching himself practical mathematics and was soon able to work as a surveyor. When the directors of the Library Company engaged him in 1734 as librarian (at £6 a year), he was called "scrivener."[3]

Meanwhile Parsons had married. Johanna Christiana Zeidig was the daughter of a Lutheran clergyman, Johann Julius Zeidig, and his wife, Salome Margaret Sprögel, of Eisleben in Saxony. At the age of 17 Johanna was sent to an uncle in Pennsylvania, and in 1722 she was married to William Parsons. She bore six children. Their life together was not a happy one, however, and they eventually separated.

Parson's account and memoranda books contain records of the boots and shoes he made and repaired at his house in Second Street, and of his sales of salt, scythes, rum, sugar, molasses, and "Very good Canary Wine, and Lime-juice." His customers—some of them fellow-members of the American Philosophical Society—included Thomas Hopkinson, William Coleman, "John Wester," William Logan, Dr. Lloyd Zachary, Lewis Evans, Anthony Benezet ("for Eight Casks of rum"), Peter Chevalier, and Benjamin Loxley.[4] Parsons made his first professional survey in 1730—"a Business SomeTimes a little profitable but on the other hand of continual Trouble and Disquietude."[5] Much of his work was done in the Tulpehocken region, but he had commissions nearer home as well, such as calculating distances in Philadelphia and laying out the park at the Proprietor's estate of Springettsbury.[6] On 22 August 1741 he was appointed surveyor general of the Province, and subscribed the oath on 10 October. His first task, he found, was to organize the rec-

---

[2] Anthony F. C. Wallace, "William Parsons, Proprietary Agent, 1701–1757" (Ms., APS) is the principal biographical source. See also John W. Jordan, "William Parsons, Surveyor General, and Founder of Easton, Pennsylvania," *PMHB*, XXXIII (1909), 340–46; J. M. Levering, "Some Notes on the Family of William Parsons, the Founder of Easton," Moravian Hist. Soc., *Trans.*, VII (1906), 41–55; A. D. Chidsey, Jr., "William Parsons, Easton's First Citizen," *Pa. Hist.*, VII (1940), 89–102; and Hubertis M. Cummings, "William Parsons," Pa. Dept. of Internal Affairs, *Bulletin*, XXX, no. 4 (1962), 24–28.
[3] *PMHB*, XXXIX (1915), 450–52. The original manuscript Articles of Agreement, 14 March 1733/4, is in Soc. Misc. Coll., Phila. Lib. Co., Box 10 B (HSP).
[4] *Pa. Gaz.*, 19 Feb. 1740/1; Parsons, Receipt Book, 1738–49, Parsons Papers (HSP).
[5] Quoted in Wallace, "William Parsons."
[6] *PMHB*, XV (1891), 241–42; XVIII (1894), 384–85.

ords of the office, which his predecessor had left in some disarray. Then, having concluded that an accurate map of Pennsylvania was badly needed, he undertook to make one; late in 1743 he announced that it was nearly completed. At the same time he projected a series of county maps, "in which every Tract of Land will be described, according to the original Surveys, and the Names of the Purchasers inserted."[7] Neither the province nor the county maps, as it turned out, was published. On 6 October 1741 Parsons was chosen a member of the Philadelphia Common Council.

As a Proprietary officer, Parsons defended the Penns' interests and opinions. Thus, although he had originally welcomed Count Zinzendorf and the Moravians to Pennsylvania and sent his children to a Moravian school, his enthusiasm cooled as he understood that reserve was more acceptable to the Penns. Another reason for his change, a personal one, also accounted for his growing dislike of the Germans. Johanna Parsons proved to be a woman of morbid piety. Nominally a Lutheran, she came in contact with Dunkards in Philadelphia, then with a group of "French Prophets"; she was attracted by the evangelism of George Whitefield, and finally found a measure of peace among the Moravians. Parsons responded to such "seeking" with scant sympathy or understanding, and in 1745 he forbade his wife to visit the Moravians anymore. The alienation deepened as the Parson children were also drawn to the Moravians. Parsons threatened to disinherit his son Robert if the young man joined them. Falling ill soon afterwards, Robert, in his weakened state, had visions and called on his Savior, while his father, seated at his bedside, urged the dying youth, "Robert, use your reason! use your reason!" The death of his oldest daughter from consumption a few months later plunged Parsons more deeply into grief; he neglected his work; and, "finding his Health declines," he resigned as surveyor-general on 10 June 1748.[8]

Taking his two youngest children, Parsons left Philadelphia and his wife and took up residence at Stonykill in Berks County. The couple were never reunited, but before his death he asked Johanna to come to him at Easton; he died before she could reach him. Johanna Parsons continued to live in Philadelphia until 1769, when she moved to Bethlehem, where she spent the last four years of her life in the Widows' House. One of their grandchildren was Thomas Horsfield, first keeper of the museum of the East India Company in London, a distinguished naturalist, and author of *Zoological Researches in Java*.

In Lancaster County Parsons was appointed a justice of the peace in 1749 and in 1752 prothonotary, register, and recorder of the courts. Taking his responsibilities seriously, he asked a friend going to England to buy him "the best English Trea-

---

[7] *Pa. Gaz.*, 24 Nov. 1743; *Franklin Papers,* II, 392.
[8] Parsons to Thomas Penn, 24 Nov. 1746 (copy), Berks and Montgomery Counties, 11 (HSP); *Col. Recs. Pa.*, V, 274; Levering, "Some Notes on the Family of William Parsons," loc. cit., 47.

tise concerning the Nature of Writs. . . ."[9] Although no longer surveyor-general, Parsons continued to make surveys for individuals and was several times given official commissions. He had the reputation of being "exceedingly exact & a real Draughtsman." He surveyed town lots in Reading and the road from that place to Easton, and was a member of the party that surveyed a portion of the Pennsylvania-Maryland boundary in 1750–51. Putting up at an inn in Chester, the men spent the night "in some philosophical Discourses, concerning Diseases, the propagation of them, the admirable properties of them. . . ."[10] In 1752 he was called on to lay out the town of Easton in Northampton County.

Hiring about twenty sturdy young Germans, Parsons levelled and laid out the streets and square, dug a well, laid out a cemetery, and eventually built a jail. Before the end of the first winter eleven families were settled in their own houses.[11] Parsons was a justice of the peace for the county, prothonotary, clerk of the courts, recorder, and clerk of the commissioners. In 1753 he was elected a representative to the Assembly.[12] He built a stone house for himself and his family, and in 1757 erected another, larger dwelling, "a pretty neat habitation very compleatly furnished," fit to accommodate the governor's party during the negotiation of the Treaty of Easton in 1757.[13] He was a trustee of the German grammar school in the new town, making it a gift of £5.

His feelings against the Germans were now abating, and he welcomed them as settlers. To Richard Peters on 8 December 1752 he expressed the hope that land would be made available to the poorer sort of Germans.

> I don't mention Dutch People from any particular Regard that I have for them more than for other People. But because they are generally laborious and conformable to their Circumstances, than some others amongst us are. I need not say who they are, but it is an old Observation, that poor Gentle Folks don't always prove the fittest to begin new Places, where Labour is chiefly wanted.[14]

Life in a new town on the edge of the frontier, however, was different from life at Stonykill, where Parsons had enjoyed "a quiet and private Life without even so much as thinking of publick Affairs." He did not know whether the back-country people were worse than city-dwellers by nature, he wrote, or because they lacked

---

[9] 2 *Pa. Arch.*, IX, 772, 774; Parsons to William Peters, 17 Nov. 1753, Lancaster County, 1724–72, 89 (HSP).
[10] Lawrence H. Gipson, *Lewis Evans* (Phila., 1939), 27, quoting Peters Papers, III, 12; ibid., 38; Sometimes the work was delayed "upon the Account of the Gnats, Musketoes, flies and other Vermin which are intolerable in the Summer Season, and especially to Horses." 1 *Pa. Arch.*, II, 41.
[11] Ibid., 95–98.
[12] 2 *Pa. Arch.*, IX, 793; 8 *Pa. Arch.*, V, 3622.
[13] 1 *Pa. Arch.*, III, 104, 208, 209; Thomas Pownall, *A Topographical Description . . . of the United States of America* (Lois Mulkearn, ed., Pittsburgh, 1949), 102.
[14] 1 *Pa. Arch.*, II, 95–98.

knowledge and had to be looked after. "But this I can truly say," he told Benjamin Franklin, "that I never saw or heard of so much Schemeing [sic] low Contrivance and Insincerity in all the Time I lived in Philadelphia as I have seen in the little Time since I left it."[15]

War erupted on the frontier in the fall of 1755, and Parsons found himself in a position of responsibility near the center of affairs. He had to cope with both the diplomacy of Indian relations and the horrors of frontier war, protecting the settlers from the Indians and friendly Indians from the frontiersmen. In particular he had to provide powder and lead from the magazine at Easton to the forts and country people. Increasing violence caused indescribable distress and confusion. "Our Roads are continually full of Travellers," he reported to Richard Peters on 31 October.

> . . . Men, Women & Children most of them barefoot, have been obliged to cross those terrible Mountains with what little they could bring with them in so long a Journey thro' ways almost impassable, to get to the Inhabitants on this side. Whilst those who live on this side near the Mountain, are removing their Effects to Tulpehocken. Those at Tulpehockon [sic] are removing to Reading, and many at Reading are moving nigher to Philada., and some of them it is said quite to Philada. This is the present unhappy Situation of Pennsylvania.[16]

A few hours later Parsons wrote Conrad Weiser:

> But how shall I find Words to discribe [sic] the Confusion & Distress of the poor unhappy Sufferers? And if I had Words My Heart would burst at the Discription [sic], which therefore I wave [sic]. I have not lived long in the World and yet I have lived too long. I have lived to see my Country almost at the Brink of Ruin and the Reins of Govermt. almost loosened through intestine Differences. I have lived to see an Enemy which we very lately dispised [sic], perhaps too much dispised, now ravaging my Country and murdering its Inhabitants. Oh! that the Almighty would be pleased to soften the Hearts of the Legislators and incline them with Pity towards the distressed miserable People of this Province.[17]

As the days and weeks passed, Parsons' appeals became more urgent. "Pray Sir, help us for we are in great distress," he called on Peters on 25 November. He had no money, no supplies; people were fleeing; "and we are now the Frontier of this part of the Country." The authorities at Philadelphia were reacting slowly, when at all. There seemed to be no plan. "Pray do something," Parsons appealed to Franklin and Governor Hamilton on 15 December, reproaching the government for inac-

---

[15] *Franklin Papers*, IV, 410–11.
[16] 1 *Pa. Arch.*, II, 443–45. For a detailed account of Parsons' acts and movements on the frontier at this period, see William A. Hunter, *Forts on the Pennsylvania Frontier, 1753–1758* (Harrisburg, Pa., 1960).
[17] Parsons to Conrad Weiser, 31 Oct. 1755, Lancaster County, 1724–72, 105 (HSP).

tivity, "or give some order for our speedy relief, or the whole country will be entirely ruined."[18]

In late December things began to change. Franklin visited the frontier with authority to lay out forts. Parsons was commissioned a major and instructed to raise a company of foot of 24 men as a garrison, guard, and watch at Easton; and on 14 May he received another commission as major in the first battalion of the Pennsylvania Regiment.[19] Not only was he responsible for the troops protecting the town, but in the summer of 1756 he made tours of inspection to outlying forts along the mountains in Northampton and Berks Counties.

All the while Parsons continued to be involved with local affairs and politics. In 1756 he was charged with withholding writs of election addressed to the sheriff, with the result that some voters were not apprised of the election in time to vote. "But you know Mr. Parsons is a Man that is not apt to forget any old Difference." He was summoned before the Assembly to answer.[20]

But when the emissary of the Assembly went to Easton to summon him to Philadelphia, Parsons was not at home. Ailing off and on for some months, he had gone to Perth Amboy in New Jersey for the fresh ocean air.[21] By mid-fall he was back in Easton, keeping an eye on defense measures. In December his illness took a turn for the worse; he wrote his will on 15 December 1757, and died two days later. In it the one-time shoemaker described himself as "gentleman." In addition to small specific bequests (including one of £100 to his nephew Stephen Woolley) and provision for his wife, he left £200 for the support of "Poor Scholars at the Academy of Philadelphia." At the time of his death he owned "a compleat Theodolite, Circumferenter, and other instruments for Surveying," which were exhibited and offered for sale by his executor at the shop of James Ham, instrument-maker, in Front Street, Philadelphia. The funeral was conducted by his son-in-law, the Reverend Mr. John Rogers, a Moravian, as Parsons had requested, and was attended by many Moravians of the town.[22]

In London Benjamin Franklin received news of Parsons' death. A friend from the days of the Junto, he was, Franklin wrote Hugh Roberts, an "odd character," "a wise Man, that often acted foolishly." Even when prosperous, Parsons was "always fretting," a man who "had always the *Means* of Happiness without ever enjoying the *Thing*"; but withal an honest man, "and that alone, as the World goes, is one of the greatest of Characters."[23]

---

[18] *Col. Recs. Pa.,* VI, 737, 761.
[19] *Franklin Papers,* VI, 313–14; 5 *Pa. Arch.,* I, 31, 42.
[20] 8 *Pa. Arch.,* VI, 4453, 4617–18.
[21] Ibid., 4635; *Franklin Papers,* VII, 206–07.
[22] Parsons, Will, 15 Dec. 1757, Book L, No. 20, cited by Wallace, "William Parsons"; *Pa. Gaz.,* 13 July 1758; Joseph M. Levering, *A History of Bethlehem, Pennsylvania, 1741–1892* (Bethlehem, 1903), 265.
[23] *Franklin Papers,* VIII, 159–60. See also Franklin's letter to his wife, 19 Feb. 1758, ibid., VII, 380.

PHINEAS BOND
By Robert Feke. *Philadelphia Museum of Art. Gift of Phyllis Cochran Derby.*

PHINEAS BOND (1717–1773)
AMERICAN PHILOSOPHICAL SOCIETY: 1743

DR. PHINEAS BOND, a young Quaker physician, was, with his brother Thomas, Benjamin Franklin, and others, a founding member of the American Philosophical Society, in which he was characterized by the broadly inclusive title of "General Natural Philosopher." That he should have joined in the enterprise was natural enough for, in addition to his medical and scientific interests, Bond had already displayed an interest in projects which the Philadelphia philosophers approved and had served from 1740 to 1742 as a director of the Library Company. Of the work of the first Philosophical Society hardly anything is known, and Bond's name appears nowhere in the scanty record. When his brother Thomas revived the long-"dormant" Society in 1767–68 to offset the upstart American Society, Phineas attended on 19 January as a member of the original group. He came to several more meetings, asked to be considered a member of the Committees on Natural Philosophy, Mathematics, Optics and Astronomy and on Medicine, Anatomy, and Chemistry; and was on the Philosophical Society's committee that negotiated the union of the two societies. His interest in the Society ceased abruptly thereafter—perhaps he was one of those disaffected by the election of Franklin as president and the defeat of the Proprietary interest—and he never attended again.

Born in Calvert County, Maryland, on 13 September 1717, the fifth son and sixth child of Richard and Elizabeth (Benson) Bond, the latter the widow of Benjamin Chew, Phineas, like his elder brother Thomas, began his medical training under Dr. John Hamilton of Calvert County;[1] and, having completed it, again like his brother and many others from southern Maryland, moved to Philadelphia. He bore a certificate of removal from Herring Creek Friends, which he promptly presented to Philadelphia Monthly Meeting on 23 Twelfth Mo. 1738/9.[2] In Philadelphia Bond received instruction from the able but ill-tempered John Kearsley, Sr., who, however, became a family friend and made bequests to Bond's daughters. By July 1740 Bond had completed one stage of his medical education, bought the apothecary shop and stock of Thomas Lloyd, and established himself at the Sign of the Golden Mortar, a few doors below the Friends meetinghouse in Second Street, where he advertised drugs and medicines for sale at the cheapest rate.[3] In the fall of 1741, Thomas Bond having returned from European studies, Phineas went abroad,

---

[1] The Cliffs Monthly Meeting, Register of Births and Deaths from 1662–1782, Book 32 (Hall of Records, Annapolis, Md.).
[2] Hinshaw, *Amer. Quaker Genealogy,* II, 468.
[3] *Pa. Gaz.,* 3 July 1740.

leaving his brother in charge at the Golden Mortar.[4] He made the usual visitor's complaint about the English weather:

> There is such a continued Fog in this Country, that the Sun does not appear once a Month. It is very common to hear them talk of its being a charming Day, when I'm shure no prudent Man in Philada. would venture to Scuilkill in such a one, unless upon the most urgent Business. They call it fine Weather if it is possible to walk half a Mile without being wet to the Skin.

London was more attractive professionally. Bond had no trouble getting permission to attend hospital practice, "where the great Variety of Sick & Lame affords not only Matter of Instruction, but Amusement."[5] From London he went first to Paris, where he attended lectures on anatomy and surgery from Claude-Nicolas Le Cat, and then to Rheims, where he received the degree of M.D. on 17 July 1742— a distinction that of itself meant very little, for Rheims was hardly more than a diploma mill. Six weeks later Bond matriculated at the University of Leiden,[6] where he made the acquaintance of the distinguished physician-botanist Gronovius, who asked him, when he returned home in 1743, to carry a letter to John Bartram, together with gift copies of Gronovius' *Index Lapideae* and Linnaeus' *Characters*.[7]

The brothers Bond soon acquired a large and lucrative practice, which ultimately included among its patients Benjamin Chew, James Hamilton, Israel Pemberton, Samuel Rhoads, William Coleman, Hugh Roberts, Edmund Physick, Provost William Smith, Benjamin Loxley, Ebenezer Kinnersley, John Vining, and Benjamin Franklin.[8] To practice, which was limited pretty largely to medicine and minor surgery, Phineas Bond added a serious experimental interest, insofar as that could be pursued in Philadelphia. Well aware that the many mineral springs in America were medically beneficial, but that reports of cures were unreliable and therefore likely to be disappointing to sufferers, the Bonds in 1747 announced that they proposed

> to examine into the real Merit of these Springs, the Share they have had in the Cures imputed to them, and in what their Excellency consists; intending, as soon as it can be done with any Certainty, to communicate to the Publick a particular Account of the Virtues of the Waters, with their Sentiments of the properest Method of using them in different Constitutions.

---

[4] Ibid., 29 Oct. 1741.
[5] Bond to Samuel Rhoads, 26 Dec. 1741 (Coll. Physicians Phila.).
[6] R.W. Innes Smith, *English-Speaking Students of Medicine at the University of Leyden* (Edinburgh, 1932), 26.
[7] Darlington, *Memorials,* 349, 353.
[8] See Phineas Bond's Day Book (HSP) and the "Co-partnership Ledgers" of Thomas and Phineas Bond (Coll. Physicians Phila.) for the extent, variety, and income of Bond's practice.

In order thereto, we shall make those Experiments which have discovered the Principles, and distinguished the Characters of the different Springs in Europe, whose Properties having been long experienced, very probable Conjectures may from thence be drawn about our own; yet as these will not be certain Conclusions . . . we are therefor obliged to desire of those Gentlemen, who, from Indisposition or Curiosity, have visited the Wells, that they would transmit to us an exact Account of the Effect of the Waters upon themselves, or others under their Observation; and let us know the Diseases for which they had Recourse to them; the Ages of the Patients; their Manner of living, both before and after the Use of the Waters, the Methods of taking them, and their immediate and consequental Effects. This Exactness is absolutely necessary to assist us in distinguishing between those Cures which have been really performed by the Springs, and such as are only the Effects of Time, Exercise, a Change of Air, Diet, or some other Accident.[9]

Doubtless the responses to this announcement, if any were made, aided the doctors in their practice, but they were too few or too inexact to publish. A few years later the Bonds displayed another instance of their taste for scientific inquiry. One of his patients having voided a 20-inch worm two days before her death, Thomas Bond obtained permission for an autopsy, at which Phineas, together with Dr. Kearsley and Dr. William Shippen, Sr., assisted. The report was sent to Dr. John Clephane of St. George's Hospital, and was published in the London *Medical Inquiries and Observations*.[10]

Other evidence testified to Bond's position in the profession and the community. He began to take apprentices—Samuel Stringer, later in charge of the military hospital at Albany, was one[11]—and he played a leading role in the Pennsylvania Hospital. He was one of the original contributors to that institution, subscribing £25; and in 1752 he, his brother, and Lloyd Zachary offered their services gratis as attending physicians. He remained on the staff until his death 21 years later, participating in all the significant decisions respecting medical care and education. In 1763, for example, the physicians proposed that students not attached to any attending physician be charged a fee for the privilege of observing the hospital practice, as was the case in Britain; and they offered to donate these fees, which traditionally belonged to them, to establish a medical library, "which we judge will tend greatly to the advantage of the pupils, and the honor of the institution."[12] On another occasion, in 1767, the Bonds and Thomas Cadwalader suggested that, to lighten the burden on the physicians, the Managers employ a "Surgeryman, as in English Hospitals, to prepare the Dressings as we direct, to be ready on all Occa-

---

[9] *Pa. Gaz.*, 6 Jan. 1746/7.
[10] *Franklin Papers*, VI, 10n.
[11] Samuel Stringer to Charles Ridgely, 28 June 1759, in Leon de Valinger, ed., *A Calendar of Ridgely Family Letters, 1742–1899*, I (1948), 84.
[12] George W. Norris, *The Early History of Medicine in Philadelphia* (Phila., 1886), 128.

sions whereby we could, or our Apprentices in our Absence, dress the Patients with more ease and advantage . . . ." The first proposal was approved, and thus the hospital library was founded; but the Managers did not appoint a surgeryman, although they did appoint a resident apothecary at the doctors' suggestion.[13] The Bonds' reputation was unsurpassed in the city; they were, John Swift told the Commissioners of Customs in America in 1770, "two as able Physicians as any we have."[14] Understandably, then, Phineas Bond was offended at not being included among the first members of John Morgan's Medical Society in 1766—but this omission was a personal and political matter, not professional.

Dr. Alexander Hamilton of Annapolis, visiting Philadelphia in 1744, was taken by Bond to the Governor's Club, which met nightly at the Tun Tavern in Water Street. "Our conversation was entertaining; the subject was the English poets and some of the foreign writers, particularly Cervantes, author of Don Quixot, whom we loaded with elogiums due to his character."[15] This is the kind of company Bond loved, for, as one biographer tells us, he "was remarkable for conviviality, but never habituated to intemperance."[16] Bond found other opportunities for conviviality at the Hand-in-Hand Fire Company, the Assembly balls, to which he subscribed, the Fishing Company of Fort St. David, and the Society of the Sons of St. George, of which he was a founding member in 1772. Doubtless he expected that the City Tavern, to which he subscribed, would provide a meeting place for other convivial groups.

In 1747 Bond was elected to the Common Council, but he attended irregularly and seems to have been called on for nothing more important than service on a committee to draft a ceremonial address to the new governor John Penn.[17] He was an original trustee of the Academy of Philadelphia, subscribed £10 a year to its support, and was a manager of the first and second Academy lotteries. Upon the establishment of the College a few years later he was named to that institution's first board, whose meetings he attended with considerable faithfulness until his death.[18]

In 1758 Phineas Bond and his brother were involved in the Pennsylvania Assembly's arrest and prosecution of William Moore, justice of the peace of Chester County, and of Provost William Smith of the College of Philadelphia. Judge Moore was summoned before the Assembly in the summer of 1757 to answer charges of improper conduct of his office brought by petitioning members of the public. The charges were heard; Moore, in a formal reply, denied both the charges and the right of the Assembly to try him on them. The Assembly, however, acting on the peti-

---

[13] Morton, *Pennsylvania Hospital,* 527.
[14] John Swift to Commissioners of Customs, 20 Dec. 1770, *PMHB,* XXX (1906), 143.
[15] Carl Bridenbaugh, ed., *Gentleman's Progress: The Itinerarium of Dr. Alexander Hamilton, 1744* (Chapel Hill, 1948), 21.
[16] James Thacher, *American Medical Biography* (Boston, 1828), I, 179.
[17] *Minutes of the Common Council . . . 1704 to 1776* (Phila., 1847), 482, 692.
[18] *Franklin Papers,* V, 437, 513.

tioners' charges, asked Governor Denny to remove him. The text of their address to the Governor, but not of Moore's defense, was printed in the newspapers. A few weeks later, after the dissolution of the Assembly, Moore addressed a letter of protest to the Governor, then published a "Humble Address," which included a counter-charge that "one of the Members, or that rather Tools, of the late Assembly," had collected petitions to effect his downfall. When this was printed, Moore was brought before the Assembly, examined, and ordered to jail.

The principal object of the Assembly's wrath, however, was William Smith, who had become a prominent figure in the Proprietary party and, thanks to a facile pen, a constant irritant to the Assembly. He was believed to have aided Moore in revising the "Humble Address." To obtain evidence the Assembly summoned both Phineas and Thomas Bond, who were present at a time when Moore and Smith could have discussed the writing. Phineas Bond was in an especially awkward position, since he was Moore's son-in-law. (Within a year Smith also married one of Moore's daughters.) Accordingly Bond refused to answer. Aware of the personal reasons for his silence, the Assembly promised him immunity. "He still obstinately persisting in his Refusal to give a direct Answer at the Time to the Question," the Assembly found him in "high Contempt," and ordered him into the custody of the sergeant-at-arms. Subsequently, when others had given the evidence the Assembly wanted and silence would no longer protect the authors of the alleged libel, Bond told what he knew.[19]

> Mr. Moore after an address published that nearly affected his Character wrote a Draught part in Town and Part at Home, tending to Clear himself. I told him I thought something of that sort Necessary and he Consulted Council upon it. The Council told him the Old Assembly were a Non Entity and you may do it safely. Otherwise I am Certain he would never have done it. I myself Consulted Council about it and was told the same thing. Without this Advice that Paper had never been published, nor Mr. Moore imprisoned. Neither Mr. Smith, my Brother nor myself brought to any trouble about it. Mr. Moore having wrote a Draught of the Address shewed it to his Friends, my Brother, Mr. Smith & myself. Our Opinions were different, but we most approv'd what he first wrote as well as done.
>
> After some Consultation various alterations were made by a Gentleman to whom it was sent, none by us, so that the Original could Scarcely be read, but thro' the whole of our Consultations upon this Paper, Mr. Smith never shewed any forwardness to alter or amend it. I advised Mr. Moore to Confine himself Chiefly to his first Draught which was copied by Mr. Livers and sent to the Governor afterwards. I was a Little Concern'd in it, but proposals were made for publishing of it. I still preferred Mr. Moore's first Draught, and did not regard the Alterations. However the Time Came when this Paper again form'd by Mr. Moore was to be published and Mr. Moore going out of Town, gave me directions to inspect the Press, which I promis'd to do. Some little Time afterwards I found a Proof of Mr. Bradfords lying on my Table. I sat down in

---

[19] 8 *Pa. Arch.*, VI, 4677–80; William Smith, Petition for habeas corpus, 4 Feb. 1758, Smith Family Mss., Case 76 (HSP).

Order to correct it, but considered at another Time how much pain it had cost me to correct a Proof and could not do it to the understanding of the Printer. I then considered who cou'd assist me and save the Trouble and Time the Other had cost me, and repaired to Mr. Smith. Upon mentioning my Errand, he said Doctor, you can do this as well as I can. Having first asked me what paper it was, I told him it was Mr. Bradford's Proof of Mr. Moore's Paper. However I prevailed on him by telling him the Printer was waiting, it must be done, & intreated him to do it. We sat down together and made some very triffleing & insignificant Corrections of the said Proof. Then I returned it to Mr. Bradford.

Q. Did Mr. Smith leave a Manuscript Copy of the said address with you?
A. I don't know that he left it, but I saw a Mss. Copy of it at my House.
Q. Did you see that Copy before or since the publication of it?
A. I cannot say.
Q. Was the Draught Livers transcribed from, in Mr. Smith's Hand Writing?
A. To the best of my Knowledge it was not.
Q. Were any of the many Alterations in Mr. Moores Draught, done by Mr. Smiths Direction?
A. Not that I know of.
Q. Were any alterations made by Mr. Smith on the sd. Address when he, Mr. Moore, Your Brother, & your self examined it?
A. There were not any made by him to my knowledge and except my self Mr. Smith said less than any other Person present.

Questions proposed by the Council
Q. At what Time was this Consultation?
A. I can't be certain, but I think it was after the last Election.
Q. Do you know whether Mr. Moore had taken the advice of Council at that Time?
A. He had, & mentioned it at that Meeting.
Q. Were the Corrections made on the Proof Sheet merely litteral?
A. They were merely so.

Some years later, Bond had another, but less unsettling, experience with the Assembly. He was one of the Philadelphia physicians who looked after the French neutrals in the city during the French and Indian War; he was paid for his services £50 in 1759 and £173 17s. in 1764. Though not officially employed to do so, he had continued to look after the unfortunates, providing them with medicines; and in 1768 he asked compensation for the cost of drugs at the rate of £25 annually for seven years. The Assembly voted an authorization of £175, but did not pay the money for five years, and that was after Bond's death.[20]

Although he was a birthright Friend, Bond's new Philadelphia associates, his European experiences, and his inclinations drew him away from the Quakers. He neglected attendance at meeting; in the winter of 1747–48 he participated in the

---

[20] 8 *Pa. Arch.,* VI, 5064; VII, 5659, 5764, 6101, 6119; VIII, 7022, 7135. Bond continued to care for the French neutrals after 1768. Thomas and Phineas Bond, Co-partnership Ledgers, V, 385.

Association; and he gave indications of intending marriage with a non-Quaker, and even spoke of joining the Episcopalian Church. He was accordingly disowned on 29 Fifth Mo. [July] 1748;[21] and on 4 August 1748 he married Williamina Moore, daughter of William Moore of Moore Hall, Chester County. They had six children: Phineas, who studied law at the Middle Temple, left Philadelphia as a Tory during the Revolution, was called to the English bar in 1779, and returned home after the war as the British consul;[22] Williamina, who married General John Cadwalader; and Ann, Rebecca, Elizabeth, and Frances. The family lived well. In 1772 Bond was one of five physicians in town who kept an "equipage"—a chariot that cost him £48 in 1770.[23] Robert Feke painted his portrait, gold-headed cane in hand, sword at his side. His daughters were sent to a dancing master,[24] which was doubtless one reason for their popularity with young British officers during the Occupation winter.

In June 1773 Dr. Bond became ill and on 11 June he died, and was buried next evening in Christ Church burying ground. The attack had probably been sudden and severe, for Bond had no time to write his will. Though the estate was large, the heirs did not quarrel over it; one of the daughters surrendered her share to her mother because, she explained, she knew it was her father's wish that his widow have everything. The administrators' reports show that they sold a copy of Boerhaave's *Institutes* for £1 15s., shop furniture for £6, and a set of medical instruments to Sharp Delany for £10.[25] The *Pennsylvania Gazette,* in its notice of Bond's passing, characterized him as "learned, judicious and rational; a sagacious Observer and diligent Follower of *Nature* . . . honest, candid, chearful and sincere . . . one of those *happy-tempered* Men, who could not be *known* without being *loved,* and therefore hardly ever had a *Patient* in whom he had not a *Friend.*"[26]

---

[21] Phila. Monthly Meeting, Rough Minutes, 29 Fifth Mo. 1748 (Haverford College).
[22] Joanne Loewe Neel, *Phineas Bond: A Study in Anglo-American Relations, 1786–1812* (Phila., 1968).
[23] "List of the Families that kept Equipages in Philadelphia . . . in . . . 1772," Du Simitière Papers (Lib. Co. Phila.).
[24] Bond, Receipt Book (HSP).
[25] Administrators' Account, Cadwalader Coll., Misc. Bond Box (HSP); Elizabeth Bond, Release, 7 March 1791, ibid.
[26] *Pa. Gaz.,* 16 June 1773.

JAMES ALEXANDER
By John Wollaston. *Museum of the City of New York.*

JAMES ALEXANDER (1691–1756)
AMERICAN PHILOSOPHICAL SOCIETY: 1744

JAMES ALEXANDER, a prominent lawyer and public figure of New Jersey and New York, was an original member of the American Philosophical Society. Warmly approving Franklin's project, he urged several of his friends, mostly New York lawyers like himself, to "send their names" as prospective members. He assured his friend Cadwallader Colden, also an early member of the Society, that he would give Franklin "all the Encouragement" in his power "to proceed in the affairs of the Society & other useful undertakings. . . ." Accomplished in mathematics and astronomy, Alexander was interested in many "philosophical" subjects and gave active support to several of New York's rising educational and literary institutions.

Born in Stirlingshire, Scotland, in 1691, a distant relation of the Earl of Stirling, James Alexander may have received his formal education at the High School of Stirling.[1] In 1707–09 he joined the Jacobite cause in support of the project of James Edward Stuart to take the throne he claimed was his; but when the Pretender's effort was aborted Alexander returned home. Still restless, however, he now joined the navy, serving on H.M.S. *Arundell* in 1712–13, where he acquired skill in navigation, mathematics, and astronomy. In August 1715 he came to New York, where he was quickly received into the company of Scots who were settled there and in neighboring New Jersey. Only three months later, on 7 November 1715, Alexander was appointed surveyor-general of New Jersey. It was the first of a number of offices in New Jersey and New York that he was to hold in the ensuing 35 years.

As surveyor-general, Alexander organized his office, collected arrearages, settled disputed titles, and inaugurated a more efficient system of record-keeping. He personally went out on surveys, making use of instruments he had brought from Scotland, including a compass made by John Rowley, whom he called "the then most noted instrument maker" in Britain.[2] Representing New Jersey in the survey of its boundary with New York in 1719, Alexander persuaded his fellow commissioners to base their lines on astronomical observations. In 1716, the year after his appointment as New Jersey's surveyor-general, Alexander was named deputy-secretary of the New York Council; in 1718 he was appointed recorder of Perth Amboy in New Jersey. His performance in these posts attracted favorable notice from Governor Robert Hunter of New York and from Lewis Morris, the Chief Justice. On recom-

---

[1] William A. Duer, *The Life of William Alexander, Earl of Stirling* (N.J. Hist. Soc., *Colls.*, II, 1847), 1–6; Henry N. MacCracken, *Prologue to Independence: The Trials of James Alexander, American, 1715–1756* (N.Y., [1964]); *DAB*.
[2] *Colden Papers,* III (N.-Y. Hist. Soc., *Colls.,* 1919), 61–63.

mendation of Governor William Burnet he was sworn to the New York Council on 2 August 1721; in 1723 he was added to the Council of New Jersey; and in the latter year was also appointed Attorney General of New Jersey, being admitted to the bar on the day of the appointment. He held the office until 1727.

When and with whom Alexander read law is not known. By 1721, however, he owned a law library of more than 140 titles. In addition, his 45 mathematical texts included Newton's *Principia, Opticks,* and *Algebra,* Descartes' *Geometry,* Kepler's *Tables,* James Gregory's *Astronomy,* J. T. Desagulier's *Course of Experimental Philosophy,* and several editions of Euclid. There were a number of books on surveying. Among the "Miscellaneous Books" were Milton, Creech's translation of Lucretius, a few other Latin authors, Johann Heinrich Alsted's *Thesaurus Chronologiae,* and some dictionaries. There were only a few works of history, two books of edification—John Scott's *The Christian Life* and Antoinette Bourignon's *Admirable Treatise of Solid Virtue*—and a single work of fiction—"Queen of Tunis a novel."[3]

Meanwhile Alexander had married on 5 January 1721 Mrs. Mary (Spratt) Provoost, daughter of John and Maria (DePeyster) Spratt and widow of the wealthy merchant Samuel Provoost, whose shop she continued to tend for many years.[4] Governor Burnet and his lady stood sponsors at the baptism of the Alexanders' first child.

For more than 30 years Alexander was engaged in the practice of law, and in political agitations and developments in New Jersey and New York. At one time or another he was lawyer, partner, agent, colleague, friend, and counsellor to Hunter, Morris, and half a score other leaders of the colonies. His work was with surveys, grants, and titles to land, with appointments and salaries, with Indian affairs and the requirements of defense. He was chairman of the commission that ran the New York-Connecticut boundary and of the committee that revised the New York city charter in 1730, and he received the freedom of the city the next year.[5] He was, Colden wrote, "the most indefatigable man of business I ever knew," and this concentration, Colden believed, ultimately impaired his health.[6] In the words of the historian William Smith, Alexander was at this time

> at the head of his profession for sagacity and penetration; and in application to business no man could surpass him. Nor was he unacquainted with the affairs of the public, having served in the secretary's office, the best school in the province for instruction in matters of government; because the secretary enjoys a plurality of offices, conversant with the first springs of our provincial economy.[7]

---

[3] Alexander, [Inventory of his Library, 1721], James and William Alexander, Records (N.J. Hist. Soc.).
[4] N.-Y. Hist. Soc., *Colls.*, 1896, 386–89.
[5] Ibid., 1885, 116.
[6] *Colden Papers,* VIII (N.-Y. Hist. Soc., *Colls.*, 1934), 335.
[7] William Smith, *The History of the late Province of New-York,* I (N.-Y. Hist. Soc., *Colls.*, IV, 1829), 212–13.

By the mid-1730s Alexander was also established as one of the leaders of the anti-government, Popular party in New York. William Cosby, on assuming the governorship in 1732, had called on Rip Van Dam, who as president of the Council had been acting governor for 13 months, to surrender half of the salary and emoluments he had received during that period. When Van Dam refused to do this, the governor sued. For this purpose he created the justices as a court of exchequer, in which they would determine the facts without the aid of a jury. The court ruled against Cosby, who retaliated by removing Chief Justice Morris from the bench and Alexander from the Council. Alexander, the governor charged, had influenced President Rip Van Dam "in every thing that was irregular and since has clog'd and perplexed every thing with difficulty's that related to the Crown"; and Mrs. Cosby was heard to express the wish that someone might do away with her husband's challenger.

This made the dispute a constitutional question of the executive's power over the courts and judges. The anti-government party now had its issue, and resolved to press it through the newspapers. Accordingly they engaged John Peter Zenger to establish the *New-York Weekly Journal* in November 1733, and employed it as a vehicle for attacking the governor, his adherents, appointees, and party in strong, even vitriolic terms.

In the spring of 1735, the *Journal*'s attacks having increased in volume and intensity, Zenger was arrested on a charge of seditious libel. When the jury would not indict, the attorney-general secured Zenger's arrest "on information." Alexander and his colleague William Smith challenged the jurisdiction of the court, and were promptly disbarred by Chief Justice De Lancey. Zenger being now left without a defense in New York, his attorneys summoned Andrew Hamilton from Philadelphia. Hamilton argued successfully that a jury might not only decide as to the fact of publication but, from their own knowledge, determine whether the publication was false, scandalous, and seditious, and therefore punishable as libel. An account of Zenger's case and trial was prepared and published by Alexander. Two years later Alexander and Smith were restored to the bar, and the former was recalled to the New York Council. His removal from the New Jersey Council had never been made effective, and so he continued in his position there.

Alexander now erected a large house in New York City. Its size and the character of its furnishings may be judged from the inventory of Mrs. Alexander's will in 1760 and from the theft by burglars in 1755 of £200 in gold, silver, and paper that were in the house.[8]

Alexander's interest in astronomy had been a natural outgrowth of his work as a surveyor. After 1740 he seems to have had more time to devote to this favorite pursuit. He observed the comets of 1742 and 1748, and corresponded about them

---

[8] I. N. Phelps Stokes, *The Iconography of Manhattan Island, 1498–1909* (N.Y., 1915–28), IV, 560, 666.

with Dr. John Betts of University College, Oxford, later the Savilian professor of geometry there. Through Colden he was drawn into the circle of Peter Collinson, who filled his and Mrs. Alexander's orders and sent him a copy of Gowin Knight's treatise on attraction and repulsion and a little tract entitled "Thoughts on Philosophy." He owned the *Abridgment of the Philosophical Transactions* and ordered current issues of the *Philosophical Transactions* from London. In 1751, after some effort, he acquired a copy of Edmund Halley's Astronomical Tables as well as Voltaire's *Elements of Newton's Philosophy*. Through Collinson he purchased instruments from Jonathan Sisson of London, among others a sector "for observing Stars in or near the Zenith to two Seconds." He was acquainted with Dr. Archibald Spencer, and in 1752 he attended Ebenezer Kinnersley's lectures on electricity, "& I assure you," he wrote Colden, "he performs them Extremely well being as Master of words as well as of the Experimants [sic]."[9]

Although Alexander published nothing himself, his knowledge and judgment were called on by, and generously given to, others. He was one of only three persons—the others were James Logan and Benjamin Franklin—to whom Colden felt he could submit drafts of his scientific writings. Lewis Evans acknowledged that Alexander's collection of maps and surveys had been "of singular Service to me, as containing Variety of Draughts not to be met with elsewhere," and he submitted his map to Alexander for correction and revision. Similarly Thomas Pownall in his *Topographical Description of . . . America* made use of papers given him by Alexander's son William.[10]

Alexander made careful plans to observe the Transit of Mercury that was to occur on 6 May 1753. "I wish you could be here Some days before the 6th of May next," he wrote his friend Colden, who was at his country place Coldengham,

> to assist in prepareing things for the observing the transit of Mercury over the Sun then, and in making the observation, for Except your Self & me, I believe there's none in the province any way acquainted with observations of that kind, and our Observing that transit might show some young men how to observe the transit of Venus in 1761.
>
> There are three reflecting Telescopes in town any of which will Serve for taking the moments of inner & outer Contacts at the End of the Transit of Mercury—my Clock has a Second hand—& the proprietors Quadrant will do to rectifie the Clock, & the other matters proposed in M^r d'Lysle's [Delisle] directions. . . .[11]

As it turned out, clouds prevented the observation, "though we were pretty well prepared" for it.

---

[9] *Colden Papers,* III (N.-Y. Hist. Soc., *Colls.,* 1919), 45–47, 48–50, 70–71, 99–100; IV (1920), 67, 104, 136–39, 204–07, 299, 336.
[10] Ibid., 107; IX (1935), 36–38; Thomas Pownall, *A Topographical Description of the Dominions of . . . America* (Lois Mulkearn, ed., Pittsburgh, 1949), 7–8; Lawrence H. Gipson, *Lewis Evans* (Phila., 1939), 18, 21–22.
[11] *Colden Papers,* IV (N.-Y. Hist. Soc., *Colls.,* 1920), 368–69.

Even as he was preparing to observe the Transit of Mercury, Alexander was thinking ahead to 1761, when the Transit of Venus would enable astronomers to determine the Sun's parallax and thus measure the distance of the Earth from the Sun. He wrote Benjamin Franklin on 26 January 1753:

> It Would be a great honour To our young Colledges in America if they forthwith prepared themselves with a proper apparatus for that Observation and made it. Which I Doubt not they would Severally Do if they were Severally put in mind of it and of the great Importance that that Observation would be To Astronomy and that the missing that One Observation cannot be retrieved for 250 years To Come.
>
> You have on so many Occasions Demonstrated Your Love To Literature and the good of Mankind in General that I thought no person so proper as your self to think of the ways and means of perswading these Colledges to prepare themselves for taking that Observation. . . .[12]

Franklin had already given thought to the coming Transit of Mercury; but Alexander's suggestion was taken up. A letter was prepared and sent out to individuals and institutions throughout the colonies; it repeated Alexander's appeal to the "Colledges" and others.[13]

With Cadwallader Colden, who was a physician as well as his good friend, Alexander sometimes discussed the illnesses from which he or members of his family suffered. "There was never So great a mortality here Since I came to this place as now," he observed of an outbreak of measles in the winter of 1729–30:

> theres no day but what theres numbers of buryings, Some of the measles but most of the pain of the Side. There's hardly a house in town but what had severals Sick of the one or other of these Distempers Some have half a Score at a time four of our children have had the Measles two almost quite recovered two Sick as yet, our negro Jupiter had them Struck out yesterday which is comeing more deliberatly than in most other familys we have three children more & three more negroes which we Expect Every day to have them, So you may Easyly think the town is in not a little Distress.[14]

Alexander was probably immune from measles, but he had other ailments, notably gout and gravel. The real or imagined properties of tar water intrigued him. He took the stuff for his troubles, but discovered to his surprise that it was better for his diarrhea. "I find that my Looseness was gone, was not troubled with wind as before. I got a keen appetite Such as I remember not to have had these twenty years . . ." He arranged with the New York printer James Parker to publish Colden's *Abstract from Dr. Berkley's Treatise on Tar-Water* (New York, 1745).[15] In the *Philosophical Transactions* he read that Chinese musk was thought to be a specific "for all

---

[12] *Franklin Papers,* IV, 417–18.
[13] Hindle, *Pursuit of Science,* 82–84.
[14] *Colden Papers,* I, (N.-Y. Hist. Soc., *Colls.,* 1917), 276.
[15] Ibid., III (1919), 102–03, 107–08.

Spasms, Convulsions and putrid fevers. . . . It Cures the Hidrophobia, in its worst State, Maniacks, Hystericks, &c."[16] He may have regarded even this marvelous cure with mingled confidence and skepticism: "So many things have been Discovered within the past Century not Dreamt of before & contrary to the theorys before in vogue," he wrote, "that we ought to be Cautious of concluding any thing impossible tho our Theorys Say so."[17]

Like Colden, Alexander looked forward to a time when New York might have its own institutions of education and public enlightenment. When the Reverend Mr. John Millington of Stoke Newington in England left his books through the Society for the Propagation of the Gospel to create a library in New York, Alexander rejoiced that one of his friend's schemes for the city might be realized. Twenty-five years later Alexander was one of the original trustees of the New York Society Library in 1754. Its organizers, who included James De Lancey, Joseph Murray, William Livingston, William P. Smith, and William Alexander (Lord Stirling), may actually have held their first meeting in Alexander's house.[18] With William Smith, Alexander endeavored to obtain funds for a free public English and mathematical school in New York in 1732.[19] In 1754 both men were chosen trustees of King's College, although both objected to the charter because it established the institution as a sectarian corporation. Shortly before his death Alexander subscribed to John Bulkeley and John Cummings' narrative of *A Voyage to the South Seas, in the Years 1740–1. . . in H.M.S. Wager* (Philadelphia, 1757).

At the time of the Albany Congress in 1754 Alexander "had some conversation" with Franklin and Dr. Richard Peters on the subject of colonial union "and the Difficulties thereof by effecting our liberties on the one hand, or being ineffectual on the other." Franklin accordingly drew up a draft of the scheme he had in mind and sent it to Alexander, who examined it carefully:

> Some difficulties stil remain—For Example there cannot be found men tolerably skilled in Warlike Affairs to be chosen for the Grand Council, and there's danger in communicating to them the schemes to be put in execution for fear of a discovery to the Enemy. Whether this may not be in some measure reminded [sic: "remedied"?] by a Council of state of a few persons to be chosen by the Grand Council at their stated meetings which Council of state to be allways attending the Govr General, & with him to digest before hand all matters to be laid before the next Grand Council, and only the General but not the particular plans of operation.[20]

---

[16] Ibid., IV (1920), 18–19; J. Wall, "On the extraordinary Effects of Musk in Convulsive Disorders," *Phil. Trans.*, XLIII (1746), 213–25.
[17] *Colden Papers,* IV (N.-Y. Hist. Soc., *Colls.,* 1920), 30–32.
[18] Ibid., I (1917), 280–81; Austin B. Keep, *The Library in Colonial New York* (reprint, N.Y., 1970), 64–76, 130, 132.
[19] Stokes, *Iconography,* IV, 516, 529, 555, 557.
[20] Alexander to Cadwallader Colden, 9 May [June?] 1754, *Colden Papers,* IV (N.-Y. Hist. Soc., *Colls.,* 1920), 442.

Alexander died after a short illness on 2 April. An obituary summed up his achievements as a lawyer, public official, man of science, and defender of popular liberties.

> In these Parts of the World few Men surpassed him either in the natural Sagacity of his Intellectual Powers, or in his Literary Acquirements. In the Mathematical Sciences his Researches were very great. He was also eminent in his Profession of the Law; and equally distinguished by his superior Knowledge and long Experience in Public Affairs.—He had the Honour to serve the King in several important Offices, and was a wise and faithful Councellor to his Majesty for the Provinces of New-York and New-Jersey: Always true to the Interest of his Country, well knowing that the Rights of the Crown are the Bulwark of the Liberties of the People; that the Liberties of the People are the Safety and Honour of the Crown, and that a just Temperament of both in the Administration of Government, constitutes the Health of the Political Body—His Zeal for the Defence of the Public Cause against the common Enemy, led him in COUNCIL when he was not sufficiently recovered from the Gout. From thence, he brought those mortal Symptoms that closed his Days within about a Week.

Alexander's death was "a publick as well as a private Loss," was Peter Collinson's comment.[21]

Alexander was survived by his widow, who lived until 1760, and by four daughters and a son, William, who, to the amused astonishment of his and his father's friends, made claim to the earldom of Stirling.[22] By his mother's will, William received, among other things, his parents' dwelling house and portraits of both his father and mother. As for the earldom of Stirling, the House of Lords never recognized William's claim, but he assumed the title nonetheless, and as Lord Stirling achieved some military distinction in the Revolutionary War.

---

[21] *N.Y. Mercury,* 5 April 1756; *Colden Papers,* V (N.-Y. Hist. Soc., *Colls.,* 1921), 104.
[22] Ibid., 159–60; Abstracts of Wills, V (N.-Y. Hist. Soc., *Colls.,* [1896]), 386–89.

ROBERT HUNTER MORRIS (1713–1764)
AMERICAN PHILOSOPHICAL SOCIETY: 1744

ROBERT HUNTER MORRIS, Chief Justice of New Jersey, was one of those prominent office-holders of New Jersey and New York who were numbered among the first members of the American Philosophical Society. In a letter of 5 April 1744 to Cadwallader Colden Benjamin Franklin named Morris as one of those who wished to promote the fortunes of the Society. If Morris wrote to Franklin about the Society and his membership, as he may well have done, the letter does not survive; and he died before the Society was revived in 1767–68.

The second son of Lewis and Isabella (Graham) Morris, he was born on the manor of Morrisania in New York in 1713 and named for a family friend, Colonel Robert Hunter of New York.[1] Lewis Morris was chief justice of New York and later governor of New Jersey. Robert was educated by local schoolmasters and at home by his father, who sharpened his children's minds by encouraging them to debate and dispute after dinner. In 1735–36 he accompanied his father to England as secretary and companion.[2] They visited the usual places of interest to strangers—Westminster Abbey, the Tower of London, Greenwich, Covent Garden, Vauxhall. Young Morris climbed to the top of St. Paul's, "from which I beheld a beautyfull Country devided [sic] by Hedges with small fields, and throughout this Country ran the winding river Thames, on whose surface were numbers of boats of all Kinds. It is inConsievable [sic] that [what?] a great number of Houses are to be seen from the top of that Church." Several entries testify to at least a gentlemanly interest in science and technologies.

> *8 May 1735:* [At the Chelsea water works he and his father] Saw the Contrivance of raising of water by pumps which went by water. We stayed there some time to observe the nature of the works and in what manner they performed what they Did. They have from this water work Seven Different Channels thro which they Convey the water to Hide Park upon the Hill, Which is two miles Distant and 90 foot perpendicular higher than the works. There are in All 4 water wheeles. Each of these by Cranks workes Eight pumps, So that there is in All 32 pumps which are at Least 6 inches Diameter. The water is forced from these into Learg [sic], Ledden pipes and from them into woodden ones which lye along underGround to a bason to wich [sic] the water is Conveyed and from thence by woodden and lead pipes all over the town of London.[3]
>
> *11 May 1735:* My father and I had Some Argument upon the Nature of Air and whether it was Capable of Expantion or Compressure. I argued in the Negative, he in

---

[1] N. J. Hist. Soc., *Colls.*, IX (1916), 168; *DAB*.
[2] Beverly McAnear, ed., "An American in London, 1735–1736," *PMHB*, LXIV (1940), 164–217, 356–406.
[3] Ibid., 191.

the Affirmative. One instance he brought among many Others was that, putting a bladder full of air under an air pump Tyed so as not to admit any air to Come through the passage it went in at and pump Out the air that is within the Glass and without the bladder, the air within the Bladder will Burst it and Consequently must Expand or it would not have that Effect. The instance I brought to prove it Could not Expand was one I had Collected from my own Observasion [sic] and repeated Experiments, which I found Exactly to answer. The thing is: Supposing a Bottle half full of water and Consequently half full of air. In Drinking out of that bottle, you must admitt more air in than was there before; otherwise, you Cannot Draw any water out of it. Now, if Air would Expand, the quantity of air already in the bottle would fill it, was the water taken out. You Cannot take the water out without Admitting air in to fill the Vacuety [sic] made by the water taken out, and therefore the air within Cannot Expand.[4]

15 July 1735: [At Faversham] My father and I after brakefast went to see the severall mills for making of powder, the method of refigning [sic] salt peeter, and of grinding it, as also of grinding the Cole and Brimstone. When we had seen what was worth seeing about the mills, it raining, we returned to the House where we lay, and, having Dined, we sat [sic] out on our returne to Rochister [sic]. It was at this place my father proposed the making of powder by cyllinders to turn one against the other. He also proposed an alteration in one set of mills that wanted force. This alteration was resolved upon and Mr. Hall directed to make a moddle of it.[5]

2 August 1735: [At Mr. Middleton's stables] I saw a dog He Had been trying Experiments upon in order to make Him Mad by Giving Him something He took from a woman supposed to Have died by the bite of a mad dog, and whom He op'ned. I found the thing given had no Effect upon the Dog, but, when He told me he had given it inwardly, I was no more at a Loss to guess at the reason why it Had not the Effect designed; which I take to be this: all those whose misfortune it is to go mad by the bite of a Dog never take inwardly any of that poisonous matter which is supposed and in all likelyHood does communicate the infection, but the poison is supposed to be by the bite of the Dog injected into the veins and mixed and incorporated with the blood and Has those dreadful Effects which Dayly instances sufficiently make appear.[6]

The experiences of his father (whose business in London, in addition to protesting his removal from the bench by Governor Cosby, included solicitation for a good appointment), coupled with his own observations, left young Morris with no high regard for the realities of British politics. "I could not help observing in my own mind," he wrote on 6 August 1735,

that that state or Kingdom must be Verry ill-governed, whose officers are chose because they are relations to this or that great man or because they are able to give a learg sum of money for their imployments, where a meritorious man Has no Chance if he has not a good friend. I say that government is most misserable [sic]: it has it's law ill

---

[4] Ibid., 195–96.
[5] Ibid., 213.
[6] Ibid., 361–62.

Executed; its fleets and armies ill guided; its towns and distant provinces ill goverdned [sic] and their people oppress'd; its publick money missaplyed [sic]; its trade monopolised; and its Religion subverted; it tends to introduce Ignorance, Luxury, Bribery, Corruption, and slavery, and all other inconveniences that Attend a Society.[7]

However Morris may have deplored the customary way of doing business in Whitehall, he nonetheless soon learned to play by its rules. "I had before this some slight Acquaintance with one of the Clerks of the Plantation Board," he wrote his brother on 13 February 1735/6.

> I found it necessary to Cultivate a more intimate Corispondence [sic] with him than I had had. In this I succeded by making him drunk at a scrub alehouse and with Better Liquor than he was Constantly used to. This Paved the way and soon after, by the Help of a little gold, I prevail'd upon him to place an intire confidence in me and to shew me all Cosbies [Governor William Cosby of New York, whose political opponents Lewis Morris and his party were] letters to the Board of Trade, which would Cost him his office if he should be discover'd. By this means I found out what He [Cosby] owned of the matters that were Charged against him. . . .[8]

Lewis Morris was ultimately successful in his lobbying and was appointed governor of New Jersey in 1738. At the same time his son was made a member of the Council of the Province, and later that year Governor Morris commissioned him chief justice "during good behavior" rather than, as was the case with his predecessor, "at the King's pleasure."[9] Robert Hunter Morris held the post through absences, interruptions, and challenges until his death more than 25 years later.

In the judgment of an early historian of New Jersey who knew him, Morris as chief justice "stuck to punctuality in the forms of the courts, reduced the pleadings to precision and method, and possessed the great qualities of his office, knowledge and integrity, in more perfection than had often been known in the colonies: Had no other stations engrossed his attention, his character had remained without dispute, more light than shade. . . ."[10] Like his father, Morris stoutly defended the royal prerogative, and as a member of the Council of Proprietors of East Jersey after 1742 he stood firmly for the suppression of popular dissatisfaction and of rioting over titles and grants and taxation of the Proprietors' lands. He viewed the matter as much more than a passing local concern. "If this Intention should prevail, in this province," he and James Alexander, a member of the Governor's Council, wrote,

---

[7] Ibid., 366.
[8] Ibid., 400.
[9] 1 *N. J. Arch.*, IX, 323–26, 562.
[10] Samuel Smith, *History of the Colony of Nova-Caesaria, or New Jersey* (Burlington, N. J., 1765), 439.

it will soon Spread into the Rest & may be the Spark that may raise a Flame in all the Plantations, which will Burn up & Destroy all Dependance of the Plantations on the Crown of Britain, untill the Crown Expend some Millions to Reduce them.[11]

Upon his father's death in 1746 Morris inherited not only his New Jersey lands and other property but also his position as the effective leader of the government.

In the fall of 1749 Judge Morris went to England. He had several missions—to collect arrears of salary due his father, to oppose a plan to unite the governments of New Jersey and New York, and to secure a more profitable appointment for himself, possibly replacing Jonathan Belcher as governor of New Jersey.[12] He had opportunities for more private matters. He was received at Court, and the nomination for his admission to the Royal Society was put in motion. He was elected a Fellow on 12 June 1755 after he had returned to America.[13]

Morris' hopes for the governorship of New Jersey or New York were thwarted. He accepted gratefully an offer from Thomas and John Penn of appointment as lieutenant governor of Pennsylvania. He received his commission on 14 May 1754, sailed for New York, where he spent a few days at the home of James Alexander, and then, accompanied by a "splendid retinue," proceeded to Philadelphia, where he was received on 3 October with the usual addresses of welcome and by salutes from the battery and the ships in the harbor.[14]

He brought many advantages to the post. Although not a native of Pennsylvania, he was American-born and was not without acquaintances in the city. Handsome, witty, and charming, he possessed attractive personal qualities. "He had," wrote Samuel Smith, "strong natural powers, an elevated quickness of apprehension, a memory tenacious, read much, and was uncommonly furnished in conversation on most subjects." Immediately after his arrival he was elected a member of the St. Andrew's Society and their president.[15] But neither wit nor charm could solve the serious problems he faced. Hardly was Morris settled in the city than he was in conflict with the Assembly for refusing to publish his instructions—a call Morris rejected as "irregular and unprecedented."[16] Like all the Penn family's governors, Morris was bound by his instructions, and none of these was firmer than that their lands not be taxed. In this and all subsequent disputes with the Assembly,

---

[11] 1 *N. J. Arch.,* VII, 200.
[12] Ibid., 379–80, 401–02; VIII, 102–03; *PMHB,* VII (1883), 232–33.
[13] Raymond P. Stearns, "Colonial Fellows of the Royal Society of London, 1661–1788," *Osiris,* VIII (1948), 102–03.
[14] 3 *Pa. Arch.,* IX, 64–66; 1 *N. J. Arch.,* XIX, 409, 421; 2 Mass. Hist. Soc., *Proc.,* VII (1891–92), 343.
[15] Smith, *New-Jersey,* 438–39; [Robert B. Beath], *Historical Catalogue of the St. Andrew's Society,* I (1907), 289–93; 1 *Pa. Arch.,* II, 191.
[16] *Col. Recs. Pa.,* VI, 221–22.

Morris displayed the other sides of his character—"often singular, sometimes whimsical, always opinionated, and mostly inflexible."[17]

Morris and Benjamin Franklin had been "intimately acquainted" before the former came to Pennsylvania as lieutenant-governor. They met again in New York in the summer of 1754, just after Morris' arrival there. Each knew what might await the new governor at Philadelphia.

> Mr. Morris ask'd me, if I thought he must expect as uncomfortable an Administration [as that of his predecessor James Hamilton]. I said, No; you may on the contrary have a very comfortable one, if you will only take care not to enter into any Dispute with the Assembly. "My dear Friend, says he, pleasantly, how can you advise my avoiding Disputes. You know I love Disputing; it is one of my greatest Pleasures: However, to show the Regard I have for your Counsel, I promise you I will if possible avoid them."[18]

But Morris rarely had occasion or inclination to take Franklin's advice; on the contrary, he lost no opportunity to dispute with the legislature. The exchanges between the governor and the Assembly were frequent; they were sharp, often heated, and sometimes descended to a personal level: the governor accused the Assembly of acting "to take Advantage of your Country's Danger, to aggrandize and render permanent your own Power and Authority and destroy that of the Crown"; while the Assembly charged that Morris, not being a native of Pennsylvania, was too little disturbed by the incursions of the French and Indians in the western parts.[19]

"Your claim . . . of a natural exclusive Right to the Disposition of publick money because it is the people's" he told the Assembly,

> is against reason, the nature of an English Government, and the usage of this Province, and you may as well claim the exclusive Right to all the powers of Government and set up a Democracy at once, because all power is derived from the people, & this indeed may be the true Design.[20]

"The avowed Principles" of the Assembly's messages to him, Morris told Governor De Lancey, "are Republican, and they are calculated to heat & inflame the people, to infuse into the minds of the Germans and others—that their rights & Libertys are invaded, & that they are to be made slaves & vassells."[21]

In reports to Thomas Penn Morris spelled out in greater detail the situation as he saw it. Not even Braddock's defeat and the urgent claims it laid upon the Province could make the people and Assembly act reasonably:

---

[17] Smith, *New-Jersey,* 439.
[18] Franklin, *Autobiography,* 212.
[19] *Col. Recs. Pa.,* VI, 387; 8 *Pa. Arch.,* V, 4137.
[20] *Col. Recs. Pa.,* VI, 619.
[21] 1 *Pa. Arch.,* II, 396.

tho' in consequence of this defeat the Province is exposed to imminent and immediate Danger yet no Dependance is to be had on the Assembly or people here for any Assistance of consequence, as they are in such a temper that the danger of their Country has not the effect upon them that it ought to have; The principal thing they have in view being to distress you and your Governor into a complyance with them, or to oblige you to give up your Government; the former they seem to have laid aside the hopes of, and therefore bend their force to obtain the latter.[22]

Morris recognized the "extraordinary ability and most extensive genius" of Franklin, who was the leader of the Assembly and the author of most of its addresses and replies to the governor; but, as Morris told Governor William Shirley of Massachusetts, Franklin "Has very out of the way notions of the power of the People, and is as much of a favourer of the unreasonable claims of American Assembly as any man whatever."[23]

In a long letter to Thomas Penn on 22 November 1755 Morris charged that,

Since Mr. Franklin has put himself at the head of the Assembly they have gone to greater lengths than ever, and have not only discovered the Warmth of their Resentment against your Family but are using every Means in their Power, even while their Country is invaded, to wrest the Government out of your hands, and to take the whole power of it into their own. To which *end* Mr. Franklin and others have sent Arms and Ammunition into the several countys and distributed them to such people as they thought proper without my knowledge or consent. This I esteem a very extraordinary measure, as the people will be thereby taught to depend upon an Assembly for what they should only receive from the Government, and if it is not criminal I am sure it ought to be so.

"I must think the Government at home," Morris continued, enlarging on his complaint,

have too long neglected the internal Condition of these Colonies, and have suffered Assemblys to go to such unwarrantable lengths in almost every one of them, that they have for some time thought themselves without Superiors, and if they do not by some means or other give a check to that factious spirit that too generally reigns in these provinces, they will soon find it more difficult to keep their own Colonys in order than they at present imagine. I never can think it right to punish a whole Country or to lay it under peculiar disadvantages, nor indeed is it necessary; for if the supreme Government would attend to the Conduct of the Subordinate ones and take care to discountenance and punish particular men that are bold enough to transgress the Laws & to

---

[22] *Col. Recs. Pa.,* VI, 518–19.
[23] 1 *Pa. Arch.,* II, 362.

favour and encourage those of whose principles and attachments they can be well assured, it would infallibly keep the Province in good order.[24]

Though on opposite sides of the political debate, Franklin and Morris apparently maintained an acceptable level of civility in personal relations. At least that is how Franklin remembered it 30 years later. The emollient effects of the passage of time as well as the consciousness that he had won, may explain the terms of near-respect in which Franklin recalled his old adversary when he wrote his memoirs.

> Notwithstanding the continual Wrangle between the Governor and the House, in which I as a Member had so large a Share, there still subsisted a civil Intercourse between that Gentleman and myself, and we never had any personal Difference. I have sometimes since thought that his little or no Resentment against me for the Answers it was known I drew up to his Messages, might be the Effect of professional Habit, and that, being bred a Lawyer, he might consider us both as merely Advocates for contending Clients in a Suit, he for the Proprietaries and I for the Assembly. He would therefore sometimes call in a friendly way to advise with me on difficult Points, and sometimes, tho' not often, take my Advice.[25]

Having resigned his office in 1756, Morris went to England to seek a settlement of the New York–New Jersey boundary dispute. In London he also petitioned, unsuccessfully, to receive the monopoly of the manufacture of salt in the colonies. On 15 February 1759 he attended a meeting of the Royal Society (to which he had been elected in 1755) and was formally admitted a Fellow. At the end of the year he returned to America, where, after a brief dispute whether his commission as chief justice of New Jersey was still in effect (his resignation not having been formally accepted), he resumed his post.[26] Still eager for advancement, he hoped to be appointed lieutenant governor and chief justice of New York in succession to James De Lancey, who died in the summer of 1760; but he was passed over.

Morris died suddenly of an "Apoplectick fit"—perhaps heart attack or stroke—at a dance at his house on Shrewsbury River in New Jersey on 27 January 1764. His body was taken to Morrisania, and laid in the family vault there.[27] He had never married, but left four natural children, of whom one, Robert, became chief justice of New Jersey under the state constitution of 1777 and was appointed a federal district judge by President Washington in 1789.

---

[24] *Col. Recs. Pa.,* VI, 739, 741.
[25] Franklin, *Autobiography,* 239.
[26] 1 *N.J. Arch.,* XX, 417–24.
[27] Ibid., 305, 328; *Pa. Gaz.,* 2 Feb. 1764. His house was offered for sale in 1771. 1 *N.J. Arch.,* XXVII, 175.

ARCHIBALD HOME (1705?–1744)

AMERICAN PHILOSOPHICAL SOCIETY: 1744

ARCHIBALD HOME, a member of the Governor's Council of New Jersey and a man of literary tastes and accomplishments, was one of the early non-resident members of the Society mentioned by Franklin in his letter to Cadwallader Colden of 5 April 1744. He had little time to enjoy the connection, however, for he died in the very week when Franklin wrote.

Born in Scotland, the third son of Sir John Home, Bt., of Blackadder, County Berwick, he came to New York before 1733, attracted the attention of the former chief justice Lewis Morris, and moved quickly and easily into good society. The first reference to him in official records is his bill, submitted to the New Jersey Council in 1736, for carrying Governor Cosby's commission seal from New York to Perth Amboy—an inconvenience necessitated by Cosby's holding the governorships of both New York and New Jersey.[1] In 1738 or 1739 Home was named Deputy Secretary of New Jersey (the Secretary, who lived in England, farmed the post), and in addition he acted as Clerk of the Council.[2] On recommendation of Lewis Morris, now governor of New Jersey, he was named to the Council in 1741, though "not desiring or expecting it," and took his seat on 31 October.[3] He lived at Trenton, and occasionally visited Philadelphia, where he purchased stationery and parchments at Franklin's shop and once paid 2s. to have a copy of Burnet's *Pastoral Care* bound.[4] He made at least one trip to the South, possibly as far as Charleston, where his brother James lived.

Home was a friendly, convivial man, with a sense of humor. Dr. Alexander Hamilton, who had entertained him in Annapolis, encountered him again at one of the nightly dinners of the Hungarian Club—mostly Scots—at Todd's Tavern in New York, where the company remained late, drinking copiously.[5] He may have been a Freemason. With a good classical education and some literary talent Home was the principal figure in a circle of literary-minded friends in Trenton, women as well as men, including David Martin and Robert Hunter Morris, who wrote verses, songs, epigrams, satires, and translations, in both English and the Scottish dialect. He wrote the prologue spoken by the actors at the opening of the theater in New

---

[1] 1 *N.J. Arch.*, XIV, 534.
[2] N.J. Hist. Soc., *Colls.*, IV (1852), 132.
[3] Ibid., 122, 132; 1 *N.J. Arch.*, XV, 220–21.
[4] Franklin, Ledger D, p. 95 (APS).
[5] Carl Bridenbaugh, ed., *Gentleman's Progress: The Itinerarium of Dr. Alexander Hamilton, 1744* (Chapel Hill, 1948), 42.

York in 1738.[6] At least two of his compositions were published. After Home's death friends collected, transcribed, and copied his writings.[7]

Home's imitation of Horace's First Satire typically voiced one of the eighteenth century's themes:

> Life's Golden Mean who steadily pursues
> Will Fortune's Gift by no Extreme abuse:
> Ten, or Ten Thousand Acres let her give
> In due Proportion still that Man will live;
> And whether Roots or Ragouts are his Diet,
> Alike will dine, alike will sleep in Quiet.
>
> * * *
>
> In Time be wise, & give your Labour o'er
> Enough acquir'd, why should you toil for more?

And he mourned a fellow-Scot in lowland Scots:

> Jersey! lament in briny tears,
> Your Dawty's gane to his Forebears:
> Wae worth him! Death has clos'd the Sheers,
>   And clip'd his Thread:
> Just in the Prime of a' his Years
>   George Fraser's dead.
>
> * * *
>
> Weel, since from weeping us he's riv'n
> Just at the Age of Forty Seven,
> May to his Hands the Staff be given
>   Which he on Earth
> Refus'd, and Constable in Heav'n
>   Be George's Berth!

Home died in the early spring or summer of 1744, and was buried in a vault in the aisle of the Presbyterian Church of Trenton.[8] By his will, dated 27 February

---

[6] George C. D. Odell, *Annals of the New York Stage* (N.Y., 1927), I, 21.

[7] N. J. Hist. Soc., *Colls.*, IX (1916), 131–33. One of these copies came to light in 1890; acquired by a New Jersey historian and collector, it was destroyed by fire in 1902, but not before several poems had been transcribed. They were printed in the *New Jersey Archives* in 1916. In 1987 another copy was found in Edinburgh University Library by Professor David S. Shields, of The Citadel, Charleston, S.C., who has generously provided a transcript of the entire volume as well as some biographical data.

[8] There is some uncertainty about the date of Home's death. John Hall, *History of the Presbyterian Church in Trenton, N.J.* (N.Y., 1859), 150–52, cites a sermon preached at the "burying of Mr. Home" on 1 April 1744. The original manuscript is preserved at the church; the correct reading is clearly 6 April. But how are we to explain Dr. Hamilton's recording his meeting Home in New York under the date of 15 June?

1743/4, of which Robert Hunter Morris, Dr. Thomas Cadwalader, and his brother James were executors, he left everything to brother James, who succeeded him briefly as Deputy Secretary of New Jersey.[9] Several friends wrote memorial elegies; one, by a lady of whose verse Home had been a friendly critic, paid tribute to

> His happy Thought, with Elegance exprest,
> Wit's winning Charms to just Advantage drest.
>
>   Yet not for Gifts like these esteem'd alone,
> In social Life the bright Companion shone,
> The candid Friend, ingenious, firm, and kind,
> Who polish'd Sense with Faultless Manners join'd,
> And ev'ry manly Virtue of the Mind.[10]

JOHN COXE (1708?–1753)
AMERICAN PHILOSOPHICAL SOCIETY: 1744

JOHN COXE, lawyer and landowner of Trenton, New Jersey, was one of the group of Jerseymen and New Yorkers named by Franklin in a letter to Cadwallader Colden on 5 April 1744 as members of the Society. From time to time business brought Coxe to Philadelphia, where he purchased books and stationery at Franklin's shop and placed advertisements in the *Pennsylvania Gazette;* but little is known of the embryonic Society at this time, and nothing of Coxe's connection with it.

His grandfather was Dr. Daniel Coxe, F.R.S. and sometime student of Jesus College, Cambridge, who established the family and its fortune in America. His father was Colonel Daniel Coxe, a member of the Governor's Council, the first Grand Master of Freemasons in North America, and author of *A Description of the English Province of Carolana* (1722) and of a plan of confederation that anticipated the Albany Plan of Union of 1754.[1] John's mother was Sarah Eckley, daughter of the late justice of the Supreme Court of Pennsylvania. Margaret Preston is the source

---

[9] Hunterdon Co. Wills, 170 J (N.J. State Library); Edgar Jacob Fisher, *New Jersey as a Royal Province, 1738 to 1776* (N.Y., 1911), 45.
[10] A Lady, "To the Memory of Archibald Home, Esq.; late Secretary of the Jerseys, &c.," *American Mag.* (July 1744), 520–21; *Pa. Gaz.,* 16 Aug. 1744.

[1] N.J. Hist. Soc. *Colls.,* IX (1916), 86; M. Atherton Leach, comp., *Some of the Ancestors and Descendants of Colonel Daniel Coxe, of New Jersey* [Phila., 1913]; Jacob E. Cooke, *Tench Coxe and the Early Republic* (Chapel Hill, [1978]), 6–9.

of a romantic tale, which she thought scandalous, of Coxe's parents' elopement and marriage.

> The news of Sarah Eckley's marriage is both sorrowful and surprising, with one Colonel Coxe, a fine flaunting gentleman, said to be worth a great deal of money,—a great inducement, it is said, on her side. Her sister Trent was supposed to have promoted the match. Her other friends were ignorant of the match. It took place in the absence of her uncle and aunt Hill, between two and three in the morning, on the Jersey side, under a tree by fire light. They have since proselyted her, and decked her in finery.

Although the ceremony was unconventional, to say the least, it was performed according to rites of the Church of England, by the governor's chaplain, by authority of a license dated 8 May 1707.[2] John was the first of the couple's four children.

He received some of his schooling in England, but not, like his grandfather, at one of the universities; and he was admitted to the New Jersey bar in 1735 and to that of Pennsylvania in 1749. In addition to a respectable practice in Trenton and Burlington, he had, after his father's death in 1739, responsibilities for extensive lands, mills, and forges in New Jersey, Long Island, and Massachusetts.[3] He was one of the proprietors of West Jersey. Coxe was appointed to the Governor's Council in 1745 and took his seat the next year. During the years of his service serious riots over land titles and the rights of squatters occurred. Jails were broken into and prisoners released. Coxe was an object of the mob's anger; both he and his property were threatened. With Governor Belcher he was soon at odds. He called the man publicly a "Scoundrel" and "an Old woman," boldly asserted that he could not obtain "common Justice at his Hands" for his clients, and promised to vote against granting the governor's salary. For his part Belcher's patience with Coxe's "insufferable insolence" soon ran out, and he suspended him from the Council on 26 July 1750. Coxe continued his attacks, however; he was reported in 1751 to be spreading a report that Belcher had been recalled.[4]

Coxe died in the spring of 1753, and was buried in St. Michael's Church, Trenton, which stood on land he had given it in 1748.[5] He had not married, and his estate was divided among his brothers, nieces, and nephews, with £50 bequeathed to any public charity his executors might designate. An inventory of personal property showed he owned 302 volumes of law books (valued at £225 16s. 9d.) and an additional 97 volumes, which probably included the prayer book and

---

[2] Watson, *Annals,* I, 50; Alexander DuBin, ed., *Old Philadelphia Families* (Phila., 1939), "Coxe," 13.
[3] 1 *N.J. Arch.,* VI, 139; XI, 587; XXX, 118–20.
[4] Ibid., VI, 139, 233; VII, 207–26, 450, 540–48, 594; John E. Pomfret, *Colonial New Jersey: A History* (N.Y., 1973) 156–63.
[5] Trenton Hist. Soc., *A History of Trenton, 1679–1929* (2v., Princeton, N.J., 1929), I, 402, 406.

a "Treatise on Whist," which he had purchased from Franklin some years before.[6] Coxe also owned, among other things, 12 prints of "Philosopher's heads," six other prints including Hogarth's *Harlot's Progress,* a clock and case, watch, and four slaves, one an 80–year-old man whom the appraisers valued at nothing.[7]

DAVID MARTIN (1696–1751)
AMERICAN PHILOSOPHICAL SOCIETY: 1744

DAVID MARTIN, High Sheriff of Hunterdon County, New Jersey, was one of the non-resident members of the Society named in Franklin's letter to Cadwallader Colden of 5 April 1744. The nature of Martin's varied achievements and activities, so typical of his place and age, would have recommended him to any society of American philosophers.

He was born at Piscataway, Middlesex County, New Jersey, 8 July 1696, the fourth child of Joseph and Sarah (Trotter) Martin.[1] Evidently he had a fair education, which he improved by reading, for at the end of his life he was said to be "a great Master of the Greek and Roman Authors, and had a most elegant Classical Taste."[2] At the age of 18, on 9 March 1714, he was married in Piscataway Baptist Church to Elizabeth Doty, daughter of Samuel and Jane (Harman) Doty of Piscataway; they had three daughters: Sarah, born 9 December 1714; Elizabeth, born 4 August 1718; and Joan, born 21 January 1719/20. The year after his marriage Martin—or another of his name—was a member of the Fourth Company of Colonel Thomas Farmar's New Jersey Regiment.[3]

Nothing else is known of him until 24 September 1736, when he was appointed sheriff of Hunterdon County.[4] He discharged his duties so humanely that he was remembered gratefully by "distress'd Families" he saved "from Ruin," and so efficiently that he was reappointed to his post by successive governors. Being sheriff, however, was not enough to keep a man busy or make him prosperous, and Martin sought other incomes. In 1739 he received a patent to operate a ferry "in

---

[6] Franklin, Ledger D, 101, 127 (APS).
[7] 1 *N.J. Arch.,* XXXII, 76; Coxe, Will, 8 April 1753, Hunterdon Co. Wills, 330J (N.J. State Lib.).

[1] Mrs. Gerald May (N.J. Hist. Soc.) to author, 15 Dec. 1962.
[2] *Pa. Gaz.,* 14 Jan. 1752.
[3] N. J. Hist. Soc., *Proc.,* n.s., IV, 38; XIII, 205; Orra E. Monnette, *Press Notices concerning First Settlers of Ye Plantations of Piscataway and Woodbridge* (4 v., Los Angeles, 1930), 239, 549.
[4] *N. J. Arch.,* XIV, 535.

the Forks of Delawar," near modern Easton; in 1745 he was made marshal of Trenton under its first charter of incorporation;[5] and apparently about this time, as Franklin reported, he came into "this Country"—Pennsylvania—"on a Scheme for making Potash in the Russian manner"—a manufacture which engaged a succession of entrepreneurs in eighteenth-century America.[6] He was elected to the Philadelphia St. Andrew's Society in 1750, helped draft their first rules and bylaws, and owned a St. Andrew's cross when he died. In 1750, when he was planning to retire to his Hunterdon County farm named "Sharon," the trustees of the Academy of Philadelphia invited him to become their rector.

To the twentieth century there is something incongruous and almost humorous in a sheriff's becoming the head of an academy; but the eighteenth century saw nothing inconsistent or improper in a scholar's being a public servant, even a sheriff or jail-keeper. Confident that Dr. Samuel Johnson of Connecticut would accept their invitation to head the institution, the trustees in the early spring of 1750 had ordered that the Academy should "be opened as soon as possible by accepting the most suitable Person that can be procured for a Rector"; and forthwith offered the post to Martin, who had been favorably recommended. He accepted, took lodging at Mrs. Gibbs', and fell to work that summer at a salary of £200 per annum.[7] Richard Peters judged him "a perfect good scholar, and a man of good temper."[8]

As rector of the Academy, Martin was the senior professor, teaching Latin and Greek, but without responsibility for policy and administration. His assistant as tutor in Latin and Greek was Charles Thomson. By all accounts Martin was successful. "He did not follow any one beaten Method of Teaching, but was at Pains to consult the particular Capacities of his Scholars, and from thence form'd his different Plans for instructing them."[9] His acquaintance with Benjamin Franklin became closer, and the two men spent many evenings together over the chess board. Franklin, who had learned the game some 15 years before as an adjunct to his study of Italian, found Martin so formidable an opponent that, to improve his game, he ordered from London Philip Stamma's manual, *The Noble Game of Chess* (London, 1745). The men's pleasant association did not last long. Martin contracted "a kind of Quinsey"—possiby diphtheria—and died suddenly on 11 December 1751. Franklin cancelled the order for Stamma's book soon afterwards.[10]

---

[5] *PMHB,* XXI (1897), 104–5; XXXVIII (1914), 110–12; Trenton Historical Society, *A History of Trenton, 1679–1929* (2 v., Princeton, 1929), I, 84.
[6] *Franklin Papers,* IV, 214.
[7] Montgomery, *University of Pennsylvania,* 136; Academy of Philadelphia, Minutes, 29 March, 17 Dec. 1750; 9, 16 April, 14 May 1751.
[8] Hubertis M. Cummings, *Richard Peters* (Phila., 1944), 146.
[9] *Pa. Gaz.,* 14 Jan. 1752.
[10] *Franklin Papers,* IV, 196, 214, 323.

Richard Peters' funeral sermon gave Martin "the just and honourable Character he deserved"; his body was laid in Christ Church burying ground, but no stone survives to mark his grave. Martin left his books to the Academy; the remainder of his small personal estate included a pair of doctor's scales, some surgical instruments, "a Microscope, Snuff box, twizers, Spectaters . . . & a Nutmeg Grater," and also a sword with a silver hilt. His estate in New Jersey, after the administrator had sold the real property, amounted in 1758 to £1495 4s 8d.[11]

RICHARD NICHOLLS (?–1775)
AMERICAN PHILOSOPHICAL SOCIETY: 1744

RICHARD NICHOLLS, lawyer of New York and postmaster of that city, may have been one of the earliest non-resident members of the American Philosophical Society. At least, he gave Franklin the names of several gentlemen "that incline to encourage the Thing,"[1] and it is not unreasonable to infer that a man who made such recommendations was himself a member. Certainly Nicholls would have been eligible by his position in New York life, his educational attainments, and his associations with Cadwallader Colden, James Alexander, Joseph Murray, and others who were members of the Society.

He was the son of William and Jane Nicholls of Garth in the parish of Guildsfield, Montgomeryshire, North Wales; and he was settled in New York before 1720. He read law with William Sharpas, who became town clerk; and on 7 October 1720 he was married in Trinity Church to Margaret Tudor, daughter of John Tudor, an attorney, who had been a lieutenant in one of the Independent Companies of Fusileers stationed in New York.[2] In 1731 Nicholls offered his fellow citizens the services of a loan and investment broker:

---

[11] Ibid., 222; *N. J. Arch.*, XXXII, 216. The inventory of his estate is in N.J. State Archives (Hunterdon Co. Wills, 318 J).

[1] *Franklin Papers*, II, 407.
[2] Robert Lurting, Certificate, 25 Sept. 1731, with supporting deposition of Thomas Tannant, 13 Aug. 1731; Rev. William Vesey, Certificate, 25 Sept. 1731, Richard Harison Papers (N.-Y. Hist. Soc.). In 1720–21 Nicholls' name appears as witness on a number of apprentices' indentures. N.-Y. Hist. Soc., *Colls.* (1909), 127, 128, 129, 145.

> Whereas many Persons in this Province have often Occasion to borrow Money at Interest, and others have Sums of Money lying by them which they want to put out, Some want to Purchase Houses, Lands and other Things, and others frequently want to sell; but for want of knowing where to apply on these Occasions are often disappointed in their Designs, to their very great Prejudice. *Wherefore* in Order that all Persons may know where to apply, Publick Notice is hereby given, That Richard Nicholls, Attorney at Law, near the Fort, in New-York, (at the Request of several Persons of Note) Negotiates all such Affairs for such Persons as desire the same, for a reasonable Reward, and with the greatest Secrecy and Integrity.
>
> N.B. He Advertises if desired (not otherwise) without Charge, unless Successful.
> A person has Four Hundred Pounds to put at Interest.
> Another has Fifty Pounds to put out on good Personal Security.[3]

Like many other ambitious and enterprising persons in eighteenth-century America, Nicholls increased his income and his influence by appointments to a variety of offices. By 1725 he was postmaster of New York; in 1731 he was also serving as coroner; in 1739 he was deputy receiver of quit-rents; in 1751 as land waiter ("a triffling Appointment" that he resigned in 1764) he petitioned that a schedule of fees be established.[4] No less an indication of his reputation and influence was his appointment in 1732 to the vestry of Trinity Church, on which he served until 1766, for some of the time as clerk.[5] On 18 February 1730/1 Nicholls was admitted a freeman of the city.[6]

Nicholls was a close personal friend of Colden and his family. On one occasion Mrs. Nicholls cared for one of Colden's daughter during an attack of measles; on another, when young John Colden had just been named town clerk of Albany, the elder Colden sought Nicholls' advice on the laws and practices that governed the office. "I cannot express the cordial Friendship that all of that Family have shown on many occasions," Colden wrote feelingly of the Nichollses at his daughter's recovery.[7] Though Nicholls was acquainted with all the members of Colden's philosophical circle, only a few scraps survive to suggest the nature and extent of his own intellectual interests. There is, for example, reference to a "Globe at Newburgh" in which James Alexander had some interest.[8] From Franklin he borrowed a copy of

---

[3] I. N. Phelps Stokes, *Iconography of Manhattan Island,* (6v., N.Y., 1915–28), IV, 524, quoting *N.Y. Gaz.,* 23 Aug. 1731.

[4] Ibid., 559, 719; Martha J. Lamb, *History of the City of New York* (N.Y., 1896), I, 522, 546n; *Letter Book of John Watts* (N.-Y. Hist. Soc., *Colls.,* 1928), 310.

[5] Herbert and Carol Schneider, eds., *Samuel Johnson, President of King's College: His Career and Writings* (4 v., N.Y., 1929), I, 172; IV, 180, 324, 331.

[6] N.-Y. Hist. Soc., *Colls.* (1885), 116.

[7] *Colden Papers,* III, 213; IX, 4–5, 14–15. Colden's daughter, Mrs. Elizabeth De Lancey, asked Nicholls to take her son John (his grandfather Colden's favorite) into his office. Ibid., 156.

[8] *Colden Papers,* III, 195.

Bishop Berkeley's *Siris* for the Reverend Dr. Samuel Johnson of Stratford, Connecticut.[9] His own library, of respectable size, contained no works of science, but many titles in history, literature, and old divinity, including *Universal History* in 43 volumes, *Ancient History* in 20 volumes, Humphrey Prideaux' *Connection of the Old and New Testament* in three volumes, *The Devout Christian's Exemplar,* Dean Sherlock's *Sermons,* Dean Stanhope's *Paraphrase and Comment upon the Epistles and Gospels* and his "St. Austin" (St. Augustine's (*Pious Breathings* ?), Young's *Night Thoughts,* Sir William Dawes' *Duties of the Closet,* Thomas Comber's *Companion to the Altar,* and a handful of magazines.[10] Not least of Nicholls' services to science, however, was as postmaster. Colden, Alexander, even Franklin, sent and received safely through his hands their letters, books, and philosophical communications.

Despite his years, Nicholls continued to hold his offices and to seek others. He was register of the Admiralty, submitting at last to the appointment of a deputy only in 1774, when he was "too feeble to act." In 1769 he sought appointment as recorder.[11]

Mrs. Nicholls died in 1772 at the age of 73. Nicholls followed her on 19 August 1775, and was buried in his vault in Trinity Church.[12] He was survived by four daughters—a son had died before; they were Mary, then wife of the Reverend Dr. Samuel Auchmuty of New York, and mother-in-law of Captain John Montresor, of the British Army, a member of the American Philosophical Society; Jane, wife of George Harrison; Elizabeth, who was married to Alexander Colden; and Susannah, whose second husband was the prominent physician Peter Middleton, professor in the Medical College of New York. The inventory of Nicholls' estate mentioned, in addition to real estate in New York, three houses in London (possibly the same houses in Fenchurch Street and Crooked Lane inherited from his father). Personal property included a quantity of plate, accounts receivable, his books, a plaid night gown, "1 Doz Hunchaback [i.e., huckaback] Towels," and a mosquito net. By his will he provided care for his aged and feeble Negro servants, bequeathed £25 to the Corporation for the Relief of Widows and Orphans of Clergymen of the Church of England, and left his gold watch to Dr. Middleton "in Testimony of the affectionate regard I entertain for him & the Sence I have of his Tenderness to my Grand Children."[13]

---

[9] Ibid., 206.
[10] Nicholls, Inventory, n.d.; Peter Middleton, Account with Estate of Richard Nicholls, 1775 (copy), Richard Harison Papers (N.-Y. Hist. Soc.).
[11] William Smith, *Historical Memoirs, 1763–1776,* (W. H. W. Sabine, ed., N.Y., 1958), 57, 193.
[12] N.Y. *Weekly Post-Boy,* 29 July 1772; Kenneth Scott, comp., *Rivington's New York Newspaper: Excerpts from a Loyalist Press, 1773–1783* (N.-Y. Hist. Soc., *Colls.,* LXXXIV), 120–21.
[13] Nicholls, Will, 6 Sept. 1772; Nicholls, Inventory, n.d., Richard Harison Papers (N.-Y. Hist. Soc.).

CADWALLADER COLDEN

Attributed to Matthew Pratt. *New York State Office of Parks, Recreation and Historic Preservation, Schuyler Mansion State Historic Site.*

CADWALLADER COLDEN (1688–1776)
AMERICAN PHILOSOPHICAL SOCIETY: 1744

CADWALLADER COLDEN, physician, botanist, Surveyor-General of New York, and member of the Council of that province, was one of the earliest and most enthusiastic members of the American Philosophical Society. He was proposed for election, probably by John Bartram, with whom he had corresponded on botanical matters for several years, and was elected a member at some time before June 1744. Thereafter he wrote frequently to Bartram, Benjamin Franklin, John Mitchell, and European scientists about the Society. But, as the Society soon collapsed, he never attended a meeting. Some thirty years after his election, however, "remarks" of his "on some obvious Phenomena of Light" were presented to the philosophers, but he was then too old and too deeply involved in public affairs to resume seriously the philosophical studies that had engrossed and gratified his middle years. His name was still on the roll of members of the Society in 1769 when it united with the American Society.

The first of 12 children of the Reverend Mr. Alexander Colden, a minister of the Church of Scotland, and of Janet (Hughes) Colden, he was born in Ireland on 7 February 1688 (n.s.), possibly at Enniscorthy, County Wexford, where Alexander Colden was minister until 1693, when he was called to the church at Duns in Berwickshire.[1] The Reverend Mr. Colden was the minister at Oxnam, near Jedburgh, at the time young Colden entered the University of Edinburgh; Cadwallader's expenses there were paid by the Duke of Roxburgh, who was a family friend.

At the university an interest in botany was awakened in Colden. He gave up plans for the ministry, decided to study medicine, and, after graduating in 1705, went to London, where he attended lectures in anatomy, chemistry, and other medical subjects. Without capital to begin practice successfully in England or Scotland, he accepted the invitation of his aunt Elizabeth Hill, a well-to-do childless widow, to come to Philadelphia. In that town in 1710 he opened a medical practice, but at the same time engaged in trade to increase his income. He visited Charleston, Jamaica, and Antigua for commercial purposes; he traded in flour, wine, and slaves; but found that "Rum is the only thing that brings ready Money."[2] He made

---

[1] Hew Scott, *Fasti Ecclesiae Scoticanae* (new ed., Edinburgh, 1915–28), II, 136; *Colden Letters,* I, vii–viii; VIII, 96, 101–07; Alice M. Keys, *Cadwallader Colden: A Representative Eighteenth Century Official* (N.Y., 1906); Alexander Colden to Colden, 15 Sept. 1728, Gratz Coll. (HSP); Saul Jarcho, "Biographical and Bibliographical Notes on Cadwallader Colden," *Bull. Hist. Med.,* XXXII (1958), 322–34; Hindle, *Pursuit of Science,* 39–48; *DAB; DSB.*
[2] *Colden Letters,* I, 3–5, 12.

of letters to his son Colden reviewed Smith's work, correcting and adding to the narrative as it recalled persons and events to his mind.[31] He refuted Smith's hostile account of the Dutch regime, he defended Colonel Andros, William Burnet, and other governors, and he presented his own conservative political philosophy in opposition to Smith's. "Perhaps you'l think that I write with resentment to Mr Smith the Historian," he told his son by way of explanation and apology.

> He is so assuming in his manner especially in giving characters of the most distinguished persons often unfair allwise partial whether his characters be favourable or otherwise biassed by his connections either as to family or religious sect, that some resentment is unavoidable. It is not fit that Mr Smith's history should pass for a chronicle of the Province of New York.[32]

In 1761 Colden was appointed lieutenant governor of the Province, succeeding James De Lancey, who had died the preceding year. Although he continued to write to Dr. Robert Whytt in Edinburgh about medical matters, his scientific correspondence now necessarily dropped off. His public business was about defense, Indian affairs, land, trade, and imperial policies, and his correspondents were General Amherst, governors of other provinces, the Board of Trade, and the Secretary of State. As he now had to be more constantly at New York, residence at Coldengham was no longer convenient, and in that year Colden moved to a farm at Flushing on Long Island that he named "Spring Hill."[33] In the ensuing 15 years Colden served as acting governor on four occasions. His tenure was troubled, and he was increasingly unpopular. He had little sympathy with the local opposition to British policies and laws. Frustrated and angered by the popular resistance, he advocated creation of a new court in which there would be no jury. "I told the old Gentleman," John Watts wrote to a friend, "a Jury was the Bulwark of English Freedom, he coldly answerd & with seeming indifference 'that there were no Jurys in Scotland & he did not see but Justice was as well Administer'd as in England.'"[34] Small wonder that when Colden put himself in the center of the controversy over the Stamp Act in 1765, he and the devil were publicly hanged in effigy together.

Robert Lettice Hooper, Jr., described Colden's appearance in these latter years of his life in 1774:

---

[31] N.-Y. Hist. Soc., *Colls.* (1868), 181–235.
[32] Ibid., 214.
[33] A. J. Wall, "Cadwallader Colden and his Homestead at Spring Hill, Flushing, Long Island," N. Y. Hist. Soc., *Quarterly Bulletin,* VIII (1924–25), 11–20.
[34] John Watts, *Letter Book* (N.-Y. Hist. Soc., *Colls.,* 1928), 313.

> The Governor is the best real Picture of an Old Man that I ever saw. He is 87 years old, has his hearing & sences [sic] as well as ever he had without marks of Age, except in his Eyes which are grown dim & his Head covered with strong white hair. His mind is excellent and he is no churl, indeed he pushed me so hard that I was obliged to shear off.[35]

The next year Colden's world collapsed. The government, he wrote on 3 May 1775, was "entirely prostrated"; royal authority was effectively ended. Soon afterwards Colden retired to his Flushing farm; and there on 20 September 1776 he died and was buried. He was 88 years old, had outlived almost all his generation, and was one of the last survivors of that earlier world in which he had played so large a part. Before his death Colden had given Coldengham to his son Cadwallader and Spring Hill to his youngest son David. To David also he bequeathed all his manuscripts and printed books.

The younger William Smith characterized Colden as only a political enemy could: duplicitous, proud, crafty, obstinate, vain, petulant, ambitious, vindictive, avaricious, "rather a Man of Genius than Erudition," who was "anxious for Preheminence [sic] on all Topics of Conversation."[36] The Reverend Dr. Ezra Stiles of Rhode Island angrily denounced him as "an avowed Enemy to American liberty" and "a haughty Tyrant," but grudgingly remembered that he had been a philosopher: "He affected to be a Friend to Literature, & wrote & I think printed a Piece to overthrow the Newtonian Philosophy—I saw & perused it. He had a superlative Contempt for American Learning."[37] An anonymous writer some years later offered a more balanced judgment.

> When it is considered how large a portion of his life was spent in the labours or the routine of public office, and that, however great might have been his original stock of learning, he had, in this country, no reading public to excite him by their applauses, and few literary friends to assist or to stimulate his inquiries, his zeal and success in his scientific pursuits will appear deserving of the highest admiration.[38]

---

[35] Robert Lettice Hooper to Reuben Haines, 10 Aug. 1774, Wyck Papers, Corres. (APS).
[36] William Smith, Jr., *Historical Memoirs, 1776–1778* (W. H. W. Sabine, ed., N.Y., 1956–), 29–33.
[37] Ezra Stiles, *Literary Diary* (Franklin B. Dexter, ed., N.Y., 1901), II, 77–78.
[38] V., "Biographical Memoir of Cadwallader Colden, M.D. F.R.S. [sic]," *Analectic Mag.,* IV (1814), 307–12.

Lancey's position was strengthened still more when Governor George Clinton made him his principal adviser and in 1744 gave him a new commission as chief justice "during good behavior" rather than "at pleasure." Soon afterwards, De Lancey broke with Clinton. The Governor tried to remove him as chief justice and to confer the lieutenant governorship on one of his own supporters. Instead, thanks to his "interest" at Whitehall, De Lancey received the appointment as lieutenant governor on 24 October 1747. Nonetheless, Clinton continued to seek De Lancey's removal from that office, and took his revenge by withholding the commission for seven years until 1753, when he left the governorship. Clinton was succeeded by Sir Danvers Osborn, who, only a few days after taking office, hanged himself in a fit of depression. As lieutenant governor De Lancey now became head of the government. It is a measure of the intensity of partisan feeling that the rumor was started that De Lancey's supporters had committed murder to bring about the ascendancy of their leader.[5]

As governor De Lancey had to move delicately both to keep his two offices and to placate the ministry in London, which instructed him to obtain five-year grants from the Assembly (which would make only annual grants), while at the same time defending the authority of the Assembly, which he had been instrumental in winning and establishing. De Lancey communicated his instructions to the Assembly; the Assembly enacted its annual bill, as was its custom; and De Lancey refused to sign it. In 1756 the Ministry gave up. There was no problem, his old enemy William Livingston believed, that De Lancey could not solve "with a smile, or a joke, or a promise, or a bottle."[6]

As governor De Lancey presided over the Albany Congress in 1754, and the next year he attended a conference of governors that General Braddock called at his headquarters in Alexandria, Virginia.

Meanwhile, a proposal to establish a college in New York raised partisan passions to a new high. The issue was whether the institution should be Anglican. De Lancey's position was ambivalent: he was the royal governor, whose patrons in England were of the Anglican hierarchy; but his party was in power in the Assembly. Once again De Lancey and Livingston and their Anglican and Presbyterian followers were arrayed against one another.[7] Trustees were named in 1751; a charter was finally granted by the Assembly in 1754 and signed by the Governor; but it was not delivered until 1755. De Lancey did not attend trustees' meetings, saying wryly that he had contributed enough to the institution in the loss of reputation and popularity. Regarded as a creation of De Lancey and the Episcopalians, the course of King's College was for many years troubled and insecure.

[5] Ibid., 153.
[6] Quoted by Leopold S. Launitz-Schürer, Jr., "Whig-Loyalists: The De Lanceys of New York," N. Y. Hist. Soc., *Quar.,* LVI (1972), 181.
[7] William Livingston and others, *The Independent Reflector* (Milton M. Klein, ed., Cambridge, Mass., 1963), 37–38, 40–41, 44.

After the short administration of Sir Charles Hardy in 1755–57, De Lancey as lieutenant-governor moved once more to the head of affairs. He was in these years increasingly concerned with matters of military defense as Britain pressed its war with France in Canada. But his influence had begun to decline, as suggested by the story William Smith, Jr., told of a party the night before De Lancey died.

> The conversation . . . certainly put the deceased to his utmost exertions; for he was treated with the familiarity of an equal in the presence of his inferiors, who had long worshipped him as a genius and character of the first magnitude. Mr. Boone, Mr. Morris, and Brigadier Prevost played off their wit in rallying some of his arts for gaining popularity; and though not a word was uttered in a manner interdicted by good breeding, yet there was gall under the disguise of politeness and respect, which made his defence the more arduous, especially as there were three against one, with the smiles of the rest. His daily coffee-house haunts, his controversy with Clinton, his persuading Sir Charles Hardy to resign on contract for half of the salary and emoluments, the subservience of his tools, his double claim to be chancellor and chief justice, his exaction of the high fees for land grants taken by Clinton, and his receipt of £400 yearly for the garrison, after the independent companies were removed, and a tale respecting that money, all touched with delicacy and justified with anxiety, without the appearance of contention, formed the topics of a conversation concluded with evening merriment on both sides; but when they parted, Mr. De Lancey instantly grew serious, and was vexed and silent on the whole passage over the Bay.[8]

De Lancey died suddenly, probably of a heart attack, at his house in New York on 30 July 1760, the morning after the evening Smith described. A generous tribute to his achievements was printed in the New York newspapers and reprinted in other papers from Boston to Charleston. With it was printed a full account of the funeral pomp:

> . . . at three Quarters past Six, P.M. His Majesty's Ship the Winchester, of 50 Guns, Captain Hale, now in the North River, fired a Gun for the Funeral to move, which was done from his Honour's Seat, in the Bowry [sic]. At the same Instant, Minute Guns began firing from Copsey Battery, and continued to 57, the Number of his Age. The Battery was followed by the Winchester, and she by the General Wall Packet, each firing the same Number with the Battery. The Order of the Procession, from his Honour's Seat to Trinity Church, was as follows, viz.
> 1. The Clerks of Trinity-Church, and St. George's Chapel, in an open Chaise.
> 2. The Rector of Trinity-Church, in a Chaise.
> 3. The Clergy of the several Protestant Denominations in this City, two by two, in Chaises.
> 4. An open Hearse bearing the Body in a Coffin, covered with black Velvet, richly adorned with gilt Escutcheons and Furniture. The Hearse was drawn by a beautiful Pair of white Horses, belonging to his Honour, in Mourning, and were drove by his own Coachman.

---

[8] Smith, *History,* II, 231–32.

5. His Majesty's Council, in mourning Coaches, being Pall Bearers.
6. Relations, in mourning Coaches.
7. Members of the Assembly, in Coaches.
8. The Magistrates, two by two, in Coaches and Chaises.
9. All the Gentlemen of the Law in this City, two by two, in Coaches and Chaises.

The Extent of the Procession was more than Half a Mile: They moved in a very regular Manner, and with a slow Pace, until they came opposite the House of Mr. Edward Willet, in the Broadway, where the Hearse stopped. The Corpse was then taken off, and put on Mens Shoulders: The Members of his Majesty's Council then came out of their Coaches, and supported the Pall: The rest of the Gentlemen alighted from their Carriages, likewise, and followed two by two, according to their Affinity and Rank. In this Order they proceeded into Trinity-Church, which was beautifully illuminated. The Corpse was then taken from the Mens Shoulders, and placed on a Stand before the Desk; where the Reverend Mr. Barclay performed the Funeral Service; at the Conclusion of which the Body was removed a few Yards to the middle Isle [sic], where it was interred. The Whole was conducted with the greatest Decorum and Solemnity.[9]

De Lancey was married in 1728 to Anne Heathcote, daughter of Caleb Heathcote, a member of the New York Council, lord of the manor of Scarsdale, and receiver-general of H. M. Customs for the Northern Department. Anne, who had inherited half of her father's estate, which was one of the largest in the Province, was probably the wealthiest young woman in New York. To this and his own wealth, De Lancey added his share of his father's very considerable estate. The couple had three sons and three daughters. Their eldest son James, educated in England, served in the New York Assembly for many years until the Revolution, and their daughter Anne married Thomas Jones, recorder of New York and a judge of the Supreme Court.

William Smith, Jr., one of De Lancey's adversaries and therefore not an impartial judge, offered an appraisal of the man in his *History of New York.*

> Mr. De Lancey's genius exceeded his erudition. His knowledge of the law, history and husbandry excepted, the rest of his learning consisted only of that small share of classical scholarship which he had acquired at Cambridge, and by a good memory retained. He was too indolent for profound researches in the law; but what he had read he could produce in an instant, for with a tenacious memory he had an uncommon vivacity; his first thought was always the best; he seemed to draw no advantages from meditation, and it was to this promptness he owed his reputation. He delivered his sentiments with brevity, and yet with perspicuity. He rarely delivered his opinions in writing, because his compositions did not merit even his own approbation. It was a labor to him to write, and he only supplied the matter of his speeches to the Assembly, which others put into form.[10]

---

[9] *Pa. Gaz.,* 7 Aug. 1760.
[10] Smith, *History,* II, 283.

DANIEL HORSMANDEN (1694—1778)
AMERICAN PHILOSOPHICAL SOCIETY: 1744

DANIEL HORSMANDEN, Recorder of New York and a member of the Council of that province, was one of the New Yorkers who "sent their names as members" of the American Philosophical Society in 1744. Though he had had a good education in England and had personal and professional relations with Cadwallader Colden and James Alexander, he seems to have had no interest in "philosophy," never corresponded with the Philadelphia members, and is not even mentioned in Franklin's correspondence.

He was born on 4 June 1694 at Purleigh, Essex, in Old England, the eldest son of the five children of the Reverend Mr. Daniel Horsmanden and Susanna Boyer (or Bowyer).[1] The Horsmandens were long settled at Goudhurst, Kent; since the time of James I they had held the advowson of the parish of Purleigh. Like several of his forebears and one of his sons after him, the elder Horsmanden was rector of Purleigh and vicar of Goudhurst. The younger Daniel studied law and was admitted to the Middle Temple on 20 May 1721 and to the Inner Temple on 9 May 1724.[2] According to William Smith, Jr., historian of New York, Horsmanden had no prospect of establishing himself at the English bar, fell deeply into debt, and in 1729 came out to Virginia, where his cousin William Byrd of Westover lived. Two years later he was settled as a lawyer in New York, warmly recommended to Cadwallader Colden by Micajah Perry as "an old friend & acquaintance of mine."[3] Horsmanden was sworn as an attorney of the Supreme Court of the Province in March 1731/2.[4] His appearance in court created a mild stir, for he wore a barrister's gown—the first ever seen in New York; but, as most of the legal business in town was already engrossed by James Alexander, William Smith, Joseph Murray, and John Chambers, Horsmanden could not look forward to a lucrative practice.

Though some thought him inclined to overvalue himself, on the whole Horsmanden made a good impression. Governor Cosby, who thought him "a Gentn of unexceptionable merit, and one whose integrity and capacity I am well satisfyed I can depend [on]," recommended him for appointment to the Council. He took

---

[1] For a full biographical account, emphasizing Horsmanden's public career, see Sister Mary Paula McManus, "Daniel Horsmanden, Eighteenth-Century New Yorker" (Ph.D. diss., Fordham University, 1960). See also Charles W. Spencer's sketch in *DAB*. On Horsmanden's English background, see Thomas Wright, *The History & Topography of Essex* (London, 1835), II, 667–68; John Venn and J. A. Venn, *Alumni Cantabrigienses,* II, 411; Joseph Foster, *Alumni Oxonienses,* II, 748.
[2] E. Alfred Jones, *American Members of the Inns of Court* (London, 1924), 100–01.
[3] William Smith, Jr., *Historical Memoirs, 1776–1778* (W. H. W. Sabine, ed., N.Y., 1958), 39; *Colden Papers,* II (N.-Y. Hist. Soc., Colls., 1918), 47.
[4] Ibid., 59.

his seat in that body accordingly on 29 September 1733.⁵ Lewis Morris spoke of him in similar terms, as "a Gentleman of breeding and sence, superior to most of that Board [Council]," though he owned no land in the Province, had little income from his practice, and was heavily in debt.⁶ Horsmanden also cultivated his acquaintance with Colden, who, in turn, assisted him to get a grant of land. He promptly sold it to pay his debts.⁷

Horsmanden allied himself with Cosby in the stormy and circuitous politics of New York. In the Zenger case in 1735 he gave his opinion that the printer was not bailable, and he stood with the governor and the De Lancey faction against the elder William Smith, James Alexander, and the popular cause. He adhered to Governor Clarke against Rip Van Dam, and his loyalty was rewarded with appointments as recorder in May 1735, judge of the Court of Vice-Admiralty in July 1736, and as third justice of the Supreme Court in January 1737.⁸ On 17 January 1736/7 he received the freedom of the city "as a Mark of their [the City Council's] great Esteem for him and for his good services done for this Corporation."⁹ As a judge, wrote William Smith, Jr., "his chief Merit consisted in a Gentlemanlike Exterior, a strict Attention to the Formality and Decorum of the Court & a Defence of the Profession agt. the vulgar and parcimonious [sic] Prejudices of an uncultivated Populace." On the other hand, he was sometimes careless about such routine tasks as signing certificates and bills, and he was often biting and sarcastic at the expense of those found guilty in his court.¹⁰

New York had long been governed in a high-handed way by cliques of wealthy landowners who also held most of the offices of government. To acquaint the people with the law, which these oligarchs violated or ignored as pleased them, the Assembly voted that a digest of the laws be prepared; and Judge Horsmanden was commissioned to compile it.¹¹ He never completed the task, for he was soon ruthlessly suppressing the Negro Plot.

A series of burglaries and fires of unknown or mysterious origin alarmed the city in the late winter of 1741.¹² Suspicion fastened at once on the city's Negro slaves and on one John Hughson, who kept a grog shop of ill fame, to which blacks often resorted. Hughson's indentured servant girl Mary Burton accused her master, members of his family, and many others, both black and white, of being burglars, arsonists, and plotters of nameless crimes. To fears of a Negro uprising was added

---

5   *Documents relative to the Colonial History of the State of New-York,* V, 939.
6   Ibid., 958.
7   *Colden Papers,* II, 99, 103–05, 106–09, 109–11, 116–18, 151–53, et passim.
8   *Calendar of Council Minutes, 1668–1783* (N.Y. State Library, Bulletin 58, Albany, 1902), 326.
9   N.-Y. Hist. Soc., *Colls.* (1885), 500.
10 Smith, *Historical Memoirs, 1776–1778,* 40.
11 *Documents relative to the Colonial History of the State of New-York,* VII, 528; Smith, *Historical Memoirs, 1776–1778,* 41; Smith, *History of New-York* (N. Y., 1830), II, 79–80.
12 James Grant Wilson, ed., *Memorial History of the City of New-York* (N.Y., 1892), II, 252–56.

the suspicion that the Spaniards were behind it all. "Tho' the Mystery of Iniquity has been unfolding by very Smal & Slow Degrees," Horsmanden explained to Cadwallader Colden, "it has at length been discovered that popery was at the Bottom." John Ury, a non-juring Anglican clergyman who was thought to be a Roman Catholic priest,

> appears to have been a principal promoter & encourager of this most horrible & Detestable piece of Villany a Scheme wch must have been brooded in a Conclave of Devils, & hatcht in the Cabinet of Hell; so bloody & Destructive a Conspiracy was this, that had not the mercifull hand of providence interposed & Confounded their Divices, in one & the Same night the Inhabitants would have been butcher'd in their houses, by their own Slaves, & the City laid in ashes; & this was to be perpetrated under the Obligation of an infamous Oath amimistred [sic] to the Conspirators . . . by Jno Hughson, now in Chains, & this Ury the priest. . . .[13]

As the public hysteria mounted, the prosecution pressed Mary Burton into making still more accusations; her charges became increasingly wild and so improbable that sober citizens began to doubt them. Before an end could be put to this shocking episode, so reminiscent of the Salem witchcraft delusion half a century before, 154 Negroes had been imprisoned, 13 were burned at the stake, 18 were hanged, and 71 were banished to the West Indies and other places; while of 21 whites arrested, two were hanged and several pardoned on condition that they take themselves out of the Province. To justify these brutal measures and allay the doubts of those who had come to believe the reaction of the authorities unwarranted, Horsmanden prepared a record of the proceedings of the "conspiracy." Its declared purpose was to impress on readers "the Design and dangerous Depth of this *hellish Project,* as well as the Justice of the several Prosecutions." It was published in 1744.[14]

By the middle 1740s, when he became a member of the American Philosophical Society, Horsmanden had joined the opposition to Governor Clinton. He wrote some of the attacks on Clinton in the press, while the names of Horsmanden, Murray, and De Lancey are a constant refrain in the Governor's letters of complaint to the Board of Trade. Finally on 12 September 1747 Clinton suspended Horsmanden from his seat in the Council and two weeks later removed him from the office of Recorder and from the Supreme Court. Though Horsmanden had never enjoyed much popular esteem, he now "had the Reward of being toasted, as the Man who had dared to be honest in the worst of Times." The Assembly voted him £150 in compensation for his services—for "the scandilous [sic]

---

[13] *Colden Papers,* II, 225.
[14] [Daniel Horsmanden], *A Journal of the Proceedings in the Detection of the Conspiracy* . . . (N.Y., 1744), i (reprinted with an introduction and notes by Thomas J. Davis [Boston, 1971]).

libels," so Governor Clinton believed them, which Horsmanden had published against him and his administration.[15]

This reward was no compensation for the loss of income from his offices. He was still in debt and, his enemies said, threatened with debtors' prison. Fortunately for him, on 8 May 1748 he married Mrs. Mary Reade Vesey, widow of the Reverend Mr. William Vesey, rector of Trinity Church, who had died in 1746, an advantageous match that restored his fortunes.[16] In the next few years Horsmanden succeeded in reestablishing himself in the favor of Governor Clinton, who restored him to his seat on the bench in 1750. In 1755 he was restored to the Council.[17] In 1754 he was one of the original trustees of King's College.

Mrs. Horsmanden died on 21 July 1760, and on 12 July 1763 the now elderly justice married Anne Jevon, whose property included a country place on the Bloomingdale Road.[18] Named "Frog Hall," it was Horsmanden's residence until war forced him out of it fifteen years later. On 16 March 1763 he was named chief justice of the Province; and at the same time, either to gratify his new wife or support his new dignity, he purchased a chariot from General Monckton—though he was slow to pay for it.[19]

Horsmanden struck a popular note in 1764 when as chief justice he ruled that, contrary to the governor's instructions, appeals could not be taken from the Supreme Court to the Council except for error. This meant that the verdict of the jury as to the merits of a case was final—a position which supporters of the King's authority in America found intolerable. Colden, now no longer friendly with Horsmanden, expressed himself on the decision in a long letter to the Earl of Halifax, adding some remarks on the influence of lawyers in New York:

> In a young Country, like this, where few Men have any acquired learning or knowledge, where the Judges and principal Lawyers are proprietors of extravagant grants of land, or strongly connected with them in Interest, or family alliances, it is possible, that a dangerous combination may subsist between the Bench and the Bar; not only greatly injurious to private property but likewise dangerous to His Majesty's prerogative & Authority, and his Rights in this Province, in case no appeals as to the merits of the case be allowed to the King in his privy Council.

---

[15] Smith, *Historical Memoirs, 1776–1778,* 40; *Documents relative to the Colonial History of the State of New-York,* VI, 378–79, 380–82, 430, 464–65; *Colden Papers,* IV (N.-Y. Hist. Soc., *Colls.,* 1920), 45.
[16] N.-Y. Hist. Soc., *Colls.* (1895), 85; Smith, *History of New-York,* II, 139.
[17] *Documents relative to the Colonial History of the State of New-York,* VI, 947–48.
[18] I. N. Phelps Stokes, *Iconography of Manhattan Island* (N. Y., 1915–28), VI, 171; N.-Y. Hist. Soc., *Colls.,* (1870), 177; *N.-Y. Post Boy,* 24 July 1760.
[19] *Letter-Book of John Watts* (N.-Y. Hist. Soc., *Colls.,* 1928), 172, 190, 234, 245, 266, 270. A list made in 1769 of those in New York who kept carriages showed Horsmanden as owner of a coach, a chariot or post chaise, and a phaeton. "Noms de personnes qui tiennent carosse à N. Y. 1769," Du Simitière Papers (Lib. Co. Phila.).

> No Lawyer in this place will at this time assist the appellant, by appearing for him, or by giving advice. . . .[20]

The Chief Justice was aging. Younger men disrespectfully called him "Old Horsey" and "Daddy Horsmanden."[21] He had a serious illness in 1769 but, to the astonishment of most, he recovered. He had a curious aversion to mentioning his age, skilfully turning aside questions about it, and even deliberately falsifying it.[22] But he attended Council meetings regularly; and in the winter of 1772–73 made two trips to Newport as member of a commission to investigate the burning of the *Gaspée*. "The Governt [of Rhode Island] (if it deserves that name)," he reported to Lord Dartmouth, "is a downright Democracy; the Govr. is a mere nominal one, and therefore a Cypher, without power or authority, entirely controuled by the populace elected annually, as [are] all other Magistrates and officers whatsoever." He made the unrealistic recommendation that Connecticut and Rhode Island be combined and made into a royal province.[23]

Horsmanden's position as a royal official and his well-known views made him an object of interest to the rebels in the summer of 1776, but because of his age he would not have been subjected to physical abuse. In the spring of that year friends had urged him to move out of the city; but his wife was dying of cancer of the breast at the time, and Horsmanden seemed incapable of decision. In August the New York Council authorized General Washington to take over Frog Hall for a hospital. Then at last Horsmanden yielded to the pleas of friends and took refuge in a "rural grotto" in Flatbush on Long Island.[24] From there he signed a loyal address to Lord Howe when the latter occupied the city.[25] It was one of his last public acts, for he was "very old and feeble."[26] He died suddenly of a stroke at Flatbush on 23 September 1778, and was buried two days later in the yard of Trinity Church, New York, which he had served more than forty years, as a vestryman in 1734–65 and 1769–72 and as a warden in 1765–69.[27] His estate was distributed among friends, relatives, and charitable institutions. To the rector of St. Giles', Cripplegate, London, he bequeathed £1,000, to King's College £500, and to the Anglican Communion of New York £1,500, of which £1,000 was to be used to rebuild the rectory, and £200 the schoolhouse, both destroyed in the fire of 1776, £100 to

---

[20] *Documents relative to the Colonial History of the State of New-York,* VII, 677.
[21] *Letter-Book of John Watts,* 172; Smith, *Historical Memoirs, 1763–1776,* 54n, 255.
[22] Ibid., 40; 4 Mass. Hist. Soc., *Colls.,* X, 619.
[23] Horsmanden to Earl of Dartmouth, 20 Feb. 1773, *Documents relative to the Colonial History of the State of New-York,* VIII, 350–54; also ibid., 390–91, 708–09.
[24] Smith, *Historical Memoirs, 1776–1778,* 39, 41.
[25] *Documents relative to the Colonial History of the State of New-York,* VII, 528n.
[26] Ibid., VIII, 685.
[27] N.-Y. Hist. Soc., *Colls.* (1870), 296; Smith, *Historical Memoirs, 1778–1783,* 25.

purchase a bell for St. Paul's Chapel, and £200 to provide a pulpit and desk for Trinity Church "when the said church shall be rebuilt."[28]

JOSEPH MURRAY (c.1694–1757)
AMERICAN PHILOSOPHICAL SOCIETY: 1744

JOSEPH MURRAY, lawyer, member of the Governor's Council of New York, was one of those who "sent their names as members" of the American Philosophical Society in 1744.[1] Presumably he was elected, but nothing survives to indicate that he ever corresponded on "philosophical" matters with any of the Philadelphia members; and he died ten years before the Society was revived after its long "dormancy."

He was the son of Thomas Murray, gentleman, and was born in Queen's County, Leinster, about 1694.[2] He came to New York in 1716 or 1717, was admitted to the bar, and made his first appearance before the Mayor's Court in 1718. Within a few years Murray achieved the reputation of one of the ablest and most respected lawyers in the city—a reputation that was increased when he was admitted to the Middle Temple on 12 May 1725. The distinction was a source of pride, for he identified himself on his bookplate thereafter as "of the Middle Temple."[3] With increasing frequency Murray was retained by the City Council in such affairs as its boundary dispute with Harlem and its controversy with Brooklyn over ferry rights. On 30 July 1728 the Corporation expressed its thanks to this "zealous Assertor of the Rights and Priviledges of this Corporation" by conferring the freedom of the city on him.[4] Less than three years later, on 11 February 1730/1, the Corporation again voted its thanks "for that he at our Request was pleased to Revise Amend and Compleat the draught" of the Montgomerie charter, "in which he has given us a lasting Instance of his great Learning Ability and Integrity in his Profession as well as for his Regard to this Corporation."[5]

Private suitors no less than public bodies sought Murray as counsel or arbiter; and he appeared in many of the most important cases in New York and New Jersey. When a suit was entered against Henry Lloyd of Lloyd's Neck in 1731, the lat-

---

[28] N.-Y. Hist. Soc., *Colls.* (1900), 57–58.

---

[1] *Colden Papers,* III (N.-Y. Hist. Soc., *Colls.,* 1919), 82–83.
[2] E. Alfred Jones, *American Members of the Inns of Court* (London, 1924), 162.
[3] Austin B. Keep, *The Library in Colonial New York* (N.Y., 1909), 85.
[4] N.-Y. Hist. Soc., *Colls.* (1885), 111; *Minutes of the Common Council of the City of New York, 1675–1776* (8v., N.Y., 1905), III, 345, 405–06.
[5] Ibid., IV, 43.

ter's lawyers retained James Alexander and then advised, by way of thwarting the plaintiffs, "Mr. Murry has not yet been applyed to by them, and as a man would be as sure as possible in an affair of such importance I would not have you risque a Lawyer of his influence & Capacity's being against you, for a smal sum."[6] Murray represented the proprietors of the Equivalent Lands,[7] for example; he and James Alexander appeared for the plaintiffs in the suit of the Earl of Stair and other East Jersey proprietors against Bond and others in 1752.[8] He joined Alexander, William Smith, and others in a petition to the Board of Trade against an effort by New Jersey in 1734 to establish legal fees and regulate the practice of law.[9] Murray was described as "a most regular Man in all his Conduct; . . . it was the Cause and not the Person that directed his Judgment."[10] The quality was illustrated when he negotiated the agreement that rescinded the disbarment of Alexander and Smith for their parts in the preliminaries to the Zenger case;[11] and when, on the question whether Jews might vote, he argued for the affirmative on the ground that the law enfranchised all freeholders of competent estate.

In a famous and significant debate before the Assembly in 1734 on the legality of the Court of Exchequer, Murray argued that the great English courts of common pleas, King's bench, chancery, and exchequer are integral and inseparable parts of the English constitution, as much a part of the liberties and privileges of Englishmen as any other liberties and privileges. He rejected the notion that only selected elements of the constitution governed New York. "I wou'd fain know," he demanded, "what sort of Constitution must that be, that has *No Courts* to administer Laws to the People: The *Constitution of England* is with *Courts,* and shall we say that *That Constitution* extends here, but *without Courts?*"[12] To establish courts in the colonies by local law might raise doubts about the citizens' title to the rights and privileges of Englishmen, which were theirs also by immemorial custom and usage; and therefore, Murray concluded, it was inexpedient to do more than regulate them as they were regulated in England, by establishing their tenure during good behavior.[13] A modern scholar has called Murray's well-argued brief "one of the few really important contributions to legal history penned in the American colonies."[14]

---

[6] *Papers of the Lloyd Family,* I (N.-Y. Hist. Soc., *Colls.,* 1926), 312. See also *Colden Papers,* IV (N.-Y. Hist. Soc., *Colls.,* 1920), 169.
[7] *Colden Papers,* II (N.-Y. Hist. Soc., *Colls.,* 1918), 203, 232.
[8] See also *N. J. Archives,* VIII, 267–74; XI, 527, 528.
[9] Ibid., V, 404–05.
[10] *N. Y. Mercury,* 2 May 1757.
[11] William Smith, *History of New-York* (N.Y., 1830), II, 51.
[12] *Mr. Murray's Opinion Relating to the Courts of Justice in the Colony of New York* [N.Y., 1734], 4.
[13] Smith, *History,* II, 17.
[14] Richard B. Morris in *DAB.*

Murray was appointed to the Provincial Council by Governor Clinton in 1744, but soon thereafter allied himself with Chief Justice De Lancey and other opponents of the Governor. By 1747 Clinton was angrily denouncing him and Judge Daniel Horsmanden as a pair of "Wretchess," and the names De Lancey, Horsmanden, and Murray run like a litany through Clinton's complaints to the Board of Trade.[15] The De Lancey faction rejoiced when Clinton was succeeded in 1753 by Sir Danvers Osborn, but rejoicing was quickly tempered when Osborn, a few days after his arrival, while a guest at Murray's house on lower Broadway, hanged himself in the garden for reasons of private sorrow.[16] De Lancey now succeeded as lieutenant governor. In that capacity he named Murray one of the New York commissioners to settle the disputed boundary with Massachusetts, and one of the New York delegation to the intercolonial congress held at Albany in 1754.[17] De Lancey, who opposed the plan of union which the Congress adopted, persuaded Murray also to oppose it. Of this incident the historian William Smith wrote that Murray "had a great merit as a lawyer; but, unless a question in that profession arose, he was either mute as a fish, or confused, slow, and superficial—a man of pride, without ambition, or a single talent for intrigue—cold, distant, formal, and disgusting." In his unpublished historical memoirs Smith's judgment was less harsh—despite his partisanship, Murray "died with the Reputation of a Man of the strictest Integrity & Veracity, and had a Sense of Honor seldom carried to the highest Elevation, but by such proud Spirits as himself."[18]

Murray assembled a considerable personal library. At the sale of the library of Governor Montgomerie in 1732, for example, he purchased 71 volumes, and he continued to buy books throughout his life. He was one of the "strenuous churchmen" who were the original trustees of King's College in 1753, and one of the first trustees of the New York Society Library the next year.[19] Whether, however, he took much interest in academic learning, especially "philosophical" studies, is doubtful, as one anecdote illustrates: James Alexander, Archibald Kennedy, and Dr. Archibald Spencer were watching "a blazeing star" in the heavens one night at Alexander's when Murray and two others came to consult about a by-law for removing the skinners and tanners from the slips to fresh water. Their business done,

---

[15] *Colden Papers,* IV (N.-Y. Hist. Soc., *Colls.,* 1920), 2, 69; *Documents relative to the Colonial History of the State of New-York,* VI, 248–49, 254, 350–51, 666.

[16] James Grant Wilson, ed., *Memorial History of the City of New-York* (N.Y., 1892), II, 290–92.

[17] *Colden Papers,* IV (N.-Y. Hist. Soc., *Colls.,* 1920), 452; I. N. Phelps Stokes, *Iconography of Manhattan Island* (N.Y., 1915–28), IV, 652, 662.

[18] Smith, *Historical Memoirs, 1776–1778* (W. H. W. Sabine, ed., N.Y., 1958), 32–33; *History of New-York,* II, 223–24.

[19] Herbert and Carol Schneider, eds., *Samuel Johnson, President of King's College: His Career and Writings* (4v., N.Y., 1929), IV, 5; Keep, *Library in Colonial New York,* 85, 141.

the visitors departed; apparently Murray had not even asked to peer at the comet through the telescope.[20]

Murray was past 40 when he married in 1738; his bride was Mrs. Grace Freeman, widow of Thomas Freeman, daughter of Governor Cosby, and a niece of the Earl of Halifax. He died on 28 April 1757, and was buried in the chancel of Trinity Church, which he served six years as a vestryman and 31 as a warden.[21] By his will he freed his Negro Caesar (whom he had successfully protected from a charge of rape several years before)[22] and Caesar's mother; he made several personal bequests—among them £200 each to Chief Justice De Lancey and Colonel Lewis Morris; and he left £100 to Trinity Church for the poor of the parish, and to the Reformed Dutch, Presbyterian, and Lutheran churches of New York, £50, £20, and £10 respectively—a gradation that may reflect the degree of esteem in which Murray held the several communions. The remainder of his estate, including his library, amounting to £7,000–8,000, went to King's College.[23] British soldiers carried the books away in 1776—Thomas Jones recalled seeing some forty in a tavern on Long Island, where they had been traded for drinks—but a few were eventually recovered and are now preserved in Columbia University.[24]

---

[20] *Colden Papers,* III (N.-Y. Hist. Soc., *Colls.,* 1919), 46.
[21] *N. Y. Mercury,* 2 May 1757; Morgan Dix, *A History of the Parish of Trinity Church in the Province of New York* (N.Y., 1898–1906), IV, 575.
[22] *Colden Papers,* IV (N.-Y. Hist. Soc., *Colls.,* 1920), 142.
[23] N.-Y. Hist. Soc., *Colls.* (1896), 165–66; *N.Y. Mercury,* 16 May 1757; Schneider, ed., *Samuel Johnson,* IV, 44, 262.
[24] Paul M. Hamlin, *Legal Education in Colonial New York* (N.Y., 1939), 89–90, 177–79, 194; Thomas Jones, *History of New York during the Revolutionary War* (N.Y., 1879), I, 136–37; Stokes, *Iconography,* IV, 923; V, 1045–46.

WILLIAM SMITH (1697–1769)

By John Wollaston. *Historic Hudson Valley, Tarrytown, N.Y. Gift of J. Dennis Delafield.*

WILLIAM SMITH (1697–1769)
AMERICAN PHILOSOPHICAL SOCIETY: 1744

WILLIAM SMITH, lawyer of New York, can be reckoned a member of the American Philosophical Society on the strength of a statement his friend and professional associate James Alexander made to Cadwallader Colden on 12 November 1744: "I am very much of your mind that Mr Franklins proposal of a Society will prove useful—at our last Court Mr Chief justice [James De Lancey] Mr Horsmanden Mr Murray Mr Smith & Several others sent their names as members of the Society." [1] No other reference to Smith's membership has been found; his name is not on the list compiled in 1768 in anticipation of union with the American Society; but that is not evidence that he was not a member in 1744.

William Smith was born at Newport Pagnell in Buckinghamshire in Old England on 8 October 1697, the eldest of five sons of Thomas and Susan (Odell) Smith.[2] His parents were in comfortable circumstances. They were staunch dissenters in religion; grandfather Smith had fought under Cromwell. In the schools of local clergymen the boy received a decent grounding in the classics and, it is said, in the sciences as well. In 1715 the family migrated to New York, where the elder Smith later took an active part in founding the first Presbyterian church there. Young William was entered at Yale College, where he was graduated in 1719. He returned to New Haven in 1722 as a tutor after the expulsion of the rector Timothy Cutler and other faculty converts to Anglicanism. Smith's father would have preferred the young man to enter the ministry, and it is said he was considered as a candidate for rector of Yale.[3] But Smith had already begun to study law. He resigned his tutorship in April 1724, was admitted to the bar on 20 May, and began to practice on 20 July 1724. On 10 March 1726/7 he was admitted to Gray's Inn, London.[4]

Dismayed by the evil consequences arising from the large number of ill-trained and unqualified legal practitioners in New York, Smith entered into an agreement with James Alexander, Joseph Murray, and three others not to associate with such persons. In 1731 Smith received the freedom of the city.

---

[1] *Colden Papers,* III (N.-Y. Hist. Soc., *Colls.,* 1919), 82–83.
[2] Maturin L. Delafield, "William Smith, Judge of the Supreme Court of the Province of New York," *Mag. Am. Hist.,* VI (1881), 264–74, with additions and corrections, ibid., VIII (1882), 60; Franklin B. Dexter, *Biographical Sketches of the Graduates of Yale College* (N.Y., 1885–1912), I, 207–11; *DAB.*
[3] William Smith, *History of the Late Province of New-York* (N.Y., 1830), II, 113.
[4] E. Alfred Jones, *American Members of the Inns of Court* (London, 1924), 201–02.

fords" to Alston and to John Jacob Dillenius at Oxford. Among them was rattlesnake root, "a medicine generally used by our Patients; to the no small detriment of some of them; for altho its' virtues seem to be great, yet they are unknown"; he asked Alston to test it.[5] As early as 1738 Mitchell became a correspondent of Peter Collinson, the London Quaker merchant who sat at the center of an international web of naturalists whom he introduced to one another and through whom they exchanged letters and specimens. In that year Mitchell sent Collinson a short treatise on the principles of botany and zoology. A thoughtful and well-trained botanist, Mitchell had realized the importance of an objective basis of classification. Criteria of the genera, he declared, should arise *"rather* from the *laws of nature* than from the *opinion of the botanists."*[6] Accordingly he argued that plants and animals that can fertilize each other are related; his system and that of Linnaeus he regarded as mutually supportive. Three years later he prepared a supplement that identified 30 genera, 24 of them proposed as new. Collinson forwarded the manuscripts to his friend Christopher Jacob Trew at Nuremberg, who had them published in the proceedings of the Academy there.[7] Mitchell's dissertations were reprinted and published at Nuremberg in 1769.

Linnaeus, who received some of Mitchell's specimens and descriptions and included them, often without credit, in his publications, named the partridge berry *Mitchellis repens* for his Virginia correspondent. Mitchell made a careful study of the pine trees of Virginia; and though he sent copies of his treatise to some correspondents, he declined to publish it.[8]

In addition to botany, Mitchell, like European naturalists, was much interested in American zoology, in particular the opossum. At the request of Collinson or another naturalist, Mitchell studied this interesting marsupial in 1741 and sent his observations, through Collinson, to the Royal Society, where they were read on 10 February 1742. The Society then returned a series of queries about the creature, which, after carefully observing a pair that he kept for two years in his own house, Mitchell answered; his detailed reply was read on 20 March 1746.[9] For a prize offered by the Academy of Bordeaux he addressed the question of the causes of the difference in skin pigmentation. He did not complete his paper in time for the contest, but submitted it instead to Collinson, who presented it to the Royal Society, whose members discussed it during four successive meetings from 3 May to 14 June 1744,

---

[5] Mitchell to Charles Alston, 4 Oct. 1738 (Univ. of Edinburgh Lib.; photocopy in APS).
[6] Berkeley and Berkeley, *Dr. John Mitchell,* 30–37.
[7] Mitchell, "Dissertatio Brevis de Principiis Botanicorum et Zoologorum etc. etc.," Academiae Caesarea Leopoldino-Franciscanaeo, *Acta Physico-Medica Botanicorum and Zoologorum,* VIII (1748), app., 187–224.
[8] Edmund Berkeley and Dorothy Smith Berkeley, eds., *Correspondence of John Bartram, 1734–1777* (Gainesville, Fla., [1992]), 265, 272.
[9] Ibid., 135, 155, 158.

and ordered it printed in the *Philosophical Transactions*. Rejecting some current theories, Mitchell explained the differences by climate and manner of life:

> . . . the Power of the Sun's Heat in hot Countries, and its more immediate Application to the Body, or the Increase of its Force, by the Nature of the Soil, or Ways of Life, is the remote Cause of the Blackness, and the different Degrees of Blackness, of the Inhabitants of the Torrid Zone: Whereas the luxurious Customs, and the effeminate Lives, of the several Nations of white People, in the northern Climates, are the remote Causes of their respective fair Complexions.

"We do not affirm," he concluded,

> that either Blacks or Whites were originally descended from one another, but that both were descended from People of an intermediate tawny Colour; whose Posterity became more and more tawny, i.e. black, in the southern Regions, and less so, or white, in the northern Climes: Whilst those who remained in the middle Regions, where the first Men resided, continued of their primitive tawny Complexions; which we see confirmed by Matter of Fact, in all the different People in the World.[10]

Mitchell's explanation was not the correct one; but it served as a basis for Samuel Stanhope Smith's *Essay on the Causes of the Variety of Complexion and Figure in the Human Species,* which was the annual oration before the American Philosophical Society in 1787 and was printed at its request.

Dr. Mitchell visited Philadelphia for the first time in the fall of 1744. One reason was to improve his health, for his constitution was reported to be "miserably broken." By chance he met there the itinerant lecturer on electricity Archibald Spencer and also Dr. Alexander Hamilton of Maryland, who found Mitchell "a man much of my own make," with "complaints . . . near a kin to mine."[11] Mitchell spent a night at John Bartram's. The next morning Bartram took him into town and introduced him to Benjamin Franklin. "He staid in town near thre [sic] weeks," Bartram later wrote Cadwallader Colden about his guest,

> so that I had the favour of his Company many times at my house in the fields & in the woods which I was well pleased with he is an excelent Phisition & Botanist & hath dipped in the Mathematicks which inclined A Gentleman in Town well known to us to say to me that our docters was but novices to him. But another person more volatil & more extravangantly expressed his value for him [&] tould me thay had not the Milioneth part of his knowledge.[12]

---

[10] Mitchell, "An Essay upon the Causes of the Different Colours of People in different Climates," *Phil. Trans.,* XLIII (1744), 102–50.

[11] Berkeley and Berkeley, *Bartram Correspondence,* 250; *Franklin Papers,* II, 415; Carl Bridenbaugh, ed., *Gentleman's Progress: The Itinerarium of Dr. Alexander Hamilton, 1744* (Chapel Hill, N.C., 1948), 189.

[12] *Colden Papers,* III (N.-Y. Hist. Soc., *Colls.,* 1919), 79.

The gentleman who thus highly esteemed Mitchell's mathematical knowledge may have been James Logan, to whom Franklin took him.

Mitchell's health continued to decline. If he did not soon leave Virginia, John Bartram told Gronovius in December 1745, "he can't continue long in the land of the living."[13] By that time Mitchell had given up his practice and sold his house, including "a large Garden, containing many useful and curious Plants and Herbs," as well as "the Furniture and proper Utensils of an Apothecary's Shop, and a small chimical Laboratory." His library, "A Curious Collection of Books, in most Sciences, particularly Physic, Surgery, and Botany; in Greek, Latin, French, and English," was still on sale the following April.[14] That spring Mitchell sailed for England, where he believed his health would improve. The voyage was unlucky. A French privateer captured the vessel; and though Mitchell was put ashore and made his way to London, his papers, notes, and specimens were taken. The herbarium was eventually restored to him, but in a damaged and plundered state; whether his manuscripts were also returned none of his letters says.

In London Mitchell was warmly received by Peter Collinson, with whom he had long corresponded, and by Dr. John Fothergill and Mark Catesby, author of *The Natural History of Carolina*. He met the aged Sir Hans Sloane, whose library and natural history collection were soon to become the foundation of the British Museum. Catesby took him to meetings of the Royal Society, where on 9 June 1748 he was proposed for membership as "A Gentleman of great merit and Learning, who . . . from his great application to the Study of Natural History, especially Botany, is very well acquainted with the Vegetable production of North America," and he was elected on 15 December. He was formally admitted a Fellow the next week and was a useful member thereafter.[15]

He continued to correspond with his American friends. He wrote Colden on botanical matters, composed a titlepage for the London edition of Colden's *History of the Five Indian Nations* (1747), "such . . . as might please & engage the Booksellers" (though it displeased the author), and intimated that he had interest that he might employ in Colden's behalf.[16] On 29 April 1749 Franklin sent to Mitchell, who was now a Fellow of the Royal Society, his "Observations and Suppositions towards forming a new Hypothesis for explaining the several Phaenomena of Thunder Gusts"; Mitchell presented it to the Society, where it was read at successive

---

[13] Berkeley and Berkeley, *Bartram Correspondence,* 266.
[14] *Va. Gaz.,* 21 Nov. 1745; 17 April 1746. Gordon W. Jones in "The Library of Doctor John Mitchell of Urbanna," *Va. Mag. Hist. Biog.,* LXXVI (1968), 441–43, lists 29 titles of books cited in three papers that Mitchell wrote while in Virginia. These included, in addition to medical and botanical works, Newton's *Optics* and Locke's *Essay on Human Understanding.*
[15] Raymond P. Stearns, "Colonial Fellows of the Royal Society of London, 1661–1788," *Wm. & Mary Quar.,* 3d ser., III (1946), 239–40.
[16] *Colden Papers,* III, (N.-Y. Hist. Soc., *Colls.,* 1919), 367–69; IV (1920), 393.

meetings on 9 and 16 November. Though not printed in the *Philosophical Transactions,* it was included in Franklin's *Experiments and Observations on Electricity* (London, 1751).[17]

Separated from Virginia, which had provided him with so much botanical knowledge, Mitchell's scientific work took a new direction and emphasis. He could no longer collect specimens personally, but as an authority on American trees and plants he was consulted by those who wished to acquire specimens from the Western Hemisphere. The Swedish naturalist Peter Kalm, for example, sought his advice before setting out on his tour of the colonies in 1748. Mitchell gathered information from many sources, including his correspondence with Linnaeus, about the manufacture of potash, and pointed to its value as "an Improvement fit for our Colonies" in a paper that was printed in the *Philosophical Transactions* and in Franklin's *Pennsylvania Gazette* in 1750.[18] He made plans to write a comprehensive natural and medical history of North America. He became intimate with the Earl of Bute, an enthusiastic botanist and gardener, and with Bute's uncle, the Duke of Argyll, who, in addition to being a botanist, was an expert in chemistry and knowledgeable in mechanics and mathematics. He was also, as Peter Collinson was to write, a benevolent man, amiable, "plain in his dress, without pride or ostentation." As one of their principal agents—whether Mitchell was simply a friend or served the duke and his family as a physician or filled some other capacity, is not known; no record of remuneration survives to suggest a professional relationship—Mitchell ordered and imported for both Bute and Argyll some American flowering trees and shrubs, especially magnolias and white cedar. He had a hand in importing oysters to plant at Inveraray; he got the duke a Franklin stove; he took a keen interest in His Grace's program of reforestation; and at Argyll's request he asked Colden to get a buffalo bull and calf, "if it is not too much trouble."[19] Mitchell was frequently—at some periods almost weekly—a guest at the duke's London house, where other naturalists were also present—"a vast Colledge on Botany," one guest called it. Despite "a vertiginous disorder," he made a botanizing trip to the Western Isles with Argyll in 1750.[20]

With such powerful friends as these, Mitchell was in a position to do something for his friends. He hinted to John Bartram that he might be able to get him an appointment that would free him from the daily responsibilities of his farm and permit him to devote all his time to botany and plant-collecting.

---

[17] *Franklin Papers,* III, 365–77, 482; *Huntington Lib. Quar.,* X (1946–47), 411.

[18] Mitchell, "An Account of the Preparation and Uses of the various Kinds of Pot-ash," *Phil. Trans.,* XLV (1748), 541–63 and *Pa. Gaz.,* 18, 25 Dec. 1750.

[19] Colden made no reply to this request; and it is not likely that an American bison at this time ever roamed Argyll's estates in the Scottish Highlands. Mitchell to Cadwallader Colden, 25 March 1749, *Huntington Lib. Quar.,* X (1946–47), 411–17.

[20] Berkeley and Berkeley, *Bartram Correspondence,* 311–12.

a member of the Society of Arts, but seems to have taken no part in that organization's work. He also belonged to the Spalding Society.[25]

After Mitchell's resignation from Kew, he seems again to have dropped from sight for a few years. In 1762 he visited Bath and Tunbridge Wells for his health's sake. He gave John Pringle his prescription for treating dysentery, and Pringle quoted it approvingly in the fourth edition of his *Observations on the Diseases of the Army* (London, 1764). Franklin, having conceived a method of printing edifying educational and moral sentiments and scenes on chimney tiles, asked Mitchell to inquire of English manufacturers whether the process was practicable.[26] In 1767 he wrote once more on imperial relations. His *Present State of Great Britain and North America, with regard to Agriculture, Population, Trade, and Manufactures, impartially considered* (London, 1767) was essentially a restatement of many of the arguments and suggestions that he and others had made, and were making, about the economic relations of Britain and the colonies. His arguments, derived from an enlarged view of the nature of the imperial relationship, had a special relevance in 1767 because the Stamp Act had been but so recently enacted and repealed and the British government asserted its right to impose taxes in America. Mitchell rejected this policy as unwise, unprofitable, and hostile to the true interests of Britain. By imposing taxes on America and discouraging or preventing the colonists from expanding into the new territory acquired from France in 1763, British policy forced them into manufacturing, and thus into competition with Britain, while at the same time curtailing the colonists' ability to provide the products Britain required.

> The first thing . . . to be considered, in the governing of colonies, is, to enable them to subsist under the government they are subject to; which they will never be able to do by paying taxes, so long as their resources are so few, and so limited and confined. Their trade and resources are now, as they ought to be, confined to Great Britain, which does not want, and will not take, what the greatest part of North America produces; so that, to oblige them to raise money, even by the produce of their lands, is to force them into a trade with foreign Powers.
>
> Thus the repeal of the taxes imposed upon the colonies is so far from being a sacrifice of the highest permanent interests, and of the whole majesty, power, and reputation of government, as many seem to think, that it appears to be the only way to secure them. The whole income of these colonies does not amount to above ten or twelve shillings a head *per annum,* which will never pay taxes, nor even purchase *absolute necessaries.* By taxes, therefore, you first oblige the people to supply themselves, independent of Great Britain, and then to carry on a trade with other nations, in order to raise money, both of which are equally opposite to the *highest permanent interests* and *government* of Great Britain. And this is not only the case at present, but is likely to be much more so hereafter. . . .

[25] John Nichols, *Literary Anecdotes of the Eighteenth Century* (London, 1812), VI, 98.
[26] Ibid., 292–93; *Franklin Papers,* XX, 459–60.

Thus it signifies nothing, whether Great Britain has a right to tax her colonies, or not, since that right can never be worth a groat; and it would be the greatest loss and detriment to the nation, ever to exercise it. This must ever be the case, so long as these colonies depend on their mother country, without either staple commodities, manufactures, or trade, that turn to any account to them; and the whole profits of these essential resources, both of wealth and subsistence, center in, and are reaped by, Great Britain. If these things are considered, it must appear to be the greatest inconsistency, either to expect, or to take, money from these colonies. That is contrary to the very nature of *colonies,* and to the intent of settling them. The nation gets both their money, if they have any, and their effects, by trade, and can expect none by a revenue. Upon these accounts, it was absolutely necessary to repeal the taxes imposed upon them, as it was equally contrary to the very nature of things, and the interest of Great Britain, that they should ever be able to pay them, till they enjoy all the profits of their own labour, and of a trade in the produce of it; which is to make them independent. Many other regulations are as contrary to nature itself, particularly in the acquisitions; and must be repealed, when they come to be known, as the rest have been. . . .

Many indeed seem to be apprehensive, that the repeal of the Stamp-act may make the colonies less subject to a British government, and more inclinable to assert an independence; in which they shew themselves to be totally unacquainted with them in this respect, as well as in all other important concerns of the nation. The inhabitants of the colonies, like all other Englishmen, have ever had a firm attachment to their mother country, and her government, on account of the invaluable blessings they enjoy, from her happy constitution and form of government; this has hitherto secured to them those liberties and privileges, which they derive from her, and are as tenacious of, as all other Englishmen: This is the great band of union between the colonies and their mother country, which we should dissolve, by depriving them of the liberties and privileges of their fellow-subjects, which they have hitherto enjoyed, and think they are entitled to by their birth-right, in common with all other subjects of the realm. To deprive them of this constitution, is the surest way to make them think of another; but so long as they enjoy all the benefits of such a government, they can never have a better. This is so well known to all intelligent people in the colonies, that although many here imagine, they want to be independent, and to set up for themselves, yet we believe, no one among them ever once thought of any such thing, unless the people here put it in their heads. So long as they enjoy their present happy constitution, they would not be independent, if it were in their power, or left to their option.[27]

Many of the authorities that Mitchell cited for his position were familiar, and reviewers found the book's style turgid; but the work is said to have influenced the thinking of William Pitt, and thus had the effect on British policy respecting the Ohio Valley that Mitchell desired.

Dr. Mitchell died in London on 29 February 1768 in the same month that his membership in the original American Philosophical Society was confirmed by the

---

[27] Mitchell, *Present State of Great Britain and North America* (London, 1767), 357–62. Thomas R. Adams, *The American Controversy* (Providence, R.I., 1980), I, 84, shows that the pamphlet was by Mitchell.

port the Presbytery of Letterkenny made to the General Synod of Ulster on 18 June 1735 Alison was listed as a licentiate. As there was no opening for him in Ireland, however, he sailed soon afterwards, "a poor Man to the wilds of America," where he was accepted by the Presbytery of New Castle, apparently before 18 September, certainly before 20 November 1733.[4] He is said to have served for a time as tutor in the house of Samuel Dickinson at "Croisiadore" in Talbot County. Appointed by the Presbytery on 19 June 1736 to supply a new church at the Forks of the Brandywine for a month, Alison preached so acceptably that he received a second appointment, and some time before 25 May 1737 was ordained and installed as the minister at New London. The church edifice erected there in 1744 is described as the largest in the region, with long low brick walls, a Swedish hipped roof, arched doorways and windows, leaden sashes, and "pews . . . of forms, patterns, and colours as diverse as the tastes and the incomes of their respective owners."[5]

Alison's stand in the New Light-Old Light controversy that swept over the Presbyterian Church in the 1740s, was consistent with his conviction of the supremacy of learning. He stood firmly against what he called "Enthusiasm & wild disorders that were like to destroy religion, & ruin our Churches." He believed in a formally trained and educated ministry and in right doctrine and good works, confident that these would lead men to conversion and bring them spiritual grace. He rejected the idea that conversion must come first. Education, not revelation, was the principal road to truth; and schools and colleges were the most certain means to end misunderstanding and schism. Reflecting on the discussions in the church, he expressed his confidence that "as our Colleges gain credit, & as mathematicks, critical Learning, freedom of enquiry, & Acquaintance with history prevail . . . forbearance & moderation, & benevolence will take place."[6]

With these sentiments in mind Alison appealed to his co-religionists to establish a college in the Middle Colonies. The call was taken up by the Presbytery of Lewes, and in 1739 the Synod of Philadelphia approved the project. War postponed the effort, but in 1743, responding to a new call from the Presbytery of Donegal, Alison opened his own grammar school at New London. It was to be, in the words of a public announcement, "a Free-School . . . where all Persons may be instructed in the Languages and some other Parts of Polite Literature, without any Expences for their Education."[7] The Synod of Philadelphia endorsed the undertaking, whose support came from the Presbyteries of Philadelphia, New Castle, and Donegal. The school's success may be measured in part by the roster of its students—Thomas McKean, Charles Thomson, George Read, John Ewing, Paul

---

[4] Pears, "Francis Alison," loc. cit., 215, 216; Ingersoll, "Francis Alison," 33–37; *Pa. Journal,* 19 April 1780.
[5] Richard Webster, *A History of the Presbyterian Church in America* (Phila., 1857), 441–42.
[6] Stiles, *Itineraries,* 431; Alison to Ezra Stiles, 10 July 1761, quoted in Ingersoll, "Francis Alison," 71.
[7] *Pa. Gaz.,* 24 Nov. 1743.

Jackson, and Hugh Williamson, to name only those who became members of the American Philosophical Society. Alison must have been a stern master, for Thomson remembered that during the four or five years he was a student of Alison's, he "never saw him smile, nor in a good humor during that time."[8] Despite success in his academy Alison had his mind set on a college. In 1745 or 1746, with the trustees' permission, he opened a correspondence with Professor Hutcheson in Glasgow "relative to our setting on foot a Seminary in our province."[9]

Some twenty-five years afterwards Alison reflected on these events in a letter to his good friend Ezra Stiles of Newport, Rhode Island. It gave him no little satisfaction, he wrote, to recall

> that at my arrival here there was not a College, nor even a good grammar School in four Provinces, Maryland, Pensylvania, Jersey, & New York; but on the other hand all that made any pretensions to learning were branded as letter learned Pharisees; and this desperate cause, of promoting learning in this Province, I undertook, encouraged by our Synod, who allow'd me only twenty pounds currency, per ann. & fifteen for an assistant; & obliged us to teach all gratis, that were pleased to accept of learning on these terms; & in this the success was beyond our expectations; & it roused a spirit in Philada. to erect an academy, & then a College; & since that time Learning became reputable, even amongst those that gave the nickname of Letter-learned Pharisees, brought up at the feet of Gamaliel.[10]

Alison's reputation as a scholar and teacher quickly reached Philadelphia, and he was invited to become a teacher in the academy established there in 1749. The New London trustees raised his salary to keep him, but after the death of David Martin, rector of the Philadelphia Academy, in December 1751, the offer was renewed; and in January 1752 Alison came to Philadelphia as master of the Latin School at £200 a year, refusing the rectorship "or to have any thing to do with the Government of the other Schools."[11] Three years later, at the urging of Alison and Provost William Smith, the trustees obtained a new charter, establishing a college with power to confer degrees; and they made Alison vice-provost in addition to being rector of the Academy, a post he had agreed to take, despite his aversion to administrative obligations. "I think Mr. Alison qualified for any Station in any College," Smith wrote Richard Peters on 22 February 1755.[12] In 1756 Alison was appointed "Professor of the higher Classics, Logic, Metaphysicks, and Geography," and he was authorized to "teach any of the other Arts and Sciences, that he may judge himself qualified to teach, as the Circumstances of the Philosophy School may require." As if these assignments were not sufficient to fill his time, Alison was

---

[8] Benjamin Rush, *Autobiography* (George W. Corner, ed., Princeton, 1948), 284.
[9] Stiles, *Itineraries,* 433.
[10] *Ibid.,* 431.
[11] *Franklin Papers,* IV, 325.
[12] *PMHB,* XXIX (1905), 457–59.

The openness he felt towards science and learning was reflected in his view of a college. He rejected religious oaths and tests in such institutions. "Such narrowness in Colleges supported at the publick expence of a govermt. to me appears unreasonable." Nor did he like it that colleges were not governed by the professors, as "it must lessen their reputation that they have no share in the govermt."[22]

Conditions at the College of Philadelphia did not please him. In 1766 he charged that the institution had been "artfully got into the hands of the Episcopal Trustees," with the result that young men who might have entered the Presbyterian ministry were "enticed" into the Anglican church; and as for attending the College of New Jersey (a New Light citadel), that institution was "so unfit to make scholars, that we have no great pleasure to send them there. . . ." In the circumstances Alison considered quitting his post. Some Presbyterians, however, thought that the unity of the church might be promoted if it was agreed that all future ministers should study at the college at Princeton, and that John Ewing should be elected president and Alison professor of mathematics and natural philosophy. The New Light trustees, however, rejected this proposal, and, somewhat hastily, offered the presidency to John Witherspoon, minister of Paisley, Scotland.[23]

Alison's personal theology seems to have been broadly ecumenical. Deborah Franklin recorded, with some disapproval, that her nephew Benjamin Mecom "had sume Confrense" with Alison and Professor Ebenezer Kinnersley.

> I Cante helpe tellin that Dr Allison has Surprized Beney by telling him that God in his mersey has maid the rode to Heaven So wide that sume of all Reig [religious] profeshons may go to heaven nay it is so wide that thay may go abreste but Ben thinkes he is mistaken and is a verey quere man and donte seme to like him.[24]

As to Anglicans in the colonies, they wished to have a bishop in America. There were practical, ecclesiastical reasons for this; but dissenters feared a bishop's influence and civil authority. Alison was one of these. Answering Thomas Bradbury Chandler's *Appeal to the Public in behalf of the Church of England in America*, Alison as "Centinel" reviewed the case. "Every attempt upon American liberty," he asserted, "has always been accompanied with endeavours to settle bishops among us."[25] Alison's first letter appeared in Bradford's *Pennsylvania Journal* on 24 March 1768; on 8 September Provost Smith began his reply which continued for 19 weeks under the pseudonym of "The Anatomist."[26]

---

[22] Stiles, *Itineraries*, 425–26.
[23] Ibid., 428–29; Stiles, *Literary Diary*, I, 250; Butterfield, *Rush Letters*, I, 36–38.
[24] *Franklin Papers*, XV, 25.
[25] *Pa. Journal*, 7 July 1768.
[26] Carl Bridenbaugh, *Mitre and Sceptre* (N.Y., 1966), 271–72.

Possessed with this notion (namely, that God and nature designed New-England as the sole property and inheritance of the *Saints*) they have always considered those among them, who said their prayers in a different manner from themselves "as spies" . . . or as intruders into their new Canaan . . . and for half a century have pursued, with the grossest calumny and abuse, a venerable society, for having only sent a few missionaries to preach the gospel of Christ, according to the mode of the Church of England, to such members of that Church as should be found within their limits.

An American bishop was not the only issue on which Alison aligned himself against British policy. On the Stamp Act he wrote Ezra Stiles on 13 June 1765:

> I am amazed that the English Parliament has given their own Constitution such a blow, as to tax men without their consent, given by themselves or their Proxies. It is an insult on common sense to say that Persons chosen for Representatives of London & Bristol are in like manner chosen to be the representatives of Boston & Philada. Has two men chosen to represent a poor Borough in England, that has sold its votes to the highest bidder, any pretence to say that they represent Virginia or Pennsylvania; & has 400 such paltry fellows a right to take our liberties. . . . Power is a sad thing. Yet I think our Mother should remember we are children, & not slaves.[27]

As the conflict between the colonies and England intensified, Alison supported non-importation and rejoiced in Boston's resistance. "I fear the British Parliament are determined to twist the yoke around our necks," he wrote Stiles in 1769, applauding Boston's firmness and urging maintenance of non-importation.

> What can England do. We have more religion & more Political virtue than any as many people in the kings dominions, or possibly in the whole world; they may distress us, but can never enslave us; all Europe owes England a spite, & if they send their Armies to distress & destroy us, they will distress & destroy themselves at the same time; & every power that ever they offended will be their enemy.[28]

Another accomplishment that gave Alison satisfaction was his part in founding a pension fund for Presbyterian ministers. Patterned on an endowment in Scotland, the Corporation for the Relief of Poor and Distressed Presbyterian Ministers, and of the Poor and Distressed Widows and Children of Presbyterian Ministers was proposed in 1754, organized in 1756, and chartered in 1759. Alison was its first clerk, serving until his death. The fund proved to be a success, and flourishes to this day.[29]

---

[27] Stiles, *Itineraries*, 427.
[28] Ibid., 434–35.
[29] Alexander Mackie, *Facile Princeps: The Story of the Beginning of Life Insurance in America* [Phila., 1956]. The appeal to the Proprietors for a charter of incorporation, signed by Alison and Robert Cross on behalf of the Synod, 10 Feb. 1757, is in Penn Papers, Beaver Skins, XII, 54 (HSP).

Alison also warmly endorsed plans for an American magazine of literary and scientific intelligence. "Tis to be hoped," he wrote Stiles in 1757, soliciting his aid,

> that this undertaking may encourage some men of abilities to publish their sentiments or Observations, who thro modesty might otherwise deprive the world of that benefit—that it may engage our young students to become litterary adventurers, when it can be done with so much safety—that it may promote a friendly intercourse among men of Learning in our different Colonies, & possibly produce some papers worthy the approbation of Great Britain famed for Arts & Sciences.[30]

Though not himself a "litterary adventurer" of this kind, Alison played important roles in several Philadelphia cultural institutions. He was a director of the Library Company of Philadelphia from 1757 to 1765 and again from 1772 to 1778, and served as secretary of the directors from 1757 to 1759. When his old academy, now moved from New London to Newark in Delaware, was chartered in 1771, Alison was named one of the trustees. A wide reader, he is recorded as subscribing to James Burgh's *Political Disquisitions,* Bulkeley and Cummings' *Voyage to the South Seas,* and Mosheim's *Church History.* The sale of his library in 1780 was an event of some importance. Alison was especially interested in promoting domestic manufactures and other economic reforms, serving as a manager of the Silk Society, for which he was the principal dispenser of mulberry seedlings and silkworm eggs;[31] and he was one of the sponsors of a project to manufacture paper in America. In the American Philosophical Society in 1773 he exhibited samples of American wine, then offered a list of practical, detailed and specific queries on which the Society might collect and disseminate information useful to American farmers— the best materials for fencing, the best sorts of grain, "wheat & other corn," on cattle, manuring, crop rotation, the cultivation of grapes, and the improvement of pastures and meadows.[32]

The war disrupted Alison's life and work. He preached on the occasion of the blockade of Boston, and he delivered a Fast Day sermon on 20 July 1775.[33] The college buildings were taken over by American troops in 1776–77, and by the British in 1777–78, disturbing the pupils, forcing the teachers from their rooms, filling the yard with supplies and refuse, and generally interrupting "the important Business of Education." In February 1777 in a letter to his son Benjamin he voiced uncertainty about his future, saying that he had

> some notion of Removing either to the Fort [Augusta?] or to Munsey to settle for life, for provisions & all things are so dear that we cannot live on our salaries and we have

---

[30] Stiles, *Itineraries,* 421–22.
[31] *Pa. Chronicle,* 10 April 1769; *Pa. Gaz.,* 22 March, 14 June, 8 Nov. 1770, 10 Jan., 21 March 1771.
[32] Alison, "Hints for the Philosophical Society," 2 April 1773 (APS Archives); printed in Phila. Soc. for Promoting Agriculture, *Memoirs,* VI (1939), 127ff.
[33] Christopher Marshall, Remembrancer, 1 June 1774 (HSP); *PMHB,* II (1878), 66.

no hopes of getting them Enlarged. On one or the other of these places I can, by farming, have the necessaries of life while I live, & I cannot get more nor so much, as things now go in Philada.

By early fall things were worse. The British army had occupied Philadelphia, the College closed, and Alison fled the city. "I have three diffrent [sic] times changed my place of Residence, to avoid the enemy," he wrote his friend and colleague John Ewing on 24 October 1777, "& was almost as often within a few miles of these unmerciful plunderers."[34]

As it turned out he did not settle on the Susquehanna, but returned to Philadelphia. In February 1779 he joined other members in signing a call for the resumption of meetings of the Philosophical Society.

Alison died in Philadelphia on 28 November 1779. The funeral services were conducted by the Reverend Mr. Ewing. America was "greatly indebted" to Alison, Ewing declared, "for that diffusion of light and knowledge, and that spirit of liberty and inquiry, which this day places many of her sons upon a level with those of the oldest nations of Europe."[35]

Alison was survived by his wife, Hannah Armitage, daughter of Benjamin and Elizabeth Armitage, and by two daughters and two sons, Benjamin and Francis, both of whom attended the Academy and College of Philadelphia and became physicians.[36] Never accepting of the institution of slavery,[37] Alison provided that his slaves be freed.

> With respect to my black servants I cannot find that the Scriptures any where condemns Slavery as what is in all cases unjust & unlawful but rather seem to tolerate & give it Countenance, but as I am convinced that it leads bad men into Inhumanity, injustice & oppression, & is beneath the benevolence of the christian religion & that freedom & liberty in civil government that men generally desire, I will that my black wench called Rose receive her freedom dues & be free forever as soon as she is thirty years of age.[38]

His estate was small; he had never lived above "pinching poverty," but he owned busts of Shakespeare and Pope. He left also the reputation, universally held and often expressed, of being

---

[34] 1 *Pa. Arch.,* V, 198–99; *PMHB,* XXIV (1900), 122; Alison to John Ewing, 24 Oct. 1777, Dreer Coll., Am. Clergy, I (HSP).
[35] John Ewing, "A Sermon delivered . . . at the funeral of the Rev. Dr. Francis Allison," *Assembly's Missionary Mag.; or Evangelical Intelligencer,* I (1805), 458.
[36] On Francis Alison, Jr. see the sketch by Samuel X Radbill in *Bull. Hist. Med.,* IX (1941), 243–57.
[37] In 1768 Alison had objected that student disputations at Yale accepted the lawfulness of slavery. "I am assured the Common father of all men will severely plead a Controversy against these Colonies for enslaving Negros [sic], and keeping their children born British subjects, in perpetual slavery—and possibly for this wickedness God threatens us with slavery. . . ." Stiles, *Itineraries,* 434.
[38] Alison, Will, 1 July 1777, Will Book R, 316; Inventory, 26 June 1780 (Register of Wills, Phila.). Alison's books were sold at auction. *Pa. Packet,* 18 July 1780.

the first who introduced real learning, not only Latin and Greek . . . but also diffused the knowledge of all the *liberal arts and sciences,* which enlarge and improve the mind; not only through Pennsylvania, but in all the neighbouring States; so that almost all men of *real learning,* in these parts of the world, who are *natives* of the country, were either taught by him, or his *pupils,* or their scholars. . . ."[39]

JOHN TENNENT (1710–1748)
AMERICA PHILOSOPHICAL SOCIETY
(CORRESPONDING MEMBER): 1744

"DOCR. TENNANT" appears as a corresponding member on the list of "Members of the American Philosophical Society instituted in the Year 1743" which the officers of that Society sent the American Society on 12 February 1768. On the list as copied into the American Society minutes someone wrote after "Tennant" the word "Dead." When membership lists were exchanged at the time of the union of the two societies in December 1768, the name "Tennant" had been dropped from the Philosophical Society's roll, and it did not appear again in any official record.

Who "Docr. Tennant" was has been a matter of some speculation and doubt. Two names have been suggested, but neither identification is acceptable. Dr. John Van Brugh Tennent, F.R.S., professor of midwifery in King's College, New York, although otherwise an eligible candidate, was only six years old in 1743; and, as he did not die until 1770, his name would have been included in any list of members of the Philosophical Society made in 1768. "Docr. Tennant" was also identified for some years on the Society's then-current list of "Former [i.e., deceased or resigned] Resident Members" as the Reverend Mr. Gilbert Tennent, minister of the Second Presbyterian Church of Philadelphia. This seems an unlikely nomination, for as Gilbert Tennent was a resident of Philadelphia after 1743 he would have been a resident, not a corresponding, member; his interests were not those of the philosophers; and he does not appear to have been known as "Doctor." Moreover, members of the Philosophical Society would have known that this Tennent, who was a prominent Philadelphian, had died in that city in 1764, and their secretary would

---

[39] [Wilson], "The Character of the Rev. Francis Allison," loc. cit. In similar vein Jacob Duché, Jr. wrote that Alison had "the honour of being among the first that introduced Science into this heretofore untutored wilderness." (*Observations on a Variety of Subjects* [Phila., 1774], 26). He was, "in short," declared Dr. Ewing, "one of the brightest luminaries that ever shone in this western world." "Sermon," loc. cit., 459. On his poverty, see Stiles, *Itineraries,* 431–32.

not have kept his name on the membership roll prepared for the American Society in 1768. It is more than probable that the philosophers' "Docr. Tennant" was John Tennent, practitioner of physic in Virginia and London.

He was born in Scotland in 1710. Of his schooling nothing is known beyond his statement that he was bred up to physic and surgery "from his early Years." When he was 14 he was sent out to Virginia in response to a call from Dr. Mark Bannerman of Middlesex County, who needed an assistant; and upon Bannerman's death in 1728, young Tennent, then 18 years old, succeeded to the practice. He appears to have practiced satisfactorily,[1] settled at Port Royal in Caroline County, married one Dorothy Paul, and acquired some land.[2] Having learned the uses of rattlesnake root from the Indians and noted its operation in cases of snakebite, where the blood was viscid and coagulated, Tennent reasoned that the root should be useful also in cases of pleurisy or peripneumony, where the blood was in the same condition. Accordingly he administered the root to several patients in the winter of 1734–35; its apparent success convinced him of its general usefulness; and in August 1736 Tennent published an *Essay on the Pleurisy,* the first of many pamphlets that dealt directly or indirectly with the subject.[3]

Pleurisy to Tennent was "the most fatal Disease that affects the Constitution of the Inhabitants of this Country." He briefly explained its causes, effects, and common methods of cure, with an appraisal of the usefulness, deficiencies, and dangers

---

[1] Most biographical sketches of Tennent state that he was born about 1700 and came to Virginia from England in 1725. In *Truth Stifled, and an Appeal, to the Genius of the Ancient Romans* (London, 1741), 36–37, Tennent makes statements from which the facts given here are drawn. In his "Memorial . . . to the learned, impartial, and judicious World," *Va. Gaz.,* 22 Sept.–13 Oct. 1738, he quotes "Nemo me impune lacesset" as "My Country's motto," i.e., Scotland's. See also "Memorial and Remonstrance, to the Northern Colonies," *Pa.Gaz.,* 19 July–2 Aug. 1739.

Biographical data may be found in Wyndham B. Blanton, *Medicine in Virginia in the Eighteenth Century* (Richmond, 1931), 119–29, where title-pages of most of Tennent's pamphlets are reproduced in facsimile; and in Richard M. Jellison, "Dr. John Tennent and the Universal Specific," *Bulletin of the History of Medicine,* XXXVII (1963), 336–46.

[2] *Va. Gaz.,* 1 Oct. 1736.

[3] The popular medical manual *Every Man His Own Doctor,* first printed at Williamsburg and frequently reprinted there and elsewhere in the following years (see Robert B. Austin, *Early American Medical Imprints . . . 1668–1820* [Washington, 1961]), has been attributed to Tennent though not always without doubts. ("The Colonial Scene—1602–1800," Am. Antiq. Soc., Proc., n.s., LX [1950], 118–19). I doubt this was Tennent's work for several reasons: First, in none of his many publications or in his appeals to the Virginia Assembly and British Parliament did Tennent ever say or hint that he was the author of *Every Man* or indeed of any work, except the *Essay on the Pleurisy,* whose aim was to make medical knowledge more widely known and easily accessible. Second, the author of *Every Man His Own Doctor* made no change in its text after the publication of *Essay on the Pleurisy,* as would have been appropriate and might have been expected were the two pamphlets from the same pen. Third, Tennent's contemporaries seem not to have believed he was the author of *Every Man;* at least Benjamin Franklin, when he reprinted that work in 1736, wrote, on his own initiative, a résumé of Tennent's *Essay on the Pleurisy,* which he said was by "a Physician in Virginia"—from the tone and context apparently not the author of the principal text (*Every Man*). *Franklin Papers,* II, 155–58.

of each. Then, citing the writings of Dr. Richard Mead on the bite of vipers, Tennent presented snakeroot as a specific for pleurisy; he had discovered it by reasoning, and proved it by experience, to be "almost absolutely certain in that Disease, when timely apply'd." Finally Tennent gave instructions for administering the drug and treating the patient, concluding with the opinion that the root "may be managed to good Purpose in many Diseases, and that it will have extraordinary Effects in the Gout, Consumption, and Dropsy; and is certainly, an effectual Remedy against the Bite of a mad Dog." Copies of the pamphlet, with samples of the root, were sent to Mead in London and to others.[4]

Tennent's *Essay* was received by most physicians with skepticism and hostility. Some challenged his reasoning, others were unconvinced by the few case histories he could offer; while the fact that the name rattlesnake root was given to several unrelated plants led to confusion. Most persons assumed that what Tennent called rattlesnake root was "Seneca rattlesnake root" (*Polygala senega*); but he seems sometimes to have meant "Virginian snake root" (*Aristolochia serpentaria*). A basic scientific objection was that the argument from analogy and the doctrine of specifics, which Tennent used, had been generally rejected. One critic who could not accept the notion of a specific, eloquently adjured his countrymen "not to be too busy with so dangerous an Engine, lest therewith endeavouring to defend the Fort, they blow up the Capitol, the Fund of Treasure, the Magazine of Safety, and the Support of Life: Let me advise you," he continued, shifting the metaphor, "to beware how you engage in so extraordinary a Voyage, where are innumerable Rocks, and the Shipwreck Death."[5]

Personal feelings as well entered into expressions of opposition. Some older men resented that so young a man as Tennent should have won considerable fame by his pamphlet; they were understandably piqued when he published directions for using rattlesnake root, with the implied criticism of those who kept their prescriptions secret. Their resentment only increased when, a few months after the publication of the *Essay,* Tennent provided an apothecary in Williamsburg and a shopkeeper in Yorktown with supplies of rattlesnake root for free distribution.[6] Tennent's repeated explanations of his views and defense of his conduct did nothing to win him professional support, although prominent laymen were his friends. The fact is that Tennent was not his own best advocate. His scientific training

---

[4] *Essay on the Pleurisy* (Williamsburg, 1736), passim; *Va. Gaz.,* 8 Oct. 1736. Professor Joseph Ewan of the Missouri Botanical Garden has explained (1989) that *Polygala senega,* named by Linnaeus in *Species Plantarum,* 1753, is a member of the milkwort family, and is often confused with *Aristolochia serpentaria* L., which is of the birthwort family, a somewhat vine-like herb. Other reputed snakeroots were genera of the lily and mint families.
[5] Tennent, "Representation to the Public," *Va. Gaz.,* 4 March 1737; Philo-Mathesis, [Reply to Dr. Tennent's Representation], ibid., 10 June 1737.
[6] Ibid., 5 Nov. 1736.

had been meager, and his character was in some respects weak. He was young, ambitious, imprudent. He condemned the materia medica as "that overgrown and complicated *Monster*" which had "so long fed and fattened itself under the Protection . . . of our *solemn medicinal Quality,* at the Expence of our Pockets; and . . . of our Lives too."[7] He spoke no less freely about his professional colleagues on other occasions, as he later admitted, telling truths he might better have concealed, and paying neither deference nor respect to their modes of practice if he thought them wrong.[8] On the other hand, though often foolish, Tennent was not a self-seeker. He seems really to have meant to do good to the sick, and really to have believed that he was acting in their best interests. Admittedly he was eager for money; but when he appealed to the legislature it was not for the price to reveal a secret nostrum, but for a reward for having already published what he—and some others—believed was an effective remedy. He had reason to complain of a government that neglected him while it paid Joanna Stephens £5000 for a worthless "cure" for the stone. A wiser, stronger man would have avoided the paths that led Tennent to destruction; an unscrupulous one might have achieved wealth and a kind of success and social position. Tennent ended in debtors' prison and the Old Bailey, and the tragedy of his career is that he only dimly apprehended that he, not others, had put himself there.

In June 1737, just as the issue between Tennent and his Virginia critics was joined, Tennent went to England, scribbling one defense on shipboard just before the vessel sailed, sending out another the moment he came ashore in London.[9] To influential Englishmen like Sir Hans Sloane, Dr. Richard Mead, and Lord Islay (later Duke of Argyll), Tennent had letters of introduction from Governor Gooch, former Governor Spotswood, and others, testifying to the efficacy of snakeroot from personal knowledge. "We owe the knowledge of this powerful Vegetable to that Gentlemans discovery," William Byrd told Sloane. "He has acted generously in publishing it to the World for the service of mankind, and if upon Tryal it be found to merit the character he gives of it, Our Assembly will reward Him very handsomely."[10] These letters were initially of great use. Mead judged Tennent "ingenious and industrious," Islay thought Parliament should reward him for his discovery, while Sloane befriended him and undertook to test the snakeroot. Tennent had a stroke of good fortune when Dr. James Monro, a physician to Bethlehem

---

[7] Tennent, *Detection of a Conspiracy, to suppress a* General Good *in* Physic, *and to promote Error and Ignorance in that important Science: Being the Singular Case of John Tennent, M.D.* . . . (London, 1743), 4.
[8] Ibid., 8.
[9] [Reply to Philo-Mathesis], 26 June 1737, *Va. Gaz.*, 15 July 1737; [On the Rattlesnake Root], 12 Oct. 1737, ibid., 16 Dec. 1737.
[10] Byrd to Sloane, 31 May, 20 Aug., 1737, 2 *Wm. & Mary Quar.*, I (1921), 195–98; Tennent to Sloane, 28 Sept. 1737, ibid., V (1925), 107–08.

Hospital, fell ill, and, other doctors and remedies having failed, allowed Tennent to treat him with snakeroot. When Monro recovered, he, Mead, and Thomas Pellett, president of the Royal College of Physicians, joined in recommending Tennent to the faculty of the University of Edinburgh for the degree of doctor of medicine.[11]

Despite this powerful patronage, Tennent quickly became an object of criticism and opposition in Britain as he had been in Virginia. He lived extravagantly—his enemies charged he kept a coach and four and passed himself off as the great American doctor—and so fell into debt. His theories were rebutted or derided. "Nothing will go down," he complained, "but a mathematical Demonstration"; but "the Subject of Physick," he insisted, "admits of no such Method of Prosecution."[12] His sometime friends began to snub or ignore him, or pushed him over onto others, treating him, Tennent wrote, as though he were "a Dog in a Dancing-School toss'd about and bandied like a *Tennis-ball* from side to side."[13] He went to Scotland, and though he published at Edinburgh his *Epistle to Dr. Richard Mead* on snakeroot, the University faculty did nothing for him. Thereafter he affected disdain for an Edinburgh degree, which was often conferred "mercenarily," saying that the recommendation of Drs. Pellett, Mead, and Monro was all he wanted.[14] In the spring of 1738 Tennent returned home to Virginia, with little to show for his trip to Britain.[15]

Within a few weeks Tennent issued proposals for a treatise on the diseases of Virginia and the neighboring colonies, which he said he had worked on while in Britain; but subscriptions were not forthcoming and the book never appeared.[16] The medical profession remained hostile, though some laymen were convinced of the efficacy of snakeroot and occasionally one testified to its usefulness.[17] Tennent took action to defend his discovery against the criticism and attacks of his fellow-physicians, whom he now called contemptuously "Pulse Pads and Bedside Banditti." Those who opposed the introduction of snakeroot he damned as quacks "in

---

[11] Tennent, *Truth Stifled*, 21–22, 24–25.
[12] Tennent, "A Memorial, humbly addressed to the learned, impartial, and judicious World," *Va. Gaz.*, 22 Sept.–13 Oct. 1738.
[13] Tennent, *Detection of a Conspiracy*, 6.
[14] "Then I must take Notice, that in this Country, and many others, the Term graduate Physician, makes a very great Noise; and a Man under this Denomination, whether he really is such, or not, if he only with an Air of Assurance assumes it, passes instantly for a Man of great Skill, Parts, &c. 'til Experience opens the Eyes of the Credulous; and, upon a proper Scrutiny, the graduate Gentleman is detected to be lately translated from a Station in Life very different from his present State of regular *Doctor*. How far true that may be, may be known without a very remote Retrospect; for it often happens, and will be allowed, that the too great Fondness of the World to that Epithet, is the Cause of their being frequently trapp'd out of their Lives." Tennent, "A Memorial . . . to the learned, impartial, and judicious World," *Va. Gaz.*, 22 Sept.–13 Oct. 1738.
[15] Tennent, *Truth Stifled*, 26–28.
[16] *Va. Gaz.*, 30 June 1738; *Pa. Gaz.*, 10 Aug. 1738.
[17] Ibid., 16 June 1738.

the most strict Sense of the Word"—those who were educated and knew better were "volunteer Quacks," the unlettered and ignorant were "simple ones."[18] He even raised his claims for the snakeroot; and in the fall of 1738 appealed to the Virginia Assembly for a reward for having published his discovery. The Lower House, however, motivated by personal as well as scientific objections, turned him down. The Governor and Council then took the unusual step of asking the Burgesses to reconsider; and on 22 November they rather grudgingly voted £100. The vote was a vindication, but Tennent had expected—and needed—a greater sum; and even this paltry reward did him no good, for, as soon as the bill passed, two creditors appeared to claim the money, and the Council divided it between them.[19] In a long "Memorial and Remonstrance to the Northern Colonies," dated 28 March 1739, Tennent called for a reconsideration of his case.[20]

Disappointed in his prospects in America, hoping for better treatment from Parliament, Tennent determined to leave the country for good, and he returned to England in July 1739.[21] Some encouraging news awaited him. Louis Lémery, Bernard de Jussieu, and Henri-Louis Duhamel du Monceau of the Jardin de Plantes, to whom he had sent a specimen of snakeroot in January 1738, had reported on their tests of it in generally favorable terms. This report, printed in the *Mémoires* of the Académie Royale des Sciences, was summarized in the Edinburgh *Medical Essays and Observations.*[22] Jussieu himself told Thomas Bond, then studying medicine in Paris, that the snakeroot had met with surprising success and was highly regarded; and Bond sent this word to his brother Phineas, who gave it to Franklin for the *Pennsylvania Gazette,* from which other American papers reprinted it.[23] Otherwise, however, Tennent met with a cold reception. Dr. Mead was no longer friendly; and others now closed their doors to him, paid his discovery no attention, and sometimes even perpetuated slanders against him.[24] Parliament was unresponsive, and even Sloane asserted that snakeroot had proved to be less effective than had been reported, and suggested that Tennent had claimed too much for it. William Byrd, championing Tennent to the end, assured Sloane that he had found the root useful and suggested that the sea air had reduced its power; but, alluding to Sloane's other point, confessed sadly that "the misfortune is, when a Plant has some remarkable Vertue, People are apt to cry it up for a universall Remedy, which is an

---

[18] Tennent, "A Memorial . . . to the learned, impartial, and judicious World," *Va. Gaz.,* 22 Sept.–13 Oct. 1738.
[19] Tennent, *Truth Stifled,* 29–34; *Va. Gaz.,* 22 Dec. 1738; "Journals of the Council of Virginia in Executive Sessions, 1737–63," *Va. Mag. Hist. Biog.,* XIV (1907), 236–38.
[20] Dated Fredericksburg, Va., 28 March 1739, published in *Pa. Gaz.,* 19 July–2 Aug. 1739.
[21] Tennent, *Truth Stifled,* 41; Tennent, *Detection of a Conspiracy,* 7.
[22] Duhamel, "Essais sur l'usage de la Plante, nommée . . . *Polygala vulgaris* . . . ," *Hist. de l'Académie des Sciences,* 1739, pp. 135–39; *Medical Essays and Observations* (Edinburgh), V, pt. 2 (1744), 906–08.
[23] *Franklin Papers,* II, 239–40; *Va. Gaz.,* 17 Aug. 1739.
[24] Tennent, *Detection of a Conspiracy,* 7; Tennent, *Truth Stifled,* 41.

honour Providence has done to no single medicine, because it would make us lazy in our Searches into Nature." [25]

Tennent responded with more free-wheeling criticism of the profession and his fellow-physicians. He charged them with inconsistency and self-seeking, and sadly and angrily compared his case with Joanna Stephens': he had published his remedy to the world, but she had kept hers a secret and been rewarded by Parliament to boot. "To what Purpose are Men that are designed for Physicians educated at Universities," he demanded, "but to be able to reason upon Phenomena in Nature, and so make Discoveries for the Use of their fellow Creatures?" [26]

When the year 1740 opened, Tennent was in debtors' prison, "troubled with Hecktick heats, Coughs, and Nocturnal Sweats." Sloane helped him get out, and Tennent, having been recommended for appointment as physician-general to the forces in the West Indies, prepared to go to Jamaica, where he hoped to retrieve his reputation and fortune. He did not get the post, nor the lesser one of assistant to the physician-general, which he would have accepted.[27] He had exhausted his credit with men who might have helped him.

This disappointment produced a spate of new pamphlets, attacking the use of vinegar and other acids in the British West Indies fleet, a prescription recommended by the Royal College of Physicians. Vinegar, Tennent asserted in a pamphlet dedicated to the Prime Minister Sir Robert Walpole, "may do more Mischief than even *the best Spanish Ships of War*." The best preventive and remedy was, of course, Seneca rattlesnake root.[28] He made the point repeatedly in the next few years.

In America, meanwhile, rattlesnake root continued to enjoy some reputation, at least among laymen. Franklin reprinted in *Poor Richard's Almanac* "Dr. Tennent's infallible Cure for the Pleurisy," as did South Carolina almanacs as late as 1768; and Franklin sold the root at his printing office; so did James Parker at his shops at Woodbridge and New York.[29] Franklin and other Americans at this time might very well have considered Tennent's discovery sufficient to warrant its author's election to the American Philosophical Society; and Tennent may have been one of those "others" in Virginia who, Franklin told Cadwallader Colden, were expected soon to join.

About this time Tennent obtained a medical degree somewhere. At least his publications of 1742 and afterwards all identify him as "John Tennent, M.D." The

---

[25] Byrd to Sloane, 10 April 1741, 2 *Wm. & Mary Quar.*, I (1921), 199–200.
[26] Tennent, *Truth Stifled*, 43; see also, Tennent, *A Reprieve from Death*, 32.
[27] Tennent to Sloane, 1, 24 Jan., 12 Feb., 1 April 1740, 2 *Wm. & Mary Quar.*, III (1923), 211; V (1925), 108–10; Tennent, *Detection of a Conspiracy*, 8.
[28] Tennent, *A Reprieve from Death: in Two Physical Chapters* (London, 1741), 4; Tennent, *Physical Enquiries* (London, 1742), sec. 1; *N. Y. Weekly Journal*, 26 Sept. 1742.
[29] *Franklin Papers*, II, 254–56; *Pa. Gaz.*, 3 July 1740; Tennent, *An Essay on the Pleurisy* (N. Y., 1742), 40; Francisco Guerra, *American Medical Bibliography* (N. Y., 1962), 306–07, 310, 333.

honor may have seemed an empty one, for his reputation and career were on the verge of collapse. "Traduc'd, circumvented, and at last betray'd," without friends or practice to speak of, he fell more deeply into debt—in 1741 he owed a total of £500 to fifteen or sixteen creditors.[30]

For a time he earned a few guineas by selling his prescriptions to the notorious quack Dr. Joshua Ward; but Ward was too much a rascal to be trusted, and the two men soon fell out. A prospect of relief appeared in the shape of a rich widow, whom he married on 3 November 1741. They began to furnish a house in Craven Street; but this was a signal for his creditors to descend upon him. "The Consequences were, many Arrests, Uneasiness in my Wife's Relations and herself, Animosities, Vexations, and at last she left me."[31] She left him not because of his debts (which apparently he had freely admitted before the marriage), but because she discovered that he had contracted a Fleet marriage a year or two before. Mrs. Tennent sued for annulment, and Tennent was indicted for bigamy.[32]

Apparently contrite, conscious of all his follies, and freely admitting the irregularities of his conduct, Tennent on the eve of his trial wrote still another pamphlet—*Detection of a Conspiracy*—in which, however, he ended by blaming others as well as himself.

Of Tennent's life thereafter little is known. In 1745 he brought out one more pamphlet, *Physical Disquisitions.* Prepared as early as 1742 and addressed not to the Royal College of Physicians but to Charles, duke of Richmond, who was a physician as well as a peer, it was a summing up of all he had said about snakeroot and vinegar and contained a proposal for the reform of the medical profession. Medical progress, he asserted, was impeded by the selfish interest of physicians and apothecaries. Successful practice depended "principally on the *Natural Genius;* not so much on understanding of Languages." Prescriptions, he thought, should be written in plain English, and the profession regulated by law.[33]

Tennent died in London on 27 October 1748.[34] He left at least one son in Virginia, John, Jr., who attended the College of William and Mary in 1754 and appealed to the Virginia Assembly in 1760 to make him a grant in recognition of his father's contribution, so that he might continue his education. No reward was forthcoming, but young Tennent managed to get to Britain, where he studied medicine and married a Scottish girl at Edinburgh. During the American Revolution he held a surgeon's commission in the Virginia troops.[35]

---

[30] Tennent, *Detection of a Conspiracy,* 1, et passim.
[31] Tennent, *A Brief Account of the Case of John Tennent, M.D.* (London, 1742), reproduced in facsimile in Blanton, *Medicine in Virginia,* 124–25.
[32] Ibid.; Tennent, *Detection of a Conspiracy.*
[33] Tennent, *Physical Enquiries,* 69–70; Tennent, *Physical Disquisitions . . .* (London, 1745).
[34] *Gent. Mag.,* XVIII (1748), 524.
[35] Blanton, *Medicine in Virginia,* 75; 2 *Wm. & Mary Quar.,* I (1921), 142.

JOHN CLAYTON (1694–1773)

AMERICAN PHILOSOPHICAL SOCIETY
(CORRESPONDING MEMBER): 1744

JOHN CLAYTON, clerk of the courts of Gloucester County, Virginia, and author with Gronovius of the *Flora Virginica,* is believed to have been a corresponding member of the American Philosophical Society on the evidence of two letters referring to that organization and its members. On 4 October 1745 John Bartram wrote Cadwallader Colden, who, pleased at his election, had told Peter Collinson about the Society:

> I find by my correspondents in Europe that they have been informed of our Phylosophycal Society & have great expectation of fine accounts therefrom tho I durst not so much as mention it to my correspondents for fear it should turn out but poorly; but I find thee mentioned [it] to Collinson, hee to Catesby, & hee to Gronovius, which was to him from Claton these accounts I showed Franklin & he layeth the blame on us.[1]

John Bartram was no grammarian; by "which was to him from Claton" he may have meant only that Clayton, having heard of the Society, told Gronovius about it. On the basis of these letters from Catesby and Clayton, however, Gronovius believed that the latter was a member, for on 17 April 1745 he wrote Linnaeus, "In Philadelphia they have established a Literary Society, and the most worthy members adorn it, such as Clayton, Colden, Mitchell, Bartram, and all who are eager to promote natural history."[2]

On the other hand, no record or memory of Clayton's election existed in 1768, when the Society prepared a list of its surviving members of 1743–46. The names of Colden and Mitchell are on the list, as are those of John Tennent and Francis Alison; but not Clayton's. Nor was he elected to the Society after its revival, though he was probably the most distinguished botanist in the colonies at the time. It is, in short, not conclusive, despite Gronovius' belief, that Clayton was a member.

He was born in England in the fall of 1694, the first of three sons of John and Lucy Clayton, of a family of substantial means and rank. His father, who had studied at Eton and Cambridge, had been called to the bar in 1691; his uncle Jasper Clayton rose to be a lieutenant general in the army and was appointed governor of Gibraltar; his aunt Charlotte married Lord Lovelace, Governor of New York and

---

[1] *Colden Papers,* III (N.-Y. Hist. Soc., *Colls.,* 1919), 159–60.
[2] Linnaean Corres., V, 484 (Linnean Society of London), quoted by Edmund Berkeley and Dorothy Berkeley, *John Clayton, Pioneer of American Botany* (Chapel Hill, [1963]). Most of the references cited below were found before publication of the Berkeleys' biography, which this sketch follows unashamedly and gratefully.

New Jersey in 1708; while their father, the botanist's grandfather, Sir John Clayton, also a barrister, was an original Fellow of the Royal Society, a friend of John Evelyn, and a member of the court of William III. Of young John's education nothing certain has been learned. He had a sound classical training and may very well have gone to Eton, as a younger brother did, and to Cambridge, as several members of his family had, and as he hoped his oldest son should do. His name does not, however, appear in the roll of Cambridge matriculates.

Leaving his boys in England to complete their education, the elder Clayton emigrated to Virginia in 1705, possibly in the party of the newly-appointed lieutenant governor, for by the end of the year he was serving as that official's secretary. In Virginia Clayton quickly acquired a legal practice, more offices, and rank. He was appointed registrar of the Court of Admiralty in 1706, attorney general of the Province in 1713, and judge of the Court of Admiralty in 1718; and he was several times elected to the House of Burgesses. His three sons eventually followed him to America. Young John may have come out to Virginia as early as 1715, when he would have finished his formal education at home; he was certainly there in 1720, when, at the age of 26, doubtless through his father's influence, he was appointed clerk of the courts of Gloucester County, a post he held for 53 years until his death. This was no sinecure—he doubtless read some law, for at least once, in 1732, he was appointed to examine candidates for admission to the bar—but he could delegate some of the work to a deputy, and so have time for his farm, garden, and family. In 1723, at Ware Church, Gloucester Court House, he married Elizabeth, daughter of Major Henry and Ann (Beverly) Whiting of "Elmington," Gloucester County; they had eight children, of whom two died young. Major Whiting was the son-in-law of Peter Beverly, Clayton's predecessor as clerk.

Clayton lived comfortably, as orders to his London agents show. Portraits of Sir John and his family by Godfrey Kneller hung on the walls. He had the income from his 450–acre plantation, the fees of his office, and, after his father's death in 1737, a generous inheritance that included rents from lands in England. Clayton had time for scientific correspondence and for his own botanical researches. In these endeavors a marked influence was exerted on him by Mark Catesby, whom his father knew, and whom he might have met as a young man before Catesby left Virginia in 1719. Clayton provided the older man with plants and with a specimen and description of the whip-poor-will for the *Natural History of Carolina*. By 1730, when Clayton was well launched on his botanical career, however, there were only two or three other planters with whom he could share his enthusiasm—Dr. John Mitchell of Urbanna, William Byrd II of Westover, and John Custis. None of these lived close enough for frequent visits, and if Clayton corresponded with them, the correspondence has not survived. Like many other men of science in colonial America, he was physically isolated, and with one exception his closest continuing scientific ties were with Europeans.

Not later than 1736 Catesby introduced Clayton to the Dutch physician and naturalist John Frederick Gronovius; and, at Catesby's suggestion, Clayton began to send over large numbers of Virginia plants for identification. Parcels and accompanying notes went off in a steady stream to London, where Catesby forwarded them to Leiden. In 1738 Clayton sent his correspondent "A Catalogue of Plants, Fruits, and Trees Native to Virginia," in which he identified and described the species he had thus far collected. Gronovius appreciated at once the value of this list, extended and revised it, and published it at Leiden in 1739 as *Flora Virginica*. This was done without prior consultation with Clayton, Gronovius explaining rather unconvincingly that the catalogue was too valuable not to be published and that, because of distance, there had not been time to consult the author. However, both on the title page and in his introduction, which was in the form of a letter to Clayton, Gronovius gave the American full credit for his work, and their contemporaries recognized it as a joint production. Although possibly astonished, Clayton was not displeased by Gronovius' action; he continued to correspond in friendly terms as heretofore and enjoyed the reputation the book gave him in the learned world. In 1743 Gronovius issued Part II of the *Flora*, which added 300 species to the 600 catalogued in Part I. Linnaeus relied heavily upon this work in *Species Plantarum* and later works. Of eastern North American species perhaps 400–500 rest for their Linnaean typification on the specimens collected by Clayton and described by Gronovius in the first edition of the *Flora*.[3]

When Clayton began his correspondence with Gronovius, the latter was in close communication with Linnaeus, who spent the years 1735–38 in Holland, where he received the degree of doctor of medicine at the University of Harderwijk. Thus the Swedish botanist knew about Clayton's work and saw many of his specimens. He gave Gronovius aid in naming American plants, and in appreciation Gronovius frequently sent Virginia seeds and plants to Uppsala. Thus many species first described by Linnaeus were actually discovered by Clayton. Not unmindful of the latter's contribution, Linnaeus graciously acknowledged the importance of his work. He sent Clayton a copy of his *Hortus Cliffortianus* when it appeared in 1737 and named the "spring beauty" of Virginia *Claytonia;* and in 1747 he proposed him for election to the Royal Swedish Academy of Sciences. Clayton was elected at the same meeting with Peter Collinson of London and Bernard de Jussieu of Paris. Not one to scramble after honors, Clayton was pleased and grateful. "Your works," he assured Linnaeus in acknowledging the election, "especially *Hort. Clif., Gen. Plan.,* and *Fl. Lap.,* are beside me night and day."

John Clayton was soon drawn into the natural history circle that centered around Peter Collinson, the London Quaker merchant, who did more than any-

---

[3] M. L. Fernald, "The 'Flora Virginica' of Gronovius," *Chronica Botanica*, VI (1940), 27–28.

one in the second third of the century to put naturalists of every country in touch with one another. He encouraged and advised them, sent them seeds and plants and books, found them customers and patrons. He encouraged Clayton's correspondence with Gronovius, introduced Clayton to John Bartram of Philadelphia, and put him in touch with Alexander Garden of Charleston, Cadwallader Colden of New York, and the Reverend Mr. Jared Eliot of Killingworth, Connecticut, who was making experiments with wheat and barley.[4] Of his own garden at Mill Hill Collinson was pleased to say that a walk in it reminded him of absent friends—that fine spruce and larch of Colden, that "Curious Firr from Mount Ida" of the Duke of Northumberland, and for "those pretty Fringe Trees, Halesias & Stuartia all Great Beauties I must thank my Fr'd Mr Clayton the Great Botanist of America."

More lowly plants than these were sometimes in the shipments from Virginia. Clayton sent Collinson a number of specimens of moss, which the latter gave to Johann Jakob Dillenius, professor of botany at Oxford, and 20 of them were listed in Dillenius' *Historia Muscorum,* 1741. Collinson read at least one of Clayton's letters to the Royal Society. It was on the "smoky weather" of America, with comments on whirlwinds, sheet lightning, and other meteorological phenomena, and a postscript on hummingbirds. Too diffuse and merely descriptive for the *Philosophical Transactions,* it was printed in the *Gentleman's Magazine.* Rejecting commonly-held notions concerning the cause of such weather, such as smoke from the tar kilns of North Carolina and the fires made by Indians when hunting, Clayton suggested that the appearance was a "highly rarefied fog, or suspended vapours, whose minute particles, or vesiculae of water, are kept at too great a distance to coalesce, or out of the sphere of each other's attractive power, by the subtile, active element of fire, and intermixed also with dry sulphureous exhalations."[5] In the *Gentleman's Magazine,* too, appeared dissents by Clayton and John Bartram from a view propounded by Professor Charles Alston of Edinburgh that plants are not bisexual and that male and female parts are not necessary for reproduction. "Surprized" that anyone should reject the concept of sexuality in plants, Clayton mentioned botanical authorities to the contrary and cited his own observations and experiments. "Then as to specimens I sent you of the bastard quarnoclif [read: quamoclit], and other bastard or mule plants," he concluded,

> is there not all the reason in the world from thence, and a multitude of other irregular vegetable impregnations, well known to all botanists, and some gardeners, to conclude, that the same law is established in the main, tho' with some little variety in the

---

[4] Collinson to Eliot, 1 March 1754, in Harry J. Carman and Rexford G. Tugwell, eds., *American Husbandry* (N. Y., 1934), 213.
[5] *Gent. Mag.,* XXII (1752), 262–63.

circumstances, by the great author of Nature, for the continuance of the species of plants, as for that of animals.[6]

By this time Clayton and Bartram were good friends through correspondence. The first time he visited Virginia in 1738 Bartram had passed through Gloucester, but found Clayton "gone toward the mountain to seek after some land"—a business journey, apparently, which Clayton improved by botanizing. The Pennsylvanian had an opportunity to examine the garden, however; he thought Clayton's and Custis' the "best furnished with variety of plants" in Virginia, but inferior to the Pennsylvania gardens, which were supplied from England, France, Germany, and Holland. Both men regretted their not meeting; but they opened a correspondence which continued for more than a quarter of a century. In 1760 Bartram came to Virginia again; Clayton was delighted with him, and bitterly regretted that the visit was so brief. "As we were just beginning an acquaintance," he wrote Bartram, "the parting with you so soon, made me very melancholly for some time. . . ." In his excitement at his friend's coming, he had forgotten to show Bartram his "pritty large collection" of dried plants, "also a few other natural curiosities."[7]

For some years after the publication of the second part of *Flora Virginica* in 1743, Gronovius talked about issuing a third part, then of bringing out a revised and enlarged edition of the whole. Accordingly Clayton continued to send additional specimens and notes until, rather unaccountably, Gronovius bluntly told him to send no more, as the postage to Holland cost too much. As the years passed, Gronovius turned to other projects and, despite repeated prodding by Collinson, appeared to have abandoned the *Flora.* In the circumstances it was natural that Clayton, who had not stopped collecting and who must have thought himself rebuffed by Gronovius, should have proceeded to prepare a new edition himself. He completed his "Flora Virginiana" in 1757 and sent it the next year to Collinson, who gave it to John Ellis to read. Ellis agreed with the natural history illustrator Georg Dionysius Ehret to make the drawings, and seems to have assumed responsibility for seeing the book through the press. For some reason, nothing happened for three years, though the manuscript was known to be in London. Meanwhile in Leiden, Laurens Theodore Gronovius, the old naturalist's son, undertook the long-awaited revised edition from such notes and specimens of his father's as he and his father could find. Seemingly Laurens Gronovius had no idea, when he completed his father's manuscript in 1761, that Clayton's had been awaiting publication in

---

[6] Ibid., XXV (1755), 407–08. A letter from John Bartram to the same effect appeared in the same issue. Conway Zirkle has pointed out the historical importance of Clayton's letter, in which the word *bastard* is used synonymously with *mule,* which was the contemporary term for *hybrid.* "John Clayton and our Colonial Botany," *Va. Mag. Hist. Biog.,* LXVII (1959), 284–94.
[7] Clayton to Bartram, 23 July 1760, Bartram Papers, II, 1 (HSP).

London for three years. In any event, Gronovius' edition appeared in February 1762. Clayton's was never published.[8]

Like the first edition, the second amply acknowledged that the plants had been found and collected in Virginia and sent to Gronovius by the "Nobilissimus Vir D.D. Johannes Claytonus, Med. Doct. etc. etc." There was not the slightest suggestion of a claim that the work was not, like its predecessor, largely the result of Clayton's collecting and study. Though an improvement on the 1739–43 edition, the 1762 revision did not incorporate all the new specimens that Clayton had sent, the plants gathered west of the Allegheny Mountains, for example; furthermore, though Linnaeus had adopted the binomial system of nomenclature ten years before, the *Flora* unaccountably used polynomials throughout. Clayton's *Flora Virginiana* would probably have been more complete and up-to-date.

Though past 65, Clayton was still able to make botanical expeditions, but his official business and his scientific correspondence were a burden. In 1769, feeling he should have a clerk to assist him, he appealed to his London agents and they sent him a lad, the nephew of one of their employees. Though only 11 years old, John James Beckley had a good hand, was quick with numbers, intelligent, and industrious; and, what was no less important, was well-behaved, healthy, and sprightly, and a welcome companion for the old man. He stayed with Clayton until the latter's death, and went on to become a lawyer, first clerk of the House of Representatives, and first Librarian of Congress. Young Beckley's companionship was the more welcome after the death of Mrs. Clayton, which happened in late 1771 or early 1772.

In the fall of 1772 Clayton made a collecting trip to Orange County. The next year a distinct but final honor came to him. A group of local philosophers in 1773, in imitation of the society at Philadelphia, formed the Virginia Society for the Advancement of Useful Knowledge, and they chose as their first president "John Clayton, Esq., author of the *Flora Virginica*." Some thirty years later, John Page, who was vice-president of the Society, described Clayton as he appeared in his last years:

> When any one . . . described to Mr. Clayton what *he* thought a newly-discovered tree, shrub, plant, or flower, he would, in a modest manner, say, "did you not find it in such a county, and in such and such a place?" On being answered that it was found in that very spot, he would add, that it was called by the Indians (I have been told) so and so; by them used for such and such purposes, and may be found described in such a class of Linnaeus. And sometimes I have heard him say, it was described by Theophrastus, and called, by him, by such a name, in Greek. And such was his desire to obtain complete knowledge of the plants of Virginia, that, notwithstanding his great parsimony, he would offer a reward for any discovery of a plant unknown to him. There seemed to be no part of the learning of his day (I mean about the year 1773) unknown to him. . . .

---

[8] The 1762 edition was reprinted in facsimile by the Arnold Arboretum in 1946.

Clayton died on 15 December 1773—the *Virginia Gazette* of 6 January 1774 reported his death—and he was buried by the side of his wife, simply, as he directed, in the private ground of his plantation. Of his sons, John was settled as a planter at Richmond; William was clerk of the court of New Kent County and a member of the House of Burgesses; Jasper was his father's deputy clerk at Gloucester; and Thomas, who had received a medical degree from Edinburgh, a clever, cheerful, indolent fellow, after trying practice in London, had now settled in Virginia, where he had shared and fed his father's "high relish for witty conversation, and classical allusions." Clayton divided his rather considerable property in land and slaves among his six children; and to his grandsons John Clayton and Thomas Hughes he bequeathed his globes, microscope, and books. Among these, no doubt, were items later described as "two volumes of manuscript, neatly copied and prepared for the press; and a *hortus siccus,* of folio size, with marginal notes, and directions for the engraver, in preparing plates for his proposed work." These volumes may have been the manuscript of the *Flora Virginiana.* A few years later, during the American Revolution, they were sent for safekeeping to William Clayton at New Kent, who lodged them in the clerk's office.[9] They were still there in 1787 when prisoners broke out of the county jail one Sunday night, set fire to it and then set fire to the clerk's office as well. Both buildings were consumed. "Thus perished, not only the records of the county, but the labours of Clayton."[10]

His memory did not perish so quickly. The *Flora Virginica* was his book no less than Gronovius'; plants he collected are still identifiable in the British Museum and the Sherardian Museum at Oxford, while many of the American plants in Linnaeus' *hortus* at Uppsala surely came from Clayton. More than thirty years after his death botanists mentioned his name with respect; André Michaux and Frederick Pursh named new species for him; and one, Benjamin Smith Barton, began—though he did not complete—a revised and extended *Flora Virginica.*

---

[9] "Memorandums of the Life and Writings of Mr. John Clayton, the celebrated Botanist of Virginia," *Phila. Medical and Physical Journal,* II (1805), 141–42.
[10] Ibid., 140–41.

"YOUNG JUNTO"

1750–1766

CHARLES THOMSON
By Charles Willson Peale. *Independence National Historical Park Collection.*

CHARLES THOMSON (1729—1824)
"YOUNG JUNTO": 1750?

CHARLES THOMSON, schoolmaster, was probably a founding member of the "Young Junto" in 1750, as he indicated in a letter to Benjamin Franklin in 1768.[1] When the Junto determined in 1757 to purchase an electrical apparatus and an "Optical Apparatus" by Benjamin Martin, Thomson asked their fellow-member William Franklin, then about to go abroad, to make the purchases in London.[2] Thomson's name appears in the earliest surviving minutes, which begin on 22 September 1758; he was one of the five still-active members of the club when it was re-organized in the summer of 1761; and he was still a member when the Junto trans-

---

[1] *Franklin Papers,* XV, 261–62.
[2] Franklin Mss., XLVIII, 120.

formed itself into the American Society for Promoting and Propagating Useful Knowledge in 1766. Through all those years Thomson remained loyal to the institution and active in its work. He was a principal figure in defining and refining the American Society's purpose in 1767–68 and was the author of plans to enlarge its membership and the scope of its interests. He was elected secretary of the American Society in 1768. In the united Society in 1769 he was also one of the secretaries, and was constant in his attendance for three or four years. He was a member of the standing Committee on Husbandry and American Improvements. He was one of those who observed the Transit of Venus on 3 June 1769 from the observatory in the State-House Yard. As a member of the Society he collected subscriptions in 1769 for the survey of a Delaware-Chesapeake canal. In the following year he subscribed £2 to the Silk Society, in which members of the Philosophical Society were interested; and some years later, when the Silk Society was dissolved, he was on the committee that petitioned the Assembly to transfer its assets to the Philosophical Society. In the years before 1774, while he was active in Society affairs, Thomson served on a number of special committees—to find out how oil was extracted from sunflower seeds, to purchase a pair of globes for the Society's cabinet, to prepare both the first and second volumes of *Transactions,* and to design a seal for the Society. In 1774 he was invited to deliver the Society's anniversary oration, but declined, probably because he was already deeply involved in politics; the choice fell upon Dr. Benjamin Rush. Thomson was one of the members who in 1779 called for the revival of the Society after wartime interruption, subscribed $20 towards the costs of starting up again, and was elected a member of the council in 1781. He subscribed £15 towards the construction of Philosophical Hall in 1785.

Born in the townland of Gorteade in the parish of Maghera in County Derry, Ireland, in November 1729, Thomson was the third of six children of John Thomson, a Scots-Irish Presbyterian of the Plantation.[3] In 1739, shortly after his wife's death, John Thomson set out for America with four of his brood; but, sickening on the voyage, he died within sight of the coast. The captain, a conscienceless rascal, confiscated most of the children's patrimony and set them ashore at Lewes at the Capes of Delaware. Charles was placed in the family of a blacksmith, but, having early developed a taste for books, he fled the blacksmith's house lest he be indentured to that trade. Thomson liked afterwards to relate how he was befriended by the lady of a local family and was sent to the academy of the Reverend Mr. Francis Alison at New London in Chester County, Pennsylvania. He also enjoyed telling how, after a volume of the *Spectator* fell into his hands and he learned that he might

---

[3] Boyd Stanley Schlenther, *Charles Thomson: A Patriot's Pursuit* (Newark, Del., [1980]) is a detailed and critical biography. See also Lewis R. Harley, *The Life of Charles Thomson* (Phila., [1900]); J. Edwin Hendricks, *Charles Thomson and the Making of a New Nation, 1729–1824* (Rutherford, N.J., [1979]); *DAB*.

get the complete work in Philadelphia, he walked to town for the purpose. His absence from school, which would normally have brought punishment down upon him, won him instead praise for his literary ambition and enterprise. Leaving Alison's academy with a sound grounding in the classics, Thomson opened a school of his own on the farm of John Chambers in New Castle County, Delaware. These and other stories of Thomson's youthful years were well known in Philadelphia, where friends sometimes recorded them in their letters and diaries.[4]

At the end of 1750 Thomson was appointed tutor of Latin and Greek in the newly established Academy of Philadelphia, where his old teacher Francis Alison became vice-provost in 1751. The salary was £60 a year. He resigned this post in July 1755, and two months later became master of Latin in the Friends' Public School at £150 a year.[5] In the summer of 1758 Thomson married Ruth Mather, daughter of Mary (Hoskins) Mather and John Mather, a well-to-do merchant, landowner, justice of the peace, and warden of St. Paul's Church in Chester, Pennsylvania. They had twin sons, who died young.

While still a teacher, Thomson took his first steps into politics. He became deeply involved in the Indian policy of the Province and of the Quakers. His service to the Friendly Association on behalf of the Indians was encouraged and supported by the school's trustees and other Quaker leaders, notably Israel Pemberton. In their attack on the Proprietary government the Quakers cited the Penn family's policies towards the Indians, and Thomson, as their public voice, deplored the many injustices the Indians had suffered at the hands of the Province. He attended the conference at Easton in 1756 and so won the confidence of the Indians there that their chief Teedyuscung insisted, over the objections of the governor, that Thomson be appointed the Indians' secretary at the conference the next year. Adopting him into the Delaware tribe with the name Wegh-wu-law-mo-end, or "The Man who Speaks the Truth," the Indians made him one of their own.

In the course of his duties Thomson examined all the acts of the Assembly and their treaties with the Indians on the subject.

> I was obliged to enter deep into their politics and investigate their claims. This led me to enquire touching the state of this nation, and to examine all the treaties and conferences with them from the first settlement of the province.[6]

In 1759 his researches were published by Franklin in London as *An Enquiry into the Causes of the Alienation of the Delaware and Shawanese Indians from the British*

---

[4] Watson, *Annals*, I, 212; *Amer. Quar. Rev.*, I (1827), 29–32; Benjamin Rush, *Autobiography* (George W. Corner, ed., Princeton, 1948), 289–90.
[5] Univ. Penna., Trustees Minutes, 17 Dec. 1750, 14 July 1752, 17 Nov. 1753, 7 Mar. 1755.
[6] Thomson, "An Essay upon Indian Affairs," HSP, *Colls.*, I (1853), 8, quoted in Schlenther, *Charles Thomson*, 33.

Interest (London, 1759). Those causes included not only the policy of friendly inducement of the French, but more "particularly in being cheated and defrauded of their Land" by Pennsylvania's Proprietary government, as exemplified, for example, in the Walking Purchase of 1737.[7] Franklin made use of Thomson's pamphlet in his effort to secure the repeal of the Proprietary charter. Thomson, though not unsympathetic to the Indians' claims and grievances, took no further part either in the Quakers' politics or in Indian affairs.

After five years at the Quakers' school, Thomson quit teaching to become a merchant; he was succeeded in his post by Robert Proud. At his shop in Market Street opposite the Sign of the King of Prussia and a few doors below the Indian Queen tavern, he offered for sale the usual "vast assortment of goods," imported and domestic, including all kinds of cloth as well as cutlery, china, pepper, tea, gunpowder, pins, pipes, "&c. &c. &c."[8] About this time he contracted tuberculosis, but fortunately recovered; as one member of the American Society informed another in 1763, the "poor fellow has been sometime fighting for life with a powerful Consumption, that he appears like a skeleton in old tapestry. He now walks abroad and seems to mend apace."[9]

His recovery having proved complete, Thomson soon extended his financial activities. He subscribed to the short-lived "Linen Manufactory" that was projected in July 1764, partly to promote American economic independence, partly to provide employment to the poor; he bought land near Winchester, Virginia, and in 1765 advertised for a saw mill operator and a blacksmith there; he owned lands in York and Cumberland Counties in Pennsylvania; and he had a stake in the Batsto iron works in New Jersey. In 1769 he bought a distillery and opened a "cordial house" in Second Street above Arch. His Philadelphia rum, he claimed, was "of an excellent Quality," made by "a new Process"—boiled tea leaves and baked crackers were put in the hogsheads—which eliminated "the disagreeable Tang which usually accompanies Continent [i.e., American] Rum, and is so much improved in Smell and Flavour, as to be little inferior to, and scarce distinguishable from, that made in the West-Indies." At the end of 1770 Thomson gave up this business, sold the stock and fixtures of the distillery and store, and engaged in "another Way of Business."[10] The decision may have been related to Ruth Thomson's illness and death early in 1770.

The young man who walked 40 miles to Philadelphia to buy the *Spectator* essays, soon assembled a good general library. An inventory Thomson made in 1760

---

[7] Thomson, *An Enquiry into the Causes of the Alienation of the Delaware and Shawanese Indians from the British Interest* (London, 1759), 4.
[8] *Pa. Gaz.,* 20 Nov. 1760.
[9] *PMHB,* XVIII (1894), 38.
[10] *Franklin Papers,* IX, 314–16; XI, 521–22n; *Pa. Gaz.,* 11 Jan., 19 April, 25 Oct. 1770; J. Edwin Hendricks, "Charles Thomson's Philadelphia Rum," *PMHB,* LXXXIX (1965), 115.

lists 110 titles, which he valued at upwards of £65 10s. In addition to Chambers' *Dictionary* and the principal classical authors—Vergil, Homer, Aristotle, Cicero, Ovid, Tacitus, Sallust, Plautus, and Livy—the collection included such works of science as Newton's *Principia,* Peter Shaw's *Philosophical Works* of Francis Bacon, the Abbé Pluche's *Spectacle de la Nature* (in seven volumes), Richard Jack's *Elements of Conic Sections,* Gassendi's *Institutio Astronomica,* Benjamin Martin's *Philosophical Dictionary,* Isaac Barrow's *Euclid's Elements,* Alexander Malcolm's *Arithmetic,* and *Memoria Technica.* Thomson owned the works of Shakespeare (in nine volumes) and the essays and poems of Milton, Addison, Pope, Thomson, and Prior. Erasmus' *Colloquies,* the works of Boileau, La Bruyère's *Moeurs de la siècle,* and, of course, the *Spectator* were in the collection. Among serious works of political science and theory were the writings of Sydney, Justinian, Pufendorf, Grotius, Montesquieu, and Machiavelli. Thomson subscribed for John Bulkeley and John Cummings' *Voyage to the South Seas. In the Years 1740–1* (Philadelphia, 1757), Robert Bell's edition of Blackstone's *Commentaries* (Philadelphia, 1771–72), and James Burgh's *Political Disquisitions* (Philadelphia, 1775). From these and other volumes he filled a commonplace book with extracts on moral themes—good and evil, happiness, man, family and relations, pride, ingenuity, love, and friendship; specific topics like duelling, rakes, servants, and riots; and "a short Account of the origin & establishment of English Liberty & the Constitution of Parliament." He sketched the outline of a philosophy of practical education that he called the "Plan of an American University":

> Learning should be connected with Life and qualify its possessor for Action, else it is just so much lumber, serving at best as an idle Amusement. But as all habits especially the active ought to be early acquird, along with their studies at home youth should be taught to look much abroad; not to plunge into the gaieties & fopperies of the idle but to view towns, fields, forts, harbours, & magazines, & to converse with Men of all characters, professions & trades & to inform themselves of their lives, Manners & connections. To this they should learn address & agility of Body & even to wield the weapons & handle the tools of the several callings they are inspecting. Why should letters disqualify a Man to take up a foile, mount in the great Saddle or rein in the hunting horse? The ingenious Mechanic, the worker in Stone & Metals & improvers in trade, navigation & Agriculture ought to be searched out & conversed with, no less than the professors of speculative Science. Thus blending the active & contemplative life would enliven & polish both and produce such models of men as Zenophon or Sir Walter Raleigh.
>
> For want of such a plan of Education many a Man miscalled great is less useful to Society than the meanest peasant & many a gentleman of family of less consequence to it than the little boy in his kitchen.[11]

---

[11] Thomson, "A List of Books belonging to C. Thomson," 1760, Memorandum Book, 1754–74, Gratz Coll. (HSP); *Franklin Papers,* X, 386.

Meanwhile Thomson was participating in a number of the city's activities and institutions. He was an active member of the First Presbyterian Church, serving after 1762 first as secretary and treasurer, then as an elder. He made a generous gift to the Pennsylvania Hospital in 1756, was a director of the Library Company of Philadelphia from 1762 to 1771 (in which capacity he helped draft the Company's rules for the conduct of the librarian), and was a trustee and treasurer of the academy at Newark, Delaware, successor to Alison's academy.[12]

After the death of his first wife Thomson married, in 1774, Hannah, daughter of Richard and Hannah (Norris) Harrison. Hannah Norris was a niece of Isaac Norris, Speaker of the Assembly, and Richard Harrison was a rich Quaker, who had moved from Herring Creek, Maryland, to the Welsh Tract, just west of Philadelphia, where he cultivated tobacco with slave labor. Mrs. Thomson inherited her father's estate, named "Harriton," just off the main road from Philadelphia to Lancaster, and with Harriton Thomson was associated during the long years of his retirement.

But of all his activities as a young man, the Junto and its successor claimed much of his thought and energies. He was constant in attendance and regularly provided queries for discussion and debate. Many were on natural history or physics, others on politics or econmics, and one was about eating before going to bed.

> What is the Reason of the Sudden fall of the Mercury in the Barometer before Rains?
> Which is the best time to Transplant Tulips, Strawberrys, Currants, and Goosberrys?
> (4 May 1759)
>
> How may smoky Chimnies be best cured?
> Is there any Danger of a Depreciation of our present paper Currency provided no more be struck these four Years to come? (26 October 1759)
> What is Modesty?
> What is the Reason of the Difficulty of assigning the exact height of the Atmosphere, when we know that a Column of air is equal to 30 Inches of Mercury & that the proportion between Air and Mercury is as 1:14,000? (22 February 1760)
> What are the Inconveniences or ill consequences attending the going to Bed on a full Stomach?
> Is it consistent with the Principles of Liberty in a free Government to punish a Man as a Libeller when what he writes is true? (6 June 1760)
> By what means do plants propagate their Species or can a plant produce fruit that never flowered?
> What is the best Way of distinguishing the different Species of Plants?
> (18 August 1761)

Once Thomson read a paper on gossamer, "or those filmy threads which are sometimes seen in a dewy morning especially in the autumn to cover whole fields."

---

12 *Pa. Gaz.*, 10 Jan. 1771.

As a merchant Thomson was deeply involved in resistance to the Stamp Act and to British imperial policy. Thereafter he was increasingly, and finally totally, engrossed by politics. His letters describing the strong resistance to the Stamp Act—he was one of the committee that forced John Hughes to promise not to discharge his duties as Stamp Agent—and his arguments against it both as law and policy were sent by Franklin to the London press and influenced Franklin to change his mind about the law. The obnoxious act was repealed in the spring of 1766, but when Parliament enacted new laws in 1767, Thomson was once more active in resistance. He was a principal organizer of public meetings of protest, promoted the non-importation agreement in response to the Townshend Acts, and developed an intercolonial network of committees of correspondence.

In this growing political and economic movement he appreciated the usefulness of the Junto. Within two weeks of the arrival in Philadelphia of news of the repeal of the Stamp Act in the spring of 1766, the Junto resumed its meetings; and, fashioned into an "American Society," it began to elect corresponding members outside Philadelphia and in other colonies. Queries offered for discussion now dealt increasingly with issues of trade and imperial politics. On 6 February 1767, for example, Thomson proposed the question, "What is the best method of Securing to the port of Philadelphia, the Trade of those Countys that lie to the Westward of Susquehannah?" As a merchant, a patriot-improver, and a member of the American Philosophical Society, which was interested in the project, he subscribed £2 towards the cost of a survey for a Delaware-Chesapeake canal in 1769. His concern for colonial economic independence continued. On 13 March 1767 he read a paper on the importance of agriculture and its improvement that was intended to be the first of several essays of the kind. The Society thought his ideas "Highly Judicious and likely to answer to Publick Spirited Intentions of the Society." On 18 September 1767 Thomson proposed that the Society systematically examine American natural resources, beginning with agriculture, since relations with Great Britain were "declining" and the future growth of the colonies was "likely to be opposed by increasing Obstacles from abroad." On 1 January 1768 he developed the idea still further in "Proposals for enlarging the Society in order that it may the better answer the End for which it was instituted, namely the promoting and propagating useful Knowledge." After a short sweeping introductory survey of American physical and social assets and potentialities, especially in agriculture, he listed a number of specific products—such as rice, whisk, Chinese vetch, and silkworms, all grown in China, which lay in the same latitude as America—and asked, "Why then should we despair of introducing others, even the Tea shrub, if we have it not already?" Americans should investigate the virtues of American trees, plants, and roots, of the persimmon, magnolia, and spicewood. "Considering the richness of many of our grapes even in their uncultivated State, and the improvement they must receive from Culture," he went on, "there is reason to hope that in a very little

part in reviving the Society after wartime interruption, served on a special publication committee within the Committee on Trade and Commerce, helped draft the bill that transferred the assets of the Silk Society to the American Philosophical Society in 1781, contributed £5 towards the cost of building Philosophical Hall, and was elected to the Council three times, serving from 1781 to 1790.

George Bryan was born in Dublin on 11 August 1731, the third of five children of Samuel and Sarah (Dennis) Bryan.[1] The elder Bryan was a merchant, trained his son to follow him in that business, and in 1752 sent him to Philadelphia, "with the best founded prospects," to get experience and, apparently, gentlemanly polish. In partnership with James Wallace he offered for sale at their store on Market Street wharf the usual variety of imported articles—dry goods, household wares, tea, rum, molasses, and Irish beef. One of the advertisements of Bryan and Wallace was of "a parcel of likely men and women servants, among whom tradesmen of different sorts."[2] The partnership expired in 1755. Bryan continued in business, importing principally from Ireland. One of his first advertisements as an independent merchant lists, among other things, checks, Irish linens, lawns, cambrics, muslins, silk handkerchiefs, calicoes, watch crystals, shirt buttons, butchers' knives, razors, thimbles, fountain pens, cork drawers, pins, shoe buckles; as well as Daffy's elixir, Stoughton's drops, lavender water, "beautifying water," and tooth powder; and also weeding hoes, earthen ware, and clover seed.[3] Political enemies later charged that he added to his income by smuggling.[4]

Young Bryan quickly made friends in Philadelphia. He became a member of the Hibernia Fire Company and in its circle established a reputation for a prodigious memory, with a head full of minute, obscure, and out-of-the-way facts, "insomuch," Alexander Graydon remembered, "that a bet was once offered, that he could name the town-cryer of Bergen-op-Zoom." This talent was widely known and sometimes derided: "You were frequently found in the Swedes Church burying-ground," it was once charged against him, "decyphering and getting by rote antique inscriptions on tomb-stones."[5] A report of George's social activities was not long in reaching Dublin. His father was swift with reproach and advice.

> I am informed that Your Evenings are taken up in boating on the River & down to Mr. Bleakly, this can in no way improve you as a man coming into Life. I recommended to you the best of company to keep, Men in Business, Men of Conversation & good Manners—that when I meet you again I may not meet with the Rustic or Tar,

---

[1] Burton A. Konkle, *George Bryan and the Constitution of Pennsylvania, 1731– 1791* (Phila., 1922); *DAB.*
[2] *Pa. Gaz.,* 6 Aug. 1752, 5 Feb. 1754.
[3] Ibid., 17 April 1755, 25 Aug. 1763; William Bryan to George Bryan, 10 Aug 1756, George Bryan Papers, Box 1, f.1 (HSP).
[4] *Pa. Gaz.,* 8 Oct. 1783.
[5] Alexander Graydon, *Memoirs of his Own Time* (Phila., 1846), 287–88; *Pa. Gaz.,* 8 Oct. 1783.

but the genteel pretty agreeable fellow as well as the compleat sensible Merchant, & this will never be the case if you proceed in your present course, for you take the readiest method to lock yourself from what I have been recommending you to do. Mr. Bleakly is an honest man but he is not a man of all men I should choose for my companion, he never saw anything in his young days that could polish his person & manners & I am afraid he has not improved either by going to Philadelphia. I gave you long letters before recommending your going into all companies where men of manners, Sense, &c. were to be found, the Expence I valued not, & those as good or better than yourself. Low mean company are a Scandal & a disgrace & nothing can so effectually lessen you in the opinion of Mankind—the amusements of Dancing, fencing, the use of the Small Sword, taking a glass of wine or Punch with a few of Such I am recommending at particular evenings, this would after business is over be shewing yourself to Mankind to be known & regarded. Away with boating & Let me never hear more of such a thing unless on business or on a party of pleasure with good company.

Let not the carelessness of the world about you with respect to God & religion have any effect on you for if once you can lose sight of this you will be an easy prey to every vice which offers. . . . I am doing everything in my power to advance you in the world and establish you as my son. Do not defeat it in any one Instance. . . .[6]

On 21 April 1757 Bryan was married in the Second Presbyterian Church of Philadelphia to Elizabeth, daughter of Samuel and Mary Smith. They had nine children, of whom seven survived their father. Within the Presbyterian Church Bryan soon rose to prominence. In 1759 he was chosen a member of "The Corporation for the Relief of Poor and Distressed Presbyterian Ministers and of the Poor and Distressed Widows and Children of Presbyterian Ministers," and in 1760 was elected president of the board. He was a lay representative to the Synod, and was treasurer of a committee to raise money to erect a house for David Brainerd's Indian school in New Jersey. In 1767 he was elected a trustee of the College of New Jersey at Princeton, serving until 1778, when he resigned. He subscribed to Gilbert Tennent's *Sermons on Important Subjects* (Philadelphia, 1758).[7]

All the while Bryan was becoming increasingly active in local politics, to which his position in one of the larger religious denominations gave him an introduction. Although he declined to serve as constable in 1758 and was fined for his refusal, in 1762 he accepted appointment on a committee to oversee the construction of piers and other improvements in the harbor and at Reedy Island in the Delaware River below the city. Two years later, as a supporter of the Proprietary party, he was elected to the Assembly with Thomas Willing, defeating Benjamin Franklin and Joseph Galloway. He was one of the members who voted against sending Franklin to London again as the Assembly's agent to seek the end of proprietary rule. In

---

[6] Samuel Bryan to George Bryan, 23 Sept. 1752 (typescript copy), George Bryan Papers, Box 1, f.1 (HSP).
[7] *Records of the Presbyterian Church . . . embracing the Minutes of the General Presbytery and General Synod, 1706–1788* (Phila., 1904), 315, 317, 324, 447, 449.

1764 Bryan was appointed a justice of the peace, and was reappointed to that office several times.[8] In 1765 he was on the committee that drafted instructions to Pennsylvania's delegates to the Stamp Act Congress, of whom he was one. That year he was defeated for reelection to the Assembly in a run-off against James Pemberton.[9]

Bryan signed the Non-Importation Agreement in 1765 and continued for some years to support non-importation. He was a member of the Philadelphia company that received a grant of 200,000 acres at Pictou in Nova Scotia.[10] His own business in these years suffered, and the failure of his Irish correspondents in 1770–71 brought him down. Thereafter, as his memorialist put it, "he became more than ever devoted to an honest and honorable simplicity, worthy of the best and purest days of the old republics."[11] From this time on, Bryan was almost constantly in public service, and never again in good financial circumstances.

Bryan's services during the American Revolution were entirely on the state level. He was not a soldier, and apparently he never aspired to office under the Continental Congress. Although he was elected commissioner of the Board of Admiralty in 1779, for example, he declined the office.[12] His most memorable contribution to the revolutionary spirit was a real but elusive role in drafting the Pennsylvania constitution of 1776. Although not a member of the convention that wrote the document, he was generally considered, even in his own day, as the principal author, with James Cannon of the College of Philadelphia, of its radical provisions. The constitution vested power in a unicameral legislature elected annually. There were no property qualifications for either voters or office-holders. The executive was weak, composed of twelve persons, and had no power of veto. A Council of Censors was to meet every seven years to review legislation, compare it with the constitution, and, if necessary, recommend amendment or repeal. Judges' terms were limited to seven years, with the possibility of reappointment.[13] Bryan defended the convention's work until at last the Revolutionary constitution was replaced in 1790.

In June 1776 Bryan received the post—for which he applied—of "Officer to superintend the Imports and Exports, and other naval Affairs, of the Port of Philadelphia."[14] In the new state government he was elected in February 1777 a member of the Supreme Executive Council and its vice-president. In the following October he was added to the Council of Safety. Though not a member of the Conway Cabal, Bryan added his voice to the "general murmur" in the winter of 1777–78

[8] 3 *Pa. Arch.* XXX, 405.
[9] 8 *Pa. Arch.,* VI, 5365; VII, 5669, 5687, 5690, 5775–76, 5788, 5795, 5799, 5800.
[10] *PMHB,* LI (1927), 280.
[11] Dunlap's *Amer. Daily Advertiser,* 31 Jan. 1791.
[12] *Jour. Cont. Cong.,* XV, 1339, 1344, 1357.
[13] J. Paul Selsam, *The Pennsylvania Constitution of 1776* (Phila., 1936), 169–204.
[14] 8 *Pa. Arch.,* VIII, 7516, 7536.

against the "weak conduct . . . slackness and remissness" of Washington, speaking so openly about the general's unfitness to command an army that one citizen called him to account and forced him to apologize.[15]

Upon the sudden death of Thomas Wharton, Jr. in May 1778 Bryan became in effect the chief executive of the state, serving until December, when Joseph Reed was elected president. In the spring of 1779 he was appointed with David Rittenhouse and Dr. John Ewing to survey and adjust the Pennsylvania-Virginia boundary. From Baltimore, where the commissioners met, Bryan wrote President Reed an interesting description and analysis of the neighboring state.

> The town, filled with industrious people, has suddenly sprouted out to the sum of 1000 buildings in a country of indolence. The country hereabouts is a poor gravelly soil. They talk of fine land in the necks which lie eastward towards the Bay, and of good farms ten or twelve miles northwest or inland. But I fancy the town is rather too large for the neighboring people, slothful as they seem, to supply. . . . This inattention of the Marylanders to the vast advantage of the Baltimore market is easily accounted for, from looking back to the fettered state of trade formerly, as conducted by a combination of little Scotch dealers, who kept the people in such bondage as stifled all industry. The cash trade of the land and the building this town has indeed removed many obstacles, but the habits of a whole people, educated and confirmed in indolency, are hardly surmountable. The readiest remedy certainly would be to introduce some new farmers, bred in a land of industry. Against this the difficulty of getting lands for them is urged, for the law of inheritance in the eldest son, the difficulty of selling real estate for common debts, entails, and the shame of parting with paternal lands, combine against strangers. An unaccountable jealousy too against this collection of strangers, as the inhabitants of the town generally are, is no small embarrassment.[16]

Elected again to the Assembly in October 1779, Bryan was chairman of committees that drafted several far-reaching acts of legislation. One stripped the Penn family of much of their property in Pennsylvania. A second removed the property of the trustees of the College of Philadelphia and vested it in another board of another institution, called the University of the State of Pennsylvania. Except that it confiscated much of the private wealth and financial prospects of the Penns, the Divestment Act had little effect on the life and growth of commonwealth; while the act concerning the College was eventually reversed and the old College and the upstart University of the State were united in 1791 as the University of Pennsylvania.

Of greater and permanent effect was the Pennsylvania law for the abolition of slavery, passed in 1780 and revised in 1788. Slavery, Bryan believed, was "disgraceful to any people, and more especially to those who have been contending in the great cause of liberty themselves." The Council had referred the question of aboli-

---

[15] Christopher Marshall, *Extracts from the Diary . . . 1777–78* (William Duane, ed., Albany, N.Y., 1877), 159; "A Citizen of Pennsylvania" in *Pa. Gaz.,* 25 Aug. 1784.
[16] 3 *Pa. Arch.,* X, 489–90; Bryan to Joseph Reed, 31 Aug. 1779, in William B. Reed, *Life and Correspondence of Joseph Reed* (Phila., 1847), I, 133–34.

tion to the Assembly in 1777, but no action was taken then. In the Assembly, to which he was returned in October 1779, Bryan pressed for action, and on 29 February 1780, the law was passed, not without opposition, ironically enough, from some of the radicals who talked most loudly of freedom.[17]

Of Bryan's political stance and views in these years Alexander Graydon wrote that "his passion or his policy" was to identify himself with the *people* against the *well-born*. He was in other respects, Graydon continued, "well enough: let us say, a well-meaning man, and even one, who, in the main, felt he was acting the patriot. . . ."[18]

On 3 April 1780 Bryan was appointed a justice of the Supreme Court of the state.[19] His years on the bench were filled with political controversy. The conservatives were beginning to regain their power; they challenged Judge Bryan, whom they regarded as the principal leader of the radicals, calling him "an archpartisan and brawler," and denouncing his conduct as a "democrat." His appointment to the Council of Censors on 21 June 1784 provided another point of attack: that it was a conflict of interest, if not worse, for Bryan to sit in judgment as a censor on acts he had done or approved as a member of the Supreme Executive Council or Assembly. Nonetheless, Bryan sat on the Council of Censors and continued to champion and defend the state constitution. It was consistent with his principles and prejudices that he should strongly attack the movement towards a strengthening of the Articles of Confederation and oppose the Federal Constitution of 1787. He called at once for another convention to revise and amend it. But his was now a minority voice and little heeded. He survived the adoption of the Federal Constitution by only three years, and died only five months after Pennsylvania replaced his constitution of 1776 with a conservative and more conventional instrument. He remained a state judge until his death.

For several years until 1788 Bryan lived at the corner of Third and New Streets in the Northern Liberties of Philadelphia in a three-story brick house described as having "two commodious well furnished rooms on a floor, connected by the piazza with a convenient back room (over which is a nursery) and the kitchen." There was "a pump of good water" in the yard.[20] Bryan then moved to a house in Arch Street, where, after a brief illness, he died on 27 January 1791. His friend Dr. John Ewing, provost of the University, delivered the funeral sermon, and his body was laid in the Arch Street Presbyterian burying ground.[21] He was, read the inscription on his

[17] *PMHB*, XXVI(1902), 339–40.
[18] Graydon, *Memoirs*, 287–88.
[19] 3 *Pa. Arch.*, X, 495–96.
[20] *Pa. Packet*, 3 Nov. 1788.
[21] Extracts from Ewing's sermon are in *American Museum*, IX (1791), 81–82, where the obituary from Dunlap's *Amer. Daily Advertiser*, 31 Jan. 1791, is reprinted (pp. 82–83).

tombstone, "among the earliest and most active and informed friends of the rights of man before the Revolution."[22]

FRANCIS RAWLE (1729–1761)
"YOUNG JUNTO": BEFORE 22 SEPTEMBER 1758

FRANCIS RAWLE, a prosperous young Quaker merchant in 1758, was the only child of William and Margaret (Hodge) Rawle of Philadelphia, and a grandson of the Francis Rawle who wrote a pamphlet in favor of paper currency in 1721. The elder Rawle, a lawyer with pronounced literary tastes, was an early member and director of the Library Company and the first American benefactor of that institution, presenting a copy of Edmund Spenser's works in six volumes.[1] Francis was born in Philadelphia on 10 July 1729; his mother died a month later; and in 1741 his father also died. Fortunately, the boy was adequately provided for; he was given a good secondary education and learned the merchant's business. In 1755 he made a trip to England and Ireland; this experience is said to have set a pattern for other well-to-do young Philadelphians who made the Grand Tour in the following decades.[2] Of economic conditions in rural Ireland he wrote:

> There seem to be but two degrees of people in this country—the gentry and slaves. These rent small pieces of land of the former, and pay high rents for them, from twenty shillings, to sixty shillings per acre a year. On these they build themselves miserable cottages or cabins of dirt and straw, or strengthen or cement them better, without any chimney or fire-place; a door of withes or Wickerwork serving them for a chimney, window, and door. To build better houses were they able, they have no encouragement; for perhaps, if they make any considerable improvement, they are directly turned off for the sake of a higher rent, brought about by their industry and good management. Their cabins are equally free to them, and their fellow creatures the cattle, hogs, sheep, goats, and poultry; of which, indeed, each house has very few to its

---

[22] Quoted in Konkle, *George Bryan,* 358. Bryan's body was moved in the nineteenth century to Laurel Hill Cemetery. Mrs. Bryan survived until 1799.

[1] Frank Willing Leach, "Old Philadelphia Families, III. Rawle," (Phila.) *North American,* 23 June 1907; Edwin J. Rawle, *Records of the Rawle Family* (Taunton, England, 1898), 183–85; Frederick B. Tolles, *Meeting House and Counting House* (Chapel Hill, 1948), 177n, 200.
[2] "Early Minutes of Philadelphia Monthly Meeting of Friends," Geneal. Soc. Pa., *Pubs.,* XI (1934), 10; Carl and Jessica Bridenbaugh, *Rebels and Gentlemen* (N.Y., 1942), 194.

share. They walk in and out in as familiar a manner as their masters, and seem to be no more regarded while there than if they were the natural occupants.[3]

Rawle returned to Philadelphia in the spring of 1756 and at once advertised for sale at his store opposite the Ferry House in Water Street near Arch, an assortment of linens, Irish sheets, oznabrigs, garlix, lawns, cambrics, muslins, "China and Persian taffeties," handkerchiefs, stockings, mitts, mittens, gloves, bed ticks, pillows, buttons, thread, pins, needles, nutmegs, cinnamon, cloves, writing paper, shot and lead, "and a variety of cutlary [sic] ware, &c. &c. &c.," which he had purchased presumably while he was abroad.[4] He was married in December 1756 to Rebecca Warner, daughter of Edward and Anna (Coleman) Warner; Edward Warner was a carpenter, merchant, and member of the Assembly.[5]

Rawle quickly settled into business and began making his way in the town. He was a partner in the Pennsylvania Land Company, held the lease of one of the Delaware ferries, and shortly before his death was elected a director of the Philadelphia Contributionship. He was appointed to the Governor's Council, but did not serve.[6] Rawle made a generous contribution to the Pennsylvania Hospital and in 1756 subscribed £20 to the Friendly Association.[7]

Elected to membership in the "Young Junto," he attended its meetings regularly, served it as treasurer, and submitted a number of queries for discussion and debate, among them:

> Why are tumultuous uneasy Sensations united with our Desires.   (12 October 1759)
> Is the Trade now [1759] carried on with the French under the Colour of Flags of Truce of Advantage to the public Weal, Provisions, naval & military Stores being wholly excluded?   (12 October 1759)
> May we Place Rods on our Houses to guard them against Lightening without being guilty of Presumption?   (18 January 1760)

In 1760 Rawle and his brother-in-law Joshua Howell bought the 76-acre tract on the east bank of the Schuylkill where Thomas Shute had erected a handsome country seat called "Laurel Hill." Rawle and Howell divided the tract, the former taking 35 acres, including the house.[8]

---

[3] Thomas I. Wharton, *A Memoir of William Rawle, LL.D.* (Phila., 1840), 6.
[4] *Pa. Gaz.,* 20 Nov. 1755, 3 June 1756.
[5] "Early Minutes of Philadelphia Monthly Meeting of Friends," loc. cit., 16.
[6] 2 *Pa. Arch.,* IX, 625; 3 *Pa. Arch.,* IX, 284–90; *Minutes of the Common Council of Philadelphia* (Phila., 1847), 609.
[7] Morton, *Pennsylvania Hospital,* 394.
[8] William B. Rawle, "Laurel Hill and some Colonial Dames who once lived there," *PMHB,* XXXV (1911), 387–89; Harold D. Eberlein and Cortlandt Van Dyke Hubbard, *Portrait of a Colonial City: Philadelphia, 1670–1838* (Phila., 1939), 292–300.

Early in June 1761 while hunting at Point-no-Point in Frankford, Rawle accidentally discharged his fowling piece into his left arm. He was brought home, wrote his will, and died a few days afterwards on 7 June.[9] He was buried next day in the Friends burying ground, Philadelphia.

Rawle left three young children—Anna, William, who became a distinguished lawyer, and Margaret. His estate was valued at more than £10,000. Each child received £1000, the Pennsylvania Hospital £50, and his widow the rest. Among the household goods were 30 maps and a lanthorn, valued together at £1 and "1 Escrutoire [sic] & Sundry Books" worth £50.[10] His widow remarried in 1767, her second husband being Samuel Shoemaker.

STEPHEN WOOLLEY (1724–1776)
"YOUNG JUNTO": BEFORE 22 SEPTEMBER 1758
"YOUNG JUNTO" (AGAIN): 19 SEPTEMBER 1766

STEPHEN WOOLLEY was a medical practitioner in Philadelphia when he was elected a member of the "Young Junto." He was born in Philadelphia on 10 December 1724, the first child and only son of Edmund and Mary (Parsons) Woolley; and was baptized in the First Presbyterian Church there on 25 September 1725.[1] Stephen's father, a native of England, was a master carpenter, who was in charge of construction of the Pennsylvania State House and built the tabernacle for George Whitefield that became the home of the Academy and College of Philadelphia. The lad's mother was a sister of William Parsons, shoemaker, who, in his spare time during the years when his nephew was growing up, studied mathematics and surveying.[2] Edmund Woolley gave his son a respectable education. Franklin's shop book of 1736–39 records sales to father or son of a dictionary, John Clarke's *Introduction to the Making of Latin,* a Horace, and other schoolbooks.[3] In 1743,

---

[9] Elizabeth Drinker, *Journal* (Phila., 1889), 18. A prayer found on Rawle's body made a deep impression on friends; it was copied and circulated among them, even in the latter years of the eighteenth and nineteenth centuries. Rawle, Prayer, 1760, Rawle Family Papers (HSP).

[10] Will, dated 5 June 1761, probated 15 June 1761; Inventory, 26 Aug. 1761 (Register of Wills, Phila.).

[1] Geneal. Soc. Pa., *Pubs.,* XIX (1952–54), 289.
[2] Virginia W. Cute, "Edmund Woolley, 1695–99?—1771," unpublished paper, University of Pennsylvania, 1962 (copy in Independence National Historical Park, Phila.).
[3] Benjamin Franklin, Shop Book, 1735–39 (APS).

EDMUND PHYSICK

By Charles Willson Peale. Reproduced from a phototype by Frederick Gutekunst of the unlocated painting. *Courtesy of the American Philosophical Society.*

EDMUND PHYSICK (1727–1804)
"YOUNG JUNTO": BEFORE 22 SEPTEMBER 1758

EDMUND PHYSICK, one of the Receivers-General of Quit-Rents of Pennsylvania, was already a member of the "Young Junto" when its earliest surviving minutes begin on 22 September 1758; he was one of the five active members who reorganized the society in the summer of 1761; and was a member when the Junto transformed itself into the American Society in 1766. He was active in both the Junto and the American Society, and was fairly regular in attending the united American Philosophical Society for several years after 1769. His attendance fell off after 1774, he came to one meeting in 1780, and never appeared again. During the years of his active membership he proposed many questions for discussion and debate—moral, political, and scientific. A few of Physick's queries illustrate the content and character of the societies' meetings in those days.

> How may the Burthen of a Vessel be computed? (28 September 1758).
> What is the Reason why men generally receive Advice with Reluctance? (16 December 1759).
> What would be the easiest & best method of procuring to the Poor of this City, a Supply of Fire Wood at a moderate Price? (17 September 1760)
> What are the common Causes that occasion the Downfall of an Empire? (7 August 1761).
> What is the best Method of making Black Ink? (20 June 1766).
> Is it consistent with Reason & Justice to punish a Commanding Officer with the loss of Life for not fighting an Enemy on terms of Advantage when deterd [sic] therefrom by an invincible fear?
> [The company answered this query in the affirmative.] (16 January 1767).

Physick was a member of the Library Company of Philadelphia (in which he inherited the share of his father-in-law Philip Syng). In 1772 he contributed £5 to the College of Philadelphia. He became a member of the Philadelphia Society for Promoting Agriculture when that society was founded in 1785. He was a vestryman of St. Peter's Church.

Physick was born in England in 1727, the sole surviving son of Timothy and Martha Physick.[1] At the age of 15 he was bound as a clerk to Thomas Penn in London and soon afterwards was sent to Pennsylvania. "Edmund Physick is a very Industrious Sober honest Lad," Lynford Lardner, the Receiver-General of Quit-Rents, wrote Penn in 1747. "I think my Self very Fortunate in having such an one in the Office, he writes a pretty good hand but is Extream slow in every thing

---

[1] *PHMB*, V (1881), 359–60.

them. There were other proofs of continuing friendship and respect: Physick was given a painting of Governor Penn, and the family asked him to sit for his own portrait by "Mr. Peal's Brother."[11]

Meanwhile, with Physick's indispensable help in searching out and compiling records, the Penns submitted a petition to the Loyalist Claims Commission for compensation for their losses. Physick's presence in London was necessary, and he made two trips there for the purpose. On the second, in the fall of 1788, he took along his son Philip, a medical student. In London he assisted once more in presenting the Penns' case to the Commission, he installed his son as a pupil with the famous surgeon-anatomist John Hunter, and he performed an important errand for Mrs. Physick.

Abigail Syng, daughter of Philip Syng, the goldsmith, and Edmund Physick were married in 1758. With the passing years Mrs. Physick had been drawn towards the Quakers and became a member of the Society of Friends a few years after the Revolution. Under the necessity of altering her clothing to conform to the sober Quaker style, she had given her husband a sky-blue dress to have dyed dark brown in London—"a Colour better adapted to the Taste of Freinds [sic]."[12] And there were errands to perform for English acquaintances on his return to Philadelphia. Fascinated by the opossum, as all European naturalists and anatomists were, Mr. Hunter had asked Physick to send him male and female specimens. With some difficulty Physick procured a nursing opossum, which he forwarded to London with instructions for feeding—meat, eggs, greased bread, turnips, and boiled potatoes—and for handling. "When it is necessary to move them from one place to another," he warned, "they should be lifted by the Tail, or they will bite."[13]

In addition to the lands they continued to own in Pennsylvania and were now selling, the Penns claimed the right to sell and convey their vacant land in Delaware and to collect quit-rents that were in arrears in the Lower Counties. To this end Physick and Thomas McKean received powers of attorney, and issued *A Calm Appeal to the People of the State of Delaware* (1793) in the case. The state rejected the claim, and so denied to the Penn family thousands of pounds of arrearages.[14]

Physick was now past 65 years of age; his wife was dead; he was ready to retire. The Solitude, he found, was too far away conveniently to conduct the Proprietary business; and so he returned to town in 1795, letting the house for £120 for its owner's benefit. He continued acting as the Penns' agent, receiving their instruc-

---

[11] John Penn to Physick, 8 Aug. 1788, Penn-Physick Mss., I, 193; Physick to [John Penn], 20 Dec. 1787, 24 Oct. 1788, 4, 29 June 1795, Ibid., III, 219, 240, 285; Harold D. Eberlein and Cortlandt Van Dyke Hubbard, *Portrait of a Colonial City: Philadelphia, 1670–1838* (Phila., 1939), 434–37.
[12] Physick to Abigail Physick, 31 March 1789, Penn-Physick Mss., II, 3.
[13] Physick to John Hunter, 20 May 1790, Letter Book, Ibid., III, 274–75.
[14] Richard S. Rodney, "The End of the Penns' Claim to Delaware, 1789–1814," *PMHB,* LXI (1937), 182–203.

tions, forwarding remittances and reports, fulfilling their orders and requests. As a former Proprietary officer, in the first years of the nineteenth century he became an object of respect and a symbol of olden and, as some would have it, happier times.

Physick died on 7 June 1804 and was buried at his request (which the Friends granted) in the Quakers' burying ground next to his wife, who had died on 8 April 1792.[15] He was survived by two sons, Henry White, who became a merchant in Delaware, and Philip Syng, destined to be hailed as "the father of American surgery."

WILLIAM FRANKLIN (1731?–1813)
"YOUNG JUNTO": BEFORE 22 SEPTEMBER 1758
AMERICAN PHILOSOPHICAL SOCIETY: 8 MARCH 1768

WILLIAM FRANKLIN, Clerk of the Pennsylvania Assembly, Postmaster of Philadelphia, and a student of law, was one of the first members of the "Young Junto," perhaps as early as 1750. When he went to England with his father in the summer of 1757, the Junto was flourishing and William Franklin asked to be retained as a member during his absence; at the same time he was requested to purchase electrical and optical instruments for the Society.[1] In the earliest surviving minutes of 22 September 1758 his name appears among the members, but as "absent." He probably continued in this status for several years, but in 1761, when the Junto was reorganized and he was still in London, he was no longer listed on the membership roll. Nearly six years passed before Franklin returned to America, and not until 1767, after some of his father's friends had revived the old American Philosophical Society, does he appear to have been in contact with some of his former associates. In the decade since Franklin last met with them, the Junto had become the American Society for Promoting Useful Knowledge; and the American Philosophical Society, which his father had founded 25 years earlier, had been revived by Dr. Thomas Bond, Provost William Smith, and Dr. John Ewing of the College of Philadelphia. William Franklin's sympathies were with the Junto and the American Society and their members, as he was sure his father's were, and he resented what he regarded as a transparent attempt by members of the Proprietary party to use Dr. Franklin's name and reputation in support of the revived Philosophical Society. Apprised of

---

[15] Penn-Physick Mss., III, 325, 466; Elizabeth Drinker, *Diary* (Elaine F. Crane and others, eds., Boston, [1991]), I, 481; III, 1748.

[1] Charles Thomson to Franklin, [June 1757], Franklin Mss., XLVIII, 120.

WILLIAM FRANKLIN

By Mather Brown. *Collection of Mrs. Jackson C. Boswell.* Photograph courtesy of Frick Art Reference Library.

their actions by his father's friend Dr. Cadwalader Evans, William Franklin, now governor of New Jersey, expressed disapproval of the way in which the old Philosophical Society was reassembled and of the political motives of its sponsors. He would have none of it, he assured Evans.

> I am at a Loss to know with what Propriety they can talk of reviving the old Society begun by my Father, for they are not I believe in Possession of any of the Papers &c. which belong'd to it. I think I saw them all some Years ago in my Father's Possession, & have no doubt but that they are so still. I question whether any of the Persons who met to revive it were ever Members, except Dr Bond and S Rhoads; & I think before they attempted to revive it they should have summoned a Meeting of all the old Members, & consulted them on the Occasion. If they refus'd to join in the Measure, then the others might have endeavor'd to form a new Society, either upon the old Plan or some other. But I fancy their Scheme in calling this a Revival of the old Society is, to induce my Father to countenance it, or by making use of his Name to engage his Friends & Connections to join them. However, you may rely that the Bait won't take with me, & I am very happy to find that it has not with you.[2]

Informed of these sentiments, the American Society on 12 February 1768 invited Governor Franklin, as "the only Member of the Antient Society, who has not signed the rules," to attend a meeting, sign the by-laws, and resume his membership. He responded that when he was next in town he would "make it my business to attend as often as I possibly can." At the same time the revived Philosophical Society elected Franklin a member on 8 March 1768. There is no record that he ever attended a meeting of either the American or the American Philosophical Society. He was, however, considered a member of the united American Philosophical Society after 1769, and his name is on the roll of members printed in the first volume of its *Transactions* in 1771.

William Franklin was born in 1730 or 1731, the son of Benjamin Franklin and an unknown woman, probably a maid or servant.[3] As a child he was tutored by Theophilus Grew, later an instructor in the Academy and College of Philadelphia; and for several years before 1743 he attended the academy of Alexander Annand. Except that he was indulged by his father, little is known of his life at home until 1745, when he tried to join the crew of a privateer for wealth and adventure. His father "fetched" him back from this venture and got him instead a commission as ensign in Captain John Diemer's company of Pennsylvania militia. The troops were sent to New York destined for Canada, but got no farther than Albany, and

---

[2] Franklin Mss., XLVII, 43.
[3] Sheila L. Skemp, *William Franklin: Son of a Patriot, Servant of a King* (N.Y., 1990); Willard S. Randall, *A Little Revenge: Benjamin Franklin and His Son* (Boston, 1984); a useful short sketch by Larry R. Gerlach, *William Franklin: New Jersey's Last Royal Governor* (N.J. Hist. Commission, 1975); *DAB*.

On the date of William Franklin's birth, see the ingenious speculation in *Franklin Papers,* III, 474n.

saw no action. Nonetheless young Franklin quite liked soldiering. "Billy is so fond of a military Life," his father observed, "that he will by no means hear of leaving the Army." The return of peace in 1748, however, put an end to William's martial ambitions and, promoted captain, he returned to Philadelphia. In August of that year he accompanied Conrad Weiser and George Croghan to Lancaster and then to Logstown near the forks of the Ohio and Monongahela rivers, where they negotiated a treaty with the Miami Indians. The journal Franklin kept on this occasion proved a "principal Help" to Lewis Evans in ascertaining the longitude of the forks for his *General Map of the Middle British Colonies, in America* (London, 1755).[4]

Young Franklin was by all accounts intelligent, good looking, with pleasing manners, and such experiences beyond his years as made him interesting company everywhere. He subscribed to the Philadelphia Assembly balls. "As to your Grandchildren," Franklin told his own mother,

> Will. is now 19 Years of Age, a tall proper Youth, and much of a Beau. He acquir'd a Habit of Idleness on the Expedition, but begins of late to apply himself to Business, and I hope will become an industrious Man. He imagin'd his Father had got enough for him: But I have assur'd him that I intend to spend what little I have, my self; if it please God that I live long enough: And as he by no means wants Sense, he can see by my going on, that I am like to be as good as my Word.[5]

James Bowdoin, who met William in Boston in 1751, complimented Franklin on his son's "good sense, and Gentlemanly Behaviour," which had recommended him "to a considerable acquaintance."[6]

Will was now ready, his father thought, to enter upon serious business. Accordingly he began the study of law with Joseph Galloway. His father ordered Coke's *Institutes,* Wood's *Institutes of the Laws of England,* Matthew Bacon's *New Abridgment of the Law,* Viner's *General Abridgment of Law and Equity,* and Danvers' *General Abridgment of the Common Law* from London for him. William's name was entered on the roll of the Middle Temple in London on 11 February 1750/1.[7] In the unabashed way of the eighteenth century Benjamin Franklin provided for his son. He saw to it that, when he was elected to the Assembly in 1756, William should succeed him as clerk of that body. When the elder Franklin became deputy postmaster general for North America in 1753, he made William postmaster of Philadelphia, and in 1754 he appointed him comptroller of the Post Office as well. In addition, young Franklin acquired a variety of other experiences. He attended the Albany Congress with his father in 1754. In 1755 he accompanied his father to

---

[4] *Col. Recs. Pa.,* V, 348; Lawrence H. Gipson, *Lewis Evans* (Phila., 1939), 57, 154; *Franklin Papers,* III, 89n, 119, 303, 320, 323.
[5] *Franklin Papers,* III, 474–75; Watson, *Annals,* I, 284.
[6] *Franklin Papers,* IV, 220.
[7] C. E. A. Bedwell, "American Middle Templars," *Amer. Hist. Rev.,* XXV (1919–20), 684; *Franklin Papers,* IV, 78.

western Pennsylvania and Maryland to collect wagons for General Braddock; and, with Richard Peters, he himself issued an appeal to the farmers of Berks County to provide forage for the troops. At the end of the year William was at Bethlehem and Gnadenhütten, where he had command of troops and assisted his father in erecting and strengthening the frontier defenses. He had even joined his father in electrical experiments, participating in the famous kite experiment in 1752 and offering suggestions on electrical phenomena. He witnessed the thrashing Franklin gave a whirlwind in Maryland in 1755, an episode that Benjamin reported in a letter to Peter Collinson.[8] Observing the close relations of father and son, the London printer William Strahan, Benjamin's friend, remarked perceptively that Benjamin was "at the same time his [William's] friend, his brother, his intimate, and easy companion."[9]

Young William subscribed towards the cost of the Christ Church steeple in 1751 and was a contributor to the Pennsylvania Hospital in 1754; he was one of the managers of a lottery for the benefit of a church in Trenton, New Jersey; and he took in subscriptions for Governor Jonathan Belcher's proposed "Observations upon the Provinces of New York, the Jersies, Pennsylvania, Maryland and Virginia."[10] He was made a Freemason.

In the summer of 1757 William accompanied his father to London as secretary and companion. The great city was filled with attractions for a personable young colonial, and the elder Franklin's position gave the son entrée into many circles. He was, Strahan wrote Deborah Franklin, "one of the prettiest young gentlemen I ever knew from America," with "a solidity of judgment, not very often to be met with in one of his years."[11] Hardly was he in London than he wrote a defense of Pennsylvania's Quaker Assembly and of his father's policy towards the Penn family. The essay was reprinted in Philadelphia; Isaac Norris pronounced it a "manly performance."[12] In 1759 he gave "great Assistance, and furnish'd most of the Materials" for the *Historical Review of the Constitutions of Pennsylvania*.[13] In 1762, when Benjamin Franklin received the degree of doctor of civil law from Oxford University, William was awarded an honorary master's degree. He and his father were elected to the Philosophical Society of Edinburgh, and so he became an honorary foreign member of the Royal Society of Edinburgh, when it succeeded the Philosophical Society. His portrait was painted by Benjamin Wilson. After a year in London, on 10 November 1758, William was called to the bar.[14]

[8] *Franklin Papers*, IV, 368; V, 4–7, 15; VI, 13–19, 64n, 168.
[9] Ibid., VII, 297.
[10] Ibid., IV, 116; *Pa. Gaz.*, 20 June 1751, 8 May 1755.
[11] *Franklin Papers*, VII, 297.
[12] Ibid., 255–63, 281.
[13] Ibid., VIII, 402.
[14] *PMHB*, XXXV (1911), 422; E. Alfred Jones, *American Members of the Inns of Court* (London, 1924), 78–83.

and was so listed in the first volume of *Transactions* in 1771. In 1785 he contributed £5 towards the construction of Philosophical Hall.

Born on 7 June 1726, the ninth of the eleven children of Jacob Howell of Chester, a tanner by trade and also a minister among Friends, and Sarah (Vernon) Howell, his wife, Joshua was trained for the shop and counting house.[1] At 22 he went to Barbados as supercargo in one of John Reynell's ships.[2] Soon after his return he formed a partnership with John Pole, who, however, died untimely in 1754. Continuing business alone, Howell moved to the store formerly occupied by Edward Penington, where in February 1755 he offered for sale a typical, if improbable, assortment of dry goods, mackerel, gunpowder, wigs, and boat anchors.[3] Family connections, his father's wealth, and his own competence and character soon brought him satisfying amounts of business. By the late 1750s he was in a position routinely to lend or borrow sums of £1000–2000 at a time.[4]

Meanwhile, on 27 November 1753, Howell married in Friends Meeting Catherine, daughter of Edward and Ann (Coleman) Warner. The couple were uncommonly unlucky; most of their children died in infancy, and only three survived to maturity. These were Catherine, who married Johns Hopkins of Maryland, Elizabeth, who married Jesse Tyson, and Edward, who lived long but never married.[5] In 1760 Howell and his brother-in-law Francis Rawle purchased land on the Schuylkill a few miles from town; they divided the tract, Rawle keeping the part he called "Laurel Hill," while on his acres Howell built "Edgely," a comfortable country seat. His friends Henry and Elizabeth Drinker occasionally visited there and the Howells were frequently at the Drinkers' house in Philadelphia.[6] Some years before, he had been admitted a member of the Fishing Company of the Colony [later State] in Schuylkill.

Upon Rawle's untimely death in 1761, Howell succeeded him in some business responsibilities. He and Samuel Shoemaker (who married the widow Rawle in 1767) were named agents of the Pennsylvania Land Company, and Howell was elected a director of the Philadelphia Contributionship (Rawle had been elected just before he died) in 1762, and again (this time in his own right, as it were) in

---

[1] Frank W. Leach, "Old Philadelphia Families, XCIII. Howell," (Phila.) *North American,* 14 Jan. 1912; *Pa. Gaz.,* 24 March 1768. Most writers say Howell was born in June; Leach gives August—which may be correct, for Howell's birth was doubtless recorded as "6 mo.," which would be August in the Old Style calendar.

[2] Frances Howell, *The Book of John Howell & his Descendants* (N. Y., privately printed, 1897), I, 113; Hinshaw, *Amer. Quaker Genealogy,* II, 556.

[3] *Pa. Gaz.,* 25 Feb., 8 May 1755. In 1770 he offers for sale choice old imported Madeira. Ibid., 19 July 1770.

[4] See, for example, Howell's notes and accounts in Norris of Fairhill Mss., Griffitts Estate (HSP).

[5] Hinshaw, *Amer. Quaker Genealogy,* II, 377–78; Leach, "Old Philadelphia Families," loc. cit.

[6] *PMHB,* XXXV (1911), 387–88; Elizabeth Drinker, *Extracts from the Journal* (Phila., 1889), 15, 117–18.

1766; he served until 1785. He was one of those who petitioned for a road from Philadelphia to Strasburg as likely to promote trade and commerce.[7] Wealth, leisure, and his Quaker principles led him to serve the community in other ways. He was one of the earliest contributors to the Pennsylvania Hospital.[8] He was elected a member of the Common Council of the city in 1767 and an alderman three years later, and he often served on committees for improving the wharves and harbor.[9] He was several times a signer of paper currency, turning over his fees for charitable purposes,[10] and for several years after 1769 he was treasurer of the Corporation for the Relief and Employment of the Poor.[11] He subscribed £2 towards the survey of a Delaware-Chesapeake canal in 1769, and £3 to the Silk Society in 1770. Through all the years he took an active role in the business of the Society of Friends, being one of those appointed by his Meeting in 1774 to deal with difficult cases of Friends keeping slaves.[12] He gave the Friendly Association £25 in 1756.

On a visit to New York and Long Island in 1763, Howell heard reports that the British Government intended to station men of war in America "to Look after the Sweet Traders, &c, and that we are to have waiters and Other Officers . . . which will make Trade something more difficult to the fair Dealer as well as to Endeavour to keep the other sort from Importing goods without Paying Dutys &c."[13] Two years later Howell was one of the signers of Philadelphia's Non-Importation Agreement.[14] But this was not to be a first step towards rebellion—Howell was too good a Quaker pacifist for that. In the face of war, he endeavored to maintain strict neutrality, but that was hard. Some of his friends were arrested and carried off into exile in Virginia in 1777—he did what he could to comfort and relieve their families—and a few weeks later, with feelings of mingled fear and sorrow, from his neighbor Elizabeth Drinker's housetop he watched the burning of John Dickinson's Fairhill and other country seats. In 1779 he accepted election to the Board of Managers of the Pennsylvania Hospital, and served three years.[15] But in the summer of 1781 he moved his family out of the city to Edgely, partly to get away from swaggering rebels. When the news of Cornwallis' surrender reached Philadelphia,

---

[7] Nicholas B. Wainwright, *A Philadelphia Story: The Philadelphia Contributionship for the Insurance of Houses from Loss by Fire* (Phila., 1952), 234; Trustees of Pennsylvania Land Company to Joshua Howell and Samuel Shoemaker, 13 Aug. 1761. Rawle Papers (HSP); 6 *Pa. Arch.*, XIV, 287–89.

[8] Morton, *Pennsylvania Hospital,* 387; 8 *Pa. Arch.,* VI, 5199.

[9] *Minutes of the Common Council . . . 1704 to 1776* (Phila., 1847), 722, 751, 761, 809.

[10] 8 *Pa. Arch.,* V, 4262; VIII, 6926.

[11] *Pa. Gaz.,* 17 May 1770, 28 Feb. 1778; *Pa. Chronicle,* 20 May 1771; 8 *Pa. Arch.,* VII, 6564.

[12] Northern District Monthly Meeting, Minutes, 24 Eleventh Mo. 1772, 22 Second Mo. 1774, 22 Eleventh Mo. 1774, et passim.

[13] Howell to William Fisher, 27 May 1763, Society Coll. (HSP). Several letters, chiefly on business, from Howell to his nephew and former apprentice John Ladd Howell, 1762–63, are in Howell, *Book of John Howell,* I, 147–54.

[14] Scharf and Westcott, *Philadelphia,* I, 272–73.

[15] Morton, *Pennsylvania Hospital,* 406.

he stayed up most of the night, anxiously hoping against hope that the report might be proved false.[16]

Howell was now a wealthy man—his name appears in a census of carriage-owners in 1782.[17] He continued active in Quaker matters, but after the Revolution seems to have taken little part in public affairs, and his private ones required but little attention. He became a member of the Agricultural Society in 1785. He fell ill and after a long sickness died on 22 May 1797, and was buried in Friends ground two days later.[18] By his will Howell left a life interest in Edgely to his wife, who survived until 1810; his share in the Library Company went to his son.[19]

WILLIAM HOPKINS (?–?)
"YOUNG JUNTO": BEFORE 22 SEPTEMBER 1758

WILLIAM HOPKINS was already a member of the "Young Junto" on 22 September 1758, when its earliest surviving minutes commence. Although unquestionably interested in the Society and its business, he was frequently absent from its meetings, being reported "in the Country." When the laws revised in the summer of 1761 were presented to him, he "approved and cheerfully signed them." A few weeks later he proposed two queries for discussion:

> Is it consistent with Justice for the Princes of Europe to support the Maltese in their Resolutions to maintain perpetual War with the Turks?
> What is the best Way of distinguishing the several Genuses of Plants?
> (11 September 1761).

He maintained his interest and attendance for some months, serving the Junto as treasurer in 1762. His last recorded attendance was on 22 October 1762, but that may mean little because no further minutes of the Junto survive until 1766. Hopkins, however, seems not to have been a member of the Junto in December 1766, when it renamed itself the American Society for Promoting and Propagating Useful Knowledge. And that is all that has been learned for certain about him.

He may have been the baker William Hopkins, who sold "Midling Bread" to the trading firm of Baynton & Wharton in 1761 and who, five years later, asked to

---

[16] Drinker, *Journal,* 66, 135; *PMHB,* XXXV (1911), 401.
[17] "Quaker Families that Keep Coaches, Coach-Waggons or Chariots," 1782. Du Simitière Papers (Lib. Co. Phila.).
[18] Drinker, *Journal,* 304.
[19] Joshua Howell, Will, 16 Fifth Mo. 1796, Will Book X, No. 439, p. 653 (Register of Wills, Phila.).

be appointed to the post of inspector of flour exported from Philadelphia.[1] A person named William Hopkins, possibly the same, petitioned the Pennsylvania Assembly in 1756 to be named a signer of paper currency for any sum that might be voted for the completion of the Pennsylvania Hospital.[2]

PAUL JACKSON (1729–1767)
"YOUNG JUNTO": BEFORE 22 SEPTEMBER 1758

PAUL JACKSON, teacher, soldier, and physician, was born in 1729, the son of Samuel Jackson, a Scots-Irishman of Oxford in Chester County, Pennsylvania.[1] He was given a good schooling, possibly at Francis Alison's academy; may have taught for several years; and in 1752, at the age of 23, on Alison's recommendation, was appointed a tutor in the Latin School of the Academy of Philadelphia at £60 a year. The trustees raised his salary £10 the next year, and in 1754 gave him the added duties of collecting the moneys owed the institution, keeping its accounts, and serving the Board as clerk. In 1756 Jackson was appointed professor of languages, with special responsibility for the Grammar School and for such Latin and Greek classes as Alison did not conduct. His salary was now £150 a year, a figure which expressed the trustees' appreciation of his remaining at the Academy despite a tempting invitation from the Friends School.[2] In 1757, when the first class was graduated from the College of Philadelphia, Jackson delivered the Latin salutatory and received the degree of master of arts.[3]

Meanwhile, having become deeply interested in the physical sciences, Jackson announced "a Course of Experimental Philosophy, for the Entertainment of the Curious." The thirteen weekly lectures, composed with such "a special Regard . . . to Plainness, Perspicuity and Method, that with a moderate Degree of Attention, 'tis hoped they will prove satisfactory to common Capacities," covered mechanics, pneumatics, hydrostatics, optics, meteorology, fire, geography, and astronomy, including the use of the globes and the orrery. "A Proposal of this Kind whether the Utility or Amusement of it be considered," Jackson's proposal continued,

---

[1] Hopkins, Invoice of 40 Barrels of Midling Bread for Baynton & Wharton, 18 March 1761, Gratz Coll., Business Papers Misc., 1744–69 (HSP); 8 *Pa. Arch.,* VII, 5870–71.
[2] Ibid., V, 4262.

---

[1] Montgomery, *University of Pennsylvania,* 292.
[2] U. of Pa., Trustees' Minutes, 21 April 1752, 17 Nov. 1753, 10 June, 11 July 1755, 13 April 1756.
[3] *Pa. Gaz.,* 12 May 1757; William Smith, *A Charge, delivered May 17, 1757 . . . in the College and Academy of Philadelphia . . . To which is added, in Latin, a Salutatory Oration* (Phila., 1757).

has some Claim at least to general Encouragement. The Study of Nature is undoubtedly the best Preparative for a successful Prosecution of any Art liberal or mechanical. It opens to the Mind a spacious and delightful Field of Knowledge equally fruitful of the most pleasing Entertainment for the Imagination, and the noblest Improvement of the Judgment. It gives a Man an acknowledged Superiority over the rest of the Species, as he is not so liable to be surprized by uncommon Appearances, nor consequently misled by the partial Conceptions of Ignorance, as practised on by the Artifice of Imposture.[4]

Although the advertisement was continued for some weeks, the number of subscribers was insufficient, and the lectures were not given.

But teaching had undermined his health, and Jackson determined to retrieve it by a vigorous, outdoor life. On 9 May 1758, as the trustees' minutes record, "Professor Jackson for some time past, having found himself consumptive, requests of the Trustees his Discharge from the Care of the Latin School, & their Interest with the Governor to obtain for him a Commission in the Levies now raising for the Expedition against Fort DuQueyne." The trustees let him go reluctantly, but recommended him to the governor, as he had requested, and he was commissioned a captain on 11 May.[5] Jackson accompanied General Forbes' forces across Pennsylvania to the Ohio, his health improved, and, finding a profession more to his liking than teaching, he began to study medicine under British military surgeons.

While still a teacher in the College, Jackson had been elected one of the twelve members of the "Young Junto." In the surviving minutes, which commence on 22 September 1758, his name first appears on 29 September, when he was marked as "out of town" with the army. When he returned at last from the western expedition and appeared in the Junto on 29 December the members set aside their scheduled business "to do ourselves the Pleasure of discoursing with him on that Affair." Jackson's attendance through 1759 was erratic. On 9 February he proposed two questions for discussion: "What state of Life bids fairest for happiness?" and "Which is the best Method of Calculating Annuities on Lives?" On 30 November

---

[4] *Pa. Gaz.*, 6 Nov. 1755. Within a few weeks of Jackson's first announcement Ebenezer Kinnersley announced his course on electricity in two lectures, and Henry Bridge brought his "Microcosm" to Philadelphia, with lectures on it.

[5] U. of Pa., Trustees' Minutes, 9 May 1758; 5 *Pa. Arch.*, I, 185. John Beveridge, a colleague in the Academy and College, and T. H., "student of philosophy," saluted Jackson in Latin and English verses on his entering the army.

> But in the rolls of lasting fame
>   Wouldst thou distinguish'd be,
> And boldly vent'ring, give thy name
>   To glorious immortality?
> Be active. Nurse the heav'nly fire,
> Like those fam'd bards before you, snatch the lyre,
> Like them to glory—deathless fame aspire.

Epistolae Familiares (Phila., 1765), 49–50, 85.

he proposed two more: "Is it for the Advantage of Great Britain to Keep up her Connections with the King of Prussia?" and "Why doth the flame of the Candle tend upwards in form of a Spire?" After this meeting he never attended again; and when the Society was reorganized in 1761 his name had been dropped from the roll.

The reason for his continued absences was that, having received a certificate from "the Royal [Army] Hospital (at that time the only medical School on the Continent),"[6] he had settled in Chester to practice. There in 1760 he married Jane, daughter of John Mather of Chester;[7] and two years later he was commissioned a justice of the county court and elected chief burgess. His interest in literature did not abate, however, and for the College commencement of 1763 he prepared at the faculty's request a poem hailing the British military victory and the return of peace:

> May Britain's Glory still increase,
>   Her Fame immortal be,
> Whose Sons make War to purchase *Peace,*
>   And conquer to set free.
> Such Pow'r like the bright Star of Day,
>   Invades the Realms of Night,
> Before whose Beam, each Beast of Prey
>   To Darkness speeds his Flight.
> Still may it grow, till round the earthy Ball
> *Science* and *Liberty* illumine all![8]

Dr. Jackson died at Chester on 22 September 1767, and was buried in St. Paul's churchyard there. Recalling him as "a Gentleman of great Learning, and acknowledged Abilities," the *Pennsylvania Gazette* declared that he had "had a clear Understanding, sound Judgment, and tenacious Memory, which he greatly improved by Reading, Observation and Study."[9] Because Jackson had been both a "practitioner in physick and shopkeeper,"[10] the inventory of his estate showed both shop goods (£388 4*s.* 11*d.*) and utensils of his "doctor's shop" (£22 7*s.*6*d.*). It also showed that he had owned "Physical Books" worth £16 12*s.* and a "Library" valued at £95 10*s.* 6*d.*[11]

He left three young children—John Mather, Mary, and Charles; but they did not remain orphans long, for his widow in 1770 married his brother Dr. David Jackson.[12]

---

[6] *Pa. Gaz.,* 1 Oct. 1767.
[7] 2 *Pa. Arch.,* II, 151.
[8] *An Excercise, containing a Dialogue and Ode on Peace . . . May 17th, 1763* (Phila., 1763); *PMHB,* X (1886), 350.
[9] *Pa. Gaz.,* 1 Oct. 1767; *Pa. Chronicle,* 28 Sept. 1767.
[10] 3 *Pa. Arch.,* II, 288.
[11] Chester Co., Register of Wills, Inventories, No. 2398. He subscribed for two copies of Gilbert Tennent's *Sermons on Important Subjects* (Phila., 1758) and for Bulkeley and Cummings' narrative of *A Voyage to the South Seas, in the Years 1740–1* (Phila., 1757).
[12] John Hill Martin, *Chester (and its Vicinity), Delaware County* (Phila., 1877), 129, 130.

GEORGE CLYMER

By Charles Willson Peale. *Pennsylvania Academy of the Fine Arts. Gift of the artist.*

GEORGE CLYMER (1739–1813)

"YOUNG JUNTO": 9 FEBRUARY 1759
AMERICAN PHILOSOPHICAL SOCIETY: 21 JULY 1786

GEORGE CLYMER, a Philadelphia merchant and trader, was elected a member of the "Young Junto" on 9 February 1759, but, as there is no record that he attended any meeting, it is likely that he did not accept election. He was not considered a member when the Junto's minutes resume in 1762, nor was he a member of the American Society when it united with the American Philosophical Society in 1769. Some years later, however, on 19 January 1781, he was proposed by James Wilson for membership in the American Philosophical Society, but was not elected. In 1786 his name was presented again, and on 21 July of that year he was chosen a member. He promptly subscribed £5 towards the cost of erecting the Society's new hall.

Though a man of wide reading, interested in agriculture and the fine arts as well as politics, Clymer had few contacts with the Society and, except once in 1812, rarely, if ever, attended a meeting. In 1802 he submitted an essay on the healthfulness of Philadelphia, which concluded, after a comparison of that city's mortality statistics with the tables of Dr. Richard Price and Albrecht von Haller, that the city enjoyed a greater degree of healthfulness than London, Paris, Vienna, "or the countries generally of Europe."[1] After Clymer's death his son George, inventor of the Columbia printing press, gave the Society some forty volumes from his father's library, which he had inherited: they included the *Historical Review of the Constitution and Government of Pennsylvania* (1759), Andrew Mackay's *Mathematical Tables* (1804), John Morgan's Edinburgh dissertation on the formation of pus (1763), George Costard's *History of Astronomy* (1767), *Histoire politique du siècle . . . depuis la paix de Westphalie jusqu'à la dernière paix d'Aix la Chapelle inclusivement* (1754–56), and the thirty-volume *Histoire de France* of Paul-Francois Velly, Claude Villaret, and Jean-Jacques Garnier (1765–85).[2]

Clymer was born in Philadelphia on 16 March 1739, the only surviving child of Christopher and Deborah (Fitzwater) Clymer.[3] Christopher Clymer was a ship captain. Deborah Fitzwater was a birthright Friend disowned when she married out of meeting. Both parents died young (Deborah probably from complications of childbirth), leaving George an orphan at the age of seven. The lad was reared by

---

[1] Clymer, "On the Healthfulness of Philadelphia," 1802, Ms. Communications on Medicine, Anatomy &c. (APS).
[2] George Clymer, Jr. to John Vaughan, 6 Feb. 1816, Archives (APS).
[3] Jerry Grundfest, "George Clymer, Philadelphia Revolutionary (1739–1813)" (Ph. D. diss., Columbia Univ., 1973); Robert Waln, Jr., "Clymer" in John Sanderson, *Biography of the Signers of the Declaration of Independence* (Phila., 1823), IV, 173–246; James R. Macfarlane, *George Clymer: . . . His Family and Descendants* (n.p., 1927); *DAB*.

his Quaker aunt and uncle, Hannah (Fitzwater) and William Coleman, and trained to follow Coleman in his counting house. Coleman was a wealthy merchant, a friend of Benjamin Franklin, and one of the original members of the American Philosophical Society in 1743. At the age of 20 in 1759 Clymer formed a partnership with Henry and Robert Ritchie for the importation of European and East India goods.[4] In 1765 he signed the Non-Importation Agreement, and in 1770 supported the call to continue non-importation as a response to the Townshend Acts. But the young man had little taste for business and, fortunately for him, his grandfather Fitzwater made him a substantial bequest, consisting of land in Philadelphia and New Jersey, ground rents, and an interest in the Durham Iron Works. Coleman, who was childless, on his death in 1769, also left his nephew a generous bequest, estimated at £6000, in addition to his books and mathematical instruments.[5]

Meanwhile on 16 March 1765 at Christ Church, Philadelphia, Clymer was married to Elizabeth Meredith, daughter of the wealthy merchant Reese Meredith and his wife Martha Carpenter, both Quakers. For marrying out of meeting Clymer's wife, like his mother, was disowned. She was described by John Adams as "a very facetious and social Lady." The couple had eight children, of whom three died young. The eldest was named William Coleman Clymer after his father's benefactor.[6] In 1772 Reese Meredith established a partnership with his son and son-in-law as Meredith and Sons; it continued after the elder Meredith's death in 1778 as Meredith and Clymer, but dissolved in 1782.

Clymer joined some of the city's social and cultural institutions. He was a member of the Library Company, the Hand-in-Hand Fire Company, and the Mount Regale Fishing Company; in the last-named he enjoyed the company of persons like himself, members of the Proprietary party. He was a contributor to the Pennsylvania Hospital, subscribed £2 10s. to the Silk Society in 1770, and gave £10 to the College of Philadelphia in 1772. In 1767 he was elected to the Philadelphia Common Council, which named him to committees for building a road from the Middle Ferry to Strasburg in Lancaster County and for replacing the city's legal half-bushel standard for measuring wheat. Elected an alderman in 1774, he was on the committee to plan for a new city hall; completion of that project, however, was delayed fifteen years by the Revolution.[7] He was a subscriber to the City Tavern in 1776. On 27 April 1772 Clymer was commissioned a justice of the peace, one of a panel from which judges of the Courts of Common Pleas and Quarter Sessions

---

[4] *Pa. Gaz.,* 20 Sept. 1759, 8 Jan. 1761.
[5] Waln, "Clymer" in Sanderson, *Biography of the Signers,* IV, 170.
[6] John Adams, *Diary and Autobiography* (L. H. Butterfield, ed., Cambridge, 1961), II, 104–05.
[7] *Minutes of the Select and Common Council* (Phila., 1847), 744, 774–75, 781, 793–94, 799, 804, 806.

and of the Orphans Court were drawn. In addition to his house in town he had a "plantation" on the Lower Ferry Road near Province Island.[8]

In provincial politics Clymer was a member of the Proprietary party. In the movement towards independence he was a Whig. A visit to Boston, where he met Josiah Quincy, Jr., and Samuel Adams in 1773, confirmed him in his principles. On his return to Philadelphia he was chairman of the committee that demanded the resignation of the consignees of the tea ships sent to the city, and he soon joined John Dickinson, Thomas Mifflin, and Benjamin Rush in writing for the press. In 1774 he made another visit to Boston, where he saw the growing opposition to British policies and laws, which he contrasted impatiently with the caution and moderation of the Philadelphia merchants. He was chairman of the city committee appointed in November 1774 to supervise the embargo, and was appointed a delegate to the Provincial Convention that met on 23 January 1775. Affairs were moving fast now. On 25 April he was commissioned a captain in Colonel John Cadwalader's "Silk Stocking Company." Three months later, on 29 July, the Continental Congress named him joint treasurer with Michael Hillegas; he held the office for a year, resigning when he was elected a member of the Continental Congress. On 2 October Clymer became chairman of the Committee of Safety, which had authority over a variety of military matters—recruiting, casting cannon, manufacturing saltpetre, planning and constructing fortifications around the city, recruiting, building salt works, and coping with inflation. In May 1776 he was elected to the Pennsylvania Assembly and on 20 July he was one of the new delegates sent to the Continental Congress to replace those who had held out against independence. He affixed his signature to the Declaration as it lay on the secretary's desk and so won a lasting place in American history as one of the "Signers."

A few weeks after Clymer took his seat, Congress appointed him and Richard Stockton to visit Ticonderoga, Saratoga, and Albany to inquire into the condition of the Northern Army under General Philip Schuyler there, especially on the state of the medical and hospital services. Clymer wrote the report, which, strongly condemning "the neglect and ill treatment of the Sick," demanded "a strict enquiry . . . into the Conduct of the other Officers and Servants, and that exemplary Punishment be inflicted on all such as shall be found to have neglected their Duty."[9] A few weeks later, as the British army, advancing across New Jersey, seemed to threaten Philadelphia itself and Congress fled to Baltimore, Clymer, Robert Morris, and George Taylor were left behind as an executive committee to handle the necessary business of Congress, such as assembling and forwarding provisions for the army, providing for sick and wounded troops, guarding and quartering the

---

[8] *Pa. Gaz.,* 27 Feb. 1788.
[9] Quoted in Grundfest, "George Clymer."

ceptance that even Bartram forgot it: when Jeremy Belknap inquired for a copy of his paper in 1780 Bartram did not know what he might be talking about.[9]

As curator with Dr. Benjamin Rush and Owen Biddle, Bartram offered a plan to increase the cabinet of the Society. They proposed that through the newspapers of every colony they appeal to merchants, captains of vessels, army officers, and other travelers "to collect & preserve all such new & curious Plants—Animals & Fossils as they may meet with on this Continent & in foreign Countries, & to transmit them" to the Society. Public acknowledgment would be made to the donors, and their names would be recorded in the Society's books. As a first step towards augmenting the cabinet, the curators asked members to return anything they might have borrowed from it.[10]

In Philadelphia in the years before the Revolution Bartram was one of the managers of the Silk Society, specially charged with distributing silkworms gratis to anyone who wished to raise them.[11] In 1776–77 he served briefly as a director of the Library Company of Philadelphia. The war brought stresses and changes, of course. During the British occupation Bartram moved his family to Haverford, but that may have been as much because of his wife's health as due to threats of war. As a Quaker and a man past 50 years of age, Bartram was under no pressure to take up arms. Unlike his brother Moses, he did not compromise his religious principles but remained a member in good standing of the Philadelphia Monthly Meeting until his death.

With the resumption of normal activities in Philadelphia Bartram was in business again at the Sign of the Unicorn. In 1785 he was elected a member of the newly-established Philadelphia Society for Promoting Agriculture; he was a contributor to the Philadelphia Dispensary, founded in 1786; and in the next year he and Moses donated drugs worth £11 7s. 8d. to the Pennsylvania Hospital.[12]

Bartram was married on 17 December 1747 to Sarah Elfreth, daughter of Caleb and Mary Elfreth. They had nine children, of whom only three seem to have survived the diseases of infancy and childhood.[13] Sarah died at Haverford on 5 August 1778; and the next year, on 30 November 1779, Isaac was married to Mrs. Mary Steel, a widow, daughter of Richard and Ann Renshaw. Both Isaac and Mary Bartram survived the yellow fever in Philadelphia, although the former appears to have had a light case.[14] He died at his house in Third Street and was buried in Friends

[9] Jeremy Belknap to Ebenezer Hazard, 28 Aug. 1780, Belknap Papers, 5 Mass. Hist. Soc., *Colls.*, II (1877), 75; see also ibid., 77, 80.
[10] Bartram, Benjamin Rush, and Owen Biddle to APS, 20 April 1770 (APS Archives).
[11] *Pa. Gaz.*, 8 Nov. 1770, 12 March 1772.
[12] Ibid., 19 Nov. 1783; John G. Bevan to Bartram, 1 Eighth Mo. 1783; Bevan to Isaac and Moses Bartram, 7 Sixth Mo. 1783, Letter Book D, 27, 34 (Allen & Hanbury's, London); Managers Minutes, 26 Third Mo. 1787 (Pa. Hospital).
[13] Leach, "Old Pennsylvania Families," loc. cit.
[14] Bartram to Benjamin Rush, 20 Sept. 1793, Rush Corres., XXXV, 9 (HSP).

ground on 22 June 1801; Mary Steel Bartram survived until 1818 and was buried beside him.[15] To his son, Isaac Bartram bequeathed the drug business, his books, and a precious family memento, the "two handled Silver Cann engraved with these words & figures to wit. 'The Gift of Sr Hans Sloane Bart. to his Frd John Bartram. Anno 1742.'"[16]

JAMES PEARSON (1735–1813)
"YOUNG JUNTO": 9 FEBRUARY 1759

JAMES PEARSON, "house carpenter," was proposed for membership in the "Young Junto" on 2 February 1759, and was elected one week later. He was never formally introduced to the Society by his sponsor, appears not to have attended any meeting, and was not considered a member when the Junto was reorganized in 1761. Some time between 1762 and 1766, however, he began to attend, and was reckoned a member before 25 April 1766, when the surviving minutes resume after a three-year lapse. Here he found the company congenial, and he attended meetings with fair regularity except for such an inescapable obligation as that of 28 August 1767: his absence that day was excused "on account of . . . declaring his intention of marriage at meeting this day." The Society asked Pearson to construct a cabinet for its curiosities—it cost £13 12s. 4d.; and he also made "a plate and balls" for voting at elections—he charged 12s. 6d. On other occasions Pearson was appointed to examine Richard Wells' invention for pumping vessels at sea and, with Charles Thomson and Moses Bartram, to recommend a list of books on history and agriculture for a society or club at Port Penn.

In the American Philosophical Society after 1769 he enjoyed the most opportunities for usefulness. He was on three standing committees—those on Geography, Mathematics, Natural Philosophy and Astronomy; on Mechanics and Architecture; and on Husbandry and American Improvements. He was named on 7 February 1769 to the committee to prepare for the observation of the Transit of Venus that was to occur that spring, and in April he was instructed "to erect an Observatory to a plan delivered him" by the Society's committee, which included the architect Robert Smith. The structure, according to the annalist John Fanning Wat-

---

[15] Philadelphia Monthly Meeting, Minutes, 30 Fifth Mo. 1777, 30 Fourth Mo. 1779; Northern District Meeting, Minutes, 29 Tenth Mo. 1779; Elizabeth Drinker, *Journal* (Phila., 1889), 122; Hinshaw, *Amer. Quaker Genealogy,* II, 335.
[16] Bartram, Will, 29 July 1800, probated 16 July 1801, Will Book Y, 540 (Register of Wills, Phila.). The "Cann" is illustrated in Darlington, *Memorials,* 305.

son, was a platform 20 feet high and 12 to 15 feet square and was situated south of the State House. Work was completed in a month, in ample time for the observers to mount and test their instruments before "Transit-Day." It cost £64 17s. Pearson himself noted the external contact of Venus and the sun "with a small Telescope" belonging to the Proprietors.

Pearson participated in other Society activities. In 1781 he was put on a special committee of publication within the Committee on Mechanics and Architecture; but the committee seems to have made no proposal. He subscribed to the Silk Society, in which many members of the Philosophical Society were interested and whose assets it eventually received. He subscribed £5 towards the construction of Philosophical Hall in 1785, but proved slow to pay his pledge.

Born in Darby, Chester County, Pennsylvania, on 1 November 1735, James Pearson was the son of Thomas Pearson, a tanner, and Hannah Blunston, his wife, both Quakers.[1] He may have been the James Pearson who attended the Academy of Philadelphia for a few months in 1751. Then or soon afterwards he was apprenticed to a carpenter, and by 1758 was settled in his trade in Philadelphia. With other ambitious young artisans, who included Moses and Isaac Bartram, John Murgatroyd, and Thomas Pryor, he was a founder of the Amicable Library Company in 1757. The company, of which Pearson was a secretary, offered its members more than a collection of books: at its annual meeting on 20 May 1765, for example, a lecture on electricity, "accompanied with suitable Experiments," was announced "(if the Air is clear)."[2] Soon afterwards the Amicable Company joined the Union Library Company, and the Union Library, thus enlarged, was united with the Library Company of Philadelphia.

Now out of his apprenticeship, on 10 October 1758 Pearson married Mary Paschall, daughter of Dr. John and Frances Paschall of Darby. She bore two sons, and died in childbed with the second. Three years later, on 28 August 1767 at Philadelphia Monthly Meeting, the young widower declared intention of marrying Susanna Hart, daughter of Thomas and Mary (Combs) Hart of Philadelphia.[3] The couple established themselves in a house on the west side of Second Street four doors above Arch. They had eleven children, of whom seven survived their parents.

As a member of the Carpenters' Company, to which he was elected before 1763 (the date the surviving minutes begin), Pearson was active and influential. He was a warden in 1764–66, an assistant in 1770–73 and again in 1785–88. He

---

[1] J. Granville Leach, "The Record of Some Resident in the Vicinity of the Middle Ferry, Philadelphia," Geneal. Soc. Pa., *Pubs.*, IX (1926), 56–57; Sandra L. Tatman and Roger W. Moss, *Biographical Dictionary of Philadelphia Architects: 1700–1930* (Boston, 1985), 597–98.

[2] *Pa. Gaz.*, 18 April 1765. His signature is on the Articles of Agreement, Union Library Company, n.d., in Griffith & Paschall Coll. (HSP).

[3] Phila. Monthly Meeting, Minutes, 28 Eighth Mo., 30 Tenth Mo. 1767; Hinshaw, *Amer. Quaker Genealogy*, II, 404, 618.

was one of the seven trustees who purchased a lot for the carpenters' hall in 1769, was named the next year to the committee to oversee the design and construction of the building, and was frequently thereafter commissioned to repair or alter the structure. He was on many *ad hoc* committees, such as one to negotiate the admission of members of the Friendship Carpenters' Company and another to arrange accommodations in the Company's new hall for the Library Company of Philadelphia as tenant; and he served on the important standing committees on prices and "for Regulating the Rules of Measuring & Settling the Accounts of the Company."[4]

In addition to being a carpenter Pearson, like so many others in Philadelphia, kept a shop for the sale of domestic and imported goods. An advertisement of 1773 reveals him offering "the various sorts of manufactured tobacco, of an excellent Quality," rappee snuff of several sorts made by an able workman recently come from Germany; also forge hammers and anvils, "fifty-sixes and smaller weights," cart-, wagon- and chair-boxes, sash weights, tea-urn heaters, and "a few kettles, neat as those imported from Britain, &c." The advertisement also invited persons to invest as partners in an iron furnace.[5] Apparently not all these ventures were successful, and Pearson fell into debt. He was spoken to by representatives from the Meeting; but, failing to make satisfactory arrangements with his creditors and an appropriate acknowledgment to the Meeting (not to mention his continued absence from religious services), he was disowned on 24 Fifth Mo. 1774.[6]

Pearson supported the Non-Importation Agreement of 1765 and opposed the decision of a majority of the merchants in 1770 to modify it. He stood with the minority in their resolution of 27 September declaring that the Parliament's claim of a right to tax the colonies for revenue was subversive of the latter's constitutional rights, asserting that a union of the colonies was necessary, and calling on the merchants to renew their former resolutions.[7] Upon the outbreak of hostilities in 1775 Pearson threw himself unreservedly into the Americans' cause. In July of that year he was engaged in making firearms for the Committee of Safety. In the winter of 1776–77 the Board of War instructed him to make repairs and alterations to the State House.[8] Later that year he was appointed commissary of military stores in Colonel Benjamin Flower's Company of Artillery Artificers—a unit composed of armourers, black- and white-smiths, brass founders, carpenters, shoemakers, saddlers, and other skilled workers. As commissary Pearson erected a plating mill; at Blockley, across the Schuylkill River, he built a mill for boring and grinding musket barrels and one for sharpening swords and bayonets; and on the city commons

---

[4] Wardens' Book, 1769–1781, passim (Carpenters' Company of Phila., on deposit in APS).
[5] *Pa. Gaz.,* 12 May 1773.
[6] Northern District Monthly Meeting, Minutes, 26 First Mo. 1773, 24 Fifth Mo. 1774.
[7] *Pa. Gaz.,* 4 Oct. 1770.
[8] 2 *Pa. Arch.,* I, 16; Force, *Am. Archives,* 4th ser., II, 1774, 1775.

SAMUEL POWEL

By Angelica Kauffmann. *Courtesy of the private owner.*

self no longer a member of any existing organization. His old friends, however, had not forgotten. He would have been a desirable addition to any company; but the American Society claimed him as their own, and on 19 January 1768 its members extended "An Invitation . . . to Mr. Saml. Powell to come and take his place as being a Member of the Society before he went to England." Powel was pleased to accept, and on 12 February 1768 he attended and signed the Laws and Obligation of the American Society. In the November elections that year he was chosen a vice-president.

In this capacity he gave some assistance in the negotiations with the American Philosophical Society which resulted in the union of the two societies. To the opportunities the enlarged society seemed to offer for improving the country he responded warmly; and he conveyed some of his enthusiasm to Thomas Penn. The Proprietor, who had already heard that the Society had awarded a premium for the best example of viniculture, replied with the gift of John Ellis' pamphlet, *Directions for bringing over seeds and plants from the East-Indies and other distant countries, in a state of vegetation: together with a catalogue of . . . foreign plants . . . worthy of being encouraged in our American Colonies . . .* (London, 1770). "I desire you will inform me what other improvements your Society has given incouragement too [sic]," Penn continued to Powel, "& if I can be an assistant therein from hence it will give much pleasure."[1] Despite this auspicious beginning in the Society, however, Powel took no further active role. Its resumption or reactivation came at just the moment when he was assuming a variety of other, weightier, and probably more congenial obligations.

Born in Philadelphia on 28 Eighth Month [October] 1738, he was the only son of three children of Samuel and Mary (Morris) Powel, and a grandson of Samuel Powell, "the rich carpenter." From childhood he knew only comfort, for his father was a wealthy man, who had served the city as a common councillor and alderman and had donated the ground on which Pine Street Meeting was built. The second Samuel Powel had a sense of family, for, either to distinguish himself from others of the name or as a reversion to an earlier spelling, he dropped one "l" from his surname. The third Samuel was entered in the Academy of Philadelphia in 1754 and continued on into the College, from which he was graduated in 1759. Within a few months he was master of a large fortune, for his father had died in 1747 and his grandfather in 1756 (and his mother on 31 October 1759).[2] With wealth added to decent abilities and a good character, Powel's prospects must have seemed limitless. After seeing that his affairs were in order, he determined to make

---

[1] Penn to Powel, 19 March 1770, Penn Letter Book, X, 79 (HSP). Extracts from Ellis' pamphlet were printed in APS *Trans.,* I (1771), 255–80.

[2] George B. Tatum, *Philadelphia Georgian: The City House of Samuel Powel* (Middletown, Conn., 1976), 6–25 *et passim;* Robert C. Moon, *The Morris Family of Philadelphia* (Phila., 1898), I, 273; Montgomery, *University of Pennsylvania,* 548.

banker Signor Barratzi's on a sturgeon that they understood had received a papal blessing, and even had a private audience with Pope Clement. He received them, Powel reported, "with great Courteousness and Affability, asking many Questions concerning America." Powel and Morgan were elected members of the Accademia degli Arcadi, and attended at least one meeting at the villa of Cardinal Albani. From ten to two o'clock each day Powel, Morgan, and two other young Americans took a course in art and antiquities under the noted Roman antiquary James Beyers, visiting galleries, palaces, churches, all "the venerable remains of Antiquity," grand and splendid beyond conception. "The Remains of Grandeur and Magnificence still extant," he commented to his uncle, "prove that they could only have been raised to the Splendor they once enjoyed, by the united Treasures of a World." He was strongly tempted to buy paintings and statues, but did not, or at least only some inexpensive ones. "Had Fortune made me her Minion," he apologized, "America should have been enriched with some few Things worthy of Attention."[9] One painting that he did bring home, however, was of himself, done by Angelica Kauffmann: it shows him, an elegant young man, holding floor plans of a house, perhaps to suggest the one he expected soon to return to in Philadelphia. Angelica painted John Morgan, too; and later, in appreciation of his professional services in an illness, presented Morgan with a portrait of herself—which some years afterwards Morgan gave to Powel.[10]

The most unusual experience of their tour awaited them in Switzerland. Friends in Rome had given them a letter to Voltaire, and on a Sunday afternoon Powel and Morgan presented themselves at the Château of Ferney. There were other guests, and Voltaire took the occasion of the Americans' visit to proclaim his devotion to liberty:

> I beg leave to present to you two English Gentlemen. Oh, Glorious Nation, renowned Conquerors of Canada. Though they have fought against you, & well have they fought battles by land & Sea, we must now look upon them as our brave friends, since we are now at peace.

So grandiloquent an introduction, though gratifying, must have been embarrassing as well. Powel was further discomfited by being drawn into a conversation on immortality. As Morgan related it in his journal,

> A little Dog happening to cross the room stopp'd before Mr. Voltaire, wagg'd his Tail and seem'd to Notice him very attentively—on w'ch Mr. Voltaire turn'd to

---

[9] Powel to Morris, 5 July 1764, in Moon, *Morris Family,* II, 469–71; Powel, "Short Notes on a Course of Antiquities at Rome In Company with Messrs: Apthorp, Morgan & Palmer, begun May 21, 1764 under Mr. Byre Antiquarian," Robert Hare Papers (APS); Powel to Roberts, 24 Nov. 1764, "Powel-Roberts Correspondence, 1761–1765," 39–40.

[10] The painting was long afterwards given by Mrs. Powel to the Pennsylvania Academy of the Fine Arts, where it now is.

Mr. Powel, & as I thought a little abruptly ask'd him, what think You of that little dog; has he any Soul or not, & what do the People in England now think of the Soul. This Question so unexpected & before Company some of whom Mr. Powel was very sure at least of Mr. Voltaire, that they entertained some Sentiments concerning the soul very different from himself & the bulk of Mankind who have been taught at all to reason about the Soul, was a little startled at this Question put so *mal a propos.* To shew that he was not desirous of enlarging upon this Topic, his Answer was that the People of England now as well as heretofore entertained very Different Notions from each other concerning the Soul. Very true says Mons'r Beaufremont [another guest]. Everybody thinks after his own fashion.

Mr. Voltaire however did not drop the subject entirely—says he I esteem one of your Country-Men who has wrote on that subject, My Lord Bolingbroke. He has done essential Service to Mankind, but there would have been still greater had he given the Matter in fewer Words. . . . Have you not read this valuable Author? Another Question as little to Mr. Powel's gout as the former—But without hesitation he told him what appear'd to me sufficiently spirited—Whatever his Merit may be I own I have never read him. Oh read him by all Means—He is a most valuable Author & let me recommend to you when you return home to get some of y'r Fr'ds to give an abridgement of it. It will bear to be reduced to a third of its bulk & then will be a most excellent Work.

Then, after showing the men his gardens and the prospect from them, Voltaire bade them farewell with a final thundering injunction:

Behold two Amiable Young Men Lovers of Truth & Inquirers into Nature. They are not satisfy'd with mear Appearances; they love Investigation & Truth, and despize Superstition. I commend you, Gentlemen—go on, love Truth & search diligently after it. Hate Hypocrisy, Hate Masses & above all hate the Priests.

Seven years of this kind of thing might easily have drawn Powel forever away from his Philadelphia background; it did, despite Voltaire's injunction, take him out of the Meeting into the Church. Powel had never been a concerned Friend—he seems to have asked for a certificate from the Philadelphia Monthly Meeting to London only as an afterthought; and in England, unlike some other Friends, he did not seek out the Quaker society that revolved closely around Gracechurch Street Meeting, but found his social life instead among the more fashionable and worldly. The change in attitudes and manners was perceptible to his Quaker relations in Philadelphia, never more so than when they received a miniature portrait and at first hardly recognized Samuel in his fashionable attire.[11] When he returned to London from the Continent in 1764, Powel was ready to embrace the Church of England, a step that John Morgan, son of a Quaker mother, had already taken and was therefore eager to see Powel take as well. Fortunately, in London at this time

---

[11] Phila. Monthly Meeting, Minutes, 31 Tenth Mo. 1760; Hinshaw, *Amer. Quaker Genealogy,* II, 626; Morris to Powel, 9 March 1765, in Moon, *Morris Family,* II, 472–75.

3 October 1775 Powel was chosen mayor.[23] The mayor of Philadelphia had never had much to do; even the ceremonial functions were few. But Powel, elected just as the Revolution was breaking out, had both more and less to do than his predecessors; more, because unprecedented problems and emergencies arose; less, because even the normal functions of government were being assumed by Congress, revolutionary conventions, and committees. Some time in the summer of 1776 the city government of Philadelphia simply disappeared. Powel kept the records but no one called for them in five years.[24]

Samuel Powel, of course, was no bawling patriot or "furious Whig." Like many other Philadelphia gentlemen of property—he paid the largest Provincial Tax of any citizen in 1772—he was aristocratic, conservative, and took his stand with the rebels slowly, deliberately, and doubtless with some distaste for their company. He stayed in Philadelphia during the British occupation; the Earl of Carlisle was quartered in his house, something Powel's descendants, if not he, regarded as conferring distinction upon it. Their relationship was anything but that of victor and vanquished. His Lordship, embarrassed, as he privately confessed, to be "coming into a gentleman's house without asking his leave, taking possession of all the best apartments and placing a couple of sentries at his door, using his plate, etc.," paid a formal call each day on his hosts, talked politics a little, "and we are the best friends in the world."[25] This gracious interlude ended for Powel with the British withdrawal, and on 24 June 1778 he took the oath of allegiance to the Commonwealth.[26]

Civic obligations that Powel had assumed before the war continued and increased after the return of peace. He was one of the Pennsylvania representatives at the Episcopal church convention at New York on 6–7 October 1784, which restored and reorganized that church in America, and was named to a committee instructed to correspond with English bishops on a plan to obtain the consecration of American bishops. At the same time he helped to reestablish the Corporation for the Relief of Widows & Children of Clergymen, whose treasurer he had been since 1773 and continued to be until 1786, when he resigned.[27] He was not long without a church trusteeship, however. When Francis Hopkinson died, Bishop William White recommended Powel to serve as trustee of the school for Negro children in Philadelphia supported by Bray's Associates of London. He was, Bishop White assured the London board, "a Gentleman eminent among us for his Integrity his Tal-

---

[23] *Minutes of the Common Council,* 799, 809; Street Commissioners, Minutes, 8 Sixth Mo. 1771 (Independence National Historical Park).
[24] Pa. Executive Council, Extract of Minutes, 1 Aug. 1781, Powel Coll. (HSP).
[25] H. D. Eberlein and Horace M. Lippincott, *The Colonial Homes of Philadelphia and its Neighbourhood* (Phila., 1912), 54.
[26] 2 *Pa. Arch.,* III, 24. In HSP is an oath of allegiance signed by Powel and dated 22 May (Misc. Mss., Brayton Coll.).
[27] Perry, *American Episcopal Church,* I, 655–66; II, 28, 47, 61–64.

ents & his Fortune & who besides his other Qualifications for the Trust, has this in a very singular Degree . . . that he is minutely attentive to whatever Business he undertakes." He was accordingly appointed in 1791.[28] Powel was elected in 1778 a manager of the Pennsylvania Hospital, to which he had made a generous gift in 1759; but resigned in two years. He was a manager of the Philadelphia Dispensary in 1786, a vice-president of the Pennsylvania Society for Promoting Manufactures in 1787, and a director of the Library Company in 1792. With the restoration of the College of Philadelphia to its trustees in 1789, Powel spent many hours in the business of reestablishing that institution, making rules for the trustees, choosing masters and tutors, finding rooms for the schools, and putting the funds in order. When the College and the University of the State of Pennsylvania were merged in 1791, he continued as a member of the new board, and often served as chairman. And, after fifteen years during which he had neither attended a meeting nor otherwise demonstrated any interest in the Society, he made a contribution towards the erection of Philosophical Hall in 1785, accepted appointment to a committee to procure building materials, attended a meeting and signed the charter and new by-laws. In 1793 he subscribed $10 to an exploration of the Missouri River that the French naturalist André Michaux proposed to make under the Society's auspices.

Powel was also in 1785 a founder and first elected president of the Philadelphia Society for Promoting Agriculture. Like most members of that society, his interest in agriculture was not as a practical farmer, but as an economist and investor. He appreciated the economic importance of agriculture and the significance of new crops and improved methods for increasing agricultural production and national prosperity. On his own farm west of the Schuylkill he experimented with both crops and machinery, and once took President Washington there to see Colonel Alexander Anderson's new threshing machine at work.[29] Powel greatly admired Washington, as did Mrs. Powel, who commissioned a portrait of the General from Joseph Wright in 1784. The Agricultural Society, which elected Washington a member in August 1785, brought the two men more closely together. The normal exchange of civilities on the occasion was followed in this case by an exchange of seeds and of reports on their growth. Washington sometimes asked Powel to execute some commission or other at Philadelphia, and he invited the Powels to pay a visit to Mount Vernon. In 1787, when he spent several months in Philadelphia as president of the Federal Convention, Washington was often at the Powels' house for tea, supper, or dinner; and during the recesses of the convention he and Powel occasionally rode out into the surrounding countryside to inspect interesting farms.

---

[28] Edward L. Pennington, "The Work of the Bray Associates in Pennsylvania," *PMHB,* LVIII (1934), 21.
[29] Washington to Powel, 21 Aug. 1791, in John C. Fitzpatrick, ed., *Writings of George Washington* (Washington, 1931–44), XXXI, 343.

One day in this way they visited Bartram's gardens, then the farm of "one Jones," where plaster of Paris was being tried; and so they continued on to Powel's farm and ended the jaunt at Robert Morris' place "The Hills." On 19 August, in company with Powel, Washington "rode up to the White Marsh, traversed my old Incampment, and contemplated on the dangers which threatened the American Army at that place." That is one of Washington's few personal entries in his diary; in what it suggests but does not say, it is deeply moving even now. Upon his return to Virginia Washington renewed his warm invitation to Mount Vernon, and this time the Powels accepted, spending several days there in the fall of 1787. On one day Powel inspected each of Washington's farms, the "work going on as usual"; on another Washington and Powel and their wives rode over to view the ruins of Belvoir.[30] The next summer, as president of the Agricultural Society, riding behind a banner showing a ploughman (representing Industry) followed by the Goddess of Plenty bearing a cornucopia, with the motto "Venerate the Plough," Powel led its members in the Grand Federal Procession, which celebrated on 4 July with incomparable pageantry the ratification of the Constitution.

Though he may have held no office in government during the Revolution, it was perhaps inevitable that eventually Powel would be returned to public life. He had lived much of his life on the fringes of it. He was, of course, a Federalist from the start. On 11 April 1789 he was elected mayor of Philadelphia again, a signal triumph of conservatives over the revolutionary radicals;[31] and in 1792 he was elected to the State Senate, where he was chosen its presiding officer.[32] As it fell out, however, Powel's service in any capacity was soon cut short. Yellow fever broke out in the city in August 1793; and on 1 September he anxiously inquired of Rush whether to adjourn the Assembly or keep it in session. "I know of but one certain preventive of the disorder," Rush wrote in answer, "& that is to keep at a distance from infected persons & places."[33] Three weeks later Powel himself was down with the fever, lying in a small building at his farm west of the Schuylkill. Rush visited him, and his nephew Samuel Powel Griffitts, now a doctor, stayed with him night and day; but his case was fatal, and at six o'clock in the morning of 29 September he died "in a small room in a small farmhouse," attended only by Dr. Griffitts and an old Negro coachman.[34] On the stone over his grave in Christ Church burying

---

[30] Fitzpatrick, ed., *Diaries of George Washington,* II, 426; III, 222–23, 233, 242, 243, 263; Fitzpatrick, *Writings,* XXVIII, 200–01, 306–07, 367, 441–42; XXIX, 322; XXX, 90–91, 99. At the conclusion of the Federal Convention, so goes the story related by James McHenry, Mrs. Powel asked Dr. Franklin whether the Convention had fashioned a republic or a monarchy. "A republic," replied the Doctor, "if you can keep it." *Am. Hist. Review,* XI (1905–06), 618.
[31] 2 *Pa. Arch.,* III, 719.
[32] *PMHB,* LXVI (1942), 448.
[33] Powel to Rush, 1 Sept. 1793, Rush Mss. Corres., XXXVIII, 21 (Lib. Co. Phila. in HSP).
[34] Butterfield, *Rush Letters,* II, 685, 686; Powel to Rush, n.d., Rush Mss. Corres., XXXVI, 6 (Lib. Co. Phila.); John H. Powell, *Bring Out Your Dead* (Phila., 1949), 196.

ground was inscribed: "He was the enemy of all exorbitant Powers and a sincere Friend to the Liberties of his Country. To all this was added a Taste for Science, for the Fine Arts and for all the Improvements of Civil Life."[35]

To his sister Abigail Powel Griffitts Powel bequeathed a small annuity and a life interest in the house she then occupied in Burlington, New Jersey, after which it was to go to her son; otherwise, except for a few small bequests, the whole of the estate, real and personal, went to his widow. "She is supposed to be worth $200,000," wrote the lawyer Edward Burd, whom such things interested.[36] Childless, Mrs. Powel adopted her nephew John Powel Hare as her heir; in acknowledgment he changed his name to Hare Powel, and as John Hare Powel he enlarged his uncle's country place into the magnificent "Powelton", which was a showplace of West Philadelphia for half a century. Now one of the wealthiest women in the city, mature, cultivated, in every way attractive, Elizabeth Willing Powel seemed to many well suited to a second marriage; but she rebuffed all suitors and emissaries of suitors for, one of her friends explained, none but a Washington would satisfy her. It was in fact for President Washington, at his birthday ball in 1797, the last before he retired from the presidency to Mount Vernon, that she broke the resolution she had formed after her husband's death of not going out in public; and on that occasion, gowned handsomely in black velvet, Mrs. Samuel Powel moved with gracious dignity among her friends and neighbors as they did honor to the national hero, who was also her and her husband's friend.[37] She survived Powel nearly forty years, dying in 1830 at the age of 88.

---

[35] Edward L. Clark, *A Record of the Inscriptions . . . in the Burial Grounds of Christ Church, Philadelphia* (Phila., 1864), 128–29.
[36] Powel, Will, 20 June 1788 (Register of Wills, Phila.; copy in Society Coll. [HSP]); Lewis B. Walker, ed., *The Burd Papers* (n.p., 1899), 184.
[37] Mrs. Williamina Cadwalader to Mrs. Ann Ridgely, 20 Feb.–8 March 1797, in Mabel L. Ridgely, ed., *The Ridgelys of Delaware & their Circle: What Them Befell* (Portland, Me., 1949), 103. A gossipy, unfriendly portrait of Mrs. Powel in the years of her widowhood is in Sophia Cadwalader, ed., *Recollections of Joshua Francis Fisher, written in 1864* (Privately printed, 1929), 205–09.

The Powels' portrait of Washington by Joseph Wright is fully described, with its history, by Nicholas B. Wainwright in *PMHB,* XCVI (1972), 419–23.

THOMAS WHARTON

By Charles Willson Peale. *Philadelphia Museum of Art. Given in memory of Marianna Lippincott O'Neill by her children.*

THOMAS WHARTON, JR. (1735–1778)
"YOUNG JUNTO": 2 OCTOBER 1761

THOMAS WHARTON, a young merchant of Philadelphia, was proposed by Charles Thomson for membership in the Young Junto, and was elected on 2 October 1761. No record survives that he was informed of this action, or accepted election, or ever attended a meeting of the Junto or its successor societies. His name was not on the list of resident members printed in the first volume of the Society's *Transactions* in 1771. Perhaps Wharton should not be considered to have been a member at all.

    He was the second of five children of John Wharton, a saddler, of Chester County, Pennsylvania, and of Mary Dobbins, his wife, both members of the Society of Friends.[1] Of his early education nothing is known, but by 1755 he was ap-

---

[1] Anne H. Wharton, "Thomas Wharton, Junr., First Governor of Pennsylvania under the Constitution of '76," *PMHB,* V (1881), 426–39; VI (1882), 91–105; *DAB.* The chapter in William C. Armor,

prenticed to the Philadelphia merchant Reese Meredith. To distinguish himself from an older cousin with the same name, he called himself thereafter "Thomas Wharton, Junior."

After leaving Meredith's service, Wharton entered into business on his own; in 1765 he advertised that he had moved his store to Water Street above Walnut, where he offered choice Madeira wine by the pipe, hogshead, and quarter cask; also sugar, molasses, coffee, pepper, allspice; and a parcel of copper for stills. "N.B. He continues to keep an Insurance Office." [2] Later he was in partnership with Anthony Stocker. Wharton signed the Non-Importation Agreement of 1765 and was an advocate of non-importation in the ensuing years.

As a merchant and businessman he supported various projects for internal improvements, subscribing £2 to the Silk Society in 1770 and a like sum (which, however, he seems not to have paid) towards expenses of the survey of a Delaware-Chesapeake canal. He was also a contributor to the Pennsylvania Hospital in 1765 and one of the managers of the Society for Inoculating the Poor in 1774. He was a member of the Fishing Company of Colony in Schuylkill. He belonged to the Union Library Company, and thus became a member of the Library Company of Philadelphia when the latter absorbed the former in 1769. He owned a country place called "Twickenham" near Abington Meetinghouse north of the city.

On 4 November 1762 Wharton married Susannah Lloyd, daughter of Thomas and Susannah (Kearney) Lloyd and great-granddaughter of the Thomas Lloyd who had been William Penn's colleague and an early governor of Pennsylvania. The ceremony was conducted by "a priest" in Christ Church, and for this violation of the Quaker discipline both Thomas (after being "lovingly treated with") and Susannah (who had been "precautioned") were promptly disowned by Philadelphia Monthly Meeting on 25 Third Month 1763. This was not the first time that Wharton had challenged Friends' advices: on several occasions in the preceding three or four years he had been brought to the attention of the Overseers for buying and selling slaves.[3]

Thomas and Susannah Wharton had five children. Susannah died in 1772, and Thomas remarried two years later. By his second wife, Elizabeth, daughter of William and Mary (Tallman) Fishbourne, he had three children.[4]

With the rise of resistance to British imperial policies, Wharton was increasingly involved in politics. He was a delegate to the Provincial Convention of 15 July 1774 that denounced Britain's retaliatory acts against Boston as unconstitutional, and

---

Lives of the Governors of Pennsylvania (new ed., Phila., 1873), 193–210, is principally an account of military events in 1775–78.
[2] *Pa. Gaz.,* 2 May 1765.
[3] Philadelphia Monthly Meeting, Minutes, 25 Eighth Mo. 1758; 23 Second Mo., 31 Eighth Mo. 1759; 30 Seventh Mo. 1762; 25 Third Mo. 1763.
[4] 2 *Pa. Arch.,* II, 308; "Early Minutes of Philadelphia Monthly Meeting of Friends," Geneal. Soc. Pa., *Pubs.,* XII (1938), 159.

was made a member of its committee of correspondence. He was appointed to the Provincial Committee of Safety in 1775 and to the Council of Safety, which superseded the Committee on 24 July 1776; he was chosen president of the Council on 6 August. At the organization of the new state government in the winter of 1777 Wharton was elected a member of the Supreme Executive Council and its president on 4 March. He was proclaimed with pomp and ceremony that included a public procession, a thirteen-gun salute from brass field pieces captured from the Hessians at Trenton, and a banquet at the City Tavern, where seventeen toasts were offered and drunk.

1. The United States of America.
2. The Congress.
3. The Commonwealth of Pennsylvania.
4. General Washington and the Army of the United States of America.
5. The Navy of the United States.
6. The Friends of Liberty in all Parts of the World.
7. Perpetual Union and strict Friendship among the States of America.
8. The Arts and Sciences.
9. Agriculture.
10. Trade and Navigation.
11. The Memory of the brave Patriots, of all Ranks, who have gloriously fallen in their Country's Cause.
12. May every American know his true Interest.
13. May Justice, Firmness, and Humanity, ever characterize Americans.
14. May Human Knowledge, Virtue and Happiness, receive their last Perfection in America.
15. May every private Consideration give Way to the Means of our public Defence.
16. General [Charles] Lee, and all our Friends in Captivity.
17. Doctor Franklin.[5]

As president of the Supreme Executive Council, Wharton was, in effect, governor of Pennsylvania. In addition to normal and expected executive functions, there were the special requirements of wartime. A Board of War was appointed. The defenses of Philadelphia had to be provided. General Washington importuned the governor and his state for troops and supplies. "The Necessities of the Service, Sir," Washington wrote him from Valley Forge on 7 March 1778,

> are great the Duty Required I acknowledge is burthensome and difficult at this inclement Season but it cannot be dispensed with. The Army and the Country have a mutual Dependence upon each other and it is of the last Importance that their several Duties should be so regulated and enforced as to produce not only the greatest Harmony and good Understanding but the truest Happiness and Comfort to each.[6]

[5] *Pa. Gaz.,* 12 March 1777.
[6] John C. Fitzpatrick, ed., *Writings of George Washington* (Washington, 1931–44), XI, 45–48.

Wharton had also to cope with real and imagined enemies within the state. In this latter role he authorized the arrest and banishment of some twenty of his fellow-citizens, most of them Quakers, all of them acquaintances, many of them friends, and a few close relatives. The action was arbitrary and at best dubious. Writing from his exile in Virginia, Edward Penington told Wharton it was "Evident thou has been our Enemy" and charged him in strong Quakerly terms with "a base Desertion of the Cause of the Innocent & Oppressed. But . . . thy Crime is of a deeper die [sic]," Penington continued.

> Thou signed orders for our Removal under Escort of two of the Troop. Now what Evidence hadst thou against us, whereby thou couldst Justify thyself in Signing this Decree. Did the General charge of the Congress, published in all the newspapers against the People called Quakers, Convince thee of our Guilt. A most senseless performance, and which we could have fully answered in a Short time, had we been allowed our undoubted right, of being heard in our Own Defence—And now I put it to thy Conscience—What could Induce thee to consent to our being Banished for Life? Thou couldst not believe we had been Guilty of any Crime, that could deserve such Punishment. To complete this Scene of Iniquity, orders were issued from the War Office, to our Conductors, not to Suffer us to distribute our remonstrances—at the same time those charges against us, Published by order of Congress, were dispersed about with the greatest Assiduity—a memorable Instance of Injustice.
>
> A few words more and I have done. Before thou signed this unjust decree, did it not occur to thee That thou wast well acquainted with a great number of us, and that thou knew us to be a Quiet, Peaceable People That were by no means likely to be concerned in Plots, or in giving Intelligence to the Enemy. But if any such thoughts took place in thy mind, It is Evident they were not long Cherished Therein.[7]

The governorship was no easy position to hold, especially as Pennsylvania was sharply divided over the government established by the Constitution of 1776. Although Wharton held office under that government, he was not one of its louder partisans, but held moderate views and enjoyed general respect. He explained himself in a letter to Arthur St. Clair.

> It is too true, that the differences amongst ourselves have been attended with bad consequences, and I am much afraid they will not be soon at an end. People have different purposes to answer; and I doubt much, if all those that are taking an active part against the present frame of government, are actuated by a love of [*torn*]. True it is, there are many faults which I hope one day to see removed; but it is true that, if the Government should at this time be overset, it would be attended with the worst consequences, not only to this State, but to the whole continent in the opposition we are making to

---

[7] Edward Penington to Wharton, 25 March 1778, *PMHB*, VI (1882), 364–66.

the tyranny of Great Britain. If a better frame of government could be adopted,—such a one as would please a much greater majority than the present one,—I should be very happy in seeing it brought about; and any gentleman that should be thought by the public qualified to take my seat, should have my hearty voice for it. My ardent ambition never led me to expect or ask for it; if I have any, it is to be thought, and to merit, the character of an honest man. I feel myself very inadequate to the station I am in; but some that were fit for it have either withdrawn themselves entirely, or are opposing the Government. However, as it is in the power of every man to act with integrity and uprightness, he that does that, will at least have the approbation of his own conscience, and merit that of the public.[8]

As the British army advanced on Philadelphia in the late summer of 1777, the state government withdrew to Lancaster. There, adversity was relieved by such diversions as could be provided locally. Christopher Marshall, a Philadelphia druggist and an early and strong advocate of American rights, who was one of the refugees, noted with stern disapproval some of Council President Wharton's conduct. "Last Sixth Day," he wrote on 4 March 1778, "another Ball or Assembly in Lancaster, where, it's said, cards were played at a hundred dollars a game. President [Wharton] there. O poor Pennsylvania!" That the managers of the ball paid a Hessian band £15 for the evening, as Marshall learned later, made the affront to republican virtue even worse.[9]

In mid-May Wharton was taken ill, and after several days he died on 23 May 1778 "of an inflammation, it's said, in his head." Trinity Lutheran Church offered a place of burial, and Wharton was interred with military honors in the nave of the church on 24 May.[10] His will, written on 18 September 1777, mentions his wife and six children, who were his heirs.[11]

The painter Charles Willson Peale, who was "ever fond of perpetuating the Remembrance of the Worthies of my time, as . . . a means of exciting an Emulation in our Posterity," offered the Council a portrait of its late president. Accepting it for the state, Joseph Reed, Wharton's successor as head of the Council, wrote:

A Character so amiable and distinguished in this great Contest cannot be too much honoured or his remembrance too well preserved. It will therefore be placed near the portrait of our Excellent General with whom in his Station he so nobly and faithfully co-operated.[12]

[8] Armor, *Lives of the Governors,* 209–10.
[9] William Duane, ed., *Extracts from the Diary of Christopher Marshall* (Albany, N.Y., 1877), 170.
[10] Ibid., 183.
[11] Wharton, Will, dated 18 Sept. 1777, probated 19 Aug. 1778, Wills 1778–88 (Register of Wills, Phila.).
[12] Charles Willson Peale, *Selected Papers* (Lillian B. Miller, ed., New Haven, 1983–), I, 347–48.

DANIEL WISTER (1739–1805)
"YOUNG JUNTO": 16 OCTOBER 1761

DANIEL WISTER, a young Quaker merchant of Philadelphia with some taste for books, was proposed to the "Young Junto" by Charles Thomson and elected a member on 16 October 1761. Whether he accepted election or attended any meeting is not known because no minutes survive for a period of eleven months after that date. Nor is he recorded as either present or absent between 3 September 1762, when the minutes resume, and the date of the Junto's demise. He was not considered a member of the American Society, whose forerunner the Junto was; and his name was not printed in any contemporary list of members of the American Philosophical Society.

First of the five of children of John Wister and his second wife Anna Catherina Rübenkam, Daniel was born in Philadelphia on 4 February 1738/9 "precisely at half-past three o'clock, and when the planets, the sun and Jupiter were in the sign of the steer."[1] John Wister was a well-to-do merchant who became a wealthy landowner in Germantown, where he built a large comfortable country place on the Germantown road known for three generations as "Wister's Big House." John Wister sent his son to the Academy of Philadelphia[2] and then, because he wanted the lad to speak and write fluent German, to school in Lancaster County. Throughout his life Daniel Wister used his German education. He read German newspapers, sometimes sent their editorial opinions to Benjamin Franklin in London,[3] and was an ardent admirer of Frederick the Great, "a very fine copy" of whose history "in the original" he owned "and never grew weary of reading."[4] Wister was a member of the Union Library Company, which was absorbed by the Library Company of Philadelphia in 1769.

In 1762 Wister was in business with Owen Jones, offering for sale "a Variety of European and East-India Goods."[5] Wister's house and store were in Market Street between Third and Fourth and until recently had been let by Wister's father to Franklin. When Wister moved in, he found the house fitted with a lightning rod that was connected with a chime of bells in a bedroom, which were agitated whenever a storm passed overhead. The bells remained in place for some time but were eventually removed to calm his wife's fears at their alarms.[6]

---

[1] *PMHB*, V (1881), 385–89.
[2] Montgomery, *University of Pennsylvania*, 553.
[3] *Franklin Papers*, XIII, 429.
[4] Charles J. Wister, Jr., *The Labour of a Long Life: A Memoir of Charles J. Wister* (Germantown, 1866–68), I, 21, 46, 200.
[5] *Pa. Gaz.*, 20 Dec. 1762, 16 Feb. 1764.
[6] Watson, *Annals*, I, 532.

In the Stamp Act controversy, he was one of several friends who offered protection to Mrs. Franklin against the mob that threatened her house in resentment against Franklin. Thereafter he defended Franklin's conduct among the Germans in Philadelphia and Pennsylvania. He signed the Non-Importation Agreement in 1765.

But business was by no means the whole of Wister's life. Travelling with a sporting crowd, he fancied horses, attended races, and joined the Jockey Club. He loved dogs, owned a great mastiff named "Nero," and imported several spitzes from Germany. He attended the theater, went shooting, and liked rich food so much that, as his friend Jacob Hiltzheimer recorded on New Year's Eve 1767, he weighed 270 pounds.[7]

All this was quite un-Quakerly. Wister had already shown a rebellious disposition when, disregarding the requirements of the Friends' Discipline, on 5 May 1760 he was married "by a priest"—apparently in an elopement—to Lowry Jones, daughter of Owen and Susannah (Evans) Jones of Lower Merion; they had nine children.[8] Although he and Lowry condemned their conduct in marrying out of meeting and remained members of Philadelphia Monthly Meeting, Wister continued to behave in a manner increasingly disapproved of by Friends. He overextended himself in business and fell deeply into debt. Bringing all the complaints against him together, the Monthly Meeting in 1770 charged that "by great Extravagance of Conduct in lavishly spending his time & Money in dissolute Company and without prudence contracted many heavy Debts" that he could not pay, Wister had behaved contrary to temperance, justice, and truth; and he was accordingly disowned. He assigned his assets to his creditors, but that was not enough. In 1773 he was in debt to the amount of £30,000, and he appealed to Franklin to intercede with his London creditors.[9]

In the fall of 1777, when the British army's advance into Pennsylvania threatened Philadelphia, Wister moved his family to the house of the widow Hannah Foulke in Gwynedd; and there his daughter Sally kept the sprightly journal that presents a charming and vivid picture of country life during the winter of the British occupation.[10]

After the war John Wister's business in Philadelphia grew yet more prosperous, and the Germantown lands, which he had refused to sell, became ever more valuable. At his death in 1789 Daniel inherited much of this real estate, including "Wister's Big House." Though he continued to keep a house in town—the city directories for years until his death identify him as "gentleman" residing at 141 High

[7] *Extracts from the Diary of Jacob Hiltzheimer* (Jacob Cox Parsons, ed., Phila., 1893), passim.
[8] 2 *Pa. Arch.,* II, 317; Hinshaw, *Amer. Quaker Genealogy,* II, 690.
[9] Ibid.; *Pa. Gaz.,* 21 June, 12 July 1770; Phila. Monthly Meeting, Minutes, 29 Sixth Mo. 1770; *Franklin Papers,* XX, 187–88, 316.
[10] Albert C. Myers, ed., *Sally Wister's Journal* (Phila., 1902).

Street—Daniel spent much time at Germantown. There he cultivated flowers, including tulips, hyacinths, and carnations, six species of which "in pots," his garden book records, were "got . . . from Matlack." He named one of these varieties for its donor Timothy Matlack ("Matlack's Brick colr.") and a species of *Ranunculus* for Benjamin Franklin.[11]

Wister died in Germantown on 27 October 1805. In his final illness his mind often strayed; he muttered Latin words and phrases.[12] He had made his peace with the Quakers and was buried in Friends ground beside his wife, who had died the year before.[13] One of their sons, Charles Jones Wister, after a short turn in the business he inherited, settled in the big house in Germantown, which he named "Grumblethorpe," and there he passed his days as a respected amateur of science and patron of local scientists.

GEORGE ROBERTS (1737–1801)
"YOUNG JUNTO": BEFORE 3 SEPTEMBER 1762
AMERICAN SOCIETY: 12 FEBRUARY 1768

GEORGE ROBERTS, an attractive, successful, and respected young merchant, "having been formerly approved," took his place in the "Young Junto" on 3 September 1762. Nothing is known of his career there, for no minutes survive for the long period from 22 October 1762 to 25 April 1766. However, he probably lost his membership by repeated absences in this period, for he was no longer considered a member in 1766, when the minutes resume. On 12 February 1768 he was formally elected a member of the American Society, whose meetings he attended with some regularity and where he gave promise of becoming a valuable member. At the first meeting of the united American and American Philosophical Societies on 2 January 1769 he was appointed one of a committee "to essay a draught of Laws for the Government of the Society." He served on one committee to have a cabinet made for the Society's curiosities and on others to examine Richard Wells' pump and to make an experimental planting of Chinese vetches. In 1770 he was elected one of the secretaries. But his interest soon waned; in 1775 he attended only a single meeting, and never came again. Yet he was keenly interested, as were many other members, in internal improvements, being a subscriber to the Silk Society, a mem-

---

[11] Wister, Garden Book, Eastwick Coll. (APS); Suzanne W. Eastwick, *The 'Grumblethorpe' Garden: An Historic Sketch* (Herb Society of America, 1963), 4–5.
[12] Poulson's *Amer. Daily Advertiser,* 29 Oct. 1805.
[13] Hinshaw, *Amer. Quaker Genealogy,* II, 438.

ber of the Agricultural Society and of the short-lived Society for Promoting the Manufacture of Sugar from the Sugar Maple, and a supporter of road construction to tap the products of the interior of the Province.[1]

Second of eleven children of Franklin's dear friend Hugh Roberts and of Mary (Calvert) Roberts, George was born into a Quaker family on 6 June 1737. As a youth he suffered from rheumatic fever, but recovered, and in 1760 went abroad to study iron manufacturing in England.[2] His father recommended him diffidently to Franklin as "a Lad of steady behaviour and . . . an Obedient Child." Franklin, who offered George counsel, was pleased to see that the boy he had known in Philadelphia had "grown up a solid sensible young Man."[3] Roberts conscientiously visited the iron foundries of Birmingham and, fortunately, was able to travel and sightsee elsewhere with several other Philadelphians then in Britain, notably Samuel Powel and John Morgan.

Solid and sensible Roberts may have been, but he was young too: after finishing "the grand Design which some Americans expatiate on, viz. the Monument, Tower and Lyons," he told his sister, he surveyed the fair maidens of England, then proceeded to Holland, where, he said, he expected to view "those Beauties that go by Bulk and Weight."[4] He returned home unencumbered in the summer of 1762, but with some taste for European goods: from Philadelphia on 5 November 1763 he begged Powel to send him from Paris "every article that's Modern, for since Whitefield's visitation we are grown so queer that a foreigner would think his lot was cast among worshippers of the First Age. On his pulpit persuasion we are forsaking every amusement and in a little time, we (I say we, because I sometimes foresake my business to attend his pretty tales) shall become no less than praying societies."[5]

Roberts never joined one of the evangelist's "praying societies"; he was already associated with his father in the ironmongery business in Grindstone Alley, their warehouse being "particularly distinguished from any other in the City, by having many of the Articles painted on the Window Shutters."[6] The business was a good one; and in the next few years, thanks to his abilities and personal charm and to his father's influence, George moved rapidly ahead in the city's mercantile establishment. He was a contributor to the Pennsylvania Hospital in 1765 and was elected a manager of the institution in 1774, resigning in 1776. He served on the Corpo-

---

[1] 6 *Pa. Arch.,* XIV, 287–89.
[2] "Early Minutes of Philadelphia Monthly Meeting of Friends," Geneal. Soc. Pa., *Pubs.,* XI (1932), 232; *Franklin Papers,* VIII, 84; Frank Willing Leach, "Old Philadelphia Families. CXXIII. Roberts," (Phila.) *North American,* 11 Aug. 1912.
[3] *Franklin Papers,* IX, 116, 280.
[4] Roberts to Polly Rhoads, 27 Jan. 1761, Charles Morton Smith Mss., II, 24 (HSP).
[5] *PMHB,* XVIII (1894), 37–38.
[6] *Pa. Gaz.,* 18 Aug. 1763, 6 Dec. 1770.

ration for the Relief and Employment of the Poor in 1769 and later,[7] was a city assessor in 1767,[8] a director of the Philadelphia Contributionship from 1774 to 1799, a manager of the Society for Inoculating the Poor in 1774, and a member of the Union Library Company, which was absorbed by the Library Company of Philadelphia in 1769. He was a member of the social Colony in Schuylkill and had a country place at Richmond.

Meanwhile, on 20 February 1772, Roberts was married at Philadelphia Monthly Meeting to Thomasine Fox, daughter of Joseph and Elizabeth (Mickle) Fox, a sedately grand affair attended by the visiting English Quaker preacher Joseph Oxley and by many of the most prominent Friends in the city, including such members of the American Philosophical Society as John Reynell, Edward Penington, Joshua Howell, David Evans, Abel James, John Morris, Jr., Richard Hockley, James Bringhurst, Thomas Clifford, and Samuel Preston Moore. Five children survived their father: George (who was disowned in 1799 for neglect of attendance, deviation in dress and address, and studying the art of war), Hugh, Charles, Elizabeth, and Mary.[9]

George Roberts and his father signed the Non-Importation Agreement of 1765, and George was one of the merchant committee set up under the Non-Importation Agreement of 1769 who protested the next year against weakening it.[10] When Boston was blockaded in 1774 Roberts collected subscriptions for the relief of the sufferers.[11] Religious scruples held him back from more overt acts after 1775, and he remained in Philadelphia during the British occupation and accepted appointment by General Howe to select and supervise the members of the night watch.[12] This service under British authorities, even in so necessary and nonpolitical a duty, may have created suspicion and resentment among citizens that made his company not entirely congenial to the philosophers—or theirs to him.

Increasingly, as time passed, Roberts branched out from ironmongery into land, and became wealthy. At the time of his death, he owned a fine town house in Church Alley, the country place at Point-No-Point called "Pine Grove," where he planted strawberries and gooseberries sent him from England by Robert Barclay,[13] a plantation and stone quarry on Ridley Creek, other lots, farms, and plantations, and large tracts of land in Luzerne, Lycoming, Mifflin, Northumberland, Hunt-

---

[7] Ibid., 11 May, 1769; *Pa. Chronicle,* 20 May 1771.
[8] Philadelphia City Commissioners, Minutes, 6 Oct. 1767, 6 Feb. 1768 (Independence National Historical Park).
[9] Marriage Certificate, 20 Second Mo. 1772, Charles Morton Smith Mss., IV (HSP). On George junior, see Philadelphia Monthly Meeting, Minutes, 28 Third Mo. 1798, 29 Third Mo. 1799.
[10] Scharf and Westcott, *Philadelphia,* I, 272–73; *Pa. Gaz.,* 20, 27 Sept., 4 Oct. 1770.
[11] 2 *Pa. Arch.,* XIII, 278.
[12] Wilbur H. Siebert, *The Loyalists of Pennsylvania* (Ohio State University *Bulletin,* XXIV, No. 23, 1920), 44.
[13] I. Bush to Roberts, 25 Feb. 1790, Charles Morton Smith Mss., II, 86.

ington, "and other Western Counties in this State, (which Lands at present are call'd unimprov'd, or back Lands.)"[14]

For many years Roberts suffered from a cancerous growth on his face. It killed him at last on 17 September 1801, and he was buried next day from his place at Point-No-Point.[15]

MOSES BARTRAM (1732–1809)
"YOUNG JUNTO": BEFORE 25 APRIL 1766

MOSES BARTRAM, second of the nine children of John Bartram by his second wife Anne Mendenhall, was born on 25 Sixth Month [August] 1732 on his father's farm at Kingsessing, just across the Schuylkill River on the road to Darby.[1] He grew up in the years when his father's reputation as a botanist was steadily growing, and the elder Bartram tried to introduce his sons to botany by taking them on his plant-collecting journeys. Neither farming nor natural history, however, appealed to Moses, and not much else either. He was a restless lad, without a goal, unable to settle down to any task or calling; and he spent ten years, in Peter Collinson's phrase, "tumbling and tossing about the world," before he returned to Philadelphia and entered business with his brother.

In 1751 he went to sea as a common sailor; the vessel was sold in London, and Moses, stranded in a strange land, sought out his father's friend and correspondent, who befriended him. The young man struck Collinson as honest, well-intentioned, and industrious; to Collinson's evident satisfaction Moses, upon being asked to survey the former's garden at Mill Hill, pointed out "many things wanting." Eventually Moses found a berth in a ship bound for the West Indies, but Collinson intervened, fearing the influence of profligate London sailors and Creole life and manners on an unsettled young colonial Quaker. He succeeded in dissuading Moses from going, bought him clothes, and paid his passage home to Philadelphia.[2]

But Moses still wanted to wander. In 1755 as master of the snow *Corsley*, belonging to James Child, he made a voyage to the Mediterranean, which provided him with a question and data that some years later he offered to the American So-

---

[14] Roberts, Will, 30 Dec. 1800. Will Book Y, No. 89 (Register of Wills, Phila.); *Pa. Gaz.*, 23 April 1777.
[15] George W. Corner, ed., *Autobiography of Benjamin Rush* (Princeton, 1948), 257, 311.

---

[1] Randolph Shipley Klein, "Moses Bartram (1732–1809)," *Quaker History*, LVII (1968), 28–34, is based on manuscript and other original sources. I am much indebted to it.
[2] Darlington, *Memorials*, 184–88, 202.

ciety. Apparently the years at sea offered great dangers and gruelling hardships, for in 1759 Collinson wrote John Bartram:

> I am concerned for poor Moses. Now he has eat his brown bread, his white will come next. I wish he would write a little Journal in his own way and style, from his first going to sea to this present time. *Short hints will do.* I question if it is to be paralleled. We don't know what human nature will bear until it is tried.[3]

The white bread was in fact almost on his plate. In 1760, home at last in Philadelphia, Moses joined his half-brother Isaac in the business of chemist and apothecary at the Sign of the Bottle and Three Bolt Heads in Second Street between Arch and Race. Their father, worried about another son, expressed the wish that William could "gain credit, as Isaac and Moses have. They began with a little, and have unexpectedly dropped into fine business."[4]

Besides the usual drugs, "chymical and galenical medicines," patent medicines such as Godfrey's cordial, Bateman's drops, Daffey's elixir, Lockyer's, Anderson's and Hooper's female pills, the Bartrams sold painters' colors, flasks, jars, retorts, crucibles, gallipots, vials, and other shop furniture. They offered practitioners pocket instruments, lancets in cases, small scales and weights, pewter syringes, and flint glass mortars and pestles. They would make up medicine chests for sea captains and country residents. In 1762 they advertised to buy "the Oil of Mint, Bucks Horn, and Rattlesnakes."[5] They were soon doing enough business to take on apprentices, one of whom, James Hutchinson,[6] became apothecary at the Pennsylvania Hospital, studied medicine at the College of Philadelphia and surgery in London, and ultimately became a professor in the Medical School of Philadelphia. In 1765 the brothers signed the Non-Importation Agreement. They dissolved their partnership in 1772, Isaac moving to the Sign of the Unicorn in Third Street, while Moses remained at the "Old Medicinal Shop" as sole proprietor.[7]

The store was not the only sign that Moses had settled at last. On 10 July at Bank Meetinghouse in Philadelphia he was married to Elizabeth Budd, daughter of Thomas Budd, a cooper, of New Jersey, and his wife Rebecca Atkinson, who, after she was widowed, married Thomas Say. Moses and Elizabeth Bartram had thirteen children, one stillborn.[8] The "Old Medicinal Store" prospered sufficiently both to support this brood, sending one to college and medical school, and to enable

---

[3] Ibid., 222; Frank Willing Leach, "Old Philadelphia Families. LXXX. Bartram," (Phila.) *North American,* 20 Dec. 1908.
[4] *Pa. Gaz.,* 28 Feb. 1760; Ernest Earnest, *John and William Bartram* (Phila., 1940), 97.
[5] *Pa. Gaz.,* 28 Jan., 10 June 1762, 24 May 1770.
[6] Cadwalader Evans to Managers of Pennsylvania Hospital, 19 April 1773, Hutchinson Papers (APS).
[7] *Pa. Gaz.,* 9, 16 Dec. 1772, 23 June 1773 suppl.
[8] Photocopy of entries in Bartram's New Testament (in Genealogical Soc. Pa.); Genealogical Soc. Pa., *Pubs.,* XIII (1941), 26; *PMHB,* XXIX (1905), 221.

Bartram to acquire a "plantation" on the Wissahickon Road between the second and third milestones.[9]

Some time between 22 October 1762, when the minutes of the "Young Junto" cease, and 25 April 1766, when they resume, Bartram was elected a member. On the latter date he attended as a member, and he signed the by-laws of the American Society soon afterwards. In that society and in the American Philosophical Society after 1769 he found a gratifying outlet for his interests. Three queries that he submitted to the members for discussion are recorded in the minutes:

> What becomes of that vast Quantity of Water that is continuously rushing into the Mediterranean Sea?
> How is it that Men in their Sleep or out of their Senses walk or climb in such dangerous places that it is not possible for a man to walk or climb in when awake, or in their proper senses and awake?   (10 October 1766)
> Have the fresh Water lakes to the Northwest of us a Tendancy [sic] to make this Climate Colder or Warmer?   (6 March 1767)

What may have been Bartram's own answer to the first of these queries survives in the archives of the American Philosophical Society. It is an explanation of why the Mediterranean has not become one great block of salt. Because that ocean is saltier than the Atlantic, the heavier Mediterranean water flows into the Atlantic far below the surface. In other words, while on the surface the current flows from the Atlantic into the Mediterranean, below the surface the flow is in the opposite direction.[10]

Bartram remained in correspondence with Collinson after his settlement in Philadelphia. In 1766 he sent the latter observations and conjectures on "the American mole locust." He had seen the insects laying their eggs on the branches of trees. He put some twigs with eggs attached in empty vials, some in vials with water, and still others he left on the twigs, which he stuck into a pot of earth, which he kept moist. On the eighteenth day the eggs in the water and moist earth hatched, but those in the vials without water dried up and died. The locusts hatched in water died after 24 hours, but those hatched on the twigs in the pot of earth "entered the earth as eagerly as they could, to escape from the light." Under a microscope, he continued, they appeared as perfect at the moment of hatching as "when they emerge from the earth." He had not yet learned how deep in the earth they burrowed, but some had been found at 30 feet, and he had seen them at 10 .[11]

---

[9] *Pa. Gaz.,* 10 Feb. 1779.
[10] "On the Current of Water running through the Straits of Gibraltar," Ms. Communications, Philology, II, 66 (APS).
[11] Bartram to Peter Collinson, 27 July 1766, in Samuel Hazard, *Register of Pennsylvania,* XIV (1834), 76.

In the negotiations between the two societies which resulted in their merger as the American Philosophical Society, held at Philadelphia, for Promoting Useful Knowledge, Bartram served on the American Society's committee. Unlike some members of the old societies, he attended meetings of the united Society regularly, was a member of the standing Committees on Natural History and Chemistry and on Husbandry and American Improvements. He took a large part in the Society's efforts to encourage the cultivation of native silkworms.

This was a subject in which Bartram had been interested since 1766. In the early spring of that year he gathered some cocoons along the Schuylkill, put five in the garret of his house facing the sun, and waited for them to hatch. The experiment began inauspiciously: the first "fly" to hatch escaped through an open window and the eggs that the others laid dried up over the winter. He made "another trial with more caution and circumspection," collected cocoons from swamps and uplands, and took precautions against escape. He kept daily notes on the period of dormancy and on the life span of the "impregnated fly," whose eggs remained "plump and fine," while unfertilized eggs shrivelled. Much to his surprise Bartram found that the worms "did not seem fond" of mulberry leaves but that, after being offered several substitutes (these changes of diet, he noted, were bad for the worms), they accepted apple leaves. Bartram had by now acquired a good deal of practical knowledge on the subject, and was ready to offer advice to those who would raise silkworms for profit. In particular he recommended native American worms as easier to raise than Chinese or Italian worms: they hatched late, after the danger of frost was past; they yielded more silk; they were accustomed to the North American climate and diet; and they were not disturbed, as foreign worms were said to be, by thunder and lightning. He concluded that silkworms "might be raised to advantage, and perhaps, in time, become no contemptible branch of commerce."

These conclusions Bartram presented in a paper to the American Society on 11 March 1768. It was ordered published in the *Pennsylvania Chronicle,* was reprinted by Lewis Nicola in the *American Magazine* in 1769, and was included in the Society's *Transactions,* which appeared in 1771.[12] The result was that a number of persons began to experiment with silkworms as a new crop and a new source of wealth and income for the colonies. The largest of these projects was within the American Philosophical Society itself.

This was the kind of American improvement the members of the old American Society were particularly interested in promoting; while the merchants who had come into the American Philosophical Society were no less eager to explore the possibilities. In 1770, under the Society's auspices, a Society for promoting the Cultivation of Silk was formed. Bartram was elected one of the managers, and con-

---

[12] "Observations on the native Silk Worms of North-America," APS *Trans.,* I (1771), 224–30.

tributed £2 to the Society's stock. Humphry Marshall of Chester County obtained worms from Bartram and made 335 pounds of cocoons the first year. The Society opened a filature on Seventh Street between Market and Arch, advertised for persons skilled in reeling and sorting silk, announced it would buy cocoons brought to its agents (Bartram was one), and announced premiums.[13] The flurry the Silk Society created just before the Revolution was short-lived, but from time to time thereafter the prospect of a native silk industry excited Americans, not least Peter S. Du Ponceau, president of the American Philosophical Society from 1828 to 1844.

The war of the American Revolution shattered Bartram's quiet life of shop and cabinet and, perhaps, awakened his old love of adventure. In the spring of 1776 he was chairman of a committee of the Second Battalion, Pennsylvania militia, to look after the families of soldiers in the field. The following year, when the invasion of Pennsylvania impended, he enlisted in the Third City Battalion under Captain Conrad Rush. Two years later he was called into "actuale service."[14] Meanwhile, this non-pacific conduct had come under the notice of his Monthly Meeting. On 28 Fifth Month 1776 a committee was named to treat with Moses Bartram for engaging in warlike activity, learning the use of arms, and "shewing the disposition to use them."[15] He would not confess his error, and on 23 July 1776 he was disowned. Considering himself a Friend in every other respect, in 1781 Bartram joined other disowned Quakers in forming a new religious society.

The members of the Society of Free Quakers believed that they had acted conscientiously; they genuinely regretted the separation from friends and relations which their conduct had brought upon them; and they had no wish to create and perpetuate a schism. Their first act, therefore, was to seek readmission to the Society of Friends, and to this end they quietly visited several meetings. But as they could not bring themselves to condemn their own conduct and the Meetings could not condone it, they were met everywhere with coolness and even hostility. At Bank Meetinghouse, where he had been married, Bartram and his colleagues tried to present a paper of explanation and defense, but were ordered out by the clerk, Henry Drinker. Their approach to the Yearly Meeting was fruitless, and so was a petition for permission to use the Fourth Street Meetinghouse for their own religious meetings. Rebuffed everywhere, the Free Quakers accepted the division as permanent. Moses Bartram was on the committee to govern the new Society, played a prominent role in constructing the meetinghouse at Fifth and Arch Streets, served as trustee of the building and burying ground until his death, and generally took an active part in all the Society's affairs.[16]

---

[13] *Pa. Gaz.,* 22 March, 14 June 1770.
[14] Leach, "Old Philadelphia Families," loc. cit.; 6 *Pa. Arch.,* I, 193, 214.
[15] Northern District Monthly Meeting Minutes, 28 Fifth Mo., 23 Seventh Mo., 1776.
[16] Society of Free Quakers, Minutes, 20 Second Mo., 1781, et passim (APS).

Bartram contributed $20 towards the costs of reviving the American Philosophical Society in 1779 and 1780. He attended some meetings, signed the new by-laws, and was put on a special publications committee within the Committee on Natural History. His interest in natural phenomena was unabated; he remarked on the results of an inadvertent freezing of oil of sassafras, and asked Dr. Benjamin Rush for an explanation.[17] He became a member of the Philadelphia Society for Promoting Agriculture. He belonged to the Humane Society, and in 1787 he and Isaac made a joint gift of drugs to the Pennsylvania Hospital. He was named one of the street commissioners in 1779, and on several occasions urged that trees and shrubs be planted in the public squares and in front of buildings like his own meetinghouse, to improve the healthfulness and beauty of the city.[18]

One by one Bartram's sons had died—Moses, the doctor, in 1791, just as his career was opening; Benjamin, drowned in the Schuylkill in 1793; Robert, carried off by the yellow fever in the same year; Thomas Say Bartram in 1803; and in 1808 Archibald, who was a printer. Only one was left, born in 1784, whom he had named George Washington, perhaps with mingled feelings of patriotism and defiance of his erstwhile co-religionists. On 9 Seventh Month 1808, after lingering with a "Dropsy in the Chest," his wife died.[19] Bartram was now 77 years old. He turned over the management of the "medicinal store" to George Washington Bartram and moved to another, smaller house at 69 Arch Street. Within a week of moving in, a day after he attended weekly First Day services at the Free Quakers' meetinghouse, he was stricken with apoplexy and died on 25 December 1809.[20]

---

[17] Bartram to Benjamin Rush, 22 Feb. 1789, Rush Mss., XXI, 10 (Lib. Co. Phila. in HSP).
[18] Street Commissioners, Minutes, 16 Oct. 1779 (Independence National Historical Park); "Petition to the Mayor . . .", [1792?], Phila. General Petitions, Box 4 (HSP); Society of Free Quakers, Minutes, 5 Fourth Mo., 1804 (APS); Pa. Hospital, Minutes, 26 Third Mo., 1787.
[19] Poulson's *Amer. Daily Advertiser,* 18 July 1808.
[20] Ibid., 27 Dec, 1809; Bartram, Will, 9 March 1809, Will Book 3, No. 51 (Register of Wills, Phila.).

Academy's sincere wish for the success of the society of which Biddle was a distinguished member.

> I doubt not, these two Societies will harmonize, in their exertions to promote public advantage. They are formed upon a liberal and extensive plan, and the ends of their institution being properly pursued, as I hope will ever be the case, they cannot but be of great utility, and an honor to our country.[30]

The oration to the Philosophical Society, election to the American Academy, and appointment as one of the commissioners to survey the boundary between Pennsylvania and Virginia in 1782[31] were the final events in Biddle's career as a natural philosopher. The remaining years of his life were a career of another kind.

While engaged in public service during the war Biddle had neglected his personal affairs. Trade with Britain had stopped, and several vessels in which he had invested were captured. By the fall of 1782 Biddle "could not wind up with that satisfaction which I could wish." In short, he faced bankruptcy. The prospect unnerved him. He was, a friend wrote, "reduced to great distress of mind," and in this state was for a time incapable of doing any business at all. In addition to simply knowing that he was overextended, he came to believe that this was a consequence of abandoning Quaker principles to serve in the war, and that that service was also a culpable act. Both debt and bearing arms violated the Friendly precepts he had been taught as a youth. Under these growing convictions he withdrew from all his usual activities—the Philosophical Society saw him no more. He thought briefly that he might find peace in the Society of Free Quakers, attended a few organizing meetings, but then dropped out.[32] Soon he began to attend his old Friends meeting again, and sought and accepted Friends' advice.[33] He turned his property over to trustees for the benefit of his creditors, Peel Hall was put up for sale, his wife considered opening a shop to support the family, and he offered himself to the Overseers of Friends schools as a teacher, which he said he had long wished to be.[34] On 30 May 1783 in Philadelphia Monthly Meeting Biddle publicly proclaimed sincere repentance for his "deviation from the Paths of Righteousness" by disregarding the advice of Friends, who had cautioned him eight years before against joining in measures that led to war,

---

[30] Joseph Willard to Biddle, 8 Feb. 1782. Biddle Papers (Friends Hist. Lib.). Biddle's membership certificate was delivered in 1790. Benjamin Rush to Biddle, 24 March 1790; Biddle to Rush, 2 Fourth Mo. 1790, ibid.
[31] *Col. Recs. Pa.,* XIII, 193.
[32] Religious Society of Free Quakers, Minutes, 8, 13 Third Mo. 1781 (APS).
[33] James Pemberton to John Pemberton, 15, 29 Twelfth Mo. 1782; 1, 22 First Mo. 1783, Pemberton Papers, XXXVII, 120, 140, XXXVIII, 6, 7 (HSP).
[34] Same to same, 15 Second Mo. 1783 (copy), ibid., 29; *Pa. Gaz.,* 15 Oct. 1783.

by which means I became instrumental in some measure to a series of public Calamities & private Distress . . . . A Conduct so unguarded and contrary to the peaceable Principles of Christianity in wch I was Educated has brought Remorse and sorrow for the same, and has been attended with such Disappointmts. [sic] and losses, as have involv'd my outward Affairs in Difficulties, brought Distress on my family, and disabled me from fulfilling my Contracts in a seasonable Time altho' I am desirous to satisfy the just Demands of my Creditors, and am abt. [sic] to take measures for that purpose, which I hope with the divine Assistance to be enabled to accomplish to your satisfaction, and to be restor'd again to membership with you . . . .

The meeting heard Biddle with deep sympathy and, satisfied with his "full clear & solid acknowledgment," restored him to membership.[35]

In the Yearly Meeting Biddle soon became a strong and influential member. He was one of those who presented an address to Congress in 1783 on the suppression of the slave trade; he signed the Yearly Meeting's appeal to the Indians for peace in 1795 and supported efforts to educate the Indians' children, introduce agriculture, and control the trade in spiritous liquors. In these sentiments Biddle was warmly supported by his brother-in-law General James Wilkinson, who was critical of the government's policy towards the Indians. In 1797 Wilkinson sent the Chickasaw chief Wolf's Friend to Biddle, "& through you I wish to recommend him to the only community on Earth, who seek to do good purely for the love of good." The next year Wilkinson sent another chief, Little Turtle of the Miamis, on a similar mission, "in the hope that you may think proper to recommend him to the patronage of the benevolent Society of which you are a member." A few craftsmen, husbandmen, and a schoolmaster, if sent to the Indians as they wished, "would produce speedy & happy Effects, upon their manners, morals & utility."[36] But Biddle's deepest concern during the last ten years of his life was with education and the establishment of a country boarding school by the Yearly Meeting.

He first raised the matter with some Friends in 1788 or 1789. With their encouragement he drafted an essay on the subject and sent it to John Dickinson, who he understood had "a warm desire to promote the education of the rising generation." Dickinson approved the idea, and in 1790 Biddle printed *A Plan for a School on an Establishment similar to that at Ackworth, in Yorkshire.* After a review of Quaker educational efforts in Britain, with generous quotations from Dr. John Fothergill, Biddle described the school at Ackworth, its physical plant, discipline, and financ-

---

[35] James Pemberton to John Pemberton, 31 Fifth Mo. 1783, Pemberton Papers, XXXIX, 7 (HSP); Joseph Bringhurst to John Pemberton, 2 Sixth Mo. 1783, ibid., 12; Phila. Monthly Meeting, Minutes, 30 Fifth Mo. 1783.

[36] *Jour. Cont. Cong.,* XXV, 660; "Address of the People called Quakers . . . To our Brothers the Shawanese, Delawares, Wyandots, Miamis and other Nations of Indians," 22 Fifth Mo. 1795, Wayne Mss., XLI, 13 (HSP); James Wilkinson to Biddle, 24 Dec. 1797, 6 Sept. 1798, Dorothy Biddle James Coll. (HSP).

ing; then presented his own plan. The school should be under the care of the Yearly Meeting, receiving its financial support from that and subordinate meetings. It would be open free to the children of poor Friends; those in better circumstances would pay tuition and board. The curriculum would be designed "to suit the Circumstances" of the young people who would attend. "Besides useful learning, the boys and girls are to be instructed in such manual business and domestic employments of every kind, as may be consistent with Friends' prospects of usefulness and improvement, or redound to the benefit and reputation of the institution." With this in mind, artisans and mechanics should be included in the school community because they might be required for labor and instruction. The boys and girls would attend classes in separate school houses and would board in separate houses—"yet not so far separated but that an innocent and cheerful intercourse may be allowed and encouraged under suitable inspection at proper seasons." Thus the children would be reared "in a healthy part of the country, under the care of sober, well qualified friends, where they may be instructed and supported, free from the corrupt examples, which cities and too many schools afford, whilst they are in a state of incapacity to form a proper judgment or take suitable care for themselves."[37]

The concern moved slowly through the committees of the Yearly Meeting. In 1794 the decision was taken, John and Mary Dickinson made a "handsome donation," and a tract of land in Chester County was purchased. Five years later the school was opened at Westtown. Biddle had died a few weeks before, but he remembered it in his will.

Meanwhile Biddle had his own affairs to look after. He became a merchant apothecary and appears in city directories from 1785 until his death as "Druggist" or "Apothecary and Druggist" at 85 Market Street, between Second and Third. For a number of years his son John was in partnership with him. As for his debts to English merchants, apparently they were not discharged until 1812, years after both he and his creditors were dead.[38]

Biddle died after a brief illness in Philadelphia on 10 March 1799. One of his survivors was Owen, Jr., "house carpenter and teacher of architectural drawing," author of *The Young Carpenter's Assistant* and designer of the Friends Meetinghouse at Fourth and Arch Streets in 1804.[39]

---

[37] [Biddle], *A Plan for a School on an Establishment similar to that at Ackworth, in Yorkshire* . . . (Phila., 1790); Biddle to John Dickinson, 4 Seventh Mo., Tenth Mo. 1789; Biddle to John and Mary Dickinson, 3 Eleventh Mo. 1794, Biddle Papers, formerly Society Coll. (HSP); John Dickinson to Biddle, 21 Tenth Mo. 1797, Logan Papers, XII, 77 (HSP); Biddle to Humphry Marshall, 25 Second Mo., 16 Third Mo. 1795, Dreer Coll., Humphry Marshall Corres., II, 31, 32 (HSP).

[38] Biddle, Correspondence, 1771–75 [concerning indebtedness to John Ewer and William Neate, merchants, of London], Cadwalader Coll.—Phineas Bond (HSP).

[39] Biddle, Will, dated 2 Third Mo. 1799 and probated 28 March, Will Book Y, No. 129 (Register of Wills, Phila.).

WILLIAM BETTLE (1734–1773)

"YOUNG JUNTO": 19 SEPTEMBER 1766

WILLIAM BETTLE, tanner, was elected a member of the Junto on 19 September 1766. He was admitted on 10 October, signed the Obligation and Laws, and shortly afterwards proposed two questions for discussion.

> Have the Diversions of the Stage a tendency to improve or corrupt the Morals of Mankind?
> Whether Man, considered as a being whose views are confined to this life, would be happier in a State of Nature than in a civil Society?

On the first of these questions the majority of the company felt that, "under proper Regulations," plays tended to improve morals. "The best things may be abused and when abused often become the worst," the secretary wrote in summary of the discussion. "But the abuse of any thing is or ought to be no argument against the right use of it." As for the second query, the members were decidedly of the opinion that men are happier in civil societies than in a state of nature. Bettle attended meetings irregularly for nearly two years; after May 1768 he never appeared again.

Born in Birmingham township, Chester County, Pennsylvania, on 10 March 1733/4, Bettle was the first son and second of the nine children of Samuel Bettle, a prosperous tanner, and of Ann (Brinton) Bettle, both Quakers.[1] The family moved to Philadelphia in 1749, bearing a certificate from the Concord Monthly Meeting of Friends to Philadelphia Monthly Meeting. William, now a tanner like his father, was married in the meeting on 12 March 1761 to Mary Lewis, daughter of Robert and Mary (Pyle) Lewis of Philadelphia. Mary Bettle died within three months of her marriage; and on 15 May 1764 William married Sarah Beakes, of Philadelphia, daughter of Nathan Beakes of Trenton. There were no children of either marriage.

Bettle's tanyard was on Long Lane, just north of Pegg's Run in the Northern Liberties, where several other tanneries were located. It consisted of a bark-house capable of holding 200 cords of bark, a mill-house, currying shop, and beam house, 37 vats and other facilities of a tanyard, as well as other buildings including a stable and chaise house.[2] Bettle also owned a small brick house on Turner's Lane several miles from the city, perhaps his own residence, with a young orchard and a well of

---

[1] Lewis D. Cook, "Bettle of Stepney, County Middlesex, England, of Salem County, N.J., and of Philadelphia," Geneal. Soc. Pa., *Pubs.,* XIX (1954), 188; Hinshaw, *Amer. Quaker Genealogy,* II, 463.
[2] *Pa. Gaz.,* 17 March, 21 April 1773. Apparently no purchaser appeared for the tanyard, for it was offered for sale again, as late the property of William Bettle, deceased, in 1783. Ibid., 12 March 1783.

NICHOLAS WALN
By an unidentified artist. *Friends Historical Library, Swarthmore College.*

NICHOLAS WALN (1742–1813)
"YOUNG JUNTO": 19 SEPTEMBER 1766

NICHOLAS WALN, an intelligent and popular young lawyer, was elected a member of the "Young Junto" on 19 September 1766 and was formally admitted a member on 3 October, when he signed the Laws. He attended meetings with some frequency until 1769, but after the union of the American and American Philosophical Societies did not come again. Having read law in Philadelphia and at the Inns of Court in London, Waln, at the time of his election to the Junto, was launched on a career that promised considerable professional and financial rewards; but he soon forsook both law and science to become a plain Quaker, wholly devoted to the concerns of the Society of Friends and its members. In the history of the American Philosophical Society Waln played no significant role, but in the Society of Friends he is remembered as a representative of that generation which, coming to maturity after the end of the Holy Experiment, turned its attention inward and led Friends into a period that was marked by devotion to moral reforms, but was conservative of ancient traditions and doctrines, separated from the world and introversive in spirit.[1]

The second of two sons of Nicholas and Mary (Shoemaker) Waln, born at Fair Hill, near Philadelphia, on 19 Ninth Mo. 1742, he came of a well-to-do family, closely connected with half a dozen other distinguished Quaker families.[2] After an early education at the Friends' Public School, he studied law with Joseph Galloway, and was admitted to the bar on 8 October 1762. In the ensuing February term of Chester County court he appeared successfully in no fewer than eight cases, though he had not reached his majority. Realizing, however, that the highest road to professional success in Philadelphia lay through London, he set off to England, where he was enrolled in the Middle Temple on 16 December 1763.[3] He returned home after a year and settled in Philadelphia. With his connections and formal training, his lively wit, and his knowledge of German, which brought him many clients from among the Pennsylvania Dutch, he was quickly launched into a profitable practice. He often appeared in the courts of Bucks, Berks, and Lancaster counties; he was consulted by lawyers in other provinces; and young men applied to read law in his office. By 1771 his income was said to be between £1500 and £2000 a year.

During these years at the bar Waln led the comfortable life of a prosperous, worldly Friend. He dressed well, relished good food and fine wines, drove about town in a bright yellow carriage, and had a country house in Frankford. In this period he was a member of the Library Company, and from 1769 through 1771 one of its directors; he subscribed £3 to the Silk Society; and he was elected a corresponding member of the Society of Arts in London.[4] He also became a member of the Junto, although, except for fairly regular attendance, he discharged few of the obligations of membership. When, on 22 May 1771 at Pine Street Meeting, he married Sarah Richardson, the only child of the wealthy merchant Joseph Richardson,

---

[1] Rufus M. Jones, *The Quakers in the American Colonies* (N.Y., 1911), 579; Frederick B. Tolles, *Meeting House and Counting House* (Chapel Hill, 1948), 238–39.
[2] Morris L. Kirk, "The Life of Nicholas Waln (1742–1813)" (M.A. thesis, 1951, Haverford College). See also "Biographical Memoirs of Nicholas Waln," *Friends' Miscellany,* V (1834), 97–144; *Biographical Sketches and Anecdotes of Members of the Religious Society of Friends* (Phila., [1870]), 381–95. On Waln's family connections, see John W. Jordan, ed., *Colonial and Revolutionary Families of Pennsylvania,* (N.Y., 1911), I, 200–25.
[3] E. Alfred Jones, *American Members of the Inns of Court* (London, 1924), 212–13; Hinshaw, *Amer. Quaker Genealogy,* II, 675.
[4] Royal Society of Arts, *Trans.,* II (1784), 269.

it must have seemed that his future was assured, for Sally Waln, indulged all her life by a devoted father, had a taste for good living that matched her husband's.[5]

Within a year, however, Nicholas was a changed man. Even before his marriage, for reasons only half acknowledged to himself, he had sometimes drawn back from rounds of gaiety. His associates ascribed this conduct to penuriousness; it was in fact something quite different. The story is that one evening in the winter of 1771–72, after winning a case for a client he thought guilty, he was overcome by a sense of wrong-doing and remorse. A few days afterwards he appeared at the Youth's Meeting in Philadelphia, where an English travelling Friend, Joseph Oxley, noted his strange behavior. "He sat under an awful weighty exercise of mind from the early sitting down of the meeting, and removed his seat into the ministering Friends' gallery; he appeared to be agitated, and trembled very much: after sitting about half an hour, he kneeled down and prayed":[6]

> Oh Lord God! arise, and let thine enemies be scattered! Baptise me,—dip me,—yet deeper in Jordan. Wash me in the laver of regeneration.
>
> Thou has done much for me, and hast a right to expect much;—therefore, in the presence of this congregation, I resign myself, and all that I have, to thee, Oh Lord!—it is thine: and I pray thee, Oh Lord! to give me grace to enable me to continue firm in this resolution!
>
> Wherever thou leadest me, Oh Lord! I will follow thee; if through persecution, or even to martyrdom. If my life is required, I will freely sacrifice it. Now I know that my Redeemer liveth, and the mountains of difficulty are removed. Hallelujah!
>
> Teach me to despise the shame, and the opinions of the people of the world. Thou knowest, Oh Lord! my deep baptisms. I acknowledge my manifold sins and transgressions. I know my unworthiness of the many favours I have received; and I thank thee, Oh Father! that thou hast hid thy mysteries from the wise and prudent, and revealed them to babes and sucklings. Amen.[7]

So extraordinary and unexpected was this outburst that older Friends at first were moved to adjourn the meeting; but, after some commotion, the meeting settled again, "and ended to the edification of many." For some weeks thereafter Waln kept to his house. He closed out his law practice, and took on the dress and manner of a plain Friend.

Convinced of Waln's sincerity, the elders of the Meeting began to assign him small responsibilities. He was appointed an overseer of the Negro school[8] and put on the committee that waited on slave-holding Friends to persuade them to free their slaves. Soon he began to appear in the ministry, mostly in Philadelphia, but

---

[5] Robert C. Moon, *The Morris Family of Philadelphia* (Phila., 1898), II, 509–15.
[6] Joseph Oxley, "Journal of his Life, Travels, and Labours of Love," in William Evans and Thomas Evans, eds., *The Friends' Library,* II (1838), 474.
[7] "Biographical Memoirs of Nicholas Waln," loc. cit. Several persons who heard it made a record of this prayer afterwards; but no written version can suggest the impact it had.
[8] Northern District Monthly Meeting, Minutes, 28 Twelfth Mo. 1773; Kirk, "Nicholas Waln."

occasionally at country meetings; and on 30 November 1774 he was formally recorded as a minister. The story of his conversion was known throughout the Society of Friends. "With what power & authority can such a man speak who has gone thro' the religious experience that he has, & whose precepts are enforced by his example," exclaimed one Friend on hearing him preach.[9] By 1776 Waln was counted as one of the more valuable members of the Philadelphia Yearly Meeting.

During the Revolution the lead sash-weights of his house were stripped off to make bullets, as they were from the houses of other citizens; and, like other citizens, after the war Waln claimed compensation from the state. On occasions of national celebration he and his fellow-Quakers would not illuminate their houses, but stood impotently by as boisterous rebels smashed the unlighted windows.[10] But Waln did not incur the particular wrath of the rebels, or seek persecution by unnecessary acts of defiance. He was never arrested. Thanks to his legal training and to the respect he enjoyed among his former brethren at the bar, he was often able to aid his unlucky co-religionists. First as a member, then as clerk, of the Meeting for Sufferings, he visited, counselled, and sometimes obtained the release of Friends in jail.[11] His memorandum on the legal position of Quakers who refused to pay the military tax, prepared at the request of Governor Joseph Reed in 1780, seems to have guided the conduct of the state authorities thereafter:

> Case.
> In the Act of Assembly which grants the four Million of Dollars. Cap. 105 is the following Clause.
> §7. If any person shall willfully conceal in the Return which he makes to the Township or Ward Assessor any part of his taxable Property within such Township or Ward with Intent to screen the same from Taxation, the person so concealing shall pay four fold Taxes for all such Property so concealed, &c.
> Under this Act the following Case has arisen:
> A Number of Persons, who apprehend they are called upon to bear a Testimony against Wars and Fighting, not through Obstinacy, Fraud or Deceit, but from a real Scruple of Conscience decline giving an Account of their Estates, as they cannot actively pay a Tax to carry on War, tho' they do not use any Device to screen their property from Taxation, but expect passively to pay their Proportion.
> Qu. Are such persons within the meaning of the said Section and liable to the heavy Penalty of a four fold Tax upon all their Estate?
> A. Penal Laws which affect particular persons are to be strictly construed and not extended beyond what the clear Words will bear; it would be very unsafe to trust

---

[9] Nicholas B. Wainwright, "'A Diary of Trifling Occurrences,' Philadelphia, 1776–1778," *PMHB*, LXXXII (1958), 437.
[10] Ibid., 438; Register of Accounts, 1790, pp. 111–12 (records of Secretary of the Commonwealth, Division of Public Records, Harrisburg).
[11] Samuel and Rowland Fisher, "Journal," *PMHB*, XLI (1917), 179, 183; Philadelphia Monthly Meeting, Minutes, 26 Sixth Mo. 1778.

engaged him less frequently. He spoke more often on points of Quaker discipline and preached a strict morality. "There are two cautions which I wish to prevail in our society," he declared in Market Street Meetinghouse in a time of severe cold weather. "I wish we may give no factitious notes. I wish we may be punctual to our promises and just in the payment of our debts—and when we have paid everybody, be kind to the poor!"[18] There is an admirable frankness here, the injunctions are unexceptionable, but the emphasis and the priorities seem wrong.

By 1810 and 1811 Waln was showing signs of age and weakness. He wrote his will, but continued to attend meeting regularly, even at some effort. "I would as lief die there, as anywhere else," he told a friend who solicitously suggested that he might conserve his strength by staying home. In the summer of 1813 he went as usual with his family to his country place at Frankford; but he was failing fast and was brought home before the season changed. "I can't die for the life of me," he is said to have remarked with a returning flash of his old wit. On 29 September 1813 he died in his house on Second Street (which was the house his wife inherited from her father).[19] He was survived by his widow, who died in 1825, and by three of their seven children. Except for a few small cash bequests all his considerable estate went to her.[20]

JOHN LUKENS (1720–1789)
"YOUNG JUNTO": 3 OCTOBER 1766

JOHN LUKENS, Surveyor-General of Pennsylvania, was proposed for membership in the Junto on 19 September 1766, was elected on 3 October, and attended the meeting of 17 October, when he signed the Obligation and Laws. Two months later the Junto changed its name to the American Society for Promoting and Propagating Useful Knowledge. For most of the next year his attendance was infrequent—he was often recorded as out of town, presumably on surveys—but he did attend the Society's anniversary meeting "on the Banks of the Schuylkill" on 1 May 1767. Resuming attendance in the winter of 1767–68, on 27 January he was put on the

---

[18] "Biographical Memoirs of Nicholas Waln," loc. cit., 130.
[19] Harold D. Eberlein and Horace M. Lippincott, *The Colonial Homes of Philadelphia and its Neighbourhood* (Phila., 1912), 36–41, describes the house, which was then standing at 254 South Second Street, Philadelphia.
[20] Waln, Will, dated 8 April 1811; probated 13 October 1813, Philadelphia Will Book S, No. 115 (Register of Wills, Phila.).

initial committee to confer with representatives of the American Philosophical Society on the expediency of uniting the two societies. His name was on the list of American Society members sent to the American Philosophical Society on 2 February 1768.

Meanwhile Lukens had been elected a member of the American Philosophical Society—in November 1767 according to one list prepared in that Society. He attended a meeting on 8 March 1768, and on 21 June was put on the committee to make preparations for the observation of the Transit of Venus that was to occur the following year. Lukens was thus an active member of both societies simultaneously. The situation was unusual, as the two were rivals and it seems to have been generally understood that a member of one should not accept election by the other. There is no evidence in the minutes, however, that Lukens found his position awkward or that either society expressed an opinion in the case, much less took action.

John Lukens was born in 1720 in Horsham Township in Philadelphia (now Montgomery) County, Pennsylvania, the first of ten children of Peter and Gainor (Evans) Lukens, both members of the Society of Friends.[1] On 31 October 1741 he married his first cousin Sarah, daughter of William and Elizabeth (Tyson) Lukens, in the Presbyterian church at Horsham. For thus marrying within the prohibited degrees of consanguinity as well as being married by a "priest," John and Sarah were both promptly disowned by the Abington Friends Meeting. They were restored to membership in 1745, however, after publicly acknowledging their error. The couple had eight children, of whom two, Charles and Jesse, became surveyors like their father.[2]

Little is known of Lukens' life before 1761. There is no record of where he obtained an elementary education, and only a surmise that he learned the art of surveying from Nicholas Scull, whom he succeeded as surveyor-general of the Province. It is known, however, that in 1755 he joined three others in founding the Hatboro library, a total of £44 being subscribed to purchase the first selection of books from London.[3] The next year Lukens moved to Philadelphia, obtaining on 28 June 1756 a certificate of removal from Abington Meeting. In Philadelphia in 1759 he became a member of Masonic Lodge No. 2. The move to Philadelphia was temporary. He returned to Horsham, and on 26 August 1762, having been appointed surveyor-general of the Province, he again received a certificate from the Meeting to Philadelphia. Including his wife and children as well as himself, it was presented at Philadelphia Monthly Meeting on 27 May 1763. The nine months'

---

[1] Hubertis M. Cummings, "Surveyors General of Pennsylvania: John Lukens, 1761–1776 and 1781–1789," Pa. Dept. of Internal Affairs, *Bulletin*, XXX (1962), No. 11, pp. 24–27, 32; No. 12, pp. 24–29; Jill J. Hurd, *The Ancestors and Descendants of Jan Lucken* (Baltimore, 1989), 122–25.
[2] Hinshaw, *Amer. Quaker Geneal.*, II, 587.
[3] Chester T. Hallenbeck, "A Colonial Reading List," *PMHB*, LVI (1932), 289–340.

delay did not pass unnoticed by the Meeting, which hinted that it demanded an explanation.[4]

Lukens received his commission as surveyor-general on 8 December, succeeding Nicholas Scull, who had died. During the next fifteen years he was occupied by the many obligations of the office. In 1764 additional duties were laid upon him, when he was appointed one of the city regulators.[5] In Philadelphia he surveyed lots, streets, and water courses; and in distant and often untraversed parts of the Province he led surveying parties in laying out manors for the Proprietors and grants, large and small, for individuals and groups of investors. The Treaty of Fort Stanwix in 1768 opened up a large area for settlement, and increased the surveyor's work. Sometimes Lukens laid out a whole town, as he reported from Bedford in 1766:

> Upon my arrival at Fort Bedford June 4th, 1766, having called together the principal inhabitants to consult with them concerning the streets and the size of the lots, being also assisted by the Sheriff of the county; It was concluded the streets running east and west, should run parallel with Capt. Lewis' new house and on measuring the ground, we found that the size of the lots mentioned in the order for laying out said Town, would not answer so well as to lay them out sixty feet in breadth and two hundred and forty feet in length, which was accordingly done except the eight short lots fronting on the Great Square, and those lying between Pitt street and the Raystown Branch of the Juniata which are of various lengths.[6]

Such work was always hard, often uncomfortable and sometimes dangerous. The men worked in all weathers, in cold, snow, and "Drisling Rain." Sometimes it was so hot that the axemen "gave out with the heat" and went home. Work had sometimes to be postponed because of Indian hostility. Each day's measurements had to be carefully recorded and the calculations made, and the surveys had to be deposited in the office of the surveyor-general. Lukens had also to examine, correct, and record the surveys of his deputies. He had to collect payments due the Proprietors as well as his own fees. He appointed the deputy surveyors, among whom were numbered at various times—in the unashamed nepotism of the day—two sons, a son-in-law, and a nephew.[7]

---

[4] Hinshaw, *Amer. Quaker Geneal.,* II, 587; Hurd, *Jan Lucken,* 122–25.
[5] Scharf and Westcott, *Philadelphia,* III, 1748; 3 *Pa. Arch.,* IX, 384–86; *Minutes of the Common Council of Philadelphia . . . 1704–1776* (Phila., 1847), 699. Lukens announced in *Pa. Gaz.,* 24 December 1761, that his office was as the same place where Scull kept his; and the advertisement implied that he would retain the deputy surveyors.
[6] William H. Koontz, *History of Bedford and Somerset Counties, Pennsylvania* (N.Y. and Chicago, 1906), I, 70, quoted in Hurd, *Jan Lucken,* 124.
[7] Lukens to Richard Peters, 22 Aug. 1761, Penn Mss., Boundaries, 70 (HSP); John Penn to Lukens, 29 Nov. 1764, Dreer Coll. (In boxes) (HSP). Several of Lukens' survey books, 1761–75, are in APS.

Although the surveyor's office was in Philadelphia, Lukens often visited his "plantation" at Horsham, where he continued to make use of the Hatboro library. Its borrowing records for 1763–68 reflect his own taste in reading, as well, perhaps, as recommendations for his children: Milton, Shakespeare, Dryden's *Virgil,* Pope's *Iliad,* Smollett's *History of England,* Fielding's *Tom Jones,* Richardson's *Pamela, The Athenian Oracle,* Pope's *Essay on Man.* From the printer David Hall on 4 January 1769 he purchased a copy of *The Vicar of Wakefield* "for his son."[8]

In the American Philosophical Society after its inauguration in 1769 Lukens was a member of the standing Committees on Husbandry and American Improvements and on Geography, Mathematics, Natural History and Astronomy. He attended frequently. He was one of those whom the Society named to observe the Transit of Venus. With Provost William Smith, John Sellers, and David Rittenhouse, he made observations on 3 June from Rittenhouse's farm at Norriton, some twenty miles northwest of the city. Lukens used a 42′ refracting telescope, whose lenses had been sent from England for Harvard College; but, reaching Philadelphia too late to be forwarded to Cambridge in time, they had been fitted to Lukens' instrument. So large a telescope was difficult to use, especially when the sun was high, and Lukens had to lie on the ground on his back to peer through it, his head "bolster'd up" by assistants.[9] Later in the year, with his former associates Smith, Rittenhouse, and Biddle, Lukens observed the Transit of Mercury over the sun on 9 November.[10] The next year, at the request of the Astronomer Royal, the three men went up once more to Norriton to make terrestrial measurements of the differences in latitude and longitude between the observatories there and in Philadelphia.[11]

Lukens performed other tasks at the behest of the Society. Matthew Clarkson, John Sellers, William Rumsey, and he were appointed in 1769 to determine the best route for the proposed Delaware-Chesapeake canal. They were

> to go and examine which will [be] the most proper place for cutting the canal, to take the proper levels, to compare the respective times of high water in both bays & see whether a direct communication can be opened by a canal, whether locks and dams are necessary, & if so, what head of waters [is required] to supply those dams, to make an estimate of the probable expence that may attend the execution of the work and report their proceedings and observations to the Society.

Several years later the Society asked him to locate and survey streams flowing into the Schuylkill and Susquehanna rivers with a view to determine the most practi-

---

[8] Hallenbeck, "A Colonial Reading List," loc. cit., 311–12; David Hall, Shop Book, 18 June 1767, 4 Jan. 1768 (APS).
[9] Lukens, "Account of the Contacts," APS *Trans.,* I (1771), 28.
[10] "Account of the Transit of Mercury over the Sun," ibid., app. 50–53.
[11] Ibid., app. 5.

cable passage between them. The report, presented to the Assembly, concluded that a canal linking Tulpehocken Creek, a branch of the Schuylkill, with Quitipahilla and Swatara creeks, which flowed into the Susquehanna, was practicable and that "an inland Navigation may be formed of vast Extent and Benefit to the Province."[12] As one interested in the economic improvement of America, Lukens subscribed £2 to the Silk Society.

Lukens' reputation extended beyond the limits of his job as surveyor-general. He was asked to endorse and recommend a manuscript by Samuel Gale, entitled "The Complete Surveyor," which, nevertheless, was never published.[13] The Philosophical Society asked him to compare the maps of Bernard Romans with those of George Gauld. (He subsequently subscribed for six copies of Romans' *Natural History of East and West Florida* [New York, 1775].) When the Marquis de Condorcet sent some queries about America to his correspondent Dr. Franklin in London, Franklin forwarded them to the Philosophical Society, which assigned several committees of knowledgeable members to prepare responses. Lukens and his fellow-committeemen had two questions to answer:

> Are there any observations made in Philadelphia, or in the neighbouring Colonies, on the direction of the Magnetic needle, so that accounts may be obtained what variations it has undergone every year, in the same place? . . .
> Has the height of the Mercury in the barometer the same conformity with the change of weather as in our Continent. . . .

The Revolution broke out a few months after Condorcet's questions were received, and it does not appear that answers were ever prepared and sent him.

With the collapse of Proprietary government in Pennsylvania in 1775–76 Lukens' authority as surveyor-general expired. He was called upon from time to time in the ensuing years, however, for information in his files about grants and surveys.[14] Early in the war he supported measures to protect settlers of Northumberland and Northampton Counties from "the hostile Invasions of a Number of lawless Intruders from Connecticut, who taking an unjust Advantage of the Calamities of the Times," claimed those lands for themselves and were trying to settle on them. Lukens and his son Jesse contributed to a fund to purchase arms and ammunition for the Pennsylvania settlers' defense.[15] With the resumption of reason-

---

[12] APS Minutes, 3 May 1769; 8 *Pa. Arch.*, VIII, 6687–88, 6748, 6931–34.
[13] *Va. Gaz.* (Purdie & Dixon), 22 July 1773.
[14] *Col. Recs. Pa.*, XII, 621.
[15] Committee of Northumberland and Northampton Counties, Memorial to Committee of Safety, 12 Oct. 1775, in Robert J. Taylor, ed., *The Susquehanna Company Papers*, VI, 369–70; 2 *Pa. Arch.*, XVIII, 617.

ably normal conditions after the evacuation of Philadelphia by the British army in 1778, Lukens petitioned for his former post; he was finally appointed surveyor-general of the state in 1781.[16] On 2 February of that year he and Archibald McClean, who had been deputy surveyor for York County, were directed to complete the running of the Pennsylvania-Virginia boundary; six weeks later they received formal instructions, which were

> to extend Mason and Dixon's line due west five degrees of longitude, to be computed from the river Delaware, for the southern boundary of Pensylvania, and that a meridian drawn from the western extremity thereof to the northern limit of the said State, be the western boundary of Pensylvania forever.[17]

On 10 April Lukens was made one of the commissioners of the Land Office. In 1782 he was reappointed one of the city regulators.

The survey was slow in getting under way, partly because the Virginia commissioners were delayed. In 1783 John Ewing, Thomas Hutchins, Rittenhouse, and Lukens were commissioned to proceed; the delays continued, and Lukens was reminded that it was necessary "to close that business with all possible accuracy and dispatch." Lukens himself did not join the surveying party until the summer of 1784. How far west he went is uncertain; the work was completed by Rittenhouse and Andrew Ellicott. Lukens, now in his office in Philadelphia, was concerned with surveys of the Depreciation and Donation Lands, set aside in the western part of the state for the benefit of Pennsylvania's veterans of the war. This work, too, was delayed, partly because some western Indians were hostile, and even friendly Indians were disaffected because of the small compensation they had received for guiding earlier parties. When the work began at last, it was with the warning that some persons in Philadelphia had formed "combinations" to acquire reserved lands for themselves, and that these people might attempt to influence or bribe surveyors to misrepresent the character of the lands. "Should this be done, much uneasiness to the State & great injury to the Soldiery will follow."[18]

Meanwhile in 1779 the American Philosophical Society, whose meetings had been interrupted, then suspended, by the war, was revived. Lukens gave $20 towards the necessary expenses of starting up; and with Rittenhouse and Owen Biddle he was directed to put the observatory in repair and lodge the Society's instruments in it. He served as treasurer of the Society for a time, and in 1781 was elected a councillor for a one-year term. In 1785 he made two contributions of £5 each to-

---

[16] Ibid., III, 384–85; *Col. Recs. Pa.,* XII, 233.
[17] Ibid., 704.
[18] Ibid., XIII, 685; 1 *Pa. Arch.,* X, 65–66, 95, 740–41.

JOHN MORGAN

By Angelica Kauffmann. *National Portrait Gallery, Smithsonian Institution*

1748. The care of John, now 13, was entrusted to relatives and friends; one of the trustees of the young children was William Allen, who was soon to become chief justice of the Province.

John was sent in 1745 or 1746 to the school kept by the Reverend Mr. Samuel Finley at West Nottingham in Chester County, Pennsylvania. In 1750 he was apprenticed to Dr. John Redman of Philadelphia to study medicine. Redman encouraged the young man to enroll in the new College of Philadelphia in 1754. The next year, on Redman's recommendation, Morgan was appointed apothecary of the Pennsylvania Hospital at a salary of £15 a year. This hospital experience he was later to cite as one of the principal steps in his professional education. In 1756, his apprenticeship completed, Morgan left the Hospital and joined the Pennsylvania Provincial troops as a surgeon with the rank of ensign. Here during four years at Fort Augusta, Fort Bedford, Fort Pitt, and other places in the western country, he acquired experience and skill in treating wounds and injuries and dealing with dysentery, jaundice, scurvy, and smallpox, as well as performing a variety of military duties, such as recruiting service. In the spring of 1757, having returned briefly to Philadelphia, Morgan received his bachelor's degree at the first commencement of the College of Philadelphia.

Morgan resigned his commission in 1760 and embarked for England to continue his medical studies. He carried warm recommendations from teachers and friends, and assurance of financial support from Chief Justice Allen, who supported the foreign studies of other promising young Philadelphians, including Benjamin West. On the advice of Dr. John Fothergill, the prominent London Quaker physician and friend of Pennsylvania, to whom Benjamin Franklin sent him, Morgan enrolled as a pupil at St. Thomas's Hospital in London and for the anatomical lectures of Dr. William Hunter. From Dr. Hunter and Hunter's brother John, in whose house he lived, Morgan learned, among other things, how to make anatomical preparations by the process of corrosion.

In the fall of 1761 Morgan matriculated in Edinburgh University, where he enrolled in William Cullen's class in chemistry, Robert Whytt's in physiology and pathology, and John Hope's in botany and pharmacy. He also attended John Rutherford's clinical lectures at the Royal Infirmary, where he made at least one postmortem examination. He was elected a member of the student Medical (later Royal Medical) Society in 1762. His social success in Scotland was outstanding. He was a familiar in the home of Professor Cullen, and was often a guest in the house of George Drummond, Lord Provost of Edinburgh, and at Prestonfield, the home of Sir Alexander Dick, president of the Royal College of Physicians. In 1762, while still a student, Morgan received the freedom of the city of Stirling, and the next year he was made a freeman of the city of Edinburgh. He was graduated in 1763, a friend wrote, "with an Éclat almost unknown before." His dissertation was *De Puris Confectione*.

Morgan travelled through Holland in the summer of 1763 (in company with a law student from Edinburgh named James Boswell) and spent the winter of 1763–64 studying anatomy under the celebrated Jean-Joseph Sue, chief surgeon of the Hôtel de la Charité in Paris. In France Morgan demonstrated the technique he had learned in London for making anatomical preparations and presented his thesis on the formation of pus to the Académie Royale de Chirurgie. In the spring of 1764, accompanied by a fellow-Philadelphian, Samuel Powel, he set out for Italy. At Leghorn the young men were invited to join the party of the Duke of York, who was travelling to Rome, and so were "invited with the English Nobility & Gentry present to the Balls, Concerts, Conversations &c. made for the entertainment of his royal highness." At Rome Morgan and Powel witnessed the lavish spectacles of Holy Week, took a course of formal instruction in art and antiquities, and were elected members of the Accademia degli Arcadi, a social club of men of letters and science—physicians, lawyers, artists, and churchmen who dabbled in verse. At Naples they were conducted through Herculaneum and other ancient monuments. Both men were painted by Angelica Kauffmann. Everywhere they bought paintings and engravings and collected curious specimens of natural history. At Padua, on the return journey, Morgan paid a visit to the distinguished anatomist Giovanni Battista Morgagni, who gave him copies of two of his books. At Ferney, Voltaire received the young men, then sent them on with a ringing salute and exhortation:

> Behold two Amiable Young Men, Lovers of Truth & Inquirers into Nature. They are not satisy'd with mear Appearances; they love Investigation & Truth, and despize Superstition. I commend You, Gentlemen—go on, love Truth & search diligently after it. Hate Hypocrisy, hate Masses, & above all hate the Priests![2]

Back in London in November, Morgan was recommended by an impressive list of sponsors to the Royal Society as one "acquainted with several Branches of Philosophical and polite Literature, & particularly . . . is a zealous Inquirer into Anatomical & Physiological Subjects." He was elected a Fellow on 7 March 1765.[3] In the same spring he passed the examination for the license of the Royal College of Physicians of London and was elected a Fellow of the Royal College of Physicians of Edinburgh.

While still a medical student in Edinburgh, Morgan had resolved to deliver medical lectures when he returned to Philadelphia, and he developed the idea during the remaining years he spent in Europe. The plan was shared by other students, notably William Shippen, Jr., who was graduated from Edinburgh in 1761, and it

---

[2] Morgan, *Journal . . . from the City of Rome to the City of London, 1764* (Privately printed, Phila., 1907), 96–98.
[3] Raymond P. Stearns, "Colonial Fellows of the Royal Society of London, 1661–1789," 3 *Wm. & Mary Quar.,* III (1946), 247–48.

was expanded in discussions with Dr. Fothergill and others in Edinburgh and London. Exactly what their expectations and understandings were is not clear; but Shippen on his return home in 1762 opened a course of lectures on anatomy, surgery, and midwifery, and Fothergill believed that Shippen would ultimately be joined by "an able assistant," namely John Morgan. But Morgan cherished ampler ideas, and his fellow-students, who knew him, believed matters would take a different turn when he returned.

So indeed they did. Morgan had now determined to establish a school of medicine in Philadelphia, and to reform medical practice in accordance with the standards of the Royal Colleges. He submitted his plan to the trustees of the College of Philadelphia, who elected him professor of the theory and practice of medicine on 3 May 1765; and on 30–31 May he presented his project for "the institution of medical schools in America" in a long, carefully thought-out address to the public.[4] It called for the establishment of the usual professorships, insisted that medical study should be based on a prior education in the liberal arts, and proposed that the degree of doctor be conferred only after the candidate had practiced for three years, written a dissertation, and submitted to an examination. As it proved, this made the course to the M.D. degree in Philadelphia longer than in Edinburgh, and the requirement was eventually dropped. In addition, Morgan pointed out that the professors could not be expected to teach if they had also to carry a full load of practice; and so he proposed that medicine be separated from "the low drudgery" of surgery and that physicians give up the compounding and sale of drugs, and charge only for advice. With this in mind, he explained, he had brought a qualified apothecary with him from London. The proposed medical school would benefit, Morgan observed blandly, from the presence of Dr. Shippen, who, as he had been informed, had already begun to offer lectures on anatomy.

All this had been thought out and done, apparently, without consulting, or even informing, Shippen and Shippen's friends among the older members of the profession. Shippen swallowed his pride, applied for appointment in the school, and on 23 September was elected professor of anatomy and surgery. But the slight was not forgotten and the resulting antagonism between the two men and their friends vexed the medical profession in Philadelphia for more than two generations.

The insult to Shippen and the older doctors was repeated the next year when Morgan founded a medical society.[5] Designed to promote higher professional standards in education and practice, the Medical Society was composed of a small number of younger doctors, presumably all Morgan's friends, who had received formal training beyond the apprenticeship. Once organized, the Society extended invita-

---

[4] Morgan, *A Discourse upon the Institution of Medical Schools in America* (Phila., 1765); reprinted in facsimile, Baltimore, 1937.
[5] Bell, *John Morgan,* 137–40.

tions to Shippen and his father, Thomas and Phineas Bond, Thomas Graeme, John Redman, and others of an older generation; most declined to join; and so another cause of dissension in the Philadelphia profession was given. Morgan's appeal to Thomas Penn for a Proprietary charter was rejected, and so his society lacked authority and prestige, even in Pennsylvania. As a result the Medical Society was far less influential than it could have been; and on 4 November 1768 it was voted into the American Society, its members becoming the Medical Committee of that Society.

In the ten years before the American Revolution Morgan enjoyed a successful practice and increasing local reputation. On 5 September 1765 he married Mary Hopkinson, daughter of the late Thomas Hopkinson and Mary Johnson, and thus became linked to one of the old and prominent families of the town. In 1766 his essay on the reciprocal advantages of perpetual union between Great Britain and her colonies won first prize in a competition at the College of Philadelphia supported by John Sergeant, M.P. The paper was printed, with three others submitted in the contest, and received favorable reviews in London. Morgan made a contribution to the Pennsylvania Hospital in 1765 and was appointed a physician to the institution in 1773 in succession to Cadwalader Evans; it was the first vacancy that opened after Morgan returned home.

His reputation as a connoisseur brought visitors to see the paintings he had acquired in Italy. One of these was the artist Henry Pelham of Boston; another was Pierre E. Du Simitière, who made "a crayon picture of an old man's head, copied from an oyle painting belonging to Dr Morgan." George Morgan gave his brother a miscellaneous lot of prehistoric bones that he had found on the banks of the Ohio River; and these too were examined and marvelled at by visitors. They were eventually sketched by Charles Willson Peale and sold to a Dutch anatomist, who used them in the process of identifying the mastodon as a distinct species.[6] In 1772 Morgan went to Jamaica in a fund-raising campaign for the College of Philadelphia. And he took a large part in efforts to obtain land grants for veterans, like himself, of the Pennsylvania Provincial troops in the French and Indian war. He was a vestryman of Christ Church in 1769 and became a warden in 1775. He subscribed £2 to the Silk Society in 1770 and was a member of the Library Company of Philadelphia. He was a corresponding member of the London Society of Arts, and in 1774 was elected a member of the Virginia Society for the Advancement of Useful Knowledge.[7]

In the American Society Morgan was active in many ways. On 16 January 1767, a month after his election, he presented a treatise on the formation of pus—prob-

---

[6] Whitfield J. Bell, Jr., "A Box of Old Bones: A Note on the Identification of the Mastodon, 1766–1806," APS *Proc.*, XCIII (1949), 169–77.
[7] (Purdie & Dixon) *Va. Gaz.,* 16 June 1774.

ably a copy of his printed Edinburgh dissertation. On 7 March he proposed for discussion the question: "Is Cold a positive Body or a Privation of Heat?" From time to time he presented specimens of natural history or descriptions of manufacturing processes, such as a method for pressing oil from sunflower seeds. Persons Morgan had known in the army, like Hugh Mercer, or had met on his travels abroad, like Isaac Jamineau, the English consul at Naples, sent him papers for the Society; and he in turn recommended them for membership. Samuel Bard, Sir Alexander Dick, Professor Cullen, Dr. John M. Butt, Lionel Chalmers, and Alexander Garden all owed their election probably to Morgan. On 4 November 1768 he was elected one of the American Society's curators,

It was the same in the American Philosophical Society after the union in 1769. Morgan was one of its three curators. He was given seeds of Chinese vetches for experimental planting. He was put on committees in 1769 and 1774 to prepare volumes of *Transactions,* and on another to design a certificate of membership.

On 17 October 1775 Congress elected John Morgan director-general of the Hospital of the Continental Army, which was then stationed at Cambridge, Massachusetts.[8] He arrived at his post on 29 November and assumed his duties at once. The tasks confronting him, both medical and administrative, were daunting. There was no organization worthy of the name. Morgan had to draft regulations and enforce them. Supplies of every sort were scarce. He had to explain and argue for the simplest needs before staff officers, the commander-in-chief, Congress, and the public. He appealed to the citizens of surrounding towns for blankets, shirts, lancets, linen, stuff for bandages, even needles and thread. Each regiment had its own hospital and surgeon, and these men, as well as the officers and privates, resisted Morgan's effort to unify the system of medical care and supply under the General Hospital. To provide qualified surgeons for the Hospital he instituted examinations. In the winter of 1775–76 smallpox broke out in the army and became epidemic in Boston in the spring.

Pressures on the medical services became more acute during the summer of 1776. The army in the north at Ticonderoga was in desperate need of supplies, and the director of its hospital called on Morgan for them. The main army, which had moved from Boston to New York, suffered casualties in several battles and engagements around that city. At the beginning of September a quarter of Washington's army was in hospitals. Meanwhile Congress did nothing to rectify the system and clarify Morgan's authority, and the regimental surgeons gave little heed to the General Hospital and its director-general. Matters only worsened when on 15 July Congress appointed William Shippen, Jr., chief surgeon and physician of the Flying Camp in New Jersey, and then followed this action with one that seemed to limit

---

[8] On the medical services of the Continental Army, see Mary C. Gillett, *The Army Medical Department, 1775–1818* (Washington, [1981]).

WILLIAM HENRY

By Benjamin West. *Historical Society of Pennsylvania.*

WILLIAM HENRY (1729–1786)
AMERICAN SOCIETY (CORRESPONDING MEMBER):
27 MARCH 1767

WILLIAM HENRY of Lancaster, Pennsylvania, gunsmith, mechanic, inventor, merchant, patron of Benjamin West, and friend of David Rittenhouse, was just such a man as would win the approbation of the American Society for Promoting Useful Knowledge and, in turn, would find the members' company stimulating and congenial. Accordingly he was elected a corresponding member on 27 March 1767; and, though unable because of distance to attend its meetings, remained active and interested in the Society's work until his death.

He was born in West Caln township, Chester County, Pennsylvania, on 19 May 1729, the eldest of eight children of John and Elizabeth (De Vinne) Henry.[1] His paternal grandparents were Scots-Irish Episcopalians; his mother's parents were Huguenots who emigrated to America through Northern Ireland. Finding themselves remote from an Anglican church, John and Elizabeth Henry joined a Presbyterian church nearby. They were never comfortable in that communion, however, and their son William joined the Anglican Church as soon as opportunity afforded. John Henry died in 1744, and young William was apprenticed to Matthew Roesser, a gunsmith in Lancaster, which was to be his home thereafter.

His apprenticeship ending in 1750, the young man probably became a journeyman gunsmith in Lancaster, which was already notable for the manufacture of excellent rifles. In time Henry opened his own shop; rather curiously, however, no guns of his making have been identified.[2] According to his son, Henry served as an armourer in Braddock's expedition in 1755,[3] but nothing has been found to

---

[1] The principal biographical account is Francis Jordan, Jr., *The Life of William Henry of Lancaster, Pennsylvania, 1729–1786* (Lancaster, Pa., 1910); it is based on two principal collections of documents: the William Henry Papers in HSP, and the Henry Papers owned (1973) by a descendant, Mrs. Thomas H. A. Stites of Nazareth, Pa., which have been microfilmed by Hagley Museum and Library, Greenville, Del. Jordan's book should be used cautiously, preferably with reference to the manuscript sources he used. Some of his statements are amplified and corrected by Herbert H. Beck, "William Henry: Progenitor of the Steamboat, Riflemaker, Patriot," Lancaster County Hist. Soc., *Papers,* LIV (1950), 65–88, which was reprinted with changes and additions as "William Henry," in Moravian Hist. Soc., *Trans.,* XVI (1955), 69–95. Henry's spiritual autobiography, translated from the German, contains some biographical facts; it was presented by S. E. Dyke as "William Henry Memoirs, 1748–1786," in Lancaster County Hist. Soc., *Journal,* LXXVI (1972), 58–68. Notes on the graves of Henry and some of his family in Greenwood Cemetery are in Geneal. Soc. Pa., *Pubs.,* XI (1934), 89–90.
[2] Beck, "William Henry," Lanc. Co. Hist. Soc., *Papers,* LIV (1950), 74.
[3] John Joseph Henry, *An Accurate and Interesting Account of the Hardships and Sufferings of that Band of Heroes who traversed the Wilderness in the Campaign against Quebec in 1775* (Lancaster, 1812), 215.

confirm this statement. Henry did serve in that capacity, however, in the Provincial forces in 1756: writing to his brother from McKee's Store on 2 June 1756, Captain Joseph Shippen complained that many of the weapons were in bad condition, splitting on firing, the locks cheap and constantly out of order, "so that we shall be obliged to take Wm Henry with us to repair them from time to time, tho' he has already taken a great deal of pains to rectifie them, & bore & straiten the Barrels."[4] In addition to making repairs, Henry provided arms and accoutrements to the garrisons at Harris' Ferry and Fort Augusta at Shamokin.[5]

In the large, well-organized army assembled by General Forbes in 1758 Henry's services as armourer were again required. After a military conference at Conococheague on 12 June Colonel Bouquet directed "the armurer Henry to go to Cumberland."[6] Thereafter he received instructions from the Virginia Colonel George Washington. At Fort Loudon on 24 June Washington directed Henry "to set about cleaning and putting all the Virginia Arms in the best repair you can."[7]

On one of these campaigns into western Pennsylvania Henry saved the life of a young Delaware warrior named Killbuck. In gratitude the latter proposed that he and his benefactor exchange names. This was the beginning of a remarkable friendship between Henry and William Henry Killbuck and their families that continued through three generations, surviving even the removal of the Delawares to the Middle West in the nineteenth century.[8]

Meanwhile in January 1756 Henry married at Lancaster Ann Wood, daughter of Abraham Wood of Darby, Pennsylvania, and his wife Ursula (Taylor) Wood. They had 13 children, of whom seven survived infancy and childhood.[9]

About 1755 a young man from Chester County who had displayed more than common talent for painting came to Lancaster under the patronage of the lawyer George Ross. He was Benjamin West, then aged 17. Henry soon made his acquaintance, engaged the young artist to paint portraits of both himself (standing with a long rifle in his hand) and his bride Ann. For a time, it seems, West lived with the Henrys, decorating his room with designs and scenes of his imagining. As he watched West at his work, Henry offered a suggestion, that he should paint historical scenes; and he proposed the death of Socrates as a subject that was both dramatic and edifying. West, who had had no classical education, asked who Socrates was. For answer Henry drew down a volume of Rollin's *Ancient History,* whose frontispiece was an engraving of the fateful scene. West made a sketch that was

[4] *PMHB*, XXXVI (1912), 386.
[5] 8 *Pa. Arch.*, V, 4373. Henry sent similar materials to Fort Augusta in 1757. Ibid., VI, 4881.
[6] S. K. Stevens and others, eds., *The Papers of Henry Bouquet* (Harrisburg, Pa., 1951–), II, 79.
[7] John C. Fitzpatrick, ed., *The Writings of George Washington* (Washington, 1931–44), II, 224.
[8] Jordan, *William Henry,* 8–9.
[9] John W. Jordon, *Colonial Families of Philadelphia* (Phila., 1911), I, 141–42.

based on, but not copied from, the engraving; then made his painting; and thus was launched on his distinguished career.[10] The Henry family long cherished their association with West. When, years later, the painter sent an agent to Lancaster to buy up examples of his juvenile work, they refused 60 guineas to part with *The Death of Socrates*.[11] Jealously retained by Henry's widow and son, West's paintings were, in fact, a principal attraction in Lancaster. The British Minister Sir Augustus J. Foster in 1806 was taken to Judge Henry's house to inspect them. Socrates, he wrote, apparently unimpressed by the "sublimity" of the subject, "looks like a Dunker, and is sitting down drinking poison while his friends stand round him with very, very rueful faces."[12] Henry named his youngest son for the artist, and Benjamin West Henry became a painter himself.[13]

In 1759 Henry formed a mercantile partnership with Joseph Simon, apparently giving up active work as a gunsmith; and in December 1760, bearing a letter of introduction from the Reverend Mr. Thomas Barton, the Anglican minister at Lancaster, he sailed to England to establish business contacts. The other passengers on the vessel included two Quaker preachers. Their conversation had a profound effect on Henry; in London he stayed with the family of one of his fellow-passengers, and in time became a Friend. Returning to Lancaster in 1761, his religious views considerably unsettled, he urged his wife also to join the Quakers, but she had come under the influence of a Moravian neighbor and was attending the services of that church. Henry accompanied his wife, and in 1765 both became members of the Unity.[14]

---

[10] William Sawitzky, "The American Work of Benjamin West," *PMHB,* LXII (1938), 448–49; John Galt, *The Life, Studies, and Works of Benjamin West, Esq.* (London, 1820), pt. 1, 35–37. The engraving was in Rollin's *Ancient History* (London, 1749), IV. See also Ann C. Van Devanter, "Benjamin West's *Death of Socrates,*" *Antiques,* CIV (1973), 436–39, and James T. Flexner, *First Flowers of Our Wilderness* (N.Y., 1969), 183, 187.
[11] Anne M. (Henry) Smith, Statements, 26, 27 March 1855, Henry Papers, II, 93 (HSP). Mrs. Smith had "a dim recollection" of another painting by West in her mother's parlor in Lancaster. It represented a fair woman in plain Quaker garb, weeping over her dead child. "My mother possessed what is usually denominated a treasure in a German domestic, excessively neat, who, objecting, I suppose, to the darker shades of the picture, to improve it applied soap, sand, & a brush and effectually consigned the beautiful memorial of the baby and mother to oblivion."
[12] Richard B. Davis, ed., *Jeffersonian America: Notes on the United States of America . . . by Sir Augustus John Foster, Bart,* (San Marino, Calif., 1954), 240–42.
[13] George Steinman, "Benjamin West Henry, a Lancaster Artist," Lanc. Co. Hist. Soc., *Papers,* XVI (1912), 270–72.
[14] "William Henry Memoirs: 1748–1786," Lanc. Co. Hist. Soc., *Journal,* LXXXVI (1972), 62, 64–65. Barton's letter is quoted in John W. Jordan to Granville Henry, 8 Nov. 1902, Henry Papers, Personal Corres. (microfilm, Hagley Museum and Library). Captain Nathaniel Falconer's receipt for £25 for Henry's passage to London, dated 17 Dec. 1760, is also in Henry Papers, Boulton Gun Works. Henry was one of the original members of the Moravian Brethren's Widows Society, signing its constitution on 19 Dec. 1770.

Simon and Henry prospered, and Henry had time to continue with his interests and studies. He dealt in ironmongery, was a "store-keeper" and "merchant,"[15] but, his son recalled, "his inclinations led him into chymical experiments. His evenings and mornings, were devoted to the laboratory," which he kept at the back of the store. "For the instruction of his children, my father would discourse upon the subjects of science, and particularly of chymistry, which was his favorite theme, and in which the names of Franklin and Priestley, were sure to stand foremost." The store, Judge Henry wrote on another occasion, "was not only the resort of mechanical men, who were generally his customers; but also of those, who in those days possessed the little science of the town and neighbouring country."[16]

Most of the possessors of the "science" of Lancaster were among the founders in 1759 or subsequent members of the Juliana Library Company, patterned after the Library Company of Philadelphia and named for Lady Juliana Penn, the Proprietor's wife. Henry was one of the first directors and the treasurer, and in 1766 became its librarian. He moved the collection into a room in his house and prepared a catalogue, which listed over 500 volumes and—certainly of great interest to Henry and the "mechanical men" and others who hung about his store—a collection of philosophical instruments. This included a small orrery, two pairs of globes, two reflecting telescopes, a solar microscope, a camera obscura, a magic lanthorn, a set of mathematical instruments, a Hadley's quadrant, a thermometer, a barometer, and an artificial magnet "of great power" made by Henry himself and presented by the maker. To these instruments, the Library catalogue announced, "an Electrical Apparatus, on the model of the ingenious Messieurs Franklin and Kinnersley, will be added as soon as possible." In addition, the Library had the beginnings of a natural history museum—a collection of minerals and fossils presented by the Reverend Mr. Barton, and "an Ostrich's Egg, preserved in a neat turned case."[17] The collection was sufficient both to stimulate and satisfy most of Henry's philosophical inclinations and projects, and he bought few instruments of his own.

Henry's first communication to the American Society was made in the spring

---

[15] For these denominations see Henry Papers, I, 3 (HSP), and the 1773 county tax list in 3 *Pa. Arch.,* XVII, 458.

[16] Henry, *Account of . . . the Campaign against Quebec,* 215; Abraham Rees' *Cyclopaedia; or, Universal Dictionary of Arts, Sciences, and Literature* (1st American edit., Phila., 1810–42), III, s.v. "Augre."

[17] Charles I. Landis, "The Juliana Library Company in Lancaster," *PMHB,* XLIII (1919), 24–52, 163–81, 228–50; also in Lanc. Co. Hist. Soc., *Papers,* XXXIII (1929), 193–245; *The Charter, Laws, Catalogue of Books, List of Philosophical Instruments, &c. of the Juliana Library-Company, in Lancaster* (Phila., 1766); *Pa. Gaz.,* 31 July 1766, 7 Sept. 1769. Henry was paid £7 10s. for repairing the borough's fire engine in 1764. Ellis and Evans, *History of Lancaster County, Pennsylvania* (Chicago, 1883), 381.

of 1768. It was the description of an automatic or sentinel register, designed to regulate the heat of a fireplace. Henry had used the device successfully for a year, and thought it might be applied to chemical and ceramic furnaces and to greenhouses and hatcheries, where uniform heat was required. "With a little alteration," he continued, "it might be applied to the purpose of opening doors, windows, and other passages, for a draught of air, and thereby preserve a due temperature of the air in hospitals, &c." The paper was reviewed by James Pearson, David Evans, and Owen Biddle, who recommended that it be published.[18] Meanwhile, at Henry's request, Dr. Cadwalader Evans of Philadelphia sent a copy of the draft of the device to Benjamin Franklin in London; favorably impressed, Franklin gave it to a printer to be published. To Franklin's French friend Barbeu-Dubourg, who doubtless also saw the description in the first volume of the Society's *Transactions,* the machine appeared "fort intéressante."[19]

A few months after sending the Society the plan of his sentinel register, Henry forwarded an account of the cultivation of sunflowers and a description of the process of expressing oil from the seeds, "which may be applyed to most of the purposes for which Olive Oil is used." The subject was one about which Dr. John M. Otto of Bethlehem, Brother Peter Miller of Ephrata, and others had written the Society; and a committee headed by Dr. John Morgan was appointed to review and consider the communications. In his report Morgan quoted Henry to the effect that, in the experience of one large grower in Lancaster County, one acre of sunflowers yielded 40–50 bushels of seed, which in turn produced as many gallons of oil. The process of manufacture was the same as that for linseed oil.[20]

For some time Henry, like other mechanics, had felt the need for a bit that would extrude the chips as it bored into wood. In the summer of 1771, after several attempts, Henry made a screw auger of lead; it worked well enough on turnips, but was unsatisfactory with hard woods. After further experimentation he soon produced a tool of tempered iron. Henry now engaged Henry Rauch, a mechanic of Lititz, Pennsylvania, to perfect a method of manufacturing the tool; Rauch succeeded in this, and for several years was the sole manufacturer. News of the invention spread rapidly. It was much in demand by builders, but for some years was not obtainable everywhere. In 1775 Henry's son John Joseph, marching to Canada as a soldier in Arnold's expedition, noticed ship's carpenters on the Kennebec using the

---

[18] The description of the register was printed in Lewis Nicola's *American Magazine,* 13, and in APS *Trans.,* I (1771), 286–89.
[19] Evans' letter to Franklin, 11 June 1769, and Franklin's reply, 7 Sept. 1769, are in *Franklin Papers,* XVI, 156, 199. Dubourg's comment, in a letter to Franklin, 25 Nov. 1773, is in Mass. Hist. Soc., *Proc.,* LVI (1922), 145.
[20] APS *Trans.,* I (1771), 235–39.

screw auger. He told them his father had invented it and asked where they had obtained theirs. "In Philadelphia," was the reply.[21]

The Society and the Assembly were both much interested in the feasibility of a water route linking the Delaware and the Susquehanna. In 1771 the Assembly named a corps of surveyors for the task; when Benjamin Lightfoot resigned, William Henry was named to replace him. The committee's report was presented on 30 January 1773.[22] Another concern shared by both the Society and the Assembly was the cultivation of silk; Henry subscribed £2 to the Silk Society.

From the beginning of the Revolutionary movement in Pennsylvania William Henry was fully engaged by various civil employments. He was a member of the town council for ten years after 1765, and was elected burgess in 1766. He was chosen a member of the Committee of Correspondence and Observation for Lancaster County on 15 July 1774. He was treasurer of the county committee that collected subscriptions for the relief of the distressed poor of Boston, to which he contributed £3.[23] With the outbreak of hostilities he was called on to supply rifles, bayonets, gunpowder, drums, and other accoutrements.[24] He was elected to the Assembly under the new state constitution of 1776. He served on the Council of Safety in 1777; and in that year was appointed treasurer of Lancaster County. His commission as justice of the peace, first received in 1770, was renewed also in 1777.[25]

Henry was now one of the most influential and responsible men in Lancaster County, with a widening reputation for usefulness and zeal in the American cause. Workmen in his employ were exempted from military service.[26] His appointment as superintendent of arms and military accoutrements in April 1778 was widely approved. "I am exceedingly glad," Washington told the Board of War, "to hear that so active a Man as Mr. Henry is universally represented to be, has succeeded Butler in the Armourer's department, which had been long shamefully con-

---

[21] A full account of the invention of the screw auger, written by Henry's son John Joseph Henry, is in Rees' *Cyclopaedia,* III, s.v. "Augre." In 1772 Charles Read of Etna Furnace asked Henry for information on the process of anealing nails; a mutual acquaintance had assured him that Henry would communicate the information "from a patriotic Spirit & a desire to assist a particular Undertaker." Read to Henry, 7 Sept. 1772, Potts Family Papers, General Corres. (MG 104, Pa. State Archives, Harrisburg).

[22] 8 *Pa. Arch.,* VIII, 6721, 6931–34.

[23] Henry, Receipt to Jasper Yeates, 10 Aug. 1775, Gratz Coll. (HSP); Ellis and Evans, *Lancaster County,* 373.

[24] The Committee of Safety contracted for 200 rifles on 23 March 1776. *Col. Recs. Pa.,* X, 523. Simon & Henry were paid £6 9s. 6d. for drums on 25 Sept. 1776—a fact whose only significance is that it indicates the partnership lasted longer than has sometimes been stated. *Jour. Cont. Cong.,* V, 826.

[25] 2 *Pa. Arch.,* III, 686, 740; XIII, 275; 6 *Pa. Arch.,* XI, 216.

[26] *Col. Recs. Pa.,* XI, 380.

ducted."[27] The Commander-in-Chief had already written the Board in a long report from Valley Forge on 29 January 1778, "A Mr. Henry of Lancaster, I am told, would contract for one, or two hundred thousand pair of shoes, annually, to be paid for in raw hides."[28] Though Henry never produced shoes at anything like that rate,[29] his performance was apparently impressive enough to induce the Board of War on 5 August 1779 to name him "Commissary of Hides for the States of Pennsylvania, Delaware and Maryland," with responsibility for procuring "immediate and constant supplies of shoes for the troops." For some years Henry's life was punctuated by importunate calls from the army for supplies.

On 31 July 1777, fearing imminent attack on Philadelphia from the Delaware River, President Wharton called on Henry and other county magistrates "Immediately [to] order 600 wagons out of your County to repair [sic] to this City, for the purpose of removing Stores, Provision, &c. &c. As you value the Interest hapiness [sic] and peace of your County, I intreate [sic] you to exert yourselves in this matter, and forward them as fast as possible without waiting for any particular number to come together."[30] Three weeks later General Washington ordered Henry to impress for the army's use all blankets, shoes, stockings, and other articles of clothing that could be spared by the inhabitants.[31] On 1 October Henry was directed to "expedite the March of any Troops in Lancaster so that they may join the General as speedily as possible."[32] The demands continued without remission. "How soon could you furnish me with One Hundred and Eighty *Spontoons* for Officers," General Wayne asked from Valley Forge on 28 March, "neatly made and about 8 feet long."[33] On 19 May the Board of War required 100 "*common* Rifles (without Bayonets) if you have or can procure that number speedily," and added that a light corps was expected at Lancaster, which Henry would want to provide with "what they want for frontier Business."[34] On 1 June General Washington needed 1700 cartridge boxes—"Pray send to him immediately all you have, and set as many hands at work as possible in making more. . . ."[35]

---

[27] *Jour. Cont. Cong.,* X, 380–81; Washington to Board of War, 1 May 1778, Fitzpatrick, ed., *Writings,* XI, 334.
[28] Ibid., X, 387.
[29] Henry, Return of Shoes, Boots, Hats, &c., 9 June 1778–12 Sept. 1779 (Henry Papers, II, 34 [HSP]) shows he delivered 15,727 pr. shoes, 700 pr. boots, 2,283 hats, 265 pr. hose, 206 pr. breeches, 546 sheets and 126 yds. linen.
[30] Henry Papers, II, 23 (HSP).
[31] Fitzpatrick, ed., *Writings,* IX, 269n.
[32] Richard Peters to Henry, 1 Oct. 1777, Henry Papers, I, 19 (HSP).
[33] Wayne to Henry, 28 March 1778, Wayne Papers, IV, 117 (HSP).
[34] 1 *Pa. Arch.,* VI, 558.
[35] Timothy Pickering to Henry, 8 June 1778, Henry Papers, I, 21 (HSP). See generally "Letters to Williams Henry, of Lancaster, Pennsylvania, 1777–1783," *PMHB,* XXII (1898), 106–113.

Other problems, sometimes more complicated, were laid on Henry's desk, usually with no warning. Spies had to be apprehended;[36] prisoners had to be housed and fed. "There will be 500 from Cowpens here in a Day or two," he informed a colleague. "What shall be done with them? There is . . . no roome in the Prison."[37] Even the bolstering of civilian morale might fall to him—could Henry arrange for the Count de Deux Ponts, President Reed asked in 1780, to meet some German clergymen and other Germans so he might have the opportunity to "convince them of the Utility & Honour of our Independence, shew them the Certainty of its being established, & the Necessity of their supporting cheerfully the War for the attainment of that glorious Object—reconcile them to a Government founded thereupon. . . ."[38]

All the while Henry was treasurer of the county, and after 18 November 1780 he was judge of the courts of common pleas and quarter sessions as well.[39] Collecting taxes was no easy task, with Continental currency depreciated, out-of-state currency of doubtful value, and currency of any kind hard to come by. In response to questions by the Supreme Executive Council concerning tax collections in Lancaster County Henry replied,

> . . . I shall not only be obliged to accuse my Imployers but myself also. The Board have been rather remiss, but they have their Excuses. Their Pay will not support their Horses while in Town, much less themselves and pay for their Services. I have often observed, when they come to Town, they hurry home before the Business is done, which I thought ought to have been done. I have often taken the Liberty to tell them so, and received for Answer, their Pay would not support them. I do not say their Reasons were good, but it is a Certainty, they are such as influence the Minds of most Men. I could wish the Assembly could be convinced, "that it is private Interest that executes Government," as well with Regard to the Board as the Treasurers. My pay will scarce clear the expenses twice to Philadelphia. There are a Number of Difficulties to be encountered in this County which none of the others have to strive with. There are several of the Townships, which have not more than two or three Persons which have taken the oath of Allegiance, and therefore not capable in Law to act as Assessors or Appraisers. This gives the Board much Trouble and takes much time, before People can be found, who will act and those are generally of the lowest Character. Some Collectors have imploy'd others at their own Risque and will suffer by it. I am indebted at this Time to the State between Sixty & Seventy Thousand Pound, which I have laid out in purchase of Leather and Paying Workmens Wages at the Shoe-Factory at Philadelphia, Allentown and Lancaster. Pressed by the Board of War and the Clothier General, as I am to make the utmost Exertions to furnish the Army with Shoes and Boots by the opening of the Campaign. I hope, Sir, you will excuse the Liberty I have

---

[36] Joseph Reed to [Henry], 10 Nov. 1780, Society Misc. Coll. (HSP).
[37] Henry to William Atlee, 12 April 1781, Henry Papers, I, 65 (HSP).
[38] 1 *Pa. Arch.*, VIII, 684–85.
[39] 2 *Pa. Arch.*, III, 738, 739.

taken, as it was done only with an Intent to further the Service. The whole of the Factorys must have stop'd for want of Pay and Materials, if I had not supported them with Money. I do not even draw Commissions on the Money furnish'd the Factorys. I this Day write to the Clothier General, who will draw 200,000 Dollars from Congress, and replace what I have used. There is yet Fourteen Townships out of Thirty three to settle for the first Tax for 1779—as soon as they have settled, I will go to Philadel[a] and settle with the State-Treasurer, which I expect will be about the 15th of May next or sooner, if I can settle here with the Board and Collectors.[40]

Sometimes, as he recited the difficulties he labored under, Henry felt he was not doing his job well. President Reed reassured him warmly: "Far from doubting your Zeal & activity in the Business, I can only wish that all concerned in the Collection of Taxes had half of it & am persuaded our affairs would be in a more promising Condition."[41]

If Henry carried out his duties as superintendent of arms, commissary of hides, and county treasurer with energy, he discharged other functions with intelligence and compassion. Ordered to arrest the Reverend Mr. Barton, whose parishioner he had once been, Henry arranged that his old friend and neighbor should withdraw quietly into British protection at New York. When the authorities selected the Moravian church in Lancaster as headquarters for the state lottery, Henry persuaded them the court house possessed superior advantages, thus protecting not only the Moravian church but the Lutheran and Reformed as well.[42]

During the winter of 1777–78, when the British army held Philadelphia, Congress met in York, some 90 miles west of Philadelphia. Minor Continental functionaries, state officials, and private persons driven from their homes, took refuge in Reading, Lancaster, and elsewhere in the countryside beyond the reach of Sir William Howe's troops. The Henrys gave room to Joseph Hart of the Supreme Executive Council, David Rittenhouse, and Thomas Paine. The association with Rittenhouse and Paine was agreeable to Henry, for Rittenhouse was a man very like himself, and Paine, though an inconsiderate guest, had a talent for engineering. John Joseph Henry, recovering from a wound received at Quebec, remembered how it was in his parents' house that winter:

> Paine would walk of a morning until 12 o'clock; come in and make an inordinate dinner. The rising from table was between two and three o'clock. He would then retire to his bed-chamber, wrap a blanket around him, and in a large arm-chair, take a nap, of two or three hours—rise and walk. These walks, and his indolence, surprised my parents. . . .

---

[40] Henry to Reed, 25 April 1780, 1 *Pa. Arch.,* VIII, 207–08.
[41] Reed to Henry, 19 Dec. 1780, ibid., 667–68.
[42] Beck, "William Henry," Lanc. Co. Hist. Soc., *Papers,* LIV (1950), 76; *PMHB,* XVI (1892), 434.

. . . Mr. D. Rittenhouse inhabited the front room, in the upper story, where was the library. There he kept the office of the treasury of Pennsylvania. . . .

When my wound in 1778, was so far mended, that hobbling on crutches, or by creeping up stairs, (as you may have seen me of late years do,) my greatest recreation in my distressed state of mind, was to get into the chamber of Mr. Rittenhouse where the books were. There, his conversation, (for he was most affable,) enlivened my mind, and the books would so amuse it, that it became calm, and some desperate resolutions were dissolved. While that excellent man was employing his hours in the duties of his office, for the benefit of the people, Paine would be snoring away his precious time in his easy chair, regardless of those injunctions imposed upon him by congress, in relation to his political compositions. . . . I have heard the late George Bryan, Esq. then vice-president of the council, speak of his gross neglects with remarkable harshness. I would sometimes go into Paine's room, and sit with him. His Crisis, No. V, lay on his table, dusted: to-day three or four lines would be added, in the course of a week, a dozen more, and so on.[43]

With the return of peace, without giving up many of his local civic responsibilities, Henry resumed his philosophical and mechanical experiments. "Experiments, magnetick and electrical," a visitor noted, filled Henry's leisure "in a useful and agreeable way, and show him to be a thinking and self-examining man."[44] He observed the aurora borealis and kept records of the weather, which he sent to Rittenhouse, who, comparing Henry's with his own, concluded that, if the thermometers were accurate, Lancaster must be warmer than Philadelphia.[45] In particular Henry invented a wheeled carriage propelled by wind power; those who inspected the model were skeptical, judging it practical only on a firm surface. Perhaps Henry came to share this view, for in 1785 he sent the model, apparently without comment, to the Philosophical Society (where it still is), together with two large pieces of crystal found in Lancaster County, and "an exceeding large tusk and one of the grinders of some unknown species of animals, brought from the neighbourhood of the Ohio."

More significant by far than his wind-driven carriage was another machine Henry worked on in these years. At least since 1767, when he invented the sentinel register, Henry had been aware of the implications of steam power. In 1775 he discussed his ideas with Andrew Ellicott, and three years later with David Rittenhouse at Lancaster. The Italian traveller Count dal Verme noted in 1783 that Henry showed him "a machine which moves against the wind and the current of a stream. . . ." This may have been the wind-propelled carriage or prototype of a steamboat. In any case, dal Verme thought it utterly impractical.[46] A few weeks

---

[43] John Joseph Henry, *Account of . . . the Campaign against Quebec,* 218, 219–20.
[44] Johann David Schoepf, *Travels in the Confederation* (A. J. Morrison, trans., Phila., 1911), II, 14–15.
[45] David Rittenhouse to Henry, 17 April 1783, *PMHB,* XI (1887), 503; Jordan, *William Henry,* 163.
[46] Elizabeth Cometti, trans. and ed., *Seeing America and its Great Men: The Journal and Letters of Count Francesco dal Verme, 1783–1784* (Charlottesville, [1969]), 35.

later Dr. Schoepf, physician to the Brunswick troops in America, inspected the same machine, on which he took careful notes; and learned that Henry was "about putting together another machine, which, if attached to a boat, must bring it against the current of a stream, being set in motion merely by the force of the current and of the wind." But, Henry told Schoepf, he was resolved not to publish the design until his financial stake was protected, "for he is sure that by means of it the difficult return passage on the Mississippi and the Ohio may be considerably eased, to the advantage of his country. From the plan of the first machine, however," Schoepf added, "it should not be a hard matter to divine that of the second."[47] Whether Henry at this moment had a clear idea how to apply steam power to a boat is not certain.

Nonetheless, when John Fitch laid before the American Philosophical Society on 27 September 1785 his plans for a steamboat, informed persons in Philadelphia advised him to consult Henry. This he did the next month.

> To my surprise Mr. Henry told me that he had proposed it many years ago, and had made a Draft of it, which he intended to have laid before the Philosophical Society, but that he had neglected it, and altho I gave no hint of the kind, I believe he thought I suspected him, and went out and hunted his papers and produced a Draft to me, which was to propel a Boat by a Steam Wheal [sic], and notwithstanding I had douts [sic] that he made it after I had laid it before Congress or the Philosophical Society, I could observe no marks of disimulation [sic] in him, and ever continued to have douts [sic] in my mind till I spoke with Mr. Ellicott on the Occation [sic], yet I confess it was ungenerous in me to suspect him, after the candid and generous [sic] declaration which he made, which was this, he said altho I am many years before you in the scheme, yet as long as I have not brought it to the public View, and altho mine is intirely different from yours, I will lay no claim to it, But will frankly give it up to you, as you are the first publisher of it to the world.

Though considerably "chagreaned" at learning he had been anticipated, Fitch was encouraged by this confirmation of his ideas and especially by Henry's generous relinquishment of all claims to the invention.[48] The fact was, however, that Henry's idea was different from Fitch's, as the latter recognized. "When I informed him that I could not have a conception how a Steamwheal could be made, he frankly offered to make a model at his own expence, and let me have it." Fitch was to have called for the model in a few months, but was prevented; instead he engaged a mechanic in Philadelphia to make one on Henry's principles,

> and in about 2 weeks [he] digested a truely philosophical plan, and communicated it to me and a great number of Respectable citizens of this town. . . . therefore

---

[47] Schoepf, *Travels,* II, 14–15.
[48] John Fitch, History of the Steamboat, No. 1, pp. 8–9, Fitch Papers (Lib. Co. Phila.).

> Mr. Henry is the first original inventor of a Steam Wheel, and Mr. Voight the first that I ever saw define the principles of it to bring it into use.[49]

Official duties, mechanical skill, and Henry's sense of public service were combined in two other contributions to the community. Henry supervised the construction of a new county jail in 1784 and drafted the plans for a Moravian church in Lititz, which was erected in 1787, the year after Henry's death.[50]

The last office to which Henry was elected was that of member of Congress. He was elected to that body on 16 November 1784, and reelected one year later. The journals give the record of his attendance, and of the committees he served on. One of these was named to receive Lafayette on the occasion of his taking leave of Congress in 1784; another considered a gratuity or pension for Christopher Ludwick, "baker-general" of the Continental Army; a third recommended that the newly-founded Dickinson College should be granted the use of the "public works" at Carlisle, Pennsylvania. More significant than any of these, however, was Henry's membership in 1786 on the Grand Committee to report amendments to the Articles of Confederation and on the committee that drafted an ordinance for the government of the Western Territory.[51] Death, however, kept him from seeing or participating in either the Federal Convention or the enactment of the Northwest Ordinance.

According to family tradition, Henry contracted some bronchial complaint during his service with Congress in New York in 1785 or 1786. By the end of the latter year he was seriously ill; wrote his will and spiritual autobiography, as the Moravian discipline enjoined; and on 15 December died in his house in Lancaster. He was buried in the Moravians' ground (since removed to Greenwood Cemetery) in Prince Street. He was survived by his widow, and by seven of their 13 children. Of his six sons, William carried on the gunworks at Boulton, near Nazareth, Pennsylvania; John Joseph was to become judge of the county courts, as his father had been; James settled in Pittsburgh as a watchmaker; and Benjamin West Henry, after graduating from Franklin College, became, like his namesake, a painter, studying his art with Gilbert Stuart. Henry's will and inventory revealed only a glimpse

---

[49] Ibid., 34–35. See also Fitch, *The Original Steam Boat Supported* . . . (Phila., 1788), 4, which says that Henry conversed with Thomas Paine about applying steam to vessels in the winter of 1778. Since Paine and Rittenhouse were both living with Henry at the time, it is likely both participated in the discussions, which would have intrigued each.

One regrets that no sketch or verbal description by Henry has survived to document the nature of his invention and its priority. A sketch of the "Original William Henry sternwheeler, 1763" in the Lancaster County Historical Society appears to be a rather obvious nineteenth-century attempt to document statements that were not made until long after Henry's death.

[50] Beck, "William Henry," Lanc. Co. Hist. Soc., *Papers,* LIV (1950), 78.

[51] *Jour. Cont. Cong.,* XXVII, 673; XXVIII, 374, 456; XXXI, 494, 667, 669, 700; Edmund C. Burnett, ed., *Letters of Members of the Continental Congress,* VIII, 17, 18.

of his philosophical interests: three variation and one dipping needle, one landscape and one history piece, and the following books: nine volumes of the *Journals of Congress,* Locke's *Essay Concerning Human Understanding,* Henry Crouch's *Complete View of the British Customs,* Charles Varlo's *New System of Husbandry,* Barclay's *Apology,* William Penn's *No Cross No Crown,* a Spanish grammar, *The Tryal of Doctor Henry Sacheverell,* Bolingbroke's *Idea of a Patriot King,* David Cranz's two-volume *History of Greenland* and the Moravian missions there, some German hymn books, and a few volumes of the Acts of Assembly.[52]

On 24 February 1786 David Rittenhouse had informed Henry that the second volume of the *Transactions* of the Philosophical Society was in press: "It will be a neat and valuable Book, have you not something to communicate which you wou'd wish to have inserted? If you have no time shou'd be lost."[53] Probably Henry's response was too long delayed. In any case, three years later, on 17 April 1789, Rittenhouse presented "a memoir from the late Willm. Henry of Lancaster, on the effects of Heat, in conducting the electric fluid, & explaining the phenomenon of Thunder; the Aurora Borealis &c." The paper was not published, and it is not in the Society's archives.

WILLIAM JOHNSON (c. 1726–1768)
AMERICAN SOCIETY (CORRESPONDING MEMBER):
27 MARCH 1767

WILLIAM JOHNSON, schoolmaster and lecturer on electricity, was born in Ulster about 1726 or 1727. His parents, who were members of Ballyhagen Friends Meeting, "carefully educated him" in the Quaker way and apprenticed him, when a lad, to a Quaker merchant of Lisburn. It was near Lisburn that the linen trade, once exclusively a cottage industry, was developing into the factory system requiring, among other things, chemical knowledge. Young Johnson's interest in technology may very well have been implanted or evoked at this time. In 1752 Johnson came to Philadelphia, with what hopes is not apparent, for he returned to Ballyhagen the next year; but the brief visit decided him and he came back to Philadelphia to settle in 1754. In 1755 he became a teacher in Friends public school in Philadelphia, and in 1759 he married Ruth Potts, sister of Stacy Potts, mayor of Trenton,

---

[52] Henry Will, probated 23 Dec. 1786, Will Book E 1, p. 392; Inventory, 26 April 1790 (Register of Wills, Lancaster). A copy of the inventory is in Henry Papers, Personal Corr. (Stites Coll. on film at Hagley Museum and Library).
[53] Henry Papers, II, 68 (HSP).

New Jersey, at Chesterfield Monthly Meeting in Burlington County.¹ On 8 February 1760 Johnson was proposed by Charles Thomson for membership in the "Young Junto," but he does not appear to have been elected. He was a member of Philadelphia's Union Library Company.

By 1763 Johnson was launched on a career as an itinerant lecturer. In October of that year he delivered lectures on electricity at New York in the Assembly Room of the City Arms tavern in Broadway.² Advertised as "for the Entertainment of the Curious," the two lectures presented many of the same experiments that Ebenezer Kinnersley had shown audiences in the continental and West Indies colonies ten years before, including an animated spider, "a Sort of electrical Horse–Race," a sand shower, and electrified money, "which scarce any one will take when offered." Johnson himself contrived "a diverting [but mysterious] Experiment, which cannot be well understood, but by those who try it."³ He did not, however, follow Kinnersley unquestioningly. Holding that air itself may be electrified plus or minus, he denied the existence of electrical repulsion, which Kinnersley upheld, stated his position forcefully to David Colden, and in consequence was drawn into a friendly but inconclusive argument over the meaning of his experiments.⁴

In February 1764 Johnson lectured in the Colony House at Newport, and in March in the court house in Providence.⁵ So successful was he that he printed a syllabus of the "course" that same year and reprinted it in 1765. In April he was at New Brunswick, New Jersey, in July at Baltimore, and in August and September at Annapolis.⁶ The spring of 1765 found him in Charleston, where the lectures, first scheduled for Backhouse's Tavern, were moved to the room of the Charleston Library Society, where they were several times repeated. Moving north with the season, Johnson performed his experiments in the Concert Hall in Queen Street, Boston, in August. Everywhere the lectures proved popular with many classes and both sexes.⁷

Johnson's long and frequent journeys drew him away from Quaker influences. By 1764 the Philadelphia Monthly Meeting reported that he neglected attendance of religious services "& giving way to the Allurements of vain conversation, he by

---

1   Ballyhagen Mo. Mtg., Certificates of removal, 11 Sixth Mo. 1752, 25 Fifth Mo. 1754. Original Certificates, Nos. 955, 1020, Phila. Mo. Mtg. Records, Philadelphia; Hinshaw, *Amer. Quaker Genealogy,* II, 566; Friends Free School Corporation Accounts, Reynell-Coates Papers (HSP).
2   *N.Y. Mercury,* 24 Oct. 1763; *N.Y. Gaz.,* 31 Oct. 1763.
3   Johnson, *A Course of Experiments, In that curious and entertaining Branch of Natural Philosophy, call'd Electricity; Accompanied with Lectures on the Nature and Properties of the Electric Fire* (N. Y., 1765).
4   *Colden Papers,* VI (N.-Y. Hist. Soc., *Colls.,* 1922), 249–51, 255–65.
5   *Newport Mercury,* 6 Feb. 1764; *Providence Gaz.,* 3 March, 1764.
6   *Md. Gaz.,* 26 July, 30 Aug. 1764.
7   *S.C. Gaz.,* 13 April, 4, 18, 25 May 1765; *S. C. Hist. and Geneal. Mag.,* XX (1919), 208; William N. Morse, "Lectures on Electricity in Colonial Times," *New England Quarterly,* VII (1934), 364–74.

degrees became so libertine in his sentiments as to conform to the customs of the World in his dress and Address." He repulsed the Meeting's efforts to win him back, asserting he no longer believed in Friends' principles; and on 26 July 1765 he was disowned. Probably he had already ceased to keep a home in Philadelphia, for on 28 June his wife and children had received a certificate to return to Chesterfield Monthly Meeting in New Jersey.[8]

Charleston was especially congenial to Johnson. After a second southern tour—he seems to have lectured there again in the late winter or spring of 1766 and offered his course at Williamsburg in October—he returned to South Carolina to settle permanently. In February 1767 he advertised the familiar lectures on electricity, but offered the additional attraction of experiments in magnetism, if enough subscribed for them. He lectured four days a week in the Library Society's rooms in Union Street, and the Library allowed him "to entertain the ladies with the microscope belonging to the Society."[9]

> Charlestown, Feb. 12, 1767
> For the Entertainment of the Curious,
> WILL BE EXHIBITED,
> At the Library-Room in Union Street,
>
> A COURSE OF EXPERIMENTS,
> In that Instructive and entertaining Branch of
> NATURAL PHILOSOPHY called
> ELECTRICITY;
> To be accompanied with LECTURES on the Nature
> and Properties of ELECTRICAL FIRE.
> By WILLIAM JOHNSON.
>
> The Course consists of two Lectures,—In the first of which, all the Properties of that wonderful Element, as far as the latest Discoveries have made us acquainted therewith, are demonstrated in a Number of curious Experiments, many of which are entirely new. Among many other Particulars, will be shewn that the electrick Fire, commonly procured by the Friction of Glass and other electrick Substances, is not created by that Friction; but is a real Element or fluid Body, diffused through all Places in and near this Earth: That our Bodies contain enough of it at all Times to set an House on Fire. Likewise many Errours, that have crept into this Branch of Natural Philosophy, will be expunged, and the true Theory thereof established on the solid Foundation of Reason and Experiment.
>
> In the second Lecture, this Fire is shewn to be real Lightning, from its constantly and invariably producing the very same Effects that Lightning does. In proving and

---

[8] Hinshaw, *Amer. Quaker Geneal.*, II, 566; Phila. Monthly Meeting, Minutes, 27 Fourth Mo. 1764, 26 Seventh Mo. 1765.

[9] *Va. Gaz.* (Purdie & Dixon), 17 Oct. 1766; *S. C. Gazette*, 16 Feb. 1767; the issue of 9 February noted the return to Charleston of William Johnson, "well known for his exhibition here last year."

explaining which, most of the Effects of Lightning will be imitated by the electrick Fire; such as killing of Animals, melting Metal, tearing and renting [sic] Bodies through which it passes; together with many curious Experiments, naturally representing the various Phoenemena of Thunder-Storms, accounting for their Causes, and explaining their Effects. A practical Method of preserving ourselves, our Houses and Effects, from the destructive Violence of Lightning, will likewise be shewn, the Efficacy of which will be demonstrated by such indubitable Proofs from Experience, as have not yet been exhibited to the World.

Those who desire to have their Dwellings effectually secured from the destructive Violence of one of the most awful Powers of Nature (which this Colony in particular has often felt) may learn from these Lectures and Experiments, more of the Nature and Properties of Lightning than has been known in the World, till within these few Years. They will at the same Time have an Opportunity of being fully convinced, that the Method proposed for their Security, if put in Practice with proper Precaution, will be attended with Success; and consequently, that instead of having any just Objection thereto, from a Persuasion of its being presumptuous, we have the utmost Reason to bless GOD for a Discovery so important and eminently useful.—*A prudent Man forseeth the Evil and hideth himself; but the Simple pass on and are punished.* Prov. xxiii, 3.

As the Knowledge of Nature tends to enlarge the human Mind, and give us more exalted Ideas of the God of Nature, it is presumed that this Course will prove to many, an agreeable and rational Entertainment.

The first Course will be on Tuesday and Wednesday next, to begin at Three in the Afternoon, and will be repeated on Thursday and Friday following: Likewise on the corresponding days, in the three following Weeks, provided the requisite dryness of the Air will permit.

Tickets to be had at Dillon's and Backhouse's Taverns, and of the Printer, at 40s. for both Lectures. N.B. No Person will be admitted without a Ticket, by paying at the Door, as the Inconvenience is great and must be obvious to every one.

Said JOHNSON proposes likewise to exhibit, a Course of Experiments (to be accompanied with an explanatory Lecture) in that eminently useful Branch of natural Philosophy called

MAGNETISM.

In this Course all the principal Properties of the Magnet or Loadstone will be demonstrated in a Number of curious Experiments, and a rational Theory of Magnetism founded thereon, by which the Polar Direction and Dip of the magnetical Needle may be naturally and rationally accounted for.

The Use and Application of this most surprizing natural Power to the important Purposes of Navigation will be shewn; the Defects of the common Sea-Compasses will be particularly considered and demonstrated; and the latest Improvements which the celebrated Dr. Knight has made in that useful Instrument, by which it has attained its utmost Degree of Perfection, will be explained, the Knowledge of which is of the utmost Importance to all Persons concerned in Trade and Navigation.

The Course will consist of upwards of Twenty Experiments, amongst which are those performed by Dr. Knight before the Royal Society, with many others equally surprizing and instructive: To be performed with several natural Magnets, together with large magnetical Steel Bars of a surprizing Degree of Strength, which will give a Touch four Times stronger than the best Loadstones yet known.

Shrewsbury in New Jersey, where he engaged in an abortive project to distill salt from sea water. Returning to New York, Bard found that many of his old patients inclined to shun him as having Loyalist sympathies, until Mayor Mathews, a man of unquestioned patriotism, publicly vouched for Bard's loyalty to the new nation. In consequence Bard quickly regained his practice. Nonetheless, he found congenial company among the physicians of the British army in New York, notably John Mervin Nooth, superintendent of the medical services, and Christian Friedrich Michaelis, a German army doctor, who obtained aid from General Washington to explore Orange County for remains of prehistoric creatures.

For several years after the restoration of peace in 1783 Bard, like other New Yorkers, was engaged in reviving and reorganizing institutions whose work had been suspended during the British occupation of the city. He helped reorganize King's (now Columbia) College, and was elected a trustee in 1787. He helped to prepare the New York Hospital to receive patients, which it did at last in 1791. He aided the New York Society Library to resume its operations. In 1790 he was one of the founders of the New York Dispensary. And he was, of course, deeply involved in the renewal of medical instruction in the city.

Bard was the only surviving member in New York of the original faculty, in which he had been professor of theory and practice of medicine. In 1784 he was elected professor of chemistry, a less prestigious chair. A year later he transferred to the College as professor of natural philosophy and astronomy. The position was frustrating for he lacked even basic instruments and equipment for instruction. Medical teaching, too, during the war and post-war years was limited and uncertain. Some physicians took private pupils in the time-honored way, as they had always done; and there may have been occasional lectures; but the education was without structure or system; no institution was responsible for it; and from 1774 to 1793 no medical degree was awarded. In 1792, however, the medical department of the College was reorganized. Bard was dean. Although he held no chair and delivered no regular course of lectures, he did give clinical lectures at the Hospital. After a few years, however, Bard moved to his farm at Hyde Park. There he was at such a distance from New York that he could not offer regular instruction, and finally in 1804 he resigned.

The Medical Department during these years did not flourish. Only one person was graduated in 1798, none in 1799, 1800, or 1801, only four in 1804. Only thirty degrees were conferred between 1793 and 1807. In Philadelphia, by contrast, the University of Pennsylvania in the same years awarded 210 degrees.

Soon thereafter the medical scene became confused. To the personal rivalries and antagonisms that characterized so many institutions in that period were now added bitter institutional rivalries. The College of Physicians and Surgeons was established in 1807 and the Medical Faculty of Queen's College in 1811. The natural competition between these two and Columbia College was intensified by the doctors' uncertainty about where their loyalty should lie. Some physicians held appointments in two institutions, and one was a professor in two schools and a trustee of one. Matters eased in 1811, when the Medical Department of Columbia College and the College of Physicians and Surgeons were joined. Bard, whose interest and loyalty were with Columbia and who had actually opposed the founding of Physicians and Surgeons, was elected president of the united institution. He held the office until 1820, often quarrelling with his faculty over fees that he felt he was entitled to, but which they thought he did not deserve because he so seldom attended meetings and examinations.

As a man of culture and wide reading, Bard took an interest in New York's cultural institutions and activities. When a student in London he had seen Garrick perform Shakespeare, and to the end of his life he would read the plays aloud to his family. He belonged to the New York Society Library and was one of the original members of the New-York Historical Society. "I am deep in Asiatic researches," he told his son in 1805, "and much interested in the study of that ancient and extraordinary people" in the works of Sir William Jones.[14] On a trip to New York in 1818, when he presided at a meeting of the Historical Society, he "took a peep at the range of buildings appropriated to the Fine Arts, Literary Societies, &c, which may be made a noble institution," viewed John Trumbull's historical paintings, and talked with Dr. Samuel Latham Mitchill about the native inhabitants of western America. "Such society rubs off our rust and sharpens our edge, making us not only brighter to the eye, but fitter for use."

In the post-war period of reconstruction of American society and institutions Bard proposed to Robert R. Livingston in 1785 that a philosophical society on the plan of the Royal Society be established, "which may serve to transplant into this new and rising empire the discoveries and improvements of Europe; and moreover, by freedom of inquiry, and collision of opinion, to strike out new lights to the advancement of sound knowledge."[15] No society was established exactly in response to this suggestion; but in 1791 the New York Society for the Promotion of Agriculture, Arts, and Manufactures was organized, with Livingston as its president.

The Bards, father and son, were always close; and after John Bard moved to Hyde Park, Samuel Bard completed a house for himself and settled permanently there. Now he had time and opportunity to devote himself to farming and botanical studies. He built a conservatory, a "little tropical region of his own creation," where he grew many species of plants. He introduced clover as a crop, applied gypsum as a manure, and every year he planted trees. He asked Rufus King, who was returning from London, to bring him carp and tench for his ponds. With Robert R.

[14] Ibid., 192–93.
[15] Ibid., 143.

ied at the Middle Temple. After three years with Moland the young man went to London for further training. He was enrolled at the Middle Temple on 21 December 1753.[2]

Although London struck him at first as "a social wilderness," all "noise, dirt and business," Dickinson quickly found friends among other students from America, like Robert Goldsborough of Maryland.[3] In addition, his father's correspondents and agents, like John Hanbury and David Barclay, made him welcome. The Proprietor Thomas Penn listened with interest to the news and information about Pennsylvania affairs that he brought, and invited Dickinson to dine with him and Lady Juliana. Such friends, not to mention the arrival of the English spring, brought a softening in Dickinson's judgment of the capital. "London is the place where a person may learn Truth," he confided, "where, unless he is an absolute fool, he may see human nature in all shapes."[4]

Dickinson spent more than three years at his studies in the Temple. He rose at five, read eight hours (English history—Rapin and Bolingbroke; English law—Coke's *Institutes* and Bacon), dined at four, and was in bed by ten. He attended the courts at Westminster Hall, itself a veritable "school of law," and listened to debates in Parliament. The level of oratory in the Commons was high, but the peers, who met "in a room much inferior to that appointed for the representatives of Pennsylvania," were "the most ordinary men" he had ever seen. One night at the theater he had a glimpse of the King, "a small man, but has a very grand walk." Partly from his observations and analysis of English law, politics, and manners, partly also perhaps from homesickness and a sense of inferiority, Dickinson came to feel himself more American than before. "America is, to be sure, a wilderness," he wrote, "& yet that wilderness to me is more pleasing than this charming garden."[5]

Two or three times in London Dickinson fell ill for lengthy periods, and convalesced at rural Clapham or Kingston. A growth on his cheek had to be removed; the operation was performed by Joseph Warner, surgeon of Guy's Hospital.[6] He visited Oxford, taking in Blenheim Palace on the way, took a trip to the mouth of the Thames, and made an excursion to St. Albans, where in St. Michael's church he saw the monument to "the great Bacon . . . the greatest man that ever livd."[7] Otherwise he hardly left London, never travelled to Scotland or wanted to, and had no desire to visit the Continent. He attended the theater—the performances

---

[2] E. Alfred Jones, *American Students at the Inns of Court* (London, 1924), 61–63.
[3] H. Trevor Colbourn, "A Pennsylvania Farmer at the Court of King George: John Dickinson's London Letters, 1754–1756," *PMHB,* LXXXVI (1962), 241–86.
[4] Ibid., 278.
[5] Ibid., 275.
[6] Ibid., 277.
[7] Ibid., 280.

of David Garrick and Hannah Pritchard he thought "exact pictures of life"—but in none of his letters home is there any mention of a museum or attendance at a scientific lecture or demonstration, no hint of an interest in the information, discoveries, and improvements that were being presented all around him every day. Dickinson was called to the bar on 8 February 1757. He returned home soon afterwards.

For more than fifteen years Dickinson was engaged primarily in the practice of law in Philadelphia. Success came quickly. "Money flows in and my vanity has been very agreeably flattered of late," he wrote his mother in 1763.[8] Like many lawyers, Dickinson soon entered politics, in his case with the special advantages of being a resident and landowner in both Pennsylvania and Delaware. He was one of those who, like Thomas McKean and George Read—aptly named "Philadelawareans" by John A. Munroe[9]—had roots in both colonies, held office in both, and were equally part of the urban life of Philadelphia and the rural life of Delaware. Dickinson was elected a member of the Delaware Assembly in 1759 and was chosen its Speaker the next year. In 1762 he was elected to the Pennsylvania Assembly. "I confess I should like to make an immense bustle in the world if it could be by virtuous actions," he told his friend Read on the eve of the 1762 election. "But as there is no probability of that, I am content if I can live innocent and beloved by those I love."[10] He was reelected in 1763 and 1764. On the great issues that engrossed the Province and the Assembly, Dickinson stood with the Proprietary party; Franklin was in the other.

With his appointment as a delegate to the Stamp Act Congress in 1765 Dickinson's life became inextricably part of the emerging national history. He signed the Non-Importation Agreement. The *Farmer's Letters,* first printed in the *Pennsylvania Chronicle* in 1767 and immediately reprinted throughout the colonies, gave him an intercolonial reputation—he was awarded an honorary degree by the College of New Jersey and a life-size figure in wax by Patience Wright was exhibited through the country with one of the Reverend Mr. George Whitefield[11]—and during more than a decade his pen was repeatedly called into the service of the American cause.

The same years also saw Dickinson's increasing involvement in local affairs and institutions. He made a generous contribution to the Pennsylvania Hospital in 1764; from 1762 to 1768 he was a director of the Library Company of Philadelphia; and in 1766 he was an original member of the Gloucester Fox Hunting

---

[8] Quoted in Flower, *John Dickinson,* 25.
[9] John A. Munroe, "The Philadelawareans: A Study in the Relations between Philadelphia and Delaware in the Late Eighteenth Century," *PMHB,* LXIX (1945), 128–49.
[10] Quoted in Flower, *John Dickinson,* 30.
[11] *So. Carolina Gaz.,* 31 Jan. 1771.

Society for Encouraging the Culture of Silk. Evans subscribed £3 towards the venture and was elected one of its twelve managers. During the next two years the Philadelphians imported eggs from Italy and Spain, engaged Joseph Ottolenghe from Georgia to superintend the operation, and petitioned the Assembly for assistance in establishing a filature. "Upon the whole, the experiment takes in the country, beyond our most sanguine expectations, & as to the managers of the filature, it is a hobby horse to each of them," Evans wrote Franklin in 1771.

The first season's crop was disappointing, the second promised well; and some 155 pounds of silk were sent to Franklin to be presented to the Queen, Lady Juliana Penn, and other women of the Penn family. "I am charmed with the sight of such a quantity the second year," Franklin replied encouragingly, "and have great hopes the produce will now be established."

> Let nothing discourage you. Perseverance will conquer all difficulties; and the contributors will have the glorious satisfaction of having procured an inestimable advantage to their country.[15]

But the cultivation of mulberry trees, the care of silkworms, and the reeling of silk proved more difficult than Evans, Franklin, or the others imagined; and the coming of the Revolution put a practical end to further experimentation. In 1781 ten pounds of silk "of the best kind of the produce of Penna." were ordered sent to France to be manufactured "in the most elegant manner" as a gift to Louis XVI. A year later the stock of the Silk Society was turned over to the Philosophical Society, and the hopes of the silk cultivators, though not dead, had to wait for another place and year to find expression.

In addition to being a physician to the Pennsylvania Hospital, Evans was a physician to the Almshouse; when his service began is not recorded, but he was re-elected in 1769. He made a gift to the Pennsylvania Hospital in 1768 and gave the College of Philadelphia £6 in 1772. As a member of the Union Library Company he became a member of the Library Company of Philadelphia in 1769; his share was listed in the inventory of his estate four years later. He subscribed 7*s. 6d.* to John Bulkeley and John Cummings' narrative of *A Voyage to the South Seas,* which was published at Philadelphia in 1757.

In the winter of 1772–73 Evans took his young kinsman Thomas Parke, fresh from medical studies in London and Edinburgh, as a partner. Perhaps failing health was a reason—there is correspondence with Franklin about a truss ordered from London.[16] By midwinter Evans' condition was worsening. "I am more unwell the beginning of every week," he told Israel Pemberton on 15 May 1771, as he pre-

---

[15] Ibid., XVI, 178–79, 201–02, 240–42; XVII, 96–99, 210–11; XVIII, 32, 159–61, 188–89; XIX, 68–69.
[16] Ibid., XIX, 203, 272, 413–14.

pared to travel to Bristol for the mineral waters. One of his last acts was to recommend his former apprentice James Hutchinson for the post of Hospital apothecary.

Evans died "after a lingering illness" on 30 June 1773 at the home of his friend Abel James at Frankford; and his body was buried the next day at North Wales "amongst many others of his ancient and worthy Family."[17] The inventory of his estate, which was shared by his brothers and sisters, listed several maps, a thermometer, a barometer, a copy of Albinus' *Tables,* and medical equipment valued at £34 9s. 5d. Some of his real property in the Northern Liberties and at North Wales was not sold until after the Revolution.[18]

DAVID EVANS (1733–1817)

AMERICAN SOCIETY: 19 JANUARY 1768

DAVID EVANS, house carpenter of Philadelphia, was proposed by Owen Biddle for election to the American Society on 8 May 1767. No action was taken at that time, but the following winter, when the Society was expanding, his name was again presented as one of several "who might not only be useful Members of the Society on the enlarged Plan, but also give considerable assistance in new modeling the Laws and in forming the Rules"; and he was accordingly elected on 19 January 1768. He attended on 29 January, signed the Obligation and By-Laws, and for a time thereafter attended meetings with some regularity.

David Evans was the last of the nine children of Evan and Elizabeth (Musgrave) Evans of Gwynedd, Pennsylvania; his father was a farmer and also a Quaker minister.[1] Before 1748 David was apprenticed to a carpenter in Philadelphia, for in that year Gwynedd Monthly Meeting of Friends, granting a certificate of removal to his older brother Musgrave, asked the Philadelphia Monthly Meeting to have a care for young David as well.[2] The care was not close enough, for on 10 August 1755 he and Letitia Thomas of Radnor Friends Meeting eloped to be married by a

---

[17] Evans to Israel Pemberton, 15 Fifth Mo. 1773, Pemberton Papers, XXIV, 173 (HSP); Evans to Physicians of the Hospital, 19 April 1773, Hutchinson Papers (APS); *Pa. Gaz.,* 7 July 1773.
[18] Ibid., 20 April 1774, 17 March 1784, 2 March 1785; Evans, Will, probated 17 July 1773, Will Book P, 434; Inventory, 1773, No. 304 (Register of Wills, Phila.).

[1] Howard M. Jenkins, *Historical Collections relating to Gwynedd* (2nd ed., Phila., 1897), 160–61, 172–73. A brief biographical note is in Sandra L. Tatman and Roger W. Moss, *Biographical Dictionary of Philadelphia Architects: 1700–1930* (Boston, 1985), 250.
[2] Abstract of Minutes of Gwynedd Monthly Meeting, 1714–1801, 27 Seventh Mo. 1748 (Geneal. Soc. Pa.); Phila. Monthly Meeting, Minutes, 30 Tenth Mo. 1748.

"priest." Eventually Evans admitted to this breach of the discipline, as doubtless did Letitia, for both were soon again in good standing in their meeting.[3]

"At an early period of his life," reads a biographical note sent to the American Philosophical Society about 1830, "he devoted a considerable portion of time to the cultivation of the Mathematics—and, by the application of the algebraic Calculus to Geometry, he became distinguished in that Science."[4] No evidence of such interests and accomplishments has been found—one might have expected one with such accomplishments to have had a part in the Society's observations of the Transit of Venus in 1769.

Briefly in 1769–70 Evans was active in several Philadelphia institutions. He was a member of the Union Library Company, whose building in Pear Street, next to his own house, he may have designed and erected in 1761. He gave the Library Company of Philadelphia a copy of Abraham Swan's *Designs in Architecture* in 1764,[5] and in 1769 became a director of that body. In the same year he was admitted a member of the Carpenters' Company. Soon afterwards, however, he suddenly withdrew from all these organizations. He resigned from the Philosophical Society in the spring of 1770 and as a director of the Library Company in the same year; and after 1771 he rarely attended meetings of the Carpenters' Company.[6]

The reason for these decisions seems to be that Evans underwent a religious change, which led him to spend most of his time and energy, after what his family and trade required, in the service of the Society of Friends. After 1772 he moved steadily into positions of increasing responsibility and influence in the Philadelphia Monthly Meeting for the Southern District. He was repeatedly appointed to oversee marriages or treat with transgressing Friends, including those holding slaves. The Monthly Meeting often appointed him a representative to the Quarterly Meeting, while the Yearly Meeting made him a member of its Meeting for Sufferings. With the outbreak of war in 1775 Evans' concerns deepened and his activities in behalf of Friends increased. In that year he was appointed to wait on Friends who were serving in the militia companies "and training to learn the Military Exercises." He helped raise a subscription for the relief of sufferers from the blockade of Boston in 1775, and, with John Parrish, carried the donation—more than £2500—to New England in November of that year. In 1781 he was one of the committee that visited Samuel Rowland Fisher, who had been ordered to jail for refusing Continental bills of credit as "no more than dirt in the street." The committee tried to bring Fisher to make some concession, for his imprisonment was an embarrassment to

---

[3] Ibid., 24 Sixth Mo., 30 Ninth Mo. 1757; Hinshaw, *Amer. Quaker Genealogy,* II, 518.
[4] [Biographical Note on David Evans], n.d. (Misc. Mss., APS).
[5] *Antiques,* XX (1931), 335; Scharf and Westcott, *Philadelphia,* III, 1887.
[6] Carpenters' Company, Wardens Book, 1 Feb., 17 July 1769; 21 Jan., 15 April 1771. But see ibid., 18 Eleventh Mo. 1799, when he proposed to resign on condition that his son David, Jr. be admitted in his place—a proposition that was withdrawn at the next meeting.

both the state authorities and to his co-religionists.[7] Evans was, in short, one of the "weighty" Friends.

Meanwhile he was fully occupied as a house carpenter. He did much of the work on John Cadwalader's elegant house in Second Street. He was the principal builder of the Friends School on Pine Street and of the addition to the Pine Street meetinghouse in 1773.[8] One of his best customers was John Dickinson, whose houses in Chestnut Street and at Fairhill he remodelled in 1771–73, and whom he advised on the construction of his house in Wilmington in 1800 and on the building and rebuilding (after a fire) of his house at Jones' Neck in Kent County, Delaware, in 1798 and 1804.[9] As Dickinson was a relative, Evans' importunities for payment sometimes had a homely touch: please send some money by bearer, he wrote one Second Day evening, "as what I have in the house happens to be in my Wife's Drawers who through forgetfullness hath taken the Key with her in the Country."[10]

Soon after the outbreak of the Revolution Evans took his family out of the city to Gwynedd. There, as in Philadelphia, he was serviceable to the Meeting in many ways, and there his eldest daughter Letitia was married. At the cessation of hostilities he returned to Philadelphia, receiving on 26 March 1782 a certificate to his former meeting for himself, wife, and three unmarried children, Gulielma, Charles, and David.[11] He at once resumed his former position of influence in the meetings. In 1784 he was named an elder, in succession to the aged John Reynell. Increasingly he was called on to consider and draft public statements of Friends' positions on "vain & sinful amusements" and theatrical entertainments, the state's militia law, the slave trade, or the trade in, or unnecessary use of, distilled spirituous liquors. He expressed a concern for the proper conduct of funerals, he served on a committee to fix new hours of meeting, and on another to formulate a policy on feeding the horses of itinerating Friends. In 1774 Evans had been appointed by his Monthly Meeting to collect subscriptions for John Woolman's *Journal;* in 1784 the Meeting for Sufferings asked him to inquire what progress had been made with the

---

[7] Phila. Monthly Meeting for the Southern District, Minutes, 27 First Mo. 1773, et passim; Phila. Yearly Meeting for Sufferings, Minutes, 29 Sixth Mo. 1775, et passim (both sets of minutes are well indexed); *PMHB*, I (1877), 168–69; XLI (1917), 430–31; Evans to Israel Pemberton, 16 Eleventh Mo. 1775, Pemberton Papers, XXXVIII, 108 (HSP).

[8] Nicholas B. Wainwright, *Colonial Grandeur in Philadelphia: The House and Furniture of General John Cadwalader* (Phila., 1964), 13, 32; Friends Free School Corporation, Accounts, Gratz Papers (HSP).

[9] Wainwright, *Colonial Grandeur,* 143–48; various bills for work on Dickinson's Chestnut Street house are in Logan Papers, XXX, 2–11, 29, et passim (HSP). On Dickinson's Wilmington house, see ibid., XXXI, 46; on the Jones' Neck property, see ibid., XXXIII, 59, 64, 67, 72, 73, 74, 89, 90, 91, et passim.

[10] Evans to John Dickinson, [20 July 1772], ibid., XXX, 38.

[11] Abstract of Minutes of Gwynedd Monthly Meeting, 30 Fourth Mo., 28 Fifth Mo., 1776; 23 Second Mo. 1779; 26 Third Mo. 1782 (Geneal. Soc. Pa.).

manuscript of Samuel Smith's history, which had been confided to Robert Proud, "and how far the Design of promoting such a History is likely to be answered, and what Expectation R. P. has of completing it."[12]

In 1787 Evans was employed as one of the carpenters to build Philosophical Hall. The *Pennsylvania Mercury* commented on the speed of construction:

> The expedition with which the building, intended for the use of the Philosophical Society, has been carried on, is worthy the notice of the public, as it reflects high merit on the artists employed. The brick work was completely raised from the cellars, by Mr. Richard Johnston, in twenty-five days, commencing the third of October; and the floors were laid, and the roof was raised by Messrs. David Evans and William Roberts, in thirty days from the commencement of the brick work;—a time remarkably short, considering the excellency of the work, and the dimensions of the building, which are 70 by 50 feet, and 30 feet high.

When the roof was raised, Evans gave his workmen a dinner, which cost £7 10*s.*, for which the Society reimbursed him.[13] Although he had resigned many years before, Evans contributed £5 towards the construction of the hall. In 1789 the directors of the Library Company asked him to offer them plans and an estimate for a building. Dr. William Thornton's design was accepted instead, but Evans was employed on the work as a carpenter, and, like other workmen on the job, received a share in the Library Company in part payment (Evans' share was assigned to his son Charles); its value was deducted from the several artisans' accounts.[14] In 1789 he was elected to the City Council and was at once put on a committee to plan a new city hall, whose construction thereafter he superintended.[15]

In 1794 the Managers of the Pennsylvania Hospital asked Evans to examine the plans they had drawn for the new west building of the institution and to give them an estimate of the cost of construction. They approved what he told them, accepted his offer to superintend the construction without pecuniary reward, and engaged his son David to do the carpenter work.[16] From 1794 until 1808 Evans

---

[12] Meeting for Sufferings, Minutes, 16 Twelfth Mo. 1784, 23 Eleventh Mo. 1796, et passim; Phila. Monthly Meeting for the Southern District, Minutes, 25 Fifth Mo. 1774, 4 Second Mo. 1784, 20 Third Mo. 1788, 14 First Mo. 1791, et passim. An idea of Evans' service to Friends on a more personal level is suggested by an entry in Elizabeth Drinker's *Diary* (Elaine F. Crane, ed., Boston, 1991), II, 1111: on 17 November 1798 Evans came to the Drinkers' house for an order to bury Rachel Taylor; he spent an hour "and exercised his gift which seems natural to him. WD [William Drinker] say'd when he was gone, he made him think of the old saying, Laugh and be fatt."
[13] *Pa. Mercury,* 2 Nov. 1787; "Monies Paid by S. Vaughan Esqrs. Order [on] Account Phl. Society Hall," 16 Aug.-29 Oct. 1787 (Archives, APS).
[14] Library Company, Minutes, 28, 30 May, 5 Nov. 1790 (Lib. Co. Phila.). On 24 April 1790 Evans fell from a scaffolding on Race Street. Christopher Marshall, Diary, 24 April 1790 (HSP).
[15] Lee H. Nelson, "Old City Hall: Historic Structure Report. Architectural Data Section," app. A, pp. 1–11 (Independence National Historical Park), collects many of the documentary references to Evans.
[16] Evans to Managers, 15 Jan. 1794; Building Committee, Minutes, 1794–95 (Pa. Hospital).

was a director of the Insurance Company of North America, and was frequently employed by the company to survey buildings for insurance.[17]

For some years Evans had neglected to pay his quarterly dues as a member of the Carpenters' Company. When the Managing Committee at last in 1813 pressed him, he submitted his resignation. The committee promptly responded, reminding him of the obligation he assumed on becoming a member; but, as Evans persisted in his determination to resign without discharging his debt, he was "Expeld and his name . . . erased from the List of the Company" on 16 October 1815, with but one dissenting vote.[18]

In the earliest city directories after 1785 Evans is identified as a house carpenter; after 1801 he is usually denominated "gentleman." Until 1803 he lived at 83 Union Street, then moved to Spruce Street between Seventh and Eighth; and there he died on 20 April 1817. His body was laid in the burying ground of the Arch Street Friends Meeting. His daughter Gulielma, who had never married, received the house as well as all her father's household goods, books, papers, plate, and china; she and her two brothers divided their father's other houses, lots, and quit rents.[19]

THOMAS MIFFLIN (1744–1800)
AMERICAN SOCIETY: 19 JANUARY 1768

THOMAS MIFFLIN, a young Philadelphia merchant, was first proposed for election to the American Society by Owen Biddle on 8 May 1767; but no action was taken on the nomination. On 15 January 1768, at a time when the Society was planning to expand, he was proposed again, one of seven persons who, it was thought, "might not only be useful Members of the Society on the enlarged Plan, but also give considerable assistance in new modeling the Laws and in forming the Rules." He was accordingly elected and he attended his first meeting on 26 January. For the remainder of the year he was regular in attendance, signed the Society's Obligation and By-Laws, and was promptly put on its committee to negotiate union with the American Philosophical Society. On 4 November he was elected one of the secretaries and two weeks later was made a member of another committee on union with the Philosophical Society, which was successful. In the reorganized American

---

[17] Evans to John Dickinson, 11 Fourth Mo. 1804, Logan Papers, XXXIII, 72 (HSP); Robert C. Moon, *The Morris Family of Philadelphia* (Phila., 1898), V, 363.
[18] Carpenters' Company, Minutes, 19 Tenth Mo., 1813; 8 Seventh Mo. 1814; 16 Jan., 16 Oct. 1815.
[19] Evans, Will, dated 27 Feb. 1813, proved 29 April 1817, Will Book 6, 436 (Register of Wills, Phila.).

THOMAS MIFFLIN
By Charles Willson Peale.
*Independence National
Historical Park Collection.*

Philosophical Society in 1769 Mifflin was elected one of the secretaries and was reelected the next year. He was a member of three standing committees—on Geography, Mathematics, Natural Philosophy, and Astronomy; on Trade and Commerce; and on Husbandry and American Improvements. As he became increasingly involved in political matters, his interest in Society affairs waned; after 1772 he seldom attended a meeting. But in 1779 he joined ten others in calling for a revival of the Society after its wartime interruption, and he contributed £5 towards the construction of Philosophical Hall in 1785. In 1793 he subscribed $20 towards a projected exploration of the Missouri River by the French botanist André Michaux under the Society's sponsorship.

Thomas Mifflin was born on 10 January 1744, the son of John and Elizabeth (Bagnell) Mifflin, both Quakers.[1] Thomas and his younger brother George were sent to the Academy and College of Philadelphia, from which he was graduated in

---

[1] Kenneth R. Rossman, *Thomas Mifflin and the Politics of the American Revolution* (Chapel Hill, 1952); *DAB*.

conceal his opinions on national and even international matters. In 1793 he recognized the French agent Genêt by attending a dinner in his honor at the City Tavern. Sensitive to the views of his supporters in the western counties of Pennsylvania, Mifflin at first denied the necessity for military action against the whiskey rebels in 1794, then hesitated to call out the militia, but finally did so and accepted the rank of second-in-command to General Henry Lee. In 1798 he supported preparations for a war with France. Barred by the constitution from serving a fourth term as governor, he retired in 1799 and was elected a member of the legislature from Philadelphia County.

Benjamin Rush, who had long since fallen out with Mifflin, excoriated him on the occasion of his election as governor.

> This man was known to be of a very immoral character. He had lived in a state of adultery with many women during the life of his wife, and had children by some of them, whom he educated in his own family. It is said his wife died last summer of a broken heart in consequence of this conduct towards her. Besides this vice, he was much addicted to swearing and obscene conversation. His political character was as bad as his moral. He had deserted his friends and joined with the men who slandered them. He was wholly dissipated and given to low company. His popularity was acquired by the basest acts of familiarity with the meanest of the people. He avoided the society of gentlemen and cherished that of the mechanicks. He lived beyond his income, and was much in debt.[30]

Not all his fellow-citizens, of course, described Mifflin in such harsh terms, and he was reelected governor two times, and, though his wife died in 1790, his personal and official life continued pretty much as before. He was elected vice-president general of the Society of the Cincinnati and president of the Pennsylvania State Society. He was a warm patron of the Young Ladies' Academy of Philadelphia.[31] Always a supporter of improvements, Mifflin was president of the Pennsylvania Society for the Promotion of Manufactures, and a member of the Society for Promoting the Improvement of Roads and Inland Navigation and of the Philadelphia Society for Promoting Agriculture. He was a contributor to the Philadelphia Dispensary, received the dedication of a part of John Parke's translation of *The Lyric Works of Horace* (Philadelphia, 1786), and subscribed to William Birch's views of the city of Philadelphia (Philadelphia, 1800).

Long before his third term as governor ended in 1799, Mifflin's life began to unravel, and provided evidence for Rush's characterization. He neglected his offi-

---

[30] Rush, *Autobiography,* 190.
[31] James Neal to Benjamin Rush, 7 Aug. 1800, Rush Mss., XII, 2 (Lib. Co. Phila. in HSP).

cial duties. He fell so heavily into debt that his creditors began to close in on him. On the advice of Charles Biddle, Mifflin left the city for his country place at the Falls of Schuylkill and then took refuge at Lancaster, where the legislature now met. He appeared harried and harrowed; to a fellow legislator he seemed "a worn out debauchee." "His situation," Biddle remembered, "preyed upon his spirits and rendered his life a burthen to him."[32] Mifflin died in Lancaster on 20 January 1800 and, as his friends were uncertain whether his estate could afford to take his body to Philadelphia, he was buried in the Lutheran cemetery at the state's expense.

> Thus ended the *chequered* life of Thomas Mifflin—*brilliant* in its outset—*troubled* and *perplexed* at a period more advanced—again *distinguished, prosperous,* and *happy*—finally clouded by *poverty,* and *oppressed by creditors.* In *patriotic principle* never changing—in *public action* never faltering—in *personal friendship* sincerely warm—in *relieving the distressed* always active and humane—in his *own* affairs improvident—in the business of others scrupulously just.[33]

JOHN MORRIS, JR. (1739–1785)
AMERICAN SOCIETY: 12 FEBRUARY 1768

JOHN MORRIS, designated Junior to distinguish him from his uncle John of Spring Mill (1709–1782), was born in Philadelphia on 15 Fourth Month [June] 1739, the second, and first surviving, child of the ten children of Samuel and Hannah (Cadwalader) Morris.[1] Samuel Morris was a lawyer, a member of a prominent and wealthy family; his wife was the sister of Dr. Thomas Cadwalader. Reared in solid Quaker comfort, young John was enrolled in the Academy of Philadelphia in 1751. On 25 December 1754 his name was also inscribed at the Middle Temple, London;[2] and in the spring of 1755 he entered the College of Philadelphia. He was graduated in 1759, but his father's hopes that he might study law in London were not realized. Instead the young man read law in Philadelphia, and on 8 Octo-

---

[32] Charles Biddle, *Autobiography* (Phila., 1883), 283–84; *PMHB,* LXII (1938), 89.
[33] William Rawle, "Sketch of the Life of Thomas Mifflin," HSP, *Memoirs,* II, pt. 2 (1830), 123–24.

[1] Robert C. Moon, *The Morris Family* (Phila., 1898–1909), II, 428–33.
[2] C. E. Bedwell, "American Middle Templars," *Am. Hist. Rev.,* XXV (1919–20), 685; E. Alfred Jones, *American Members of the Inns of Court* (London, 1924), 161.

ber 1760 he was admitted to the bar. A year later Edmund Physick proposed him for membership in the Junto; but the minutes of the ensuing meetings are missing, and no record survives that a vote on Morris was ever taken.

During the next decade Morris' practice and reputation grew. From Hall & Sellers' printing shop he purchased in 1767 Blackstone's *Commentaries* in two volumes quarto for £3 19s. 8d.[3] In the same year Owen Biddle proposed him for election to the American Society, and he was chosen a member on 12 February 1768. Notified of his election by Moses Bartram, he attended his first meeting on 19 February and signed the Obligation and By-Laws. In the united Society after 1769 he asked to be a member of the Committee on Husbandry and American Improvements. He had attended meetings of the American Society fairly often, but his appearance in the American Philosophical Society was infrequent. In 1772 he gave £5 to the College of Philadelphia.

From the start of the Revolutionary movement Morris' sympathies were with the American cause. As early as the summer of 1775 he fell under the disapproving notice of the Friends Meeting for assuming—in the Quakerly circumlocution—a military appearance and associating with others in training and exercising to learn the art of war; and on 21 Eleventh Month 1775 he was disowned.[4] Freed from the restraints of the Meeting, Morris threw himself into the political and military struggle, and held a succession of offices under the new government—secretary of the Convention that met on 15 July 1776 to draft a constitution for the state; justice of the peace for Philadelphia, commissioned on 3 September 1776; Recorder of Deeds and Master of the Rolls, offices to which he was commissioned on 22 March 1777; and finally clerk to the General Assembly in November 1778.[5] Inevitably he came into embarrassing and unwanted association with his former co-religionists: in the case of the Quaker pacifist Samuel Rowland Fisher, Morris chose not to be active in prosecuting.[6]

Meanwhile, in the critical fall of 1776 Morris was sent to Westchester County and Albany in New York with a view to obtaining reenlistments from Pennsylvania troops stationed there;[7] and a few weeks later he was appointed quartermaster, with the rank of lieutenant colonel, of the state militia ordered into service in Bucks County, Pennsylvania, and New Jersey. Two of his brothers fought in the battles of Trenton and Princeton, one receiving a bayonet wound in the throat and a bullet in the leg.[8]

---

[3] Hall & Sellers, Shop Book, 1767–69 (APS).
[4] Northern District Monthly Meeting, Minutes, 26 Ninth Mo., 21 Eleventh Mo. 1775.
[5] 2 *Pa. Arch.,* III, 680, 688, 719; *Pa. Evening Post,* 6 Nov. 1778.
[6] "Journal of Samuel Rowland Fisher," *PMHB,* XLI (1917), 155.
[7] Ibid., XXIV (1900), 380; Morris and others to Committee of Safety, 9 Oct. 1776, Provincial Delegates, III, 120 (HSP).
[8] *Col. Recs. Pa.,* XI, 25; 1 *Pa. Arch.,* V, 161–62.

Civil affairs in Pennsylvania were not yet everywhere re-established by midsummer of 1777, and further disintegration was likely as the state was threatened with invasion by the British army. In the circumstances it was important that courts be held wherever and whenever possible to assert the authority of the new regime. But the attorney general, Andrew Allen, had joined the British. The president of the Pennsylvania Council, therefore, turned to Colonel Morris. He was willing, and the Council authorized him to act as the state's attorney general in the several counties. Morris set out for Lancaster, assuring President Wharton that he would "do every thing in my power to strengthen the hands of Government." A few days later, having attended court in that county, he reported that "the opening the Channel of Justice seems to give a pretty general satisfaction, tho'," he added, "the countenances of some plainly shewed their dissatisfaction, however they said nothing."[9] Morris saw to it that copies of official publications went to Pierre E. Du Simitière for his historical library and museum, and this practice was continued by Morris' successors, Timothy Matlack and Thomas Paine.[10] In 1780 Mrs. Morris subscribed one half-jo to the Ladies Fund for the relief of the Continental Army.

In the American Philosophical Society Morris signed the call in February 1779 for a resumption of its meetings. Subsequently he was appointed to a special publications committee to consider papers on husbandry and American improvements and to another to review the accounts of Thomas Coombe. He was also one of the committee to collect subscriptions for the construction of a great air balloon,[11] and he subscribed £7 10s. towards the building of Philosophical Hall. This was almost his last act, however, for he was already ill of the dropsy and died of the disease at Philadelphia on 5 March 1785. He was buried two days later. In his will, by which he left everything to his wife Mary (there were no children), he referred bitterly to persons unnamed, probably his kin, who, but for their "Careless Injustice, Insult & Cruelty," would have shared his wealth.[12]

---

[9] Ibid., 481, 506; *Col. Recs. Pa.,* XI, 246, 258, 276, 294, 357.
[10] *PMHB,* XIII (1889), 364.
[11] *Pa. Gaz.,* 30 June 1784.
[12] Will Book T, 125 (Register of Wills, Phila.); *Pa. Packet,* 13 Aug. 1785.

WILLIAM BARTRAM
By Charles Willson Peale.
*Independence National
Historical Park Collection.*

WILLIAM BARTRAM (1739–1823)
AMERICAN SOCIETY (CORRESPONDING MEMBER):
19 FEBRUARY 1768

WILLIAM BARTRAM, planter, botanist, and illustrator, was elected a corresponding member of the American Society on 19 February 1768. Although he received some recognition as the son of John Bartram—he was so identified when nominated for membership—William at this time enjoyed a modest reputation of his own as an artist of natural history. As he was living as a planter in North Carolina at the time of his election, he could not attend meetings of the Society, but even after he returned permanently to Philadelphia in 1777, he never attended a meeting or took any interest in its work. However, long before his death he was widely and respectfully recognized by botanists in the United States and Europe; and in the twentieth century he has been the subject of a small library of historical, biographical, and literary studies.

He was born at Kingsessing, on the Schuylkill River just outside Philadelphia, on 9 April 1739, the third son—he had a twin sister—of John Bartram and his second wife Ann Mendenhall.[1] His father, a farmer and already famous as a collector of plants, seeds, and specimens of natural history, sent him to the newly opened Academy of Philadelphia, where the master was Charles Thomson and his fellow-students in a company of remarkable youths included Francis Hopkinson, Jacob Duché, Nathaniel Evans, Thomas Godfrey, Jr., and John Morgan. Billy's father took him, while still a student, on plant-hunting trips to the Catskills in 1753 and to Connecticut in 1755. On these long travels, as in the fields around Kingsessing, William displayed an artistic interest and talent, sketching flowers and animals that he saw with a box of paints that "a Switzer Gentleman" gave him.[2] He presented drawings to President Thomas Clap of Yale College and to the Reverend Mr. Jared Eliot of Killingworth in Connecticut. His proud father sent samples of the boy's work to his London patron Peter Collinson. Much pleased with them, Collinson gave the drawings of birds and animals to George Edwards (who reproduced them in his *Gleanings of the Natural World* [London, 1758–64]) and the drawings of oaks to J. F. Gronovius in Holland, while Collinson himself sent the turtles to the *Gentleman's Magazine,* which published them in 1758.[3] The illustrations were warmly praised. "Billy's Elegant Performance makes the shell alive," Collinson told John Bartram. "They are Dead Lumps without it."[4] And William was asked for more.

The lad did not go on from the Academy to the College of Philadelphia, though, for his plain-spoken father had no wish to make him "what is commonly called a gentleman. I want to put him to some business by which he may with care & industry get a temperate reasonable liveing. I am afraid Botany & drawing will not afford him one & hard labour does not agree with him." John Bartram would have liked Billy to study medicine and surgery, but he had not been able to get Billy to read a single page of any of the medical or surgical texts he owned, and, besides, that profession would take the boy from his drawing; surveying would afford opportunities to continue with botany, but there were already too many surveyors in Pennsylvania. Collinson suggested printing, "a pretty Ingenious Imploy," with which drawing and engraving were associated; and Franklin offered to take the young man on as an apprentice. In the end William was apprenticed to a merchant.

A less appropriate career for Billy could not have been chosen. Not only had he no taste or aptitude for commerce, botany and drawing remained his "darling de-

---

[1] Ernest Earnest, *John and William Bartram, Botanists and Explorers* (Phila., 1940); Joseph Ewan, *William Bartram's Botanical and Zoological Drawings, 1756–1788* (APS *Memoirs,* 74 [1968]), 34–43; Darlington, *Memorials; DAB; DSB.*
[2] Edmund Berkeley and Dorothy S. Berkeley, eds., *Correspondence of John Bartram, 1734–1777* (Gainesville, Fla., [1992]), 357.
[3] *Gent. Mag.,* XXVIII (1758), facing pp. 8 and 478.
[4] Berkeley and Berkeley, *Bartram Corres.,* 476.

light." After four years in the counting house William, in the summer of 1761, opened a trading store in the Cape Fear region of North Carolina, where his uncle William had settled. One of his first impressions of that region must have pleased the disowned Quaker John Bartram. "Dear Father," he wrote from Wilmington, North Carolina, "here no Preaching. But Unkle seems a Gods man and we enjoy some Pleasant & Inosent conversation—Men are allowed the Liberty to Worship God her[e] according to the dictates of right Reason." But John soon feared that William might be "ruined in Carolina every thing goes wrong with him there." Collinson believed Billy should get a wife—"Some notable Farmers Daughter who has been brought up remote from Towns for then Bill's plantation will not Seem Irksome to Her."[5]

Young William was thus living, not very happily, in Carolina when his father came through in 1765 en route to Georgia and Florida to explore the St. Johns River. William joined him. The journey, one of Bartram's modern biographers has written, "had more influence on William than any he had made up to that time."[6] When the men returned to Charleston, William, fascinated by a world so different from Pennsylvania, determined to remain behind, settling on the St. Johns River as a planter of rice and indigo. His father advised him how to plant yams, pumpkins, and "cowcumbers," sent him supplies from Charleston and, with some distaste, purchased the slaves his son would need, while warning him against the "mischievous practices" of the Negroes, whom the Carolinians generally represented to be "all either murderers runaways or robers or theeves: espetialy the Plantation negroes." William's "frolick," as his father called it, cost John Bartram some guineas.[7]

The venture was not successful, for William was no better a farm manager than he had been a country trader. The site was badly chosen, swampy and "disagreeably hot," with not another human within nine miles of him. His house was a hovel, the roof and walls leaked, and there were no workmen to repair them. He was living a precarious existence. "In fact," Henry Laurens told John Bartram, "according to my ideas, no colouring can do justice to the forlorn state of poor Billy Bartram."[8] He soon returned briefly to Philadelphia, found some sort of employment, but fell into debt, and in 1770 "absconded," his father knew "not whither."[9]

During these years William's drawings and collections of American natural history had brought him some income (although he was dilatory about sending accounts to his patrons) and increasingly warm praise. Collinson continued to show William's work to others, notably Dr. John Fothergill, who was delighted with it, promptly ordered drawings of all American land tortoises to the amount of at least

[5] Ibid., 516, 622, 680.
[6] Earnest, *John and William Bartram,* 100.
[7] Berkeley and Berkeley, *Bartram Corres.,* 661–63, 668.
[8] Ibid., 672.
[9] Ibid., 734.

20 guineas, and, after Collinson's death in 1768, became Billy's principal patron.[10] In the summer of 1771 Billy Bartram was in North Carolina once more, attempting to put his finances in order. A year later he announced that he was going to Florida again. His father thought this a "wild notion," told his son angrily that there would be no more money for any further adventures to the southward "upon any pretense whatever," and assured his son that it would be better for him to come back to Philadelphia, where relatives and friends would "endeavour to put thee in a way of profitable business if thee will take their advice & be industrious and carefull."[11]

Just at this moment Fothergill proposed that William Bartram return to Florida and gave him a drawing account for the purpose. "He draws neatly," Fothergill told William's father, "has a strong relish for natural History and it is pity that such a genius should sink under distress. Is he sober & diligent?"[12] Fothergill's letter of 22 October 1772, written just before William set out on the older man's commission, is typical in its general encouragement, precise instructions, and expression of concern for the young man's welfare.

> I received thy obliging letter, and the drawings that accompanied them. They are very neatly executed, and I should be glad to receive the like of any new plant or animal that occurs to thee. If it was possible to be a little more exact in the parts of fructification and where these parts are very diminutive to have them drawn a little magnified, I should be pleased and at the same time, if the plants or seeds of such curious plants could be collected and sent hither, it would be very acceptable.
>
> . . . I shall desire Dr. Chalmers of Charles Town to make thee a little present for the drawings, and I should be glad to contribute to thy assistance in collecting the plants of Florida, if thou would suggest what terms might be agreeable. That no time, however, may be lost, should this come to thy hands at Charles Town, I shall desire Dr. Chalmers to confer with thee on this subject, and to render thee such assistance as may be immediately wanted.
>
> The drawings I could wish to have pretty correct, and shall be willing to make due acknowledgment for them. As I imagine thou art well acquainted with the method of packing up plants and seeds, I shall say not much on this head. All bulbous roots are easily managed. Let them be taken up when the flower fades, dry them a little in the shade, put them in a box, either wrapped up in paper or in dry sand, and they will come very safe.
>
> But in the midst of all this attention, forget not the one thing needful. In studying nature forget not its author. Study to be grateful to that hand which has endowed thee with a capacity to distinguish thyself as an artist. Avoid useless or improper company. Be much alone, and learn to trust in the help and protection of him who has formed us and everything. Fear him, and He will raise thee, Friend, and keep thy foot

---

[10] Betsy C. Corner and Christopher C. Booth, eds., *Chain of Friendship: Selected Letters of Dr. John Fothergill of London, 1735–1780* (Cambridge, Mass., 1971), 289, 303, 318, 389–90.
[11] Berkeley and Berkeley, *Bartram Corres.*, 749.
[12] Ibid., 750.

from sliding. For thy Father's sake I wish thee all good, and for thy own a constant reverent heart and hope in that Power who is ever near to help those who confide in him.[13]

Setting out from Philadelphia on 20 March 1773, Bartram travelled for four years through the southern American colonies. He observed, collected, and sketched plants, trees, and flowers, like the beautiful and delicate magnolia, dogwood, and mimosa. He observed the animal life, describing birds, fish, turtles, snakes, and insects. His account of an encounter with alligators, made more memorable by a striking drawing, was so vivid—and so outside the experience of other travellers and all town-dwelling naturalists—that many would not credit it. Bartram lived among the Indians, who made him welcome, calling him Puc-Puggy, the Flower Hunter. He was to place an engraving of Mico Chlucco, "the Long Warrior, King of the Seminoles," as the frontispiece of the published account of these years in Carolina, Georgia, and Florida. Bartram made careful note of his routes and camp sites, described the landscape, mountains, lakes, streams, all natural features, and the weather. He took an interest in the evidences and remains of the Spanish occupation. Filled with all sorts of data, the notebooks are a record of strange and marvellous sights, introducing Dr. Fothergill, who received them, and the friends with whom he shared their contents, to a natural world they did not know and had only half heard of. The St. Johns River, Bartram noted,

> abounds with multitudes of Alegators or Crocadiles which are of vast size & extremely voracious; having pitch't our Camp; before night we went into the Lagoon to fish for Trout & having taken a sufficient number for supper, returning to camp; just in the mouth of the Lagoon, three alligators of a monstrous size rush't out of the weeds, & stop't before us who seemed inclin'd to dispute the pass, however we pusht on towards them. One rush't through the water at us, heaved his enormous body streight up out of the water near breast high, close by the side of our canoe, & open'd a dreadfull pair of jaws, & a bellowing throat; The other rose up behind us in like maner, pierceing the water with his strongplated Tail 5 or 6 feet high, flourishing it in the air, lashing the River into a foam, & roaring like furious waters breaking out of the earth, then plunging & rushing through the waters around us. Thus were we attacked by those River monsters & pursued to the shore where they lay threatning with terrible roaring. I jumped a shore clear, but was pursued up on land, within 3 Yards of our Tent; having a Fusee loaded with buck shott I immediatly armed myselfe & returned to the attack. He had withdrew himself in to the water but observing me approach nearer, pusht up towards me, & being within about 5 or 6 Yards I discharged my piece & blew the whole load into his body just behind his fore leg; he turn'd over & died immediately; the noise of the gun made them retire a little distance, in the mean time we got our fish out the canoe; & began to scale & clean them. Again the Allegators assembled in prodigious numbers, some rising their huge bodies out of the water, & roaring like terrible thunder & lashing the waters with mighty bodies, they drew near to us & one rise up

---

[13] Corner and Booth, *Fothergill Letters*, 391–93.

& with a sweep of his Tail had like to robbed us of our fish, which we recover'd again, he come near again & having my gun loaded with a bullet, which I discharged at his head & I believe wounded him, he plunged in the water, in a dreadfull maner, & rise up a good way off. Fireing at them several times caused them to keep at some distance. They however appeared so numerous & formidable round our port, that I began to consider my situation very desagreeable & under an absolute embargo. It is scarcely credible what an immence number of Fish these monsters destroy, especially at these passes, the River being here, as I observed before, very Narow. The Trout who pass here in their way to & from the numerous lakes & endless Lagoons & Marshes towards the head of this Vast River, where they go to spawn. The Alegator post themselves forming a line across, where we see them opening their voracious Jaws into which the fish are intrap't. They heave their heads and upper part of their body upright, opening their throats to swallow them, & I have seen them with two or three great Trout in their mouth at a time, choping them up, the fishes tail hanging out. The noise of their jaws choping together, with the water & prey in their Throats; their plunging through the water after their Prey & pursuing one another altogether exhibits a very terrifying shew.[14]

Back in Philadelphia in 1778 William made his home with his brother John, to whom their father had deeded the farm in 1771; and after John's death in 1812 he stayed on with John's daughter and her husband, Ann and Robert Carr. He entered into the life and routine of the Bartram farm and garden, collecting seeds, cultivating plants, receiving botanists and other visitors, sometimes writing a brief description of a new or unusual specimen. Manasseh Cutler, New England clergyman and botanist, who was taken to the garden on 14 July 1787, penned a long description of the place and its principal resident.

> Mr. Bartram lives in an ancient Fabric, built with stone, and very large, which was the seat of his father. His house is on an eminence fronting to the Schuylkill, and his garden is on the declivity of the hill between his house and the river. We found him, with another man, hoeing in his garden, in a short jacket and trowsers, and without shoes or stockings. He at first stared at us, and seemed to be somewhat embarrassed at seeing so large and gay a company so early in the morning. Dr. [Gerardus] Clarkson was the only person he knew, who introduced me to him, and informed him that I wished to converse with him on botanical subjects, and, as I lived in one of the Northern States, would probably inform him of trees and plants which he had not yet in his collection; that the other gentlemen wished for the pleasure of a walk in his garden. I instantly entered on the subject of botany with as much familiarity as possible, and inquired after some rare plants which I had heard that he had. He presently got rid of his embarrassment, and soon became very sociable, which was more than I expected, from the character I had heard of the man. I found him to be a practical botanist, though he seemed to understand little of the theory. We ranged the several alleys, and he gave me the generic and specific names, place of growth, properties, etc., so far as he knew them.

---

[14] Bartram, "Travels in Georgia and Florida, 1773–74: A Report to Dr. John Fothergill," Francis Harper, ed. (APS *Trans.* n.s., XXXIII, pt. 2 [1943]), 151–52.

This is a very ancient garden, and the collection is large indeed, but is made principally from the Middle and Southern States. It is finely situated, as it partakes of every kind of soil, has a fine stream of water, and an artificial pond, where he has a good collection of aquatic plants. There is no situation in which plants or trees are found but that they may be propagated here in one that is similar. But every thing is very badly arranged, for they are neither placed ornamentally nor botanically, but seem to be jumbled together in heaps. The other gentlemen were very free and sociable with him, particularly Governor [Alexander] Martin, who has a smattering of botany and a fine taste for natural history. There are in this garden some very large trees that are exotic, particularly an English oak, which he assured me was the only one in America. He had the Pawpaw tree, or Custard apple. It is small, though it bears fruit; but the fruit is very small. He has also a large number of aromatics, some of them trees, and some plants. One plant I thought equal to cinnamon. The Franklin tree is very curious. It has been found only on one particular spot in Georgia. His cider-press is singular; the channel for the stone wheel to run in for grinding the apples is cut out of a solid rock; the bottom of the press is a solid rock, and has a square channel to carry off the juice, from which it is received into a stone reservoir or vat. From the house is a walk to the river, between two rows of large, lofty trees, all of different kinds, at the bottom of which is a summer-house on the bank, which here is a ledge of rocks, and so situated as to be convenient for fishing in the river, where a plenty of several kinds of fish may be caught. Mr. Bartram showed us several natural curiosities in the place where he keeps his seeds; they were principally fossils. He appeared fond of exchanging a number of his trees and plants for those which are peculiar to the Northern States. We proposed a correspondence, by which we could more minutely describe the productions peculiar to the Southern and Northern States.[15]

On the day of Cutler's visit, half a dozen members of the Federal Convention also toured the garden. A month earlier the president of the Convention had also come; but, probably expecting a formal horticultural display, General Washington was unimpressed: the garden, he noted in his diary, though it contained many exotics, "was not laid off with much taste, nor was it large."[16] Although some of Bartram's visitors were in effect sightseeing tourists, many were serious botanists drawn by the fame of the place and of the Bartrams. William generously shared his vast knowledge with such interested and informed persons. The Brunswick army surgeon Dr. Johann David Schoepf, who went twice to the garden on his travels in America in 1783–84, learned that William had an unpublished manuscript about Florida that "should be instructive and interesting." The French botanist André Michaux frequently visited "Mess. Bartram Botanistes" during the years he was in the United States; Thomas Nuttall was there so often and for such long periods that a workspace was set apart for him that was known as "Mr. Nuttall's room";

---

[15] William Parker Cutler and Julia Perkins Cutler, eds., *Life, Journals and Correspondence of Rev. Manasseh Cutler, LL.D.* (Cincinnati, 1881), I, 272–74.
[16] Washington, *Diaries* (Donald Jackson and Dorothy Twohig, eds., Charlottesville, 1976–79), V, 166–68, 183.

while the Scots schoolmaster Alexander Wilson, who taught nearby for several years, stayed for extended periods at the garden with Bartram, who taught him a great deal about birds of the Carolinas, Georgia, and Florida, and offered sound and gentle criticism of the drawings Wilson was preparing for his great work on American ornithology. Frederick Pursh spent "happy hours" in the company of William Bartram, whom he found to be "a very intelligent, agreeable, and communicative gentleman," who gave him much information about the plants of Carolina. Sir Augustus John Foster, secretary of the British legation, visited the garden in 1805 and ordered plants and seeds for Lord Liverpool, Lord Aberdeen, and other English noblemen.[17] Even the Duke de La Rochefoucauld-Liancourt, who found Bartram rude and untidy and living in a room he likened to a pig-sty [*bauge*] (decorated, however, rather improbably, with a framed print of the ancestral arms of the English Bartrams), recognized that the botanist was a good man, honest and sensitive.[18] Other foreign visitors who rode out from Philadelphia to Bartram's garden at Kingsessing included the Polish Julius U. Niemcewicz, the Italian counts Francesco dal Verme and Luigi Castiglioni, the Frenchmen Moreau de St. Méry and Barbé-Marbois, and the English textile manufacturer Henry Wansey of Salisbury. Each left some record of the visit in his diary or journal.

Bartram spent much of the decade until 1790 turning the journals, notes, and memories of his travels in Carolina, Georgia, and Florida into a book. The *Travels through North & South Carolina, Georgia, East & West Florida* (Philadelphia, 1791) was not a botanical catalogue like Humphrey Marshall's *Arbustrum Americanum* or the record of an observant scientific traveller like Peter Kalm's *Travels in North America*. In the first paragraph the tone of the book was set. "For the first twenty-four hours," the author wrote of his departure from Philadelphia in April 1773,

> we had a prosperous gale, and were cheerful and happy in the prospect of a quick and pleasant voyage; but, alas! how vain and uncertain are human expectations! how quickly is the flattering scene changed! The powerful winds, now rushing forth from their secret abodes, suddenly spread terror and devastation; and the wide ocean, which, a few moments past, was gentle and placid, is now thrown into disorder, and heaped into mountains, whose white curling crests seem to sweep the skies!

Those who read further into the *Travels* may well have been astonished by Bartram's description of amusements of some of the natives of Florida.

---

[17] Schoepf, *Travels in the Confederation [1783–1784]* (A. J. Morrison, trans. and ed., Phila., 1911), I, 90–92; C. S. Sargent, ed., "Portions of the Journal of André Michaux," APS *Proc.*, XXVI (1889), 68; Clark Hunter, ed., *The Life and Letters of Alexander Wilson* (APS *Memoirs*, CLIV [1983]), 73; Pursh, *Flora Americanae Septentrionalis . . . The Plants of North America* (2nd edit., London, 1816), I, vii; Foster, *Jeffersonian America: Notes on the United States of America . . . 1805–6–7 and 11–12* (Richard Beale Davis, ed., San Marino, 1954), 256–57.

[18] François-Alexandre, duke de La Rochefoucauld-Liancourt, *Journal de Voyage en Amérique et d'un Séjour à Philadelphie* (Jean Marchand, ed., Baltimore, 1940), 117.

> We returned . . . through part of this high forest skirting on the meadows; began to ascend the hills of a ridge which we were under the necessity of crossing, and having gained its summit, enjoyed a most enchanting view, a vast expanse of green meadows and strawberry fields; a meandering river gliding through, saluting in its various turnings the swelling, green, turfy knolls, embellished with parterres of flowers and fruitful strawberry beds; flocks of turkeys strolling about them; herds of deer prancing in the meads or bounding over the hills; companies of young, innocent Cherokee virgins, some busily gathering the rich fragrant fruit, others having already filled their baskets, lay reclined under the shade of floriferous and fragrant native bowers of Magnolia, Azalea, Philadelphus, perfumed Calycanthus, sweet Yellow Jessamine and cerulian Glycine frutescens, disclosing their beauties to the fluttering breeze, and bathing their limbs in the cool fleeting streams; whilst other parties, more gay and libertine, were yet collecting strawberries or wantonly chasing their companions, tantalising them, staining their lips and cheeks with the rich fruit.
>
> This sylvan scene of primitive innocence was enchanting, and perhaps too enticing for hearty young men long to continue idle spectators.
>
> In time, nature prevailing over reason, we wished at least to have a more active part in their delicious sports. Thus precipitately resolving, we cautiously made our approaches, yet undiscovered, almost to the joyous scene of action. Now, although we meant no other than an innocent frolic with this gay assembly of hamadryades, we shall leave it to the person of feeling and sensibility to form an idea to what lengths our passions might have hurried us, thus warmed and excited, had it not been for the vigilance and care of some envious matrons who lay in ambush, and espying us gave the alarm, time enough for the nymphs to rally and assemble together; we however pursued and gained ground on a group of them, who had incautiously strolled to a greater distance from their guardians, and finding their retreat now like to be cut off, took shelter under cover of a little grove, but on perceiving themselves to be discovered by us, kept their station, peeping through the bushes; when observing our approaches, they confidently discovered themselves and decently advanced to meet us, half unveiling their blooming faces, incarnated with the modest maiden blush, and with native innocence and cheerfulness, presented their little baskets, merrily telling us their fruit was ripe and sound.
>
> We acepted a basket, sat down and regaled ourselves on the delicious fruit, encircled by the whole assembly of the innocently jocose sylvan nymphs; by this time the several parties under the conduct of the elder matrons, had disposed themselves in companies on the green, turfy banks.[19]

This was not the language of the *Philosophical Transactions,* Franklin, or the members of the American Philosophical Society. Most readers hardly knew what to make of it. The reviewer in the *Columbian Magazine* condemned the style as "very incorrect and disgustingly pompous."[20] Ebenezer Hazard labelled the book a "curiosity."[21] But Bartram's *Travels* was in fact one of the memorable early expres-

---

[19] Francis Harper, ed., *The Travels of William Bartram (Naturalist's Edition)* (New Haven, 1958), 1, 225–26.
[20] *Columbian Mag.,* VI (1792), 267.
[21] Mass. Hist. Soc., *Colls.,* 5th ser., III (1877), 289.

sions of the romantic spirit, a source of ideas and figures that, transmuted, appear in the poetry and novels of Samuel Taylor Coleridge, William Wordsworth, and Chateaubriand.[22]

The book was published at last (it had been announced as early as 1786) at the end of 1791. It was dedicated to Governor Mifflin of Pennsylvania after President Washington declined as a matter of policy to allow his name to be used.[23] In the next few years Bartram's work had two editions in London and one in Dublin, and was translated and published in Paris, Berlin, Vienna, and Haarlem.

Bartram spent the remaining thirty years of his life, as he had passed many of the preceding years, quietly at the famous garden, which was operated first by his brother, then by his niece and her husband. In 1785 his cousin Humphrey Marshall had proposed that the two of them make a natural history expedition to the western territories, perhaps with the endorsement or support of the American Philosophical Society. Other similar invitations were made to Bartram,[24] but he travelled no more and seems hardly even to have gone into Philadelphia. He was especially helpful to young Benjamin Smith Barton: he provided material for the latter's *Collections for an Essay on the Materia Medica,* (Philadelphia, 1798) and he made the drawings for most of the plates in Barton's *Elements of Botany* (Philadelphia, 1803). Barton stated this fact in the introduction to the work, then continued:

> While I thus publicly return my thanks to this ingenious naturalist, for his kind liberality in enriching my work, I sincerely rejoice to have an opportunity of declaring, how much of my happiness, in the study of natural history, has been owing to my acquaintance with him; how often I have availed myself of his knowledge in the investigation of the natural productions of our native country; how sincerely I have loved him for the happiest union of moral integrity, with original genius, and unaspiring science, for which he is eminently distinguished.[25]

At Barton's request Bartram wrote an account of the Cherokee and Creek Indians, but it was not published in the lifetimes of either man. In fact, Bartram published nothing except a few short descriptive notes, and he owed the appearance of some or all of these to the interest of friends. Dr. Benjamin Say in 1788 sent Bartram's "Observations on the pea fly or beetle and fruit curculio" to the Philadelphia Society for Promoting Agriculture, to which Bartram had been elected three years earlier; it was published in the Society's *Memoirs* in 1808. In 1802 Dr. Barton gave to the Philosophical Society Bartram's paper describing the native vines of America and tracing them to their original stock; but although its publication was recom-

---

[22] John Livingston Lowes, *The Road to Xanadu* (Boston, 1927); N. Bryllion Fagin, *William Bartram, Interpreter of the American Landscape* (Baltimore, 1933).
[23] John C. Fitzpatrick, ed., *Writings of George Washington* (Washington, 1931–44), XXXI, 56–57.
[24] Darlington, *Memorials,* 522–23.
[25] Barton, *Elements of Botany* (Phila., 1803), I, x–xi.

mended, it never appeared in the Society's *Transactions*. In his *Philadelphia Medical Journal* Barton published Bartram's notes on a species of Certhia or creeper, an essay on reasons for believing that the town of Bristol had once been geologically part of Jersey, and Bartram's biographical sketch of his father. Barton also printed in the same volume of this medical journal charming anecdotes of a crow, taught to answer to the name of Tom, a bird of "a happy temper, and good disposition," which Bartram had "reared from the nest."[26] Bartram was elected to membership in the Philadelphia Linnaean Society in 1806 and in the Academy of Natural Sciences of Philadelphia in 1812; but he made no contribution to either.

On the morning of 22 July 1823 William Bartram completed writing a botanical note, took a few steps outside his room, collapsed, and died. His personal possessions were few—some clothing and bedding, a few pieces of furniture, a few dollars in a purse, and "Sundry Books" appraised at $16.50.[27]

JOHN CHAPMAN (1740–1800)
AMERICAN SOCIETY (CORRESPONDING MEMBER):
19 FEBRUARY 1768

DR. JOHN CHAPMAN, a young country physician of Bucks County, Pennsylvania, was elected a corresponding member of the American Society in 1768, but he neither corresponded with it nor attended a meeting, though he had many opportunities to do so on his frequent sojourns in Philadelphia.

Born in Wrightstown Township, Bucks County, on 18 October 1740, he was the only child of John and Ruth (Wilkinson) Chapman and a grandson of John and Jane Chapman, who were the first settlers of Wrightstown.[1] Reared in a Quaker household, he attended neighborhood schools, probably read medicine with a local practitioner, and in the winter of 1762–63 went to Philadelphia, where for two years he was a private pupil of Dr. Cadwalader Evans, one of the physicians of the Pennsylvania Hospital.[2] Three of his texts can be identified in the library of the

---

[26] *Phila. Med. & Phys. Jour.*, I, pt. 1 (1804), 89–95; pt. 2 (1805), 103–05, 131–33. "Some account of the late Mr. John Bartram, of Pennsylvania" is ibid., pt. 1 (1804), 115–24.
[27] Bartram, Letters of Administration, 25 July 1823 (Register of Wills, Phila.).

[1] John Chapman, Biographical File (Bucks Co. Hist. Soc.); *Biographical Directory of the American Congress, 1774–1927* (Washington, 1928), 803.
[2] "Early Minutes of Philadelphia Monthly Meeting of Friends," Geneal. Soc. Pa., *Publications*, XII (1935), 158.

College of Physicians—Boerhaave's *Academical Lectures,* Richard Brookes' *General Practice of Physic,* and Richard Mead's *Discourse on the Smallpox and Measles.* He returned to Bucks County, producing his certificate from Philadelphia Monthly Meeting, 5 Second Mo. 1765; and soon settled into life. The Wrightstown Monthly Meeting frequently appointed him to do its business. On 25 June 1767 he married Mercy Beaumont, daughter of John and Sarah Beaumont of Upper Makefield Township, who brought him a farm of 285 acres and bore him six children.[3]

However, the political disturbances of the time, which reached even into remote Bucks County, unsettled him. Sympathizing with those who upheld America's rights, he was chosen a member of the county Committee of Safety in December 1774, and then its clerk and a member of its Committee of Correspondence. He was easy in his mind about collecting funds for the relief of the distressed citizens of blockaded Boston, but waging war was something else; and on 21 July 1775, pleading conscientious scruples, with several other Quaker members, he asked to be excused from the Committee.[4] As was true with many other Friends, however, his political convictions proved to be stronger than religious teachings: he took the oath of allegiance on 25 February 1779, and accepted the commission of justice of the peace. Shortly afterwards he was appointed judge of the Court of Common Pleas. This conduct brought him the disapproving notice of the Monthly Meeting; he refused to give satisfaction, and was thereupon disowned.[5]

For the next few years Dr. Chapman was active in public affairs. As a physician he was sometimes asked to examine sick or wounded soldiers and military prisoners. As a justice he heard an occasional criminal case and scores of suits for non-payment of small debts. One of the latter was instituted by "Negro Toney" against Benjamin Roberts for a debt of 12s.—an interesting commentary on the status of free Negroes in Pennsylvania in 1785.[6] In 1783 Chapman ran as an Anti-Constitutionalist for a seat on the State Council but was soundly beaten. Three years later, in the political revolution that was eventually to sweep the Anti-Constitutionalists into power in Pennsylvania, he was elected to the Assembly.[7]

In the spring of 1788 Chapman appeared at Wrightstown Monthly Meeting, where he "offered something in writing in order to Condemn his misconduct" in swearing allegiance, and asked to be reinstated. Perhaps his conscience had been

---

[3] Wrightstown Monthly Meeting, Minutes, 5 Fifth Mo., 25 Sixth Mo. 1767 (transcript, Bucks Co. Hist. Soc.); 2 *Pa. Arch.* IX, 276.
[4] *PMHB,* IV (1880), 161–62; XV (1891), 259–60, 264.
[5] *Col. Recs. Pa.,* XI, 708; XV, 30; Wrightstown Monthly Meeting, Minutes, 5 Ninth Mo., 3 Tenth Mo. 1780; 8 Fourth Mo. 1788.
[6] John Chapman, Justices' Docket, 1783–1786, Henry Chapman Papers, (Bucks Co. Hist. Soc.); Certificate, 26 Nov. 1782, Stauffer Coll., X, 697 (HSP).
[7] 6 *Pa. Arch.,* IX, 104; *Pa. Gaz.,* 18 Oct. 1786; *Col. Recs. Pa.,* XV, 104.

bothering him again; maybe it was only that he wanted to marry in meeting, his first wife having died in 1784. In any case, the Friends took him back, and on 17 December 1788 at Falls Meeting in Bucks County he was married to Mrs. Margery Hutchinson, widow of Michael Hutchinson and sister-in-law of Dr. James Hutchinson of Philadelphia.[8]

Meanwhile Bucks County farmers and improvers had organized a society for promoting agriculture and domestic manufactures and for reforming manners and customs, like the Philadelphia County Society for Promoting Agriculture, which Dr. George Logan presided over. The Bucks County reformers agreed specifically to report all useful experiments in agriculture, to discourage the use of articles of foreign growth and manufacture, not to use distilled spirituous liquors in their own families, and to practice strict frugality. Chapman was elected president.[9]

Dr. Chapman was reelected to the Pennsylvania Assembly annually from 1786 through 1795. In 1796 he was elected as a Federalist to the United States House of Representatives, where he voted for the Alien and Sedition laws of 1798.[10] He served but one term. He died at his farm in Upper Makefield on 27 January 1800, and was buried in Wrightstown Friends burying ground. He was survived by his widow, three sons—John, Seth, and Josiah—and three daughters—Sarah, Jane, and Mercy. To his nephew Isaac Chapman he left three medical books; his wife was to have, among other benefits, "the Priviledge of Riding to meeting and other places in my Riding Waggon," whenever son John was going there.[11]

---

[8] Wrightstown Monthly Meeting, Minutes, 8 Fourth Mo., 6 Fifth Mo., 4 Eleventh Mo. 1788; 2 *Pa. Arch.,* IX, 235.
[9] Isaac Van Horne to Reading Beatty, 8 June 1788, *PMHB,* LIV (1930), 174.
[10] Harry M. Tinkcom, *The Republicans and Federalists in Pennsylvania, 1790–1801* (Harrisburg, 1950), 182–83.
[11] John Chapman, Will, 17 Jan. 1800, Will Book 6, 254; Inventory of estate, file 2957 (Register of Wills, Bucks Co., Doylestown, Pa).

ISAAC JAMINEAU (1710–1789)
AMERICAN SOCIETY (CORRESPONDING MEMBER):
26 FEBRUARY 1768

ISAAC JAMINEAU, His Britannic Majesty's Consul at Naples, was strategically located both to observe the eruptions of Mount Vesuvius and to assist English travellers in Italy. One of the latter was Dr. John Morgan of Philadelphia, who spent several weeks in Naples in 1764, and maintained his acquaintance with Jamineau by correspondence thereafter. In 1767 the consul sent Morgan a description of Vesuvius' latest eruption; Morgan read it to the American Society on 19 February 1768; and when the reading was completed Jamineau's name was put in nomination for election as a corresponding member. He was elected at the next meeting but, since the certificate of election appears never to have been sent and is now in the Society's archives, it seems that he was never officially informed of the honor done him.[1]

Third son of Claude Jamineau of London, Isaac was educated at Westminster School under Dr. Robert Freind, and was admitted a pensioner of Trinity College, Cambridge, on 2 June 1727, at the age of 17; a few months later, on 5 October, he was admitted to the Middle Temple; but he never took a degree at Cambridge nor was he called to the bar.[2] In 1731 he subscribed for two copies of Luke Trevigar's text on conic sections. In 1742 he was given a Post Office sinecure: he had the privilege of supplying newspapers to the Post Office, particularly to the Clerks of the Roads, and of placing Post Office advertisements in newspapers. His income from this post ultimately reached £1,200 a year, from which he paid a clerk £200 to do the work.[3] Despite support from the Earl of Lincoln, he was unsuccessful in seeking the secretaryship of the Foreign Post Office;[4] but in 1753 he was named consul at Naples, retaining, of course, his Post Office appointment and emoluments. In Naples he amused himself with his garden, asking Morgan for "any curious flowers" or good fruits of the climate of Philadelphia that might grow in Naples.[5]

Several times during his first year in Naples Jamineau inspected Vesuvius, descending into the crater, measuring its depth, and noting portents of another eruption. Of the eruption in December 1754 he sent accounts to Sir Francis Hatton

---

[1] In 1773 Morgan gave young John Singleton Copley a letter of introduction to Jamineau. *Letters & Papers of John Singleton Copley and Henry Pelham, 1739–1776* (Mass. Hist. Soc., *Colls.*, LXXI, 1914), 209–11.
[2] John and J. A. Venn, *Alumni Cantabrigienses*.
[3] Treasury Letter Book, V (1789–90), 64, Post Office Records, (G.P.O., London).
[4] Jamineau to Newcastle, 4 July 1751, Add. Mss. 32724, f. 427 (British Library).
[5] Jamineau to John Morgan, 3 Nov. 1767 (Coll. Phys. Phila.).

Eyles Styles, F.R S., which were read to the Royal Society and printed in its *Philosophical Transactions*.⁶ He also sent Styles an account of the earthquake that happened at Naples at 3:17:30″ on 22 October 1756. "I can be so particular as to the time," he explained,

> because it stop'd a Pendulum of Ellicots at the Imperial Ministers. We were Eight of us at table & took it at first for the Shakeing the Beams of the house, which are considerably long, by some hasty steps in another Room but the lasting soon determin'd what it was; it Continued an Undulating Motion, at the interval of a Regular but Slow pulse, to about ten pulsations after I began to count, increasing till about the Sixth, & decreasing in like gradation after its coming to the height. My Counting was interrupted by the Company's rising to have recourse to the Door way of a thick wall at hand . . . wherein before the Number it could contain were well fix'd the motion entirly ceas'd. I am firmly of Opinion therefore that it did not last half a Minute, tho more than one person in Naples have very idly talk't of five. . . . It was neither preceeded [sic] nor attended with any Noise, and the Motion was so equable, that but for the Apprehensions of its increasing to Mischief, you might have imagined yourself riding on a Chamber Horse, if you recollect such an Elastic Machine.⁷

Jamineau's account of Vesuvius' eruption of 1767, which was read to the American Society, was printed in the *Pennsylvania Chronicle* of 28 March 1768 and in Lewis Nicola's *American Magazine,* and reprinted in the first volume of the American Philosophical Society's *Transactions*. It was remarkable only for calling attention to the periodicity of eruptions—a matter Jamineau left to "your deep naturalists" to account for.

Like most foreign service officers Jamineau had to spend far more than he earned. War reduced the income of the Naples post after 1756; and in 1760 he estimated that he had spent £3,000 of his private income, in addition to the necessary expenses of the clerks. An appeal to Newcastle produced an increase of salary but not the reimbursement Jamineau hoped for; doubtless income from consular fees increased after the resumption of peace in 1763.⁸ Jamineau resigned the consulship in 1779, but retained the Post Office job, whose income was now only £700–800 a year. In 1775 the Society for Promoting Arts, Manufactures and Commerce, of which he was a member, awarded Jamineau a gold medal "for promoting the views of the Society."⁹ He died 3 November 1789.¹⁰ He never married, and left his entire estate to his niece.

---

⁶ *Phil. Trans.,* XLIX, pt. 1 (1755), 24–28.
⁷ Jamineau to Styles, 26 Oct. 1756 (extract), Royal Society Mss., Letters and Papers, III, 230.
⁸ Jamineau to William Pitt, 22 July 1760, Add. Mss. 32908, f. 431; to Newcastle, 3 March, 18 Aug. 1761, ibid., 32919, f. 398; 32927, f. 102 (British Library).
⁹ Society for Promoting Arts, *Trans.,* I (1783) 54, 295.
¹⁰ *Gent. Mag.,* LIX (1789), 1056.

I will never oppose or disturb it; my constant study being to pass thro' Life at Peace with my own Breast and all the World.[17]

Wells stayed in the city during its occupation by the British army, as appears from his advertisement of 6 January 1778 for spermaceti lamp oil and candles.[18] After the war, in addition to keeping his wholesale store, he opened a retail hardware store in Third Street between Market and Arch Streets, which he put under the care of his eldest son. It offered forge hammers, smith's anvils and vises, nails, screws, bricklayers' tools, coach-makers' irons, hinges, bolts, spades and shovels, gridirons and frying pans, air vents, brass cocks, scale beams, steelyards, paint, and several score other articles of hardware.[19] From 1787 until 1793 Wells was in partnership in Philadelphia with William Buckley; after that year his partner was Benjamin W. Morris, his son-in-law.[20] In another venture in 1790, he was a partner of Thomas Clifford, Jr., of Bristol, England, who had invented a rolling mill for the manufacture of nails. Just at that time two Philadelphians, John Nancarrow and Henry Voight, were also developing a machine similar to Clifford's. Fearful that his competitors might obtain copies of Clifford's patent papers from England, as they were legally entitled to do, and so undercut Clifford and Wells in America, Clifford appealed to Congress against the clause in a pending bill that would have allowed individuals to receive an exclusive license in the United States for British patents, thus denying entrepreneurs like himself the benefit of industrial improvement. As it turned out, Nancarrow and Voight gave up their interest to Wells, and turned to other processes.[21] Perhaps it was searching for iron in connection with this enterprise that Wells spent much time "in the western Country . . . boring into the Bowells of the Earth," although, as it turned out, without much success.[22]

---

[17] Wells to Council of Safety, 15 Jan. 1777, 1 *Pa. Arch.*, V, 189. Wells was suspected of correspondence with the British, informing them of the location of river defenses, but the charges were groundless. Ibid., 108.

On the strength of an early nineteenth-century notation on copies in APS Library Wells has been named author of two pamphlets in the pre-Revolutionary debate—A Citizen of Philadelphia, *Political Reflections Submitted to the Consideration of the British Colonies* (Phila., 1774) and *The Middle Line: or, An Attempt to Furnish Some Hints for ending the Differences subsisting between Great-Britain and the Colonies* (Phila., 1775). No other authority has been found for this ascription, which in any case seems out of character for the man.

[18] *Pa. Evening Post*, 6 Jan. 1778.

[19] *Pa. Gaz.*, 8 June 1785; *Pa. Packet*, 28 Feb. 1782; Wells to Thomas Clifford, Jr., 27 Aug. 1784, Clifford-Pemberton Corres., VII, 94 (HSP); 2 *N. J. Arch.*, III, 203.

[20] Moon, *Morris Family*, I, 387.

[21] *New American State Papers. Science and Technology*, IV, 11–14; Wells to Thomas Clifford, Jr., 8 Jan., 24 March 1790, Clifford-Pemberton Papers, IX, 145, 205 (HSP); Abraham Rees, *Cyclopaedia; or Universal Dictionary of Arts, Sciences, and Literature* (1st Amer. ed., Phila., 1810), s.v. "Nails."

[22] Wells to William Thornton, 11 May 1792. I am indebted to Charles M. Harris for this and other references to the Thornton letters.

Wells was an early and steady supporter of John Fitch in the latter's development of a steamboat. He encouraged him, invested in his company (as did his sons), and, convinced that Fitch's claim of priority over James Rumsey was sound, helped him to assemble, organize, and edit a statement of his case in the pamphlet entitled *The Original Steam-Boat Supported* (Philadelphia, 1788). For his patron's help Fitch was grateful. Wells, he wrote, was "a truly honest man, that would speak nothing but simple truths." He was, the inventor continued, "a person of the most refined principles, and perhaps not a thousand on Earth to be found that can equal him in delicate sensation of honour."[23]

Wells was always active in Quaker and civic activities. At various times he was on the Monthly Meeting's committees on order, discipline, and poor relief. In 1776 he was one of the twelve managers of the Philadelphia Society for Alleviating Distressed Prisoners, and in 1787 was a vice-president of its successor, the Philadelphia Society for Alleviating the Miseries of Public Prisons. He was a contributor to the Pennsylvania Hospital and to the Philadelphia Dispensary for the Medical Relief of the Poor. He belonged to the Philadelphia Society for Promoting Agriculture and was a director of the Library Company of Philadelphia for twenty years until his death. In the summer of 1795 he went about the city collecting subscriptions, as Jacob Hiltzheimer noted in his diary, "towards the trees planted this spring on both sides of Market street to the Schuylkill."[24]

Wells' views in state politics in the 1780s were Anti-Constitutionalist. He supported the reformed constitution of 1790 as well as the new federal Constitution, and was elected to the Pennsylvania House of Representatives in 1790. He served two years. In 1791 he was appointed cashier of the Bank of the United States, a post he held until his death ten years later. During these years he was a friend and correspondent of Dr. William Thornton, who designed a building for the Library Company of Philadelphia and was author of a treatise on the origin of language, entitled *Cadmus*. He showed the essay to Wells, who thought it "vastly ingenious," but warned against submitting it to the "untutor'd fangs" of the Philosophical Society.[25] Thornton noted the warning but did not heed it, and *Cadmus* received the Society's Magellanic Premium in 1793. In the yellow fever epidemic of that year Wells remained in the city. Though falling ill himself, he displayed singular courage and sympathy towards other victims: the widow of Dr. John Morris, returning from the cemetery after burying her husband, found that her own father would not

---

[23] John Fitch, *Autobiography* (Frank D. Prager, ed., APS *Memoirs,* CXIII, 1976), 181–83, 194.
[24] Northern District Monthly Meeting, Minutes, 25 Seventh Mo. 1775, 24 Twelfth Mo. 1776; *Pa. Evening Post,* 6 Feb. 1776; *PMHB,* XVI (1892), 418.
[25] [Wells] to [William Thornton], 12 Nov. 1792.

let her into his house; but "Richard Wells then sayd, as one door was shut, God would open another," and took the poor woman in.[26]

Richard Wells was buried in Friends ground in Philadelphia on 14 February 1801.[27] His wife had died in 1796.

HUGH MERCER (1726–1777)
AMERICAN SOCIETY (CORRESPONDING MEMBER):
26 FEBRUARY 1768

HUGH MERCER of Fredericksburg, Virginia, who had been both a physician and a soldier, sometimes simultaneously, was proposed to the Philadelphia Medical Society by his friend and sometime fellow-in-arms Dr. John Morgan. In a letter to Morgan on 16 May 1767, replying to letters of 25 February and 2 March, he acknowledged the honor done him by election and asked Morgan to assure the Society that he would "with the utmost alacrity contribute all my very limited abilities & observation admitt of to the valuable purposes of the Institution."[1] He was elected a corresponding member of the American Society on 26 February 1768, so that, as the American Society absorbed the Medical Society on 4 November 1768, he had a double claim to membership when the American Society united with the American Philosophical Society in 1769. Though his professional interests remained reasonably keen until the outbreak of the Revolution, he lived too far from Philadelphia ever to attend a meeting, and only once did he send a formal communication.

Hugh Mercer was born on 16 January 1726, the third of the five children of the Reverend William Mercer, minister of Pitsligo, Aberdeenshire, and Anne, his wife, who was the daughter of Andrew Monro, sheriff-clerk of Elgin.[2] In 1740 he entered Marischal College, Aberdeen, where his father had gone, and was graduated in arts in 1744.[3] He must then have read medicine, for in the following year or early in 1746 he joined the army of Prince Charles as an assistant surgeon. Mer-

---

[26] Isaac Heston to brother, 19 Sept. 1793, *PMHB*, LXXXVI (1962), 205; Smith, *Letters of Doctor Richard Hill,* 162–63, 371–72.
[27] Hinshaw, *Amer. Quaker Genealogy,* II, 433.

---

[1] Mercer to John Morgan, 16 May 1767, Dreer Coll., Generals of the American Revolution (HSP).
[2] Hew Scott, *Fasti Ecclesiae Scoticanae,* VI (1926), 235.
[3] Peter J. Anderson, comp., *Fasti Academiae Mariscallanae Aberdonensis* (Aberdeen, 1898), II, 315.

HUGH MERCER

By John Trumbull. *Fordham University Library, Charles A. Munn Collection.* Photograph courtesy of Frick Art Reference Library.

cer was at Culloden Moor on 16 April 1746, and, like others who survived that bloody battle, after a period of concealment, he quit Scotland for America in the spring of 1747. Mercer passed through Philadelphia and settled at Conocoheague on the frontiers of the province, near the modern towns of Greencastle and Mercersburg in what is now Franklin County. As nothing is known of his life there during the next seven or eight years, it can only be supposed that he practiced medicine and farmed.[4] The outbreak of war in 1754 offered more exciting opportunities.

In the turmoil following Braddock's defeat at Great Meadows, Mercer volunteered his services, and on 6 March 1756 he was commissioned a captain in the provincial forces.[5] He marched with Colonel John Armstrong to Kittanning,

---

[4] John T. Goolrick, *The Life of General Hugh Mercer* (N.Y. and Washington, 1906) and Joseph M. Waterman, *With Sword and Lancet: The Life of General Hugh Mercer* (Richmond, Va., 1941) contain some useful facts, but they are always uncritical, often inaccurate, and must be used with caution.

[5] 5 *Pa. Arch.,* I, 44.

Mercer was well established in Fredericksburg, owned a house on the main street, operated a ferry two miles from town, and was sufficiently prosperous to be able to buy George Washington's Ferry Farm for about £2000.[18]

Mercer's service in the American Revolution was exclusively military. His first reaction on hearing that the British had seized the powder stores at Williamsburg in April 1775 was to offer to march to the capital at the head of a band of volunteers.[19] In September he was named colonel of the minutemen of Spottsylvania and adjoining counties, the Committee of Safety adding to the appointment a warm acknowledgment of "his publick spirit in sacrificing his private interest to the service of his country."[20] On 10 January 1776 he was chosen colonel of the Third Virginia Regiment. The Continental Congress appointed him a brigadier general on 5 June and ordered him to headquarters at New York at once. During the summer and fall, as commanding officer of the Flying Camp, Mercer was active in the defense of New York, Staten Island, and northern New Jersey.[21] With the fall of Fort Lee, Washington's army withdrew before the British, retreating across the Hackensack, Passaic, and Raritan Rivers in succession. Christmas found them on the west side of the Delaware River.

The short remainder of Mercer's story is well known. He was in the battle of Trenton, where Washington's unexpected descent on the Hessian garrison there reversed the course of the war. On the night of 2–3 January 1777, the army marched to Princeton, where, early in the morning, Mercer's troops encountered a British force under Lieutenant Colonel Charles Mawhood. There was a sharp engagement, Mercer fell, and, refusing to give up his sword, was bayonetted and left for dead. He died of his wounds on 12 January; his mutilated body was taken to Philadelphia, where it was exhibited as evidence of British savagery. He was interred in Christ Church burying ground on 16 January.[22]

By the circumstances of his death Mercer became one of the early heroes of the new republic. Congress voted to erect a monument in his honor at Fredericksburg (they did so at last in 1902); towns and counties were named for him; and in 1784,

---

[18] (Purdie) *Va. Gaz.,* 27 March 1778; Goolrick, *Hugh Mercer,* 38; Freeman, *Washington,* III, 346.
[19] Ibid., 410. In the presence of General Arthur St. Clair, Colonel Clement Biddle, and Dr. Benjamin Rush two days before the battle of Princeton, Mercer declared, "I will never submit to lose my liberty. Sooner than bow my neck to the Yoke, I will cross the mountains, & incorporate my self with the Indians. I will live & die a freeman." This is in Rush's hand on the back of a letter to him from Hugh Mercer, Jr., 25 April 1803. Rush Mss., X, 6 (Lib. Co. Phila. in HSP).
[20] (Purdie) *Va. Gaz.,* 22 Sept. 1775.
[21] Freeman, *Washington,* IV, 147.
[22] Benson J. Lossing, *The Pictorial Field-Book of the Revolution* (2 v., N.Y., 1852), II, 236–37. Dr. Jonathan Potts, who was also at Princeton, reported that British soldiers had robbed Mercer as he lay helpless, "even to taking his cravat from his neck, insulting him all the time." Potts to —, 5 Jan. 1777 (copy), Continental Cong. Papers (film M247, r100, i78, v. 18, p. 121). On the exhibition of the body, see Jacob Mordecai's recollections in *PMHB,* XCVIII (1974), 153.

on motion of Thomas Jefferson, Congress made a small appropriation to educate Mercer's youngest son.[23] In 1840 under the direction of the St. Andrew's Society of Philadelphia, which he had joined in 1757, Mercer's body was reburied in Laurel Hill Cemetery, Philadelphia.[24]

BENJAMIN RUSH (1746–1813)
AMERICAN SOCIETY: 26 FEBRUARY 1768

BENJAMIN RUSH, while still a "student of physick" at Edinburgh University, was elected a member of the American Society on 26 February 1768. Presumably about the same time he was also chosen a member of the Philadelphia Medical Society. Probably he owed both elections to Dr. John Morgan, his teacher in the medical school of the College of Philadelphia, to whom he had confided his youthful professional aspirations. Rush became a member of the American Philosophical Society when that society and the American Society united in 1769. He lost no time in associating himself with the philosophers: on 18 August 1769, only a few days after his return home to Philadelphia, he attended a meeting of the Society.

Born on 4 January 1746 (n.s.) at Byberry, ten miles north of Philadelphia, he was the fourth of seven children of John Rush, a gunsmith and farmer, and Susanna (Hall) Harvey.[1] He was sent to the academy of the Reverend Dr. Samuel Finley, an uncle by marriage, at Nottingham on the Pennsylvania-Maryland border, and then to the College of New Jersey, from which he was graduated in 1760 in the same class with Jonathan Bayard Smith. The following year he was apprenticed to Dr. John Redman of Philadelphia. He attended the first medical lectures at the

---

[23] Goolrick, *Hugh Mercer,* 61, 67; Julian P. Boyd, ed., *The Papers of Thomas Jefferson,* VII, 132; *Jour. Cont. Cong.,* XXVI, 309.

[24] Robert B. Beath, *Historical Sketch of the St. Andrew's Society* (2 v., Phila., 1907), I, 44–47; William B. Reed, *Oration delivered on the occasion of the Reinterment of the Remains of General Hugh Mercer* (Phila., 1840). (Purdie) *Va. Gaz.,* 27 March 1778, carried an advertisement by Mercer's executors of the sale of a portion of his estate, including "a choice collection of books, drugs, surgical instruments, and shop furniture and utensils."

---

[1] The literature on Rush in the last 40 years alone is enormous. One may start with Nathan G. Goodman, *Benjamin Rush, Physician and Citizen, 1746–1813* (Phila., 1934); L. H. Butterfield, ed., *Letters of Benjamin Rush* (Princeton, 1951); George W. Corner, ed., *Autobiography of Benjamin Rush* (Princeton, 1948); Richard H. Shryock, "Medical Reputation of Benjamin Rush: Contrasts over Two Centuries," *Bull. Hist. Med.,* XLV (1971), 507–52: *DAB; DSB.*

BENJAMIN RUSH

By Charles Willson Peale. *Henry Francis du Pont Winterthur Museum. Gift of Mrs. Julia B. Henry.*

College of Philadelphia in 1765, and in 1766 went to Edinburgh to obtain a doctor's degree. There, like many other students, he became an ardent admirer of Professor William Cullen, organizing his fellow students in a petition to their teacher to allow his portrait to be painted so that they might each have a print to carry home.[2] As an alumnus of the College of New Jersey, he employed his notable powers of persuasion to induce the Reverend Dr. John Witherspoon—but more especially Mrs. Witherspoon—to leave Scotland to become president of the institution at Princeton. Rush was graduated in medicine in 1768, offering a dissertation on the digestion of food in the stomach.

In London and Paris, as in Scotland, Rush sought the acquaintance of other physicians, philosophers, and the gentry. He knew Dr. Franklin, of course, was frequently at the house of Dr. Richard Huck, with whom he corresponded thereafter, and one memorable evening at the home of Sir Joshua Reynolds he found himself seated at dinner between Dr. Samuel Johnson and Oliver Goldsmith, whose thrusts and ripostes in conversation he long remembered.[3] In Paris he made the acquaintance of the chemist Augustin Roux of Rouen, whom he later proposed for membership in the American Philosophical Society.

Rush had left America in the aftermath of the Stamp Act crisis; in Britain he revealed himself to be a fervent patriot. Like Charles Thomson and other members of the American Society, he was especially concerned that the American colonies should develop their economies. "Go on in encouraging American-Manufactures," he urged Thomas Bradford on 15 April 1768.

> I have made those Mechanic Arts wch. are connected wth. Chimistry the particular Objects of my study, & am not without Hopes of seeing a China-Manufactory established in Philada: in the Course of a few Years. Yes—we will be revenged of the Mother Country. For my part I am resolved to devote my Head—my Heart & my pen entirely to the service of America, . . .[4]

During his years abroad Rush had not concealed his ambition to be appointed a professor in the newly established medical school of the College of Philadelphia, and he returned home in July of 1769 with warm recommendations from Professor Cullen and Dr. John Fothergill of London as "sensible, diligent, well acquainted with his business, and . . . very well qualified to give lectures on . . . Chemistry."[5] He was accordingly elected professor of that subject on 1 August 1769. He deliv-

---

[2] A. M. Drummond and others to William Cullen, 8 Feb. 1768, Cullen-Thomson Papers (Glasgow Univ. Lib.). I am indebted to Dr. C. Helen Brock of Cambridge, England, for this reference.
[3] Butterfield, *Rush Letters,* II, 632–33.
[4] Rush to Thomas Bradford, 15 April 1768, Misc. Mss. (APS).
[5] William Cullen to John Morgan, 18 Sept. 1768 (copy), Rush Mss., XXIV, 54 (Lib. Co. Phila. in HSP); John Fothergill to ——, 8 Fifth Mo. 1769, Gilbert Coll. of Ms. Letters, II, 141 (Coll. Phys. Phila.).

ered his first course of lectures that fall, and the next year published *A Syllabus of a Course of Lectures on Chemistry.*

Only a few months before his return, the American Philosophical Society had been formed by the union of the American Society and the revived American Philosophical Society, and so Rush became a member of the newly constituted group. He attended its meetings regularly for some years and took an active part in all its work. He was a member of the standing Committee on Natural History and Chemistry. He was elected one of the curators in 1770 and was twice reelected. Within a few weeks the curators proposed to enlarge the Society's museum by asking merchants, army officers, and ship captains to collect and send to Philadelphia any new and curious plants, animals, or fossils they might find. He was elected one of the Society's secretaries in 1773 and served in that office for another three years. He was appointed to the committee to answer questions on American natural history submitted through Dr. Franklin by the Marquis de Condorcet. He was a member of one committee to design a seal for the Society in 1770, and on another with Dr. Morgan and Pierre E. Du Simitière in 1774 to draft a certificate of membership. He read several papers to the Society on medical and chemical subjects—thorn apple, laudanum, sleep and dreams, the effects of cold, and the mineral waters of Philadelphia, Bristol, and Abington—and in 1774 was invited to deliver the annual oration in the place of Charles Thomson, who had fallen ill. The address, entitled *An Enquiry into the Natural History of Medicine among the Indians of North-America* (Philadelphia, [1774]), was dedicated to Dr. Huck in the hope, which proved vain, that this pamphlet, in addition to his communications on medical subjects[6] and Huck's influence, would win him election to the Royal Society.

Many facts in the *Enquiry,* Rush acknowledged, came from the French writers Lahontan and Charlevoix, but most of the material was provided by persons who had travelled and lived in the Indian country, especially Edward Hand, a military surgeon who had spent several years at Fort Pitt, where he had known and dealt with Indians and "directed his enquiries into their customs, diseases, and remedies. . . ." While he rejected the Indians' medicine as inferior to that of the Europeans, Rush at the same time deplored the degeneracy, luxury, and indulgence of modern times that brought diseases upon Europeans that the simpler diet and manners of their ancestors might have spared them. Health, Rush asserted, was not incompatible with civilization. He concluded with reflections on the astonishing growth of Pennsylvania in less than a century since its founding and with a compliment to the American Philosophical Society on its remarkable success in the half dozen years since its organization. Then, taking up a theme to which he was to recur repeatedly in his writings, Rush declared:

---

[6] (London) *Medical Observations and Inquiries,* IV (1771), 367–70; V (1776), 32–40.

> It reflects equal honor upon our society and the honourable assembly of our province, to acknowledge, that we have always found the latter willing to encourage by their patronage, and reward by their liberality, all our schemes for promoting useful knowledge. What may we not expect from this harmony between the sciences and government! Methinks I can see canals cut—rivers once impassable rendered navigable—bridges erected—and roads improved, to facilitate the exportation of grain.—I see the banks of our rivers vieing in fruitfulness with the banks of the rivers of Egypt.—I behold our farmers, nobles—our merchants princes.—But I forbear—Imagination cannot swell with the subject.
>
> I beg leave to conclude, by deriving an argument from our connection with the legislature, to remind my auditors of the duty they owe to the society. Patriotism and literature are here connected together; and a man cannot neglect the one, without being destitute of the other. Nature and our ancestors have completed their work among us; and have left us nothing to do, but to enlarge and perpetuate our own happiness.

The various comments on this publication, both complimentary and critical, added to the reputations of both its author and the Society under whose auspices he spoke.[7] For this and other publications Rush was elected a corresponding member of the Virginia Society for the Promotion of Useful Knowledge in 1774.[8] His private practice grew steadily, as did his reputation. Students came to Philadelphia to study with him. In 1776 he was charging 100 guineas to take an apprentice and had to admit that "contrary to my wishes I find I am growing rich." He began to speak out on public issues and was recognized as a public-spirited citizen and advocate. He wrote a tract against slave-keeping in 1773, and was one of the first members of the Pennsylvania Society for the Abolition of Slavery when it was founded the next year. He became a contributor to the Pennsylvania Hospital in 1770, subscribed £2 to the Silk Society in the same year, and in 1772 gave the College of Philadelphia £10. In 1774 he was one of the physicians of the Society for Inoculating the Poor. "The benefit of this institution to the community is great," he told Dr. Andrew Duncan of Edinburgh, "and the expence and trouble very trifling."[9] On 16 March 1775 he addressed subscribers to the newly founded Society for the Promotion of Manufactures on the necessity and benefits of manufacturing, particularly as a means of strengthening and defending the liberties of America.

> By establishing manufactories among us, we erect an additional barrier against the encroachments of tyranny. A people who are *entirely* dependent upon foreigners for food or clothes, must always be subject to them. I need not detain you in setting forth the

---

[7] (Edinburgh) *Medical and Philosophical Commentaries,* III, pt. 1 (1775), 262–72.
[8] (Purdie & Dixon) *Va. Gaz.,* 16 June 1774. Benjamin Franklin, David Rittenhouse, Provost William Smith, and Dr. John Morgan of Philadelphia, and Dr. Williams Smibert of Boston, all members of APS, were elected to the Virginia Society at the same time as Rush.
[9] *Pa. Packet,* 7 Feb. 1774; (Edinburgh) *Med. and Philos. Commentaries,* III, pt. 1 (1775), 102–05.

misery of holding property, liberty and life, upon the precarious will of our fellow subjects in Britain.[10]

Rush had resolved not to marry before he could support a wife and family; now he was able to do that; and accordingly on 11 January 1776 he married Julia Stockton, daughter of the lawyer Richard Stockton of Princeton, New Jersey. They had 13 children, of whom James became a physician and Richard had a distinguished career in public service as attorney general, secretary of state, secretary of the treasury and United States minister to England and France.

With the onset of war in 1775 Rush was appointed to a committee with Owen Biddle, George Clymer, Lambert Cadwalader, John Allen, and others to establish and superintend a factory for making saltpetre, and to this end he published directions for its manufacture that included excerpts from writings by Franklin and "M. Roux of the academy of Rouen."[11] He was appointed a surgeon to the Pennsylvania Navy Board, and was also called on to examine candidates for appointment as battalion surgeons in the army.[12] He represented Philadelphia in the Provincial Congress, which met on 18 June 1776; and on 20 July, as he told General Charles Lee, feigning reluctance, he was "thrust into Congress."[13] He had not been a member when the Declaration of Independence was voted, but signed the document shortly afterwards and so enjoys lasting fame as "a Signer." He was chairman of the Medical Committee of Congress, charged, among other things, with procuring medicines and other necessary supplies for the army. He served on several minor committees, such as one to inquire into the quality of the product of powder mills, and another to propose appropriate memorials to General Joseph Warren, who had died at Bunker Hill, and to General Hugh Mercer, mortally wounded at the battle of Princeton. (The committee recommended that monuments be erected at Boston and Fredericksburg, Virginia, respectively, and that one son of each hero be educated at public expense.) In the debate on the Articles of Confederation Rush proclaimed himself a staunch nationalist. "When I entered that door," he declared, "I considered myself a citizen of America." He argued in favor of voting by the numbers of free inhabitants rather than by states because, among other benefits, it would have "one excellent effect, that of inducing the colonies to discourage slavery and to encourage the increase of their free inhabitants."[14] Because he opposed the Revolutionary state government in Pennsylvania and the constitution the radicals had written for it in the fall of 1776, he was not

---

[10] *Pa. Evening Post,* 11, 13 April 1775.
[11] Ibid., 4 July 1775; *Pa. Gaz.,* 14 July 1775.
[12] *Pa. Evening Post,* 11 Jan. 1776; 2 *Pa. Arch.,* III, 708.
[13] Paul H. Smith, ed., *Letters of Delegates to Congress, 1774–1789* (Washington, 1976–), IV, 527.
[14] *Jour. Cont. Cong.,* VI, 1081, 1105.

returned to Congress in February 1777. Strongly opposed to that constitution, in 1779 he signed a public call for its revision.[15]

On 11 April 1777 Rush was elected surgeon-general of the Middle Department of the army, and on 1 July was given the title of physician-general of the Hospital for the Middle Department after Dr. Walter Jones of Virginia declined the post.[16] In this position he witnessed the inefficiency of the medical department and the needless suffering of the sick and wounded. "Hospitals are the sinks of human life in an army," he was to write long afterwards of his observations. "They robbed the United States of more citizens than the sword."[17] In private letters to John Adams he described and deplored the conditions, hoped that Congress would act, became increasingly critical of the Director-General William Shippen, Jr.; and, finally, despairing of seeing any reforms effected, he submitted his resignation on 30 January 1778. It was accepted promptly without discussion or debate.[18]

Meanwhile, Rush was comparing the victories of the northern army under General Horatio Gates at Saratoga with Washington's defeats at Brandywine and Germantown and his withdrawal to Valley Forge. This critical attitude owed something to Rush's reading of history and to a generally republican philosophy that made him suspicious of those who had power and popularity. He listed the reasons why he believed it unlikely that General Washington would—or should—continue as commander-in-chief to the end of the war. One of these was that "he is idolized by the people of America, and is tho't to be absolutely necessary for us to enable us to carry on the war." General Gates, he believed, should supersede Washington as commander-in-chief. These sentiments he communicated in an unsigned letter to Governor Patrick Henry of Virginia, who sent it on to Washington, who recognized the author's handwriting. Any usefulness that Rush might have had in the Revolutionary movement thereafter, or even in the army's medical services, was now at an end, and Rush retired to the home of his father-in-law in Princeton, where, in his depression, he actually thought of giving up medicine to study law. After the British army evacuated Philadelphia in June 1778, however, he returned to that city and the practice of medicine.

The quarrel with Washington cast a cloud over Rush's spirits that never quite lifted, and over his popular reputation that more than two centuries have not entirely dissipated. As to the Medical Department, Rush, in concert with his friend and former teacher, Morgan, who had been removed as director-general of the Hospital and been succeeded by Shippen, pressed charges that brought about Shippen's court-martial and led to his eventual resignation. The bitter Morgan-Shippen-Rush

---

[15] *Pa. Gaz.,* 24 March 1779.
[16] *Jour. Cont. Cong.,* VII, 254; VIII, 518.
[17] Rush, *Medical Inquiries and Observations* (2nd edit., Phila., 1805), I, 276.
[18] *Jour. Cont. Cong.,* X, 101.

feud, whose origins lay as far in the past as the founding of the Medical School, roiled and divided the medical profession in Philadelphia for thirty years, and did not wholly subside until all the principals were dead.

In the years that followed the close of the war Rush conceived or supported dozens of reforms to enhance the character of the new nation. Appreciating the indispensable role of education in the republic, he was a principal founder of Dickinson College in Carlisle, Pennsylvania, in 1783, and solicited his English friends for books for its library. He was a patron of Franklin College in Lancaster, Pennsylvania. He advocated education for women and lectured to the Young Ladies' Academy of Philadelphia. He drafted plans for a state university and for a national system of education. Long opposed to slavery, he served first as secretary, then, after 1803, as president, of the Pennsylvania Abolition Society of 1787; and as one of its representatives he attended the first convention of abolition societies of the United States in Philadelphia on 1 January 1794. In 1791 he wrote a paper on the sugar maple tree and methods of extracting sugar from it, and the next year he helped form the Society for Promoting the Manufacture of Sugar from the Sugar Maple; one of its purposes was to weaken slavery in the southern states and the West Indies by persuading consumers to give up cane sugar for maple. Always a humanitarian, he opposed capital punishment and urged more humane treatment of criminals; he was one of the physicians of the Prison Society in 1787. His paper on "the influence of public punishments upon criminals and upon society" was read to the Society for Political Inquiries, founded in 1787, of which Franklin was president and Rush one of the first members. In another paper he argued that just as there was a War Department, there ought also to be a Peace Department. An advocate of temperance from his early years as a medical practitioner, he wrote against rum, whiskey, and tobacco, and praised the healthful effects of good diet, proper dress, and sufficient exercise. In his commentary on the Grand Federal Procession of 4 July 1788, he ascribed the orderliness of the celebrating crowd to the fact that only "federal drinks," such as beer and cider, were consumed on the occasion. Many of his proposals on these subjects were collected and published as *Essays, Literary, Moral and Philosophical* (Philadelphia, 1798); the book is a veritable catalogue of republican reforms. Rush presented a copy to the Philosophical Society as soon as it was printed.

In his campaigns for reform Rush often had an ally in Dr. John Coakley Lettsom of London. In many ways the successor to Dr. Fothergill as a medical man and humanitarian reformer, Lettsom was also much like Rush, although less impulsive and emotional. The two men corresponded as long as both lived, exchanging books and pamphlets, plants and seeds, and encouraging each other in good works. "To you, after I am gone," Rush wrote his friend in 1788,

> I bequeath a continuance of the war you have begun against them [spirituous liquors]. You move in a great and extensive circle. One word from a London, will spread further

and do more good, than a thousand essays in favour of humanity from a Philadelphia physician.[19]

By the mid-1780s Rush was at the top of his profession. It gave him especial pleasure to have secured the printing of an American edition of his Edinburgh teacher Cullen's *First Lines of the Practice of Physic* in 1781, while Britain and the United States were still at war. "What has physic to do with taxation or independence?" he demanded.[20] He was appointed a physician to the Pennsylvania Hospital in 1783 and four years later was put in charge of the ward for the insane, where, regarding the mental patients as sick rather than "possessed," he introduced principles and practices of humane treatment for which his name is gratefully remembered. The results of his observations and experience were published in 1812 in *Medical Inquiries and Observations upon the Diseases of the Mind*—a work that went into five editions and was not superseded in the United States until 1883. Rush was a founder and consulting physician of the Philadelphia Dispensary for the Medical Relief of the Poor in 1786; in the first eight months of its operation the Dispensary treated 719 patients without charge, and in the twelve-month 1789–90, it treated 1,796.[21] He was vice-president of the Humane Society, established in 1780 to rescue persons from drowning and other sudden and accidental deaths. As a founder of the College of Physicians of Philadelphia in 1787, Rush laid out a program for the institution in an address to the Fellows; and to the first issue of its *Transactions* he contributed a number of medical papers of his own, as well as observations sent to him by his many correspondents in this country and abroad. He published two volumes of *Medical Inquiries and Observations* in 1789, and expanded them to four volumes in 1796; it had five editions in all.

The outbreak of yellow fever in Philadelphia in the late summer of 1793 after a lapse of more than thirty years was a crisis in the life and career of Dr. Rush as well as in the history of the city. Testing his professional knowledge and skill to their limits, the epidemic also displayed him as tireless, stubborn, sympathetic, self-righteous, strident, and heroic. "The conduct of Dr. Rush deserves, that not only the City of Philadelphia, but Humanity at large, should raise a statue of him," Dr. Jean-Georges Zimmerman wrote Lettsom from Hanover soon after the epidemic subsided.[22]

Rush was the first in the city to recognize the fever for what it was when it appeared in Water Street in August. As the disease spread and more and more citizens fell victims to it, a host of questions was asked about its origin and best methods of

---

[19] Thomas J. Pettigrew, *Memoir of the Life and Writings of the late John Coakley Lettsom* (London, 1817), II, 437.
[20] Butterfield, *Rush Letters,* I, 310–11.
[21] Goodman, *Benjamin Rush,* 158.
[22] Pettigrew, *Memoir of Lettsom,* I, Correspondence, 167.

treatment. Although no one was to know the cause of the disease for another century, Rush was firmly of the opinion that the plague was of domestic origin and that therefore quarantine was helpless to prevent it. For obvious reasons this idea was rejected by importers and other merchants, by many civic leaders, and by some physicians as well.

More significant than Rush's view that the fever was of domestic origin, were his convictions about treating it. Believing that fever was caused by an excessive amount of "excitability," Rush held that the normal balance of the body must be restored by depletion, that is to say, by bleeding, purging, and a low diet. "Ten and ten"—ten ounces of blood and ten grains of jalap—was his usual prescription. So confident was Rush of its efficacy that he was ready to bleed away four-fifths of a patient's blood to secure the victim's recovery. Many of Rush's patients survived; many did not; but the doctor firmly ascribed unfortunate outcomes to failure to bleed and purge sufficiently.

But Rush could defend his positions and combat those of his critics only by rhetoric. He kept no systematic record of his cases; he offered no experimental proof; he had only his recollections, his memory of patients, his treatment, and its results. He was passionate, eloquent, indignant, full of human feeling and concern; he wrote with fury and conviction, but it was too much and not enough. He needed incontrovertible facts to support his views and confound his critics; and these he did not have, nor, apparently, did he know how to amass them.

For more than two months Rush labored ceaselessly. He could not relax for as much as an hour, for patients and their friends brought their pleas for attendance and requests for prescriptions even to his dinner table. His house, he wrote, had become a "Lazaretto." He was himself stricken with the fever; three of his five apprentices died. Not all his fellow-physicians agreed with him; former students and colleagues in the faculty of the Medical School pursued a gentler therapy; while the Fellows of the College of Physicians were firmly of the opinion that the disease was imported.

For more than ten weeks the city was in the grip of the pestilence. Thousands fled to the more healthful areas of Germantown, Bucks and Chester counties. Government was virtually suspended; President Washington removed to Germantown; and other officers went home. Even some of the doctors retreated from the city, offering as explanation or excuse that they were only following their patients, who might need them. Mayor Clarkson played a heroic part, as did so many of the citizens, black and white, who cared for the sick in their homes or emergency hospitals, removed the dead from their houses, and buried them in hastily dug graves.

By mid-November the epidemic was over. The citizens returned to their homes and businesses. But the controversy over the origins and treatment of yellow fever continued, and was renewed each time the fever reappeared, as it did several more times during Rush's lifetime. The College of Physicians on 25 November 1793 reported to Governor Mifflin that there was no instance of the disease having originated in the city or any other part of the United States, "but there have been frequent instances of its having been imported." Wearied by his exertions and by the rejection of his ideas by other physicians, journalists, and some of the citizens, Rush had already resigned his fellowship in the College of Physicians. He organized a rival society, the Academy of Medicine, in 1797, but it did not long survive. His belief in the domestic origin of the fever never weakened, however, as he wrote Lettsom in 1806:

> The evils which flow from a belief in the importation of our American pestilence are incalculable. It has perpetuated the disease in our country. It has demoralized our citizens, as far as humanity constitutes moral character. It fosters national prejudice and hostility, and it consigns thousands every year to the grave, who might otherwise have been preserved from it.[23]

The controversy over Rush's treatment of yellow fever was reflected in a falling-off of his practice. He felt himself shunned for both professional and political reasons, and entertained the notion of moving to New York, where friends proposed him for a professorship in the College of Physicians and Surgeons. He was pleased and grateful when his friend President Adams appointed him treasurer of the Mint; the post was essentially a sinecure, paying $1200 a year. But his reputation as a teacher seems to have remained undimmed, and his name drew scores of medical students to Philadelphia every fall. During the decade of the 1780s he had lectured to between 16 and 45 each year. In 1792 the number rose to 119, after 1800 his classes exceeded 100 each season, and in the last four years of his life he lectured to more than 300 annually. During his lifetime he taught more than 3,000. In addition to addressing students in the lecture hall of the Medical School, Rush communicated his views to scores of physicians and patients throughout the country who sought his advice and prescriptions by correspondence; and they all, adopting his doctrines, methods, and treatments, established and spread his name and influence throughout the country for two generations.

In 1803 Rush joined other physicians of Philadelphia in publicly recommending vaccination as "a certain preventive of the small pox." He pronounced himself in accord with Jennerian practices and opinions "in their fullest extent."[24]

In 1779 Rush with a dozen other members called for resumption of the Philosophical Society's meetings, which had been suspended during the British army's occupation of the city in 1777–78; and he gave £5 towards the construction of Philosophical Hall in 1785. He supported the proposal to construct a great air bal-

---

[23] Ibid., III, 200.
[24] Pettigrew, *Memoir of Lettsom,* III, 199.

loon in 1784 and was one of those who received subscriptions for the project. Increasingly engrossed by practice, teaching, and his civic activities, however, Rush's attendance at the Society after the war was less frequent than before; nonetheless the members elected him repeatedly to various offices—a councillor in 1786–94, a vice-president in 1797–1800, and a councillor again from 1806 until his death seven years later. He was on the committee that drafted instructions for André Michaux's projected exploration of the Mississippi and Missouri rivers with Society support in 1793; and in 180l he favored the Society's motion to lend the artist and museum director Charles Willson Peale $500, interest free, so that Peale might complete the reconstruction of the mastodon he had found and exhumed. During these years Rush also submitted several papers as well—on fevers, tetanus, and a cancer cure announced by his former student Dr. Hugh Martin. His 1786 oration entitled *An Inquiry into the Influence of Physical Causes upon the Moral Faculty*— the second annual oration he gave before the Society—was one of the most important philosophical and physiological dissertations of the time. One thousand tickets were printed, and the venerable Franklin himself attended. The essay was reprinted in the nineteenth century (Philadelphia, 1839) at the instance of the English phrenologist George Combe. In one of the last papers he presented to the Society, on 14 July 1797, Rush argued that the color of Negroes was owing to leprosy. Were this a fact, it might have benevolent consequences: if a cure could be found, Rush concluded, and black become white, the argument for enslaving Negroes because of their color would be destroyed and "render the belief of the whole human race being descended from one pair, easy, and universal, and thereby not only add weight to the Christian revelation, but remove a material obstacle to the exercise of that universal benevolence which is inculcated by it."[25]

Rush received many honors and recognitions in this country and Europe. He was elected a Fellow of the Massachusetts Medical Society in 1787, and was the first honorary member of the Medical Society of South Carolina in 1795. He was elected to the American Academy of Arts and Sciences in Boston and to the Royal Swedish Academy of Science, and was a corresponding member of the Royal Society of Arts of London and of the Manchester Literary and Philosophical Society. To the last of these in 1785 and 1786 he sent observations made during his service as physician-general of the Continental Army hospitals and "An Account of the Progress of Population, Agriculture, Manners, and Government in Pensylvania [sic]," which in its picture of "the happiness of a Pensylvanian farmer," was virtually an emigrant aid tract.[26] He received decorations and gifts from European mon-

---

[25] Rush, "Observations intended to favour a supposition that the Black Color (as it is called) of the Negroes is derived from Leprosy," APS *Trans.*, IV (1799), 289–97.
[26] Manchester Literary and Philosophical Society, *Memoirs*, II (1785), 506–09; III (1790), 183–97; Butterfield, *Rush Letters*, I, 400–06.

archs, was made an honorary member of the Royal Humane Society in 1811, and in 1812 received the honorary degree of doctor of laws from Yale College.

From time to time Rush had been called on for an obituary notice or eulogy of a friend or colleague—Christopher Ludwick, "baker-general of the Revolution," Dr. Morgan, and Professor Cullen; now the Society asked him to deliver a memorial eulogy of its president David Rittenhouse, who died on 26 June 1796. Rush took the occasion both to rebuke mildly those who regretted that Rittenhouse during the Revolution had turned aside from philosophical pursuits to fill a political role, and also to give expression once more to his own deeply cherished republican views.

> It belongs to monarchies, to limit the business of government to a priviledged order of men, and it is from the remains of a monarchical spirit in our country, that we complain when clergymen, physicians, philosophers and mechanics, take an active part in civil affairs. The obligations of patriotism are as universal and binding, as those of justice and benevolence, and the virtuous propensities of the human heart are as much resisted by every individual who neglects the business of his country, as they are by the extinction of the domestic affections in a cell. Man was made for a republic, and a republic was made for man, . . . [27]

Rush died at his house in Philadelphia on 19 April 1813 after a short illness, and his body was laid in Christ Church burying ground. His son, Dr. James Rush, undertook to continue his father's lectures on the Institutes and Practice of Medicine, but attendance quickly dwindled away and he gave them up after four years, ascribing the failure to "the opposition of the University . . . and the aristocratic tyranny around it," as well as to their content.[28] Julia Rush remained a widow for thirty-five years, and died in 1848 at the age of 89.

---

[27] Rush, *Eulogium intended to perpetuate the Memory of David Rittenhouse* (Phila., [1796]), 35–36.
[28] James Wallace to Rush, 18 Nov. 1811, Rush Mss., XIX, 20 (Lib. Co. Phila. in HSP); card of admission to "Lectures on the Institutes and Practice of Medicine, by the late Dr. Benjamin Rush, read by his son Dr. James Rush" (Lib. Co. Phila.).

OSWELL EVE (c.1723–1793)

AMERICAN SOCIETY: 26 FEBRUARY 1768

OSWELL EVE, mariner and ship chandler, was elected a member of the American Society on 26 February 1768 and attended its meeting on 1 April, when he signed the By-laws. Meanwhile, he had been elected to the American Philosophical Society on 22 March 1768. There is no record that he declined this election; in any case he never attended a meeting of either society thereafter or of the united Society after 1769. The reason is that he left Philadelphia only weeks after his elections, and did not return for five years.

For more than twenty years Eve had been a ship captain sailing from Philadelphia to Lisbon and to Jamaica and other West Indian ports; of many of the vessels he was a part owner. He was married in Christ Church, Philadelphia, on 2 June 1744 to Anne Moore; in the ensuing years the couple produced 13 children, of whom seven, including the first, died in infancy.[1] The family appears to have lived comfortably; they had "a very pleasant seat" in the Northern Liberties; and Eve sent at least one of his sons to the Academy of Philadelphia.[2]

Eve played a part in some of the city's institutions. In 1756 he held a commission as lieutenant in the Associators of that year. He was a member of the Fishing Company of Fort St. David. He signed the Non-Importation Agreement in 1765. The next year he was elected one of the Port Wardens, who named him and Abel James to have a seal cut and a certificate engraved for their use. (They employed Henry Dawkins for the purpose.) Eve was also a founding member of the Society for the Relief of Poor and Distressed Masters of Ships, their Widows and Children in 1765, but was dropped the next year for non-payment of dues.[3] He was one of those who recommended to the public John Gordon's *Mathematical Traverse Table, &c.*, which was published at Philadelphia in 1758.

For several years before his election to the American Society Captain Eve faced mounting financial problems. Now in the spring of 1768, leaving his wife and younger children but taking his sons Oswell and John with him, he fled to Central America, where he established himself on Sand Key north of St. George's Cay in the Bay of Honduras. There he set about to recoup his fortune.[4] In Philadelphia his daughter Sarah kept a journal account of the family's retired life to show her fa-

---

[1] "Extracts from the Journal of Miss Sarah Eve," *PMHB*, V (1891), 19; 2 *Pa. Arch.*, II, 330.
[2] Montgomery, *University of Pennsylvania*, 537; *Pa. Evening Post*, 5 Aug. 1775.
[3] 2 *Pa. Arch.*, II, 524; 8 *Pa. Arch.*, VIII, 7004; *History of the Schuylkill Fishing Company* (Phila., 1889), 401–02; William Bell Clark, "The Sea Captains Club," *PMHB*, LXXXI (1957), 44; Port Wardens, Minutes, 13, 15, 30 May 1766 (transcript, Free Lib. Phila.).
[4] Charles Biddle, *Autobiography* (Phila., 1883), 44.

ther. A cloud appearing one morning when the men were cutting hay reminded her poignantly of his career: "the sun rose clear, a cloudy noon, but how it will set, lies concealed in the bosom of futurity. May it, Oh! my God, when late it sets, shine more beamingly bright than when it first arose."[5]

Sarah's wishes seemed about to be fulfilled soon afterwards. With "returning hope of independency," Captain Eve came home to Philadelphia at the end of 1773 and opened a ship chandler's shop. Young Oswell was now a master, with a ship of his own. And Sarah was engaged to that rising young physician Benjamin Rush; the date for the wedding had been set when Sarah became ill and died.[6] With the outbreak of hostilities in 1775, Eve leased his house in the Northern Liberties and moved to a 200–acre farm in Oxford Township.[7] He was undertaking a new career of powder-maker.

The Frankford Powder Mill, as Eve called his manufactory, supplied gunpowder to the Pennsylvania Committee of Safety, and on 11 January 1776 the Continental Congress contracted with him to manufacture into powder all the saltpetre delivered to it.[8] In an appeal to Congress on 22 March 1776, Eve claimed to have "spent much time in inventing Machines and making experiments for bringing that Branch of Business to Perfection." He further represented,

> That by employing his whole time and study therein he has Invented and Carried into Execution Works for Graining Powder and for other parts of Manufacturing the same which are put in Motion by Water (which is not done in any part of Europe) and by which not only many Hands may be saved . . . but that it can be completed with much more Expedition and Safety than in any other Mill.
>
> Also that he has by different Experiments improved the refining of Salt petre and Sulphur and has brought the whole to perfection and is now making upwards of Twenty-Two Hundred Weight of Powder pr Week.

For these reasons, and because so many persons—including Paul Revere—came to the Frankford Mill to inspect and copy his improvements, Eve asked Congress for a reward.[9] His estimate of the mill's production was not exaggerated; by April 1777 he had delivered 25,000 lbs. of powder to the State.[10]

---

[5] Sarah Eve, "Extracts from the Journal," loc. cit., 193.
[6] Ibid., 19; 5 *Pa. Arch.,* I, 408.
[7] *Pa. Evening Post,* 5 Aug. 1775.
[8] *Col. Recs. Pa.,* X, 301, 306, 341, 375, 398, 412, 417, 426, 458, 502, 504; 1 *Pa. Arch.,* IV, 696; *Jour. Cont. Cong.,* V, 425. For a good account of the powder manufacture, with some specific information on Eve, see David L. Salay, "The Production of Gunpowder in Pennsylvania During the American Revolution," *PMHB,* XCIX (1975), 422–42.
[9] Petition of Oswell Eve, 22 March 1776, Papers of the Continental Congress, No. 42, II, f. 378 (microfilm, M247, reel 53, National Archives). Charles Willson Peale, who was also interested at this time in the manufacture of saltpetre and gunpowder, visited and described the Frankford works in 1776. Peale, Diary, 20 Jan. 1776, Peale-Sellers Papers (APS).
[10] [Memorandum on Eve's Manufacture], 25 April 1785, RG 4, Box 3, Accounts—Forfeited Estates (Pa. State Archives); 6 *Pa. Arch.,* XIII, facing 312.

In addition to making powder for the new government Eve put his knowledge of the Delaware River and Bay at the service of both the Province and the Congress; he made surveys of the river from Marcus Hook to Philadelphia and of the inlets north of Cape May.[11] As it turned out, a year or so later he performed similar services for the British.

Why Eve became a Tory is not apparent; but by the summer of 1777 he had come to his decision, for at that time his conduct was exciting suspicion. One Edward Evans testified to it a few years afterwards:

> On Receiving Information of a Brass Hogate, in the Possetion of Oswald Eve, I was Determd to Carry the Same off on the Evacuation of this City [by the Americans]. In Serching for Which, I found a Quantity of Powder. What Powder is this Sais I to Mr. Eve. It is John Nixons Sais Eve. How Came he by Such a Quantity of Powder. It is the States he Acts for. Well then I shall take the Powder a Way. But on Questioning him further Conserning Nixon Leaving the Powder—he Said the Powder Was his One. I Rote to Mr Nixon Concerning the Powder whilst the Enemy was in the City, and on Our Returne Mr Nixon was Sent for By the Board of War, and Cleard the matter up that he had No Powder in Eves hands. The Powder Was Evedantly Deseced [destined?] for the Enamy and as Eves Property Siezed.[12]

Eve joined the British soon after they came to Philadelphia, reconnoitred Mud Island for them, and for their use he constructed a galley of his own design, which a naval officer testified was "ingenious." Upon the evacuation of the city Eve withdrew to New York and thence to the Bahamas.[13]

He was accordingly attainted of treason by proclamation of 21 May 1778, two of his sons were thrown into jail soon afterwards, and his property was confiscated and sold.[14] An inventory of Eve's personal effects at this time listed, in addition to the usual household furnishings and farm implements, "A number of old Books &c." valued at £1 5s.[15] Anne Eve continued to live on the farm, paying rent to the state until 1780, when the place was put up for sale and bought in by her son John. John Eve was unable to make the required payments, however, his request for an extension was denied, and the farm was lost. He remained in possession for several years, however, for in 1782 he advertised that he would work saltpetre into powder

---

[11] 2 *Pa. Arch.,* III, 683; *Col. Recs. Pa.,* X, 412; *Jour. Cont. Cong.,* V, 697.
[12] Edward Evans to John Nicholson, 11 July 1785, RG 4, Box 3. Accounts—Forfeited Estates (Pa. State Archives).
[13] "United Empire Loyalists," Province of Ontario, Bureau of Archives, *Second Report,* 1904, II, 1288–90; American Loyalist Transcripts, XXV, 520–31 (N.Y. Public Lib.).
[14] 3 *Pa. Arch.,* X, 522; Elizabeth Drinker, *Diary* (Elaine F. Crane, ed., Boston, 1991), I, 319, 327; *Pa. Packet,* 3 Sept. 1778.
[15] 6 *Pa. Arch.,* XII, 634–36, 766, 774; "An Account of the vendue sale of Oswell Eve Confiscated household goods and Chattles . . . ," 14 Sept. 1778, RG 4, Box 3, Accounts—Forfeited Estates (Pa. State Archives).

and buy or repair damaged powder at reasonable rates.[16] Anne Eve withdrew to New York, where her husband joined her from the Bahamas.[17]

Upon the declaration of peace, Eve led a number of Loyalists to the Bahamas, where he established a settlement on Cat Island. He appealed to the Loyalist Claims Commission for compensation for his losses, which he calculated at £7062 10s. current or £4237 10s. sterling. Though the petition was supported by Andrew Allen and Joseph Galloway, and the Commission found Eve to be a "Meritorious Loyalist," the claim was disallowed.[18] Eve died in 1793 at the home of his son Joseph on New Providence Island in the Bahamas.

Joseph had never completely lost touch with his dead sister's fiancé, and in 1794 he wrote Rush about "a Machine for the separating the seed from Cotton" which he had invented and which planters from the southern American states urgently wished to copy. He sent a model to Philadelphia with the necessary papers for securing a patent from the United States government; but Eli Whitney had already obtained one on his machine of like purpose.[19]

---

[16] Joseph Eve, Petition to Supreme Executive Council, 10 June 1780; John Eve, Petition to Supreme Executive Council, 29 Sept. 1780, RG 27, Applications for Passes, Box 1 (Pa. State Archives); *Pa. Packet,* 13 June 1780; *Pa. Gaz.,* 27 Feb. 1782.

[17] Eve (or his son Oswell) came to New York from Jamaica in the brig *Nancy,* carrying 14 four-pounders, in the fall of 1780. The vessel was captured, 9 October by the American sloop *Saratoga,* but was retaken by the British before the prize crew could get her to port. William Bell Clark, *The First Saratoga* (Baton Rouge, 1953), 93, 94.

[18] American Loyalist Transcripts, XXXII, 209 (N.Y. Public Lib.); Daniel Coxe to Edmund Physick, 23 Feb. 1789, Penn-Physick Papers, IV, 107 (HSP).

[19] Joseph Eve to Benjamin Rush, 24 Nov. 1794, Rush Corres., XXIII, 39 (Lib. Co. Phila. in HSP).

SAMUEL ELIOT (1739–1820)
AMERICAN SOCIETY (CORRESPONDING MEMBER):
26 FEBRUARY 1768

SAMUEL ELIOT, merchant, was born in Boston on 25 August 1739, the second of five children of Samuel and Elizabeth (Marshall) Eliot.[1] The elder Eliot, printer, bookseller, and publisher of the *American Magazine, and Historical Chronicle,* died in 1745. The family was left very poor, but Mrs. Eliot, a proud, independent, self-reliant woman, kept it together. Young Samuel remembered having run errands in all weathers, in thin clothing, sometimes in ragged shoes; this experience, wrote a cousin years afterwards, "gave rise to a disposition to anxiety, of which he could never divest himself."[2] The lad attended the Boston Latin School, where, under the famous Master John Lovell, he studied Greek, which he read with pleasure throughout his life, and copied into commonplace books selections from Pope, Addison, Shakespeare, Prior, and other poets, and from the *Annual Register* and *Monthly Review.* He was then apprenticed to the merchant Nathaniel Appleton. Because Appleton had little work for him, the indenture was transferred to the firm of Jonathan and John Amory. On reaching his majority in 1760, Eliot was put in charge of the Amorys' retail business; and he rented from them a house and store in Dock Square, where he installed his mother and three unmarried sisters.[3]

During the next few years Eliot was increasingly successful as a merchant. He had a head for trade, and his pleasant manner, tact, and punctuality were additional assets in the retail shop. All the while he continued to read widely, sharing his views on books with his friend Robert Treat Paine. He once wrote Paine in critical appreciation of *Tristram Shandy* and the English translation of Solomon Gessner's *Der Tod Abels*—a work that he judged suffered by comparison "with one of the noblest Efforts of human Genius Paradise lost which it is easy to see Mr. Gessner has read with Advantage."[4] In 1765 Eliot married Elizabeth Barrell, daughter of Joseph Barrell, a wealthy and noteworthy Boston citizen, who lived in a grand style. Her brother William was a prosperous merchant in Philadelphia. The Eliots soon had two children, both of whom died young.

By 1769 Eliot had left the Amorys' firm and was in business on his own. In August of that year he went abroad to establish contacts with English manufacturers, suppliers, and agents. As a visitor in London, he saw Garrick in *Much Ado*

---

[1] Walter Graeme Eliot, *A Sketch of the Eliot Family* (N.Y., 1867); [Mrs. Anna Eliot Ticknor], *Samuel Eliot* (Boston, 1869); William H. Whitmore, "Brief Memoirs and Notices of Prince's Subscribers," *New England Hist. Geneal. Reg.,* XXIII (1869), 338–39.
[2] Ticknor, *Samuel Eliot,* 5.
[3] Ibid., 7–10.
[4] Eliot to Paine, 24 June 1762, Robert Treat Paine Papers (Mass. Hist. Soc.).

SAMUEL ELIOT

By Jane Stuart after Gilbert Stuart. *Harvard University Art Museums.*

About Nothing and other plays, took tea with John Wilkes, and dined one night at Governor Pownall's, where Dr. Franklin was also a guest. In Glasgow, where he visited the High Kirk ("a most dreadful place in every respect"), Eliot was made a freeman of the city. He met Joseph Priestley in Leeds and General Paoli in Boulton's factory in Birmingham, and visited Gainsborough's studio at Bath. "Two days of Bath life were sufficient to tire me out." Of the Arundel Museum in Oxford he wrote with mixed admiration and disbelief that an archaeologist of the University had spent three months deciphering the nearly obliterated inscription on a small piece of marble that was discovered to be the "agreement with workmen for building the Temple of Apollo at Delphos!"[5] Before sailing home in April 1770 Eliot purchased some articles for his friend Paine—Blackstone's *Commentaries,* Hale's *Pleas of the Crown,* and some other law books, maps of England and London ("the best . . . you can find, for size & perspicuity"), "a Good Gun & Bayonet," and, from the mathematical instrument-maker Benjamin Martin, "a Scioptric Ball & Socket in Wood."[6] He heard Colonel Barré, Lord North, and Sir George Savile address the House of Commons, and sent Paine an account of British political attitudes and his own reaction to the repeal of the Townshend Acts:

> . . . I pass my Time in a State of dreadful Suspense, dreadful as it is a Question upon wch my Well Being, if not my Existence depends; you will therefore not wonder at my Solicitude in regard to a Determination. But however casual the final Issue of this Sessions [sic] may be I am fixed in my Resolution to take out no Goods, till I shall see the Way open for their chearful Reception, let the Consequences be as they may to my own private Interest. I think I have not been an Enthusiast in the Cause of Liberty, but I must suppose I should be grossly deficient in my Duty, if I should do any Thing wch had a Tendency to prevent a Settlement of our present Disputes, upon such a Foundation as no future villainous Administration, should have it in their Power to shake.[7]

Eliot returned home without any trading goods, and with a growing dislike of public life. He was glad to have nothing to do with politics, he wrote in 1771. "I had rather go on in a dog-trot, retailing tape and pins, lawns, cambricks, and Irish linens, than be put in any dirty office or post of Government."[8] He was a member of a Boston fire company, founded in 1763 but apparently renamed after 1765 the Anti-Stamp Fire Society, whose members, under the new appellation, may have been as eager to light fires as to drench them. The members sometimes met at his house.[9]

---

[5] Ticknor, *Samuel Eliot,* 24–42. His uncle Rev. Andrew Eliot sent him an introduction to Thomas Hollis, and William Palfrey recommended him to John Wilkes "as a firm friend to that cause in which you are now suffering." 4 Mass. Hist. Soc., *Colls.,* IV, 444; Mass. Hist. Soc., *Proc.,* XLVII (1914), 208.
[6] Paine to Eliot, 12 Jan. 1770 (draft), Robert Treat Paine Papers.
[7] Eliot to Paine, 31 Jan. 1770, ibid.
[8] Ticknor, *Samuel Eliot,* 44.
[9] Mass. Hist. Soc., *Proc.,* VIII (1864–65), 324; Anti-Stamp Fire Society, *Rules and Orders* ([Boston], n.d.). In the copy in the Huntington Library Eliot's name, along with several others, has been added to the printed list of members. His "Place of Abode" is given as Tremont Street.

Eliot's political views at this time, as well as his cultural interests, doubtless were reasons why he was recommended for membership in the American Society. He was nominated on 19 February 1768, and was elected the next week; but there is no evidence that he corresponded with the Society or took any interest in its work. On the other hand, in addition to his brother-in-law, Eliot had good friends in Philadelphia, among the dearest the Quaker merchant Thomas Mifflin and his wife. The Mifflins stayed at the Eliots' house when they visited Boston in 1773, tarrying longer than expected while John Singleton Copley painted their portrait. Of the artist's work Eliot assured his brother-in-law that "this Town will have the Honour of furnishing Phila. with one of the best Pictures it has to boast." [10]

Though he defended the "rights of America," Eliot, as he had confessed to Paine, was not "an Enthusiast in the Cause of Liberty." His moderation appeared clearly in the public part he took, against his inclination, in the controversies developing in Boston after the Tea Party and the announcement of the Port Bill. On 13 May 1774 the Town Meeting expressed itself as of the opinion that a joint resolution by the colonies interdicting trade with Great Britain until the Port Bill was repealed would "prove the salvation of North America and her liberties." Taking this vote for their authority, the Committee of Correspondence prepared and circulated among neighboring towns and colonies a Solemn League and Covenant, by which the signers should bind themselves not to trade with Britain and also not to consume any goods of British origin whenever imported, to have no commerce or dealing with those who continued to import or purchase British goods, and to expose as "contumacious" enemies of their country all who refused to sign the pledge.[11]

This was farther and faster than many in Boston were prepared to go; and at the Town Meeting of 27–28 June a motion was made to censure the Committee and disavow their action. Samuel Adams, Josiah Quincy, Jr., Dr. Joseph Warren, and others supported the Committee; Eliot was among those who opposed. His brother-in-law John Andrews described him on the occasion:

> Our brother Eliot display'd his eloquence in a long speech upon the subject, deliver'd in so masterly a stile and manner as to gain the plaudits of perhaps the largest assembly ever conven'd here, by an almost universal clap: wherein he deliver'd his sentiments with that freedom and manliness peculiar only to himself. He related his own particular case, as expecting a large quantity of goods which, should they arrive, he can't possibly qualify himself to sell according to the tenor of the Covenant, having countermanded 'em no other ways than to have 'em shipped, provided your place [Philadelphia], with New York, Rhode Island, &c., should have their goods as usual; and from the determination of those places, he has all the reason in the world to expect them.[12]

---

[10] Eliot to William Barrell, 24 Aug. 1773 (photostat from Lib. Cong.), Society Coll. (HSP).
[11] Peter Force, ed., *American Archives* (Washington, 1837–53), 4th ser., I, 331, 397–98, 489–91.
[12] John Andrews to [William Barrell], 22 July 1774, Mass. Hist. Soc., *Proc.,* VIII (1864–65), 331. See also the diary of John Rowe, 27 June 1774, 2 Mass. Hist. Soc., *Colls.,* X, 86.

The motion did not pass, and on 29 June the minority issued a public Protest against the Solemn League and Covenant and the Committee's "clandestine" conduct in the affair. The authors felt as Eliot did, that the Covenant required "the surrender of liberty, the sacrifice of property, and everything justly dear to man." Though Eliot did not sign the Protest—in fact he was not opposed in principle to either non-importation or non-consumption—he was identified with those who were. His Philadelphia brother-in-law Barrell and his friend Thomas Mifflin both criticized his conduct and wondered whether he had deserted the Whigs. Explaining his decision to the latter, he assured him,

> I am disposed to engage in any measure calculated to relieve us from the subjugation which has taken place, and which is further endeavored against us. I will exert my every power to establish the Liberty and Constitution of my Country, referring to my former conduct for the reality, and proof, of my present professions.[13]

Within a week of the battles of Lexington and Concord and the investment of Boston by the New England militia, Eliot was sure the city was no longer "by any means" safe, and determined to quit it, possibly even for England. He stored his goods, installed a reliable caretaker, and, with his wife, sister-in-law, and some others, took a vessel for Halifax. They disembarked instead at Marblehead, and after a few days' "wandering" settled at Haverhill. There they were "elegantly & commodiously Lodged" in the house of John White, and there the Eliots' third child Frances was born. Eliot bought a horse and chaise to drive about the country in; but he was restless, for he was not used to having no work to do, and he had no books. Two days after the evacuation of Boston on 17 March 1776 Eliot returned to the city, but threat of a smallpox epidemic kept him from bringing his wife and infant daughter to town until November. Meanwhile, his store of goods having come through the occupation intact, he resumed trading.[14] The profits were the foundation of what became probably the greatest fortune in Boston.

Eliot made a brief return to public life during the Revolution. In 1780 he was chosen by the Town Meeting one of four persons to draft instructions to the town's delegates to the convention ratifying the new state constitution. In ringing terms the committee directed the delegates to vote to strengthen the provisions: freedom of speech ("nothing spoken with design to give information of the State to the Public should be ever subject to the smallest restraint"), rotation in office ("Persons long in Office are apt to lose that sence of Dependance upon the People, which is

---

[13] Ticknor, *Samuel Eliot*, 56–57, 59–60; William Barrell to Eliot, 27 July, 24 Oct. 1774 (drafts), Andrews-Eliot Papers (Mass. Hist. Soc.).
[14] 2 Mass. Hist. Soc., *Colls.*, X, 86; John Andrews to [William Barrell], 24 April, 6 May, 1 June 1775, Mass. Hist. Soc., *Proc.*, VIII (1864–65), 405–07, 409; John Eliot to Jeremy Belknap, 26 May 1775, 6 Mass. Hist. Soc., *Colls.*, IV (Belknap Papers, III), 90; Eliot to William Barrell, 24 July 1775, Andrews-Eliot Papers; Eliot to Paine, 25 July 1775, 2 June 1776, Robert Treat Paine Papers.

essential to keep them within the Line of duty to the Publick"), and the right to habeas corpus (which should be suspended only in time of war, invasion, or rebellion—not on "urgent and pressing occasions," the latter term "being too indefinite and giving scope to the most powerfull Engine of Despotism, and Slavery").[15]

Mrs. Eliot died on 24 May 1783 after a long illness with dropsy. In July Eliot made another voyage to England to open and reestablish trading connections.[16] For his brother-in-law Jeremy Belknap, who was completing the first volume of his *History of New Hampshire,* he tried—unsuccessfully, as it proved—to find a London publisher. Through Belknap Eliot became acquainted with Ebenezer Hazard, who was compiling his *Historical Collections.*[17] "He is a merchant who thoroughly understands business," Belknap assured Hazard,

> and has large connexions in England, where he was about twelve years ago. He is a man of good sense, quick perception, high sensibility, pretty largely acquainted with modern authors, among whom Dr. Johnson is a great favourite. He is a person of strict integrity, has acquired a pretty considerable fortune entirely by his own industry; but these late times have given a severe check to his pursuits, as he could never give into the arts of peddling, speculation, or monopoly. . . . He is a bitter enemy to all quackery in religion or politics, and zealously attached to the West Church, of which he is a member, being initiated by the late Dr. Mayhew.[18]

Soon after his return to Boston Eliot purchased in 1785 John Amory's large dwelling house at Beacon and Tremont Streets; and the next year, after a glimpse of her in his shop, he decided he wanted to marry Catherine Atkins, daughter of Dudley Atkins of Newburyport. She was 28 at the time, and assessed her suitor realistically, noting in his favor "that his apprentices love him and apply to him as a father; his man-servant has lived with him five years, his maid-servant [since] some time before his wife's death, and he has no thought of parting with either."[19] They were married on 14 May 1786, and had seven children. The Eliots built a greenhouse and imported English roots, seeds, and bulbs; they laid out a garden, whose annual display of hyacinths, roses, and tulips brought visitors from a distance. The Eliots entertained extensively; as the housekeeper put it, it was always "all but everybody—company forever—every English man that came to town." It was Eliot's custom after 1790 to give annually one dinner, in the best style possible, for

---

[15] *Boston Town Records, 1778 to 1783* (Boston, 1895), 132–34; John Eliot to Jeremy Belknap, 23 May 1780, Belknap Papers, III (6 Mass. Hist. Soc., *Colls.,* IV), 189; Samuel E. Morison, "The Struggle over the Adoption of the Constitution of Massachusetts, 1780," Mass. Hist. Soc., *Proc.,* L (1916–17), 395.

[16] Ticknor, *Samuel Eliot,* 102.

[17] 5 Mass. Hist. Soc., *Colls.,* II, 199, 214–15, 246, 264–66, 272, 335, 355.

[18] Ibid., 222–23.

[19] Ticknor, *Samuel Eliot,* 129.

the governor and lieutenant governor of the year; and another for the judges of the Supreme Court.[20] Gilbert Stuart painted his portrait and Mrs. Eliot's.

In 1798 Eliot subscribed $4000 towards the building of the 28-gun frigate *Boston* for the United States Navy.[21] In the same year he was elected president of the Massachusetts Bank, holding the post until December 1803, when he resigned. Like his fellow-directors, Eliot was cautious and conservative, and under his direction the bank's income steadily increased.[22] He was methodical in his habits. Every day almost until his death, Eliot visited his countinghouse. He rose late, opened the day with prayer, breakfasted on a bowl of milk and two or three pieces of toast, while he walked about inspecting his books and flowers. After dinner he often retired to the library to read.[23]

Though a charitable man, Eliot disliked to have his philanthropies made public, rarely signed a public subscription, and would rebuff a request for a gift if made in the presence of others; but would send a coin or bill by private messenger an hour later. Once, on what seems an impulse, he paid the charges of all those confined for debt in the Leverett Street jail.[24] Because of this wish for anonymity, few of Eliot's charitable acts became known. His best known benefaction, made through his good friend John Lowell, was revealed only after his death; it was a gift of $20,000 to Harvard College in April 1814 to establish a professorship of Greek. The act appears to have been a memorial to his son Charles, who, having graduated from Harvard in 1809 and studied for the ministry, was about to be called to a church when he contracted tuberculosis and died in the summer of 1813.[25] On the occasion of his next son Samuel's graduation in 1815 Mr. Eliot gave a splendid dinner, to which 500 were invited; it was said to have cost him $2500.[26]

When Joseph Pope, an instrument-maker of Boston, built an orrery in 1787, friends of Harvard College determined to buy it. Private gifts proving insufficient, they asked the Legislature for authority to conduct a public lottery. This succeeded, and in March 1789 the managers, of whom Eliot was one, had the satisfaction of seeing the instrument installed at the College.[27] Eliot was elected a member of the Massachusetts Historical Society in 1804 (he gave the institution $50 in 1813) and of the American Academy of Arts and Sciences in 1806. He was also a member of

---

[20] Ibid., 136, 141.
[21] Samuel A. Drake, *Old Landmarks and Historic Personages of Boston* (Boston, 1900), 196.
[22] N.S.B. Gras, *The Massachusetts First National Bank of Boston, 1784–1934* (Cambridge, 1937), 76, 374, 530, 531, 541, 546.
[23] Ticknor, *Samuel Eliot,* 165ff.
[24] Ibid., 145–48.
[25] Josiah Quincy, *The History of Harvard University* (Cambridge, 1840), II, 312–13.
[26] John Pierce, Journal, 30 Aug. 1815, 2 Mass. Hist. Soc., *Proc.,* V (1889–90), 181.
[27] David P. Wheatland, *The Apparatus of Science at Harvard, 1765–1800* (Cambridge, 1968), 57–59; Justin Winsor, *Memorial History of Boston* (Boston, 1883), IV, 501–02.

the Humane Society of Massachusetts. He had expressed a strong opposition to slavery at least as early as 1767.[28]

In his latter years Eliot's eyes grew cataracts; he submitted at last to having them removed by Dr. Nathan Smith of Dartmouth Medical College, but the operation was not permanently successful. He died in Boston on 18 January 1820, and was laid in the Granary Burying Ground. From his fortune, estimated at $1,200,000 and more, he provided amply for his widow, children, and other members of his family. One of his sons, Samuel Atkins, became treasurer of Harvard College and mayor of Boston, and was the father of Charles William Eliot.

JAMES ALEXANDER (?–1778)
AMERICAN SOCIETY: 4 MARCH 1768

JAMES ALEXANDER, gardener on Thomas Penn's country place Springettsbury, near Philadelphia,[1] who also had his own business as a seedsman competing with John Bartram, was elected to the American Society on 4 March 1768. Having been notified of this fact by Moses Bartram, he appeared at the next week's meeting, was "duly qualifyed, signed the Rules & took his place." He was a regular attendant thereafter at meetings of the Society and of its successor. On 18 March he showed "Leaves of several plants Anatomised; which he had prepared by soaking them in Water 'til the Skin of the Leaf is a little rotted, when it peels off & the paranchyma may easily be washed out"; and the following week he presented a piece of Chester County asbestos and some leaves of the cassina plant of Carolina, "which appears to be the same with the Labradore Tea." In the American Philosophical Society in 1769 he was a member of three standing committees—Geography, Mathematics, Natural Philosophy and Astronomy; Natural History and Chemistry; and Husbandry and American Improvements—which among them pretty well covered the spectrum of science. He was named a member of the committee to observe the Transit of Venus, and to a committee to consider what improvements in agricul-

---

[28] Eliot to Robert Treat Paine, 26 Feb. 1767, Robert Treat Paine Papers.

[1] He has been called the first professional gardener in America of whom there is record, but William Penn had a Scots gardener at Pennsbury before 1687. Carl and Jessica Bridenbaugh, *Rebels and Gentlemen* (N.Y., 1942), 219–20; *PMHB,* LXXXVI (1962), 407.

ture were best adapted to Pennsylvania In 1772 he was elected a curator of the Society and was reelected the next year.

His name and church membership—Presbyterian—suggest that he was a Scot, his spelling and handwriting that his formal education was meager, and that is about all that is known or appears about his background. He was in Philadelphia before 1735. Thomas Penn, who came to America in 1732, employed Alexander to lay out the gardens, lawns, and walks of Springettsbury, which was situated on a splendid height overlooking both the Schuylkill River and the town.[2] After Penn returned home in 1741 Alexander remained in charge of Springettsbury, providing his employer with American fruits and nuts and American trees, shrubs, plants and seeds. Penn ordered magnolias, azaleas, laurel, and rhododendron, often for planting at Stoke Park, sometimes for his "planting" friends the Earls of Coventry and Litchfield, and he forwarded one assortment from his gardener as a gift to the King.[3] "Fill the Box," Alexander was directed, "with anything that is beautiful, and that has not been so commonly sent." In "the pretty bricked Green House," that Daniel Fisher thought surpassed anything of the kind that he had seen in America,[4] Alexander cultivated oranges, lemons, citron and limes. Temperatures in the hot house were recorded on "a curious thermometer of spirits and mercury." Alexander grew a particularly luscious grape in the Springettsbury vineyard; whether it was a native product or a hybrid opinions varied in the eighteenth century as they do today; but it is still known as "Alexander's grape."[5] Such a showplace inevitably attracted visitors. Ezra Stiles described his visit with Joseph and William Shippen, when, after "passing a long spacious walk, set on each side with trees, on the summit of a gradual ascent," they viewed the Proprietor's house, a modest brick one, "& walkt in the gardens, where besides the beautiful walk, ornamented with evergreens, we saw fruit trees with plenty of fruit, some green, some ripe, & some in the blossom on the same trees. . . . Spruce hedges cut into beautiful figures, &c., all forming the most agreeable variety, & even regular confusion & disorder." The whole scene, Stiles concluded, was "most happily accommodated for solitude and rural contemplation."[6] Apparently Stiles and his friends did not meet Alexander; those who did were sometimes treated to a demonstration of his orrery or allowed to peer through his solar microscope, which, John Smith reported, "magnified

---

[2] Watson, *Annals*, II, 478–79; III, 400. Alexander was in Penn's employ before 1742, when he submitted a bill to the Proprietors, 19 Feb. 1741/2. Penn Accounts, Large Folio, I, 45 (HSP).
[3] Alexander to Thomas Penn, 20 Nov. 1755, Penn Mss., Official Corres., VII, 159; Penn to Alexander, 1 July 1755, Penn Corres., IV, 126; same to same, 7 July 1757, 12 April 1759, 6 May 1761, 13 July 1764, 12 Aug. 1766, 26 July 1768, Penn Letter Book, XI, 1, 21, 30, 43, 49, 282 (HSP).
[4] Daniel Fisher, "Extracts from the Diary," *PMHB*, XVII (1893), 267–68.
[5] William Bartram, "Account of the . . . Varieties of the Vine of North America," *Medical Repository*, 2nd hexade, I (1804), 23; L. H. Bailey, *Sketch of the Evolution of our Native Fruits* (N.Y., 1898), 43.
[6] *PMHB*, XVI (1892), 374.

PETER HARRISON

By Louis Sands after Nathaniel Smibert. *Redwood Library and Athenaeum, Newport, R.I.*

PETER HARRISON (1716–1775)
AMERICAN SOCIETY (CORRESPONDING MEMBER):
1 APRIL 1768

PETER HARRISON, Collector of H. M. Customs at New Haven, Connecticut, and architect of several public buildings of distinction in Rhode Island and Massachusetts, was elected a corresponding member of the American Society on the same day as his brother Joseph; and, like Joseph, he never attended a meeting of the Society and no record survives to show that he ever corresponded with it.

Born on 16 June 1716, he was the fourth and youngest child of Thomas and Elizabeth (Dennyson) Harrison, Yorkshire Quakers of respectable lineage and status.[1] As a boy Peter often visited the home of Peter Acklam at Hornell, as well as Wyeston Hall, the house near Bawtry of a family friend and patron, Jonathan Acklam, High Sheriff of Nottinghamshire. But Thomas Harrison was not rich, and Peter was put out to learn the trade of ship-builder in the seaport town of Hull. He made at least one voyage from that place with his brother Joseph, with whom he was closely associated throughout his life; and in 1739 the brothers came to Newport, Rhode Island, where they quickly found employment with the merchant John Banister. By this time, or soon afterwards, Peter Harrison had mastered the principles of cartography, surveying, and drafting, as well as becoming skilled in wood-carving. "He was a lad that engaged my fancy," Banister wrote later, "and I took Notice of him."

Harrison soon had a ship of his own and made several voyages to Boston, Charleston, Nova Scotia, and England. In 1742 he drew "A Plan of the Harbour of St. Augustine and the Adjacent Parts of Florida," and on another voyage he produced a plan of the harbor and fortress of Louisbourg, which proved useful to the colonial forces that captured that famous bastion in 1745. On these voyages Harrison not only acquired the reputation of "an Ingeneous young commander" but began to accumulate wealth and property of his own. On several visits to England he purchased architectural works—Campbell's *Vitruvius Britannicus,* William Kent's *Designs of Inigo Jones,* Hoppus' *Palladio,* James Gibbs' *Book of Architecture,* and *Rules for Drawing the several Parts of Architecture.* Returning to Newport from England in 1745, he was asked to draw a plan for Fort George and a chart of Newport harbor; for the purpose he used *The New Method of Fortification, as practised by Monsieur Vauban.*

---

[1] This sketch rests almost entirely on Carl Bridenbaugh, *Peter Harrison, First American Architect* (Chapel Hill, 1949) and Bridenbaugh, "Peter Harrison, Addendum," *Jour. Soc. Architectural Historians,* XVIII (1959), 158–59. See also *Macmillan Encyclopedia of Architects* (N.Y., 1982), 321–23, and *DAB.*

---

able to oversee his farm, for in 1765–66 he had a serious illness and was often in

[3] *DAB.*
[4] Ibid.

Ambitious, well-spoken, personable, attractive in form and manner, a Quaker no longer, the prospering young captain aspired to be a gentleman of the kind he had known in England and at Wyeston Hall. An important step towards achieving this rank was taken in 1746 when he married Elizabeth, daughter of Edward and Arabella (Williams) Pelham, an heiress worth £20,000 sterling, not to mention land and personal property. Of necessity and to evade the disapproval of Elizabeth's

ill health thereafter. In New Haven, where he endeavored strictly to enforce the laws against smuggling, Harrison found the atmosphere increasingly uncongenial and ultimately hostile. His brother's unpopularity, arising from his seizure at Boston on 10 June 1768 of John Hancock's sloop *Liberty* on a charge of smuggling, recoiled on Peter. In addition, he became embroiled in disputes of his own, narrowly avoiding a conflict with the local people over writs of assistance. Revenue from customs duties and his own income fell; he suffered insult and abuse from the Sons of Liberty; and the deaths of a daughter and a favored son Thomas, whom he was encouraging in a career in the arts, were personal blows. An invitation to design a building for Dartmouth College in 1773 was conveyed to him in such terms as not to elicit a reply. The worsening relations between England and the colonies—mobs, riots, outrages of many kinds—were a heavy strain. On 30 April 1775 Peter Harrison died "in a fit" at New Haven. He was buried in Trinity Church there. He was, the *Connecticut Gazette* observed, "in point of family second perhaps to very few in America."[5] The *Connecticut Courant* addressed his achievement: "In his death," it commented, "learning appears veil'd: and the fine art of architecture has now in America no standard."

Death did not protect Harrison's property from the patriot mob. The Sons of Liberty broke into his house, plundering, destroying, and carrying away furniture, clothing, paintings, and, as his daughter testified, "a large and elegant Library of Books containing . . . between Six and Seven Hundred Volumes, besides Manuscripts and a large Collection of Drawings." Mrs. Harrison fled to Newport, where her property, including Harrison's Farm, suffered at the hands of both the rebels and the Hessians. Reduced to near-poverty, dependent on relatives and friends, she died in Newport in 1784, survived by two daughters.

[5] *Conn. Gaz.*, 19 May 1775.

CHARLES BENSEL (1725–1795)
AMERICAN SOCIETY (CORRESPONDING MEMBER):
1 APRIL 1768

CHARLES BENSEL was born in Germantown, Philadelphia County, on 11 April 1725, the son of George and Anna Barbara (Sagor) Benzelius.[1] The elder Benzelius is said by one author to have been a weaver, by another—not necessarily in conflict—to have been related to Bishop Eric Benzelius.[2] In his will he called himself a shopkeeper. Whatever his background, he prospered in the New World. Two years after Charles' birth George Bensel purchased a lot at what is now Germantown Avenue and School House Lane and built a house; he acquired other properties, was naturalized,[3] and at his death in 1763 made bequests to the Pennsylvania Hospital and the Reformed Church in Germantown.[4]

Young Bensel attended a local school, then studied medicine as apprentice to an older practitioner. By 1752 he was established in the profession, advertising patent and prescription medical wares for sale at reasonable prices.[5]

Occasionally he received a bit of public medical business, as when he cared for a wounded Indian under the oversight of the Overseers of the Poor; he was paid £15 for his medicines and attendance.[6] For the rest, however, little is known of his medical practice, except that it appears to have brought him both income and reputation in the town. He subscribed to one of the three fire companies formed in Germantown in 1764;[7] he was a member of the Fishing Company at Fort St. David (where his name is spelled as the Germans of Germantown may have pronounced it—Pensyl).[8] In 1759 with Christopher Sower and others he was on a committee to raise money to build a public school in Germantown. He gave £20, and in 1760

---

[1] *PMHB,* VI (1882), 388–90; S. F. Hotchkin, *Ancient and Modern Germantown, Mount Airy and Chestnut Hill* (Phila., 1889), 101 and "Errata" sheet.
[2] Charles J. Wister, Jr., *A Memoir of Charles J. Wister* (Germantown, 1866), pt. 1, 165–66; I. Pearson Willits, "The Early Physicians of Germantown," *Germantown History* (Site and Relic Society Papers, 1915), 139–41.
 Bishop Benzel's son Adolf visited America in 1750, bringing an introduction from Gronovius to John Bartram. Darlington, *Memorials,* 358.
[3] 2 *Pa. Arch.,* II, 351.
[4] George Bensel, Will, 8 July 1763, Will Book N, 60 (Register of Wills, Phila.); Harry M. Tinkcom et al., *Historic Germantown . . . A Survey of the German Township* (Phila., 1955), 7.
[5] *Pensylvanische Berichte,* 1 Jan. 1751/2.
[6] 8 *Pa. Arch.,* IV, 3495.
[7] Naaman H. Keyser et al., *History of Old Germantown* (Germantown, 1907), 103; Scharf and Westcott, *Philadelphia,* III, 1886.
[8] *A History of the Schuylkill Fishing Company of the State in Schuylkill, 1732–1888* (Phila., 1889), 401.

was chosen by the Contributors one of the trustees of the school, which opened in 1761. The Germantown Union School, as it was called (now Germantown Academy), was one of Bensel's principal interests thereafter: he was elected a trustee annually until 1763, then from 1769 to 1777, and finally from 1789 until his death.[9]

Meanwhile Bensel had married, about 1750, Sarah, daughter of Paul Engle of Germantown; their first child, Charles, was born in 1752. They had at least three others: Sarah, George, and Engle. Dr. Bensel built a house near his father's at the northwest corner of Germantown Avenue and School House Lane.[10]

Bensel's membership in the American Society seems to have brought little benefit either to him or to the Society, for he never attended a meeting, or, so far as the records show, made a communication of any kind. He was, however, an ardent horticulturalist, raising tulips, hyacinths, narcissi, and other flowers, which he sometimes shared with others;[11] and as a physician he might be thought to have had an interest in scientific matters. In addition, he may have been welcome in the American Society because of his political views. These were ardently Whig. With the outbreak of the Revolution Bensel was several times charged by the Committee of Safety with watching prisoners sent to Germantown; and he was on a committee appointed by the Council to collect leaden window and clock weights and lead from roofs. Zealous in the cause, he kept an eye on neighbors and strangers and reported suspicious actions to the authorities.[12] Young Charles Bensel, whom his father had sent to the Academy of Philadelphia and then trained in medicine, was a surgeon in the Philadelphia County militia in 1777.[13] An anecdote illustrates Dr. Bensel's enthusiasm for the American cause: having received intelligence of an American victory, he hurried to the church, played a triumphant hymn on the organ, and, when his neighbors assembled to ask the reason, announced the good news.[14]

So outspoken a rebel had no alternative but to flee on the approach of the British army in September 1777. The Bensels left Germantown the day before the enemy arrived and took refuge for the winter in Horsham. The house in Germantown was thoroughly looted: the soldiers or Tory neighbors not only carried away all the good furniture, but they removed the locks from doors and closets, and even dug up the bulbs in the flower gardens. Among the many articles that disappeared were two eight-day clocks, one with a japanned face showing the battle between the

---

[9] [Joseph Jackson], *A History of the Germantown Academy* ([Phila.], 1910), 34, 259; *Pa. Gaz.*, 5 March 1761; Bensel to Israel Pemberton, 20 May 1773, Pemberton Papers, XXIV, 177 (HSP).
[10] Keyser, *History of Old Germantown,* 334.
[11] William Logan to John Smith, 10 Third Mo. 1759, Smith Mss., V, 97 (Lib. Co. Phila. in HSP).
[12] *Col. Recs. Pa.,* X, 547, 580, 596, 637; Bensel to James Biddle, 8 June 1776, Gratz Coll. (HSP); Bensel to Owen Biddle, 13 Aug. [1776], Gilbert Coll. of Ms. Letters, I, 175 (Coll. Phys. Phila.).
[13] 2 *Pa. Arch.,* I, 35, 497; 6 *Pa. Arch.,* I, 961; Montgomery, *University of Pennsylvania,* 532.
[14] *PMHB,* VI (1882), 390.

Continental gondolas and H.M.S. *Roebuck;*[15] more than fifty "gilt and plain pictures" and six paintings of historical scenes; a pair of small globes; two reflecting burning glasses; a house organ, piano, and violin; copper and iron stills, scales, steelyards, mortars, retorts "with all the utensils belonging to the Laboratory"; and all the medicines, drugs, and furniture of the medical shop. In addition, Bensel's whole library of 600–700 volumes "of physical and historical authors" was taken, as were two skeletons, a collection of anatomical preparations, and "a small perspective shew, with 30 different pieces, viz. Vauxhall, Royal Exchange, Ranelagh, &c."[16] He replenished his professional stock by purchasing some of the confiscated property of his Loyalist neighbor Christopher Sower—a variety of drugs, "a lot of Medicine," and an article or articles identified simply as "something that beats the Doctr."[17]

Bensel was as good a Federalist after the war as he had been a patriot during it. On 21 September 1787 he presided at a public meeting at which the citizens of Germantown unanimously approved the new Constitution and urged the Pennsylvania Assembly to take steps to secure its ratification.[18] He subscribed to Carey's *American Museum.* But his Federalist principles did not keep him from refusing to lease his house to the government for President Washington during the yellow fever epidemic of 1793.[19]

Bensel died at his home in Germantown on 17 March 1795, and was buried in the Lower Burying Ground there. His son Charles, who succeeded to his practice, died in 1796, but George, who had also studied medicine, practiced in Germantown until his death in 1827.[20]

---

[15] Perhaps this painting of the recent naval action in the Delaware was made by Lt. George Ball of the *Roebuck,* a paroled prisoner of war for whom the Committee of Safety asked Bensel to provide proper boarding. *Col. Recs. Pa.,* X, 580.
[16] *Pa. Gaz.,* 10 March 1779.
[17] 6 *Pa. Arch.,* XII, 907–08.
[18] *Pa. Packet,* 22 Sept. 1787.
[19] Charles F. Jenkins, *Washington in Germantown* (Phila., 1905), 93.
[20] Charles Bensel, Letters of Administration, 2 May 1795 (Register of Wills, Phila.); I. Pearson Willits, "The Early Physicians of Germantown," loc. cit., 139–41; Wister, *Memoir of Charles J. Wister,* pt. 1, 166. Dr. George Bensel in a letter to Benjamin Smith Barton, 5 Nov. 1804, wrote "On the medical virtues of the Orobanche Virginiana, in Cancerous and other Ulcers," *Phila. Med. and Physical Jour.,* I, pt. 1 (1804), 110–11.

JOHN SELLERS (1728–1804)

AMERICAN PHILOSOPHICAL SOCIETY: 8 MARCH 1768
AMERICAN SOCIETY (CORRESPONDING MEMBER):
1 APRIL 1768

JOHN SELLERS, of Darby, Pennsylvania, farmer, surveyor, and manufacturer, was, in the words of William Barton, nephew and biographer of David Rittenhouse, "a sensible and ingenious country-gentleman, possessed of some skill in mathematical and astronomical science."[1] He had a restless mind and strong opinions, made experiments to increase the productivity of the soil, invented tools and machines to do work more efficiently and cheaply, and did all this without benefit of formal education. He was, in short, just the kind of man both the American and the American Philosophical Society counted on to promote useful knowledge.

The American Philosophical Society elected him to their fellowship on 8 March 1768. Whether he formally accepted the election is not certain, but his name was included in the list of members the Philosophical Society submitted to the American Society when the two groups were negotiating their union in 1768. Three weeks after this election by the Philosophical Society, on 1 April, Sellers was elected a corresponding member of the American Society, attended a meeting and signed its Obligation and By-laws. In the united Society after 1769 Sellers played a small but noticeable role. He was on the Society's committee to prepare for the Transit of Venus; and as a member of Rittenhouse's party at Norriton he counted the clock during the climactic moments of the transit. He was also one of the Society's committee to survey a route for a Delaware-Chesapeake canal, and in this service Sellers had a new kind of level constructed, which the Society so highly approved that it offered 50s. to defray its cost, provided he would let them use it whenever they wished. Sellers attended meetings infrequently—there is no record of any attendance after 1770—but he subscribed £3 towards the construction of Philosophical Hall in 1785.

Sellers was born on 19 September 1728, the seventh and youngest child of Samuel and Sarah (Smith) Sellers, of Darby, both Quakers.[2] The elder Sellers, a weaver by trade, was noted for mechanical ingenuity; he constructed a machine for twisting worsted and became famous for weaving coverlets and camlets. Young

---

[1] William Barton, *Memoirs of the Life of David Rittenhouse* (Phila., 1813), 227n.
[2] Short sketches of Sellers appear in George Smith, *History of Delaware County, Pennsylvania* (Phila., 1862), 499–500, and in Gilbert Cope and Henry Graham Ashmead, eds., *Historic Homes and Institutions and Genealogical and Personal Memoirs of Chester and Delaware Counties, Pennsylvania* (N.Y., 1904), I, 195–96. Both sketches appear to be heavily indebted to John Sellers, Jr., to David Townsend, 31 May 1822 (Chester Co. Hist. Soc., West Chester, Pa.). See also Frank W. Leach, "Old Philadelphia Families. CXXXIV. Sellers," (Phila.) *North American,* 27 Oct. 1912.

John learned weaving and farming, but otherwise received only limited formal education. He was, however, an enterprising lad, and on his own acquired a knowledge of surveying, in which he rapidly achieved skill and reputation. In 1766 he was appointed by the Assembly to survey a route from Philadelphia to Lancaster.[3]

Meanwhile, at Darby Friends Meeting in 1749, Sellers married Ann, daughter of Nathan and Ann (Hunt) Gibson of neighboring Kingsessing. They eventually had ten children, of whom six reached maturity.[4] In 1752 John's father assigned the family farm to him, and John took the opportunity to extend its boundaries and add to its activities. Cobbs Creek, on which the farm lay, offered abundant power. A grist mill was soon erected, then a saw mill, a press for linseed oil, and other structures. In all, Sellers is said to have constructed six mill dams and dug not less than three miles of mill race on his property.[5] The flour mills were operated profitably for more than a century thereafter.

Inevitably Sellers considered how milling practices might be made more efficient. None of the existing bolting machinery and devices was entirely satisfactory. Sellers accordingly constructed wire rolling screens and sieves to his purpose. These proved so satisfactory that he began to manufacture them for sale. In an advertisement of 1767 he called himself "the original inventor and institutor of that branch of business in America," and added that, as he had instructed no others in the art, he believed himself "in all probability . . . the best master of the work." He may well have been: at least he claimed to have made all the wire bolts used in Philadelphia and New York as well as a considerable number of the rolling screens in use anywhere for cleaning wheat.[6] Another advertisement was more specific.

> MADE and SOLD by the subscriber, in Darby, various kinds of WIRE WORK, such as twilled or plain, as may best suit their purposes; rolling screens for cleaning wheat, consisting of four various sorts of wire, each calculated to the greatest exactness, and found, from long experience, to answer the purpose; rolling screens for cleaning flaxseed from the yellow or wild seed; small bolts for separating the cockle from the flaxseed; or bolts so constructed, as for one to perfect both the said purposes, as may best suit the stores in which they are to be used; small bolts for Indian corn meal; fans, for taking out garlic, and common Dutch fans, both made in the neatest and best manner. Likewise all other kinds of wire work for standing shoe and shoot screens, wire sieves and riddles of all degrees of fineness, and short cloths for millers. Those that please to favour him with their orders, may depend on their work being done with care, and the greatest dispatch, and the work warranted, and that he is not pretending to perform that which he has not, in a great number of instances, given the utmost satisfaction,

---

[3] 8 *Pa. Arch.,* VII, 5932, 5945, 5951, 5956.
[4] *Descendants of Samuel Sellers* (Ardmore, Pa., 1962), 5; Darby Women's Monthly Meeting, Extracts of Minutes (Geneal. Soc. Pa.).
[5] The tax lists of John Sellers, "wyer weaver," indicate that he extended the farm from about 160 acres in 1771 to upwards of 350 acres in 1773. 3 *Pa. Arch.,* XI, 540, 700; XII, 16.
[6] *Pa. Gaz.,* 3 Sept. 1767.

having had long experience in the use of them, and made upwards of thirty rolling screens for wheat, and upwards of fifty for flaxseed.

He added that he stamped his name on the heads of all his bolts, rolling screens, and fans.[7]

Sellers took part in public affairs. In Darby Township he was elected constable in 1761, and served several times as overseer of the poor. In 1767 he was elected for the first of five terms in the Assembly, which appointed him, often with John Lukens, to committees for making surveys—of the Schuylkill River near Barbados Island and its channel; of a road from the Middle Ferry to Strasburg; of the branches of the Schuylkill, Lehigh, and Susquehanna rivers, to determine how far their branches were navigable "and whether the opening a Communication between them for the Purposes of Navigation or Land-Carriage be practicable at a reasonable Expence." In the last case the surveyors (Sellers and Benjamin Lightfoot) concluded that it was practicable to construct a canal of four miles between Tulpehocken Creek (which flowed into the Schuylkill) and Quittapahilla Creek (which flowed into the Swatara, which in turn flowed into the Susquehanna). In 1773, no longer in the Assembly, Sellers asked, unsuccessfully, to be appointed collector of excise for Chester County.[8] He contributed £10 to the Pennsylvania Hospital in 1769.

In the quarrel with Great Britain Sellers was an American partisan from the start. He was a member of the Chester County Committee of Correspondence in 1774, and represented the county in the Provincial Convention in July of that year.[9] After the outbreak of war, he signed paper currency and sawed wood at his mills for the Continental army, while his son Nathan was released from military service to help his father produce goods for the army. Such unneutral conduct was promptly complained of in Friends Meeting; and, as Sellers would not confess to error and wrong-doing, he was disowned. Not one to take censure meekly, he appealed to the Quarterly Meeting, then to the Yearly Meeting; but for some reason he failed to appear in his defense, and the excommunication stood.[10] He took the oath of allegiance on 2 July 1778.[11]

Sellers continued to be politically active after the return of peace. He was appointed a justice of the peace in 1776, served on a commission to build a new courthouse and jail for Chester County in 1780, and in 1784 was elected township supervisor. An Anti-constitutionalist in state politics, he declined election to the

---

[7] Ibid., 27 July 1769.
[8] 8 *Pa. Arch.,* VII, 6062, 6285, 6383, 6447, 6582; VIII, 6609–10, 6687–88, 6724, 6931–34, 7026; Darby Township Records, 52, 94 (transcript in Geneal. Soc. Pa.). Sellers' Return of a Road from the Middle Ferry on Schuylkill to the Village of Strasburg, 5 June 1773, is in Penn Mss., Warrants and Surveys (large folio), 75 (HSP).
[9] 2 *Pa. Arch.,* III, 545; Smith, *History of Delaware County,* 280.
[10] Darby Monthly Meeting Records, 29 Fifth Mo. 1777 (transcript in Geneal. Soc. Pa.); Sellers Family Association, *Proceedings of the First General Meeting . . . 1910,* 20–24.
[11] 2 *Pa. Arch.,* III, 26.

Assembly because he opposed a unicameral legislature in principle. But he represented Delaware County (now separated from Chester—he was one of the surveyors who ran the line) in the state constitutional convention of 1789, and was elected to the state senate the next year.[12] Governor Mifflin offered him appointment as associate justice of the county courts, but he preferred to stay in the Senate in order to promote pending legislation for what he called "Useful Improvements."[13]

Meanwhile Sellers had resumed the career of a practical philosopher. Elected to the Philadelphia Society for Promoting Agriculture in 1785, the next year he advocated before that body the erection of a bridge across the Schuylkill at the Middle Ferry, and brought a model to one of the Society's meetings.[14] Agricultural improvers were also interested in the observations and experiments with plaster of Paris that Sellers had made since 1786, especially as his land had been under cultivation for more than a century. Sellers' reply to the questionnaire of Judge Richard Peters, Jr., on the subject in 1796 was printed in the latter's *Agricultural Inquiries*.[15]

As he approached his seventieth year Sellers suffered increasingly from urinary obstruction. As the doctors apparently did nothing for him, he consulted medical treatises himself, concluded he had a bladder stone, and prescribed seeds of wild carrot and whortleberry (*uva ursi*). These proving ineffective, Sellers resumed his medical studies, placed the blame for his condition on his sedentary life and consumption of beer and port, and thereafter drank only water impregnated with lime from oyster shells. Relief followed—from which he deduced that "water alone is Soficiant and affectual (in health) for all the purposes of Human wants in drink; and Happy had it been for the Race of mankind had no other mixd, or Artificial Liquars ever been invented."[16] Secure in this conviction, he departed this life on 2 February 1804 in the house where he was born, where his father had lived and died, on land where his grandfather had settled.[17]

Mrs. Sellers survived her husband only fourteen months. Of their sons, John, Jr., a tanner, received the grist and merchant mills; while Nathan, who had had twenty years' experience in the wire works, carried the family tradition in technology to greater heights.

---

[12] Edward Burd to Jasper Yeates, 12 Oct. 1790, L. B. Walker, *The Burd Letters* (n.p., 1899), 166. Sellers declined appointment in 1789 as one of the commissioners for viewing the river Schuylkill, and was replaced by Benjamin Rittenhouse. *Col. Recs. Pa.,* XVI, 194.
[13] Sellers to Governor Thomas Mifflin, 15 Oct. 1791, Dept. of State, RG 26 (Div. of Public Records, Harrisburg).
[14] Jacob Hiltzheimer, *Extracts from the Diary* (Jacob C. Parsons, ed., Phila., 1893), 103; Phila. Soc. for Promoting Agriculture, Minutes, I, 5 Sept., 7 Nov. 1786, 3 July 1787 (Univ. Pa. Lib.).
[15] "Answers to Queries on Plaister of Paris," in Richard Peters, *Agricultural Inquiries on Plaister of Paris* (Phila., 1810), 46–52. Peters characterized Sellers as "uncommonly observant; and one of a strong mind, not destitute of cultivation."
[16] Sellers to Benjamin Rush, 15 March 1801, Rush Mss., XV, 59 (Lib. Co. Phila. in HSP).
[17] A copy of Sellers' will, dated 13 Sept. 1803, is in Sellers Family Papers, Peale-Sellers Papers (APS).

PIERRE EUGÈNE Du SIMITIÈRE (1737–1784)
AMERICAN SOCIETY (CORRESPONDING MEMBER):
1 APRIL 1768

PIERRE EUGÈNE DU SIMITIÈRE, Swiss-born artist, naturalist, and antiquary, the first in America who systematically collected a library and museum of American history, was elected a corresponding member of the American Society on 1 April 1768, when he was living in Boston, before he permanently settled in Philadelphia. He was introduced into the Society on 13 August and attended the next several meetings. He appears to have come occasionally thereafter, whenever he was in Philadelphia; and after the approach of war put a stop to his excursions, he attended the Society fairly regularly and took an active part in its work. On 17 December 1774 he was named to a committee with Dr. John Morgan and Dr. Benjamin Rush to draft a certificate of membership; the men did their work promptly, and Du Simitière and Thomas Bradford were directed to have the certificates engraved. Doubtless because of the war, this was not done. On 30 May 1775 he agreed to answer the queries on American geology and natural history which the Marquis de Condorcet submitted to Franklin and Franklin forwarded to the Society. Du Simitière was elected one of the curators on 5 January 1776. He was present at the first meeting the Society held after the withdrawal of the British army from Philadelphia, and was elected once again to his post of curator. He was re-elected to it in 1781. A few months before his death in 1784 he received again a former assignment—he and Major DeBrahm were appointed to get membership certificates engraved.

Born in Geneva on 18 September 1737, the son of Jean-Henri-Ducimitière (or Dusimitière), a well-to-do East India broker, and his wife Judith-Ulrique-Cunegonde Delorme, he displayed a talent for sketching and received some formal instruction from a local drawing master, who, a few years later, was the teacher of John André.[1] In his teens Du Simitière left Geneva for Amsterdam, where he was admitted to membership in the Eglise Wallone in 1754, and where he lived for

---

[1] The principal sources of biographical information are the publications of Paul G. Sifton: *Historiographer to the United States: The Revolutionary Letterbook of Pierre Eugène Du Simitière* (N.Y., 1987), which presents, though in erratic transcription, some one hundred of Du Simitière's letters; "A Disordered Life: The American Career of Pierre Eugène Du Simitière," *Manuscripts,* XXV (1953), 235–53; and "Pierre Eugène Du Simitière (1737–1784): Collector in Revolutionary America" (dissertation, Univ. of Penna., 1960). On Du Simitière's career and collections, see also Hans Huth, "Pierre Eugène Du Simitière and the Beginnings of the American Historical Museum," *PMHB,* LXIX (1945), 315–35; Martin Levey, "The First American Museum of Natural History," *Isis,* XLII (1951), 10–12; Levey, "Pierre Eugène Du Simitière—Early American Bibliophile," Société suisse des Américanistes, *Bulletin,* no. 9 (1955), 17–25; William J. Potts, "Du Simitière, Artist, Antiquary, and Natu-

four years until 10 November 1757, when he sailed for the West Indies. During the next five years Du Simitière travelled among the islands—St. Eustatius, Curaçao, and Jamaica—sketching local scenes, collecting specimens of natural history, coins, and historical data and artifacts, and supporting himself by drawing portraits of the planters and merchants. In the summer of 1763 he came to New York, where he began to collect specimens of North American flora and fauna. In the next few years Du Simitière visited Charleston, Boston, and Newport, where the Reverend Ezra Stiles showed him a copy of the inscription on Taunton Rock and quizzed him about the liberties Protestants enjoyed in France.[2] On all these journeys he kept careful meteorological records. In 1765–67 Du Simitière spent some time in Philadelphia, where he made the acquaintance of John Smith of Burlington, who, with antiquarian interests similar to his, befriended him. Du Simitière made another long visit to New York, where he was naturalized on 20 May 1769. In 1770 he settled in Philadelphia.

All the while Du Simitière was collecting books, pamphlets, newspapers, and the physical evidences and remains of American natural and civil history. Struck by the significance of American resistance to the Stamp Act, he became increasingly aware of the importance of the events happening around him; and he dunned his friends for every record of the momentous era and its backgrounds.[3] For hours at a time and days on end he labored on his collections, indexing newspapers and magazines, excerpting passages from borrowed books and manuscripts, preparing lists of names, dates, and titles on scores of subjects, and then arranging the notes under appropriate topics. He made sketches of American harbors, towns, and buildings; he copied maps; and began a gallery of portraits. By 1771 he had come to regard his collection as the source from which the history of America would eventually be written.

The museum grew along with the library. Dr. William Bryant of Trenton donated Indian artifacts; from Richard Bache came a seahorse and a stone adze from Otaheite which Dr. David Solander had given Franklin; while the eccentric Dr. Abraham Chovet presented a sketch of a view of Rome.[4]

The collection absorbed Du Simitière's resources as well as his time. Never in good financial circumstances, he often had to borrow money—he once lost a col-

---

ralist, Projector of the First American Museum, with some Extracts from his Notebook," *PMHB*, XIII (1889), 341–75; *DAB*.

Du Simitière's collections at the time of their dispersal by sale in 1785 and the contents of the major portion of surviving manuscripts are inventoried in *Descriptive Catalogue of the Du Simitière Papers in the Library Company of Philadelphia* (Phila., 1940).

[2] Du Simitière, Scraps, 116 (Lib. Co. Phila.); Franklin B. Dexter, ed., *Extracts from the Itineraries . . . of Ezra Stiles* (New Haven, 1916), 239.

[3] Du Simitière to John Smith, 6 Aug. 1767, Etting Collection, Artists, 21 (HSP); *PMHB*, XIV (1890), 90–91.

[4] Du Simitière, Memoranda, 1774–83 (Lib. Cong.).

lection of 135 coins which he had pledged as collateral but could not redeem when his creditor died and the executors demanded payment; sometimes he sold specimens to get a few pounds to go on with.[5] He could, of course, always fall back on his artist's skill. In 1771 he told a friend that he had lately begun "to draw at large in Crayons," proposing "to take very soon likenesses in that way, so that I'll have two strings to my bow."[6] He was serious about this, for the next year he purchased from the Philadelphia bookseller Robert Aitken copies of the *Art of Drawing and Painting in Water Colors* and the *Art of Drawing in Perspective*. If doing portraits in miniature of well-to-do Philadelphians gave him a modest income, he took greater satisfaction—for this was related to his historical museum—from the portrait of William Penn he made from Sylvanus Bevan's wax medallion in William Logan's possession; it was engraved in London and prints were offered for sale in Philadelphia.[7] From time to time Du Simitière received other commissions: he designed the title-page of Aitken's *Pennsylvania Magazine* in 1775 and also made some illustrations for the magazine, receiving 30*s.* each for drawings of instruments and machines, such as Arthur Donaldson's for cleaning docks and harbors. He was especially interested in heraldry (in 1772 Aitken bound for him a copy of Morgan's *Sphere of Gentry*),[8] and in 1775 the trustees of the Wilmington Grammar School asked him to design a seal for the corporation.

With the establishment of the governments of the several states and of the United States in 1776, Du Simitière found his knowledge of languages and of heraldry and his skill as an artist in demand. Congress employed him occasionally as a translator, and called on him to design a seal for the United States and the medal which Congress voted to General Washington in honor of the evacuation of Boston by the British army in 1776.[9] New Jersey, Delaware, Virginia, and Georgia had him design their new state seals; he made one for Rockingham County, Virginia, as well.

The outbreak of war in 1775 confirmed Du Simitière in the conviction that his American museum was an invaluable resource for the nation,[10] and he redoubled his efforts to collect appropriate materials. John Adams, who was on the committee of Congress which consulted Du Simitière about the seal of the United States, described the antiquary's collection and method in a letter to Abigail:

---

[5] Du Simitière to William Dillwyn, 7 April 1771 (photostat), Society Coll. (HSP).
[6] Du Simitière to Evart Bancker, Jr., 27 March 1771, Misc. Mss. (APS).
[7] *Pa. Journal,* 14 Sept. 1774.
[8] Robert Aitken, Waste Book, 17 March, 2 June, 1772, et passim, (Lib. Co. Phila.); Paul G. Sifton, "Pierre Eugène Du Simitière: illustrator of nascent America," *Antiques,* LXXVII, (1960), 576–78.
[9] *The Papers of Thomas Jefferson,* (Julian P. Boyd, ed., Princeton, 1950–), I, 495–96, 510–11.
[10] On the significance of Du Simitière's collection, see William E. Lingelbach, "An Early American Historian," in *Bookmen's Holiday: Notes and Studies Written and Gathered in Tribute to Harry Miller Lydenberg* (N.Y., 1943), 355–61.

> This Mr. Du simitière is a very curious Man. He has begun a Collection of Materials for an History of this Revolution. He begins with the first Advices of the Tea Ships. He cuts out of the Newspapers, every Scrap of Intelligence, and every Piece of Speculation, and pastes it upon clean Paper, arranging them under the Head of the State to which they belong and intends to bind them up in Volumes. He has a List of every Speculation and Pamphlet concerning Independence, and another of those concerning Forms of Government.[11]

At the same time the war created problems for Du Simitière personally and for his museum. The advance of the British army on Philadelphia put his precious books and artifacts in danger; he sent them for safe keeping to Dr. Bryant in New Jersey.[12] He himself was called to military service, and when he failed to report, was fined. He appealed—conveniently forgetting that he had become a citizen in New York in 1769—on the ground that he was a citizen of Geneva, not permanently settled in Pennsylvania, and was engaged in a work of national importance.[13] The plea was rejected. For having served Congress, he was suspect by the British; when they took Philadelphia, they threw him in prison; though they released him after three weeks without requiring him to answer charges.[14] During the occupation winter Du Simitière painted miniatures of many British officers, including Captain Stephen Adye and Captain John Montresor. In June 1778, when the army evacuated the city, Du Simitière, according to the recollections of the aged Charles Thomson, tried to dissuade his friend Major John André from carrying off some of Dr. Franklin's books.[15]

On the return of Congress and the Pennsylvania Assembly to Philadelphia, Du Simitière was once again engaged to translate foreign documents, and took the oath of allegiance to the state in 1779.[16] He redoubled his efforts in behalf of the museum. Captain Montresor gave him a collection of medals; the president of Pennsylvania, an Indian scalp; from Joseph Wharton came a medallion bas-relief of Franklin—possibly one of Nini's—and from Joseph Cooper in New Jersey an ancient stone chisel. He even secured some costumes from the Meschianza Ball. At the same time Du Simitière lost no opportunity to sketch portraits of the military and political leaders of the Revolution. Washington, John Jay, Silas Deane, the French minister Gérard, Charles Biddle, Colonel Henry Laurens, General Joseph Reed, and others sat to him. Some of the portraits were engraved at once and sold

---

[11] L. H. Butterfield, ed., *Adams Family Correspondence,* (Cambridge, Mass., 1963), II, 96.
[12] Du Simitière, Memoranda, 1774–83 (Lib. Cong.).
[13] 2 *Pa. Arch.,* III, 121–22.
[14] Du Simitière to John Lamb, 24 Nov. 1778, in Isaac Q. Leake, *Memoir of the Life and Times of General John Lamb* (Albany, 1850), 211–15.
[15] *PMHB,* VIII (1884), 430.
[16] 1 *Pa. Arch.,* VII, 212; 2 *Pa. Arch.,* XIV, 47.

individually; but a selection of thirteen was sent to France to be engraved and printed, and sets were returned to America for sale.[17]

So far Du Simitière had carried on the museum at his own expense and by the generosity of friends. He thought it time to obtain public support, and on 22 July 1779 appealed to Congress, representing

> That your memorialist has resided for upwards of twenty years, in the principal Parts of North America and the West Indies, in pursuit of the civil and natural History of those Countries—That your memorialist being in this City at the memorable Æra of the Stamp Act, was induced from the novelty and importance of the Contest, to make inquiries into the civil history of this Continent; and after having perused a variety of publications on that very interesting subject, and finding the historical accounts false & erroneous, he formed the design of rectifying those accounts, by publishing at some future period, a Work containing Memoirs and Observations upon the Origin and present State of the different parts of the Country he was acquainted with. For which purpose, your memorialist hath ever since that time, with unwearied application, great expence of money and time, and unassisted by any public bodies, collected a considerable number of Books, Pamphlets, Papers both printed & Manuscript, relating to the political, civil, municipal, & religious affairs of this continent, and also to the Trade Manufactures and the progress of the Arts & Sciences of the same, to which must be added, a Collection of Charts, Maps, Plans, Prospects &ca. both printed and manuscript of most part of this continent both ancient & modern. This Collection as far as has come to the knowledge of your memorialist, is not exceeded by any either public or private in the Continent of North America.
>
> Another branch of your Mem:'s collection consists of his own Observations, Descriptions, Memoirs, Remarks, Chronologies, Extracts from scarce books and manuscripts, Plans, Drawings, &ca. all which have been procured and brought together by your Mem: own industry and with no other assistance than the gratuity of private individuals of the different States thro' which he has travelled, and have been preserved safe notwithstanding the severe persecution he suffered while the enemy were in possession of this City occasioned by his voluntary attachment to the cause of America, and amidst the disasters and losses he sustained in consequence thereof.
>
> But your memorialist's undertaking being a work of leisure and great application, and his Situation being such as obliged him to devote the greater part of his time to the practice of an art, from the precarious emoluments of which he derived his only Support, he hath not hitherto been able to make such progress as corresponded with his ardor; and the Calamities of war increasing the difficulties of his Support, he is now induced to lay his Case before your honble house, humbly requesting that it may be taken into Consideration; and if they shall deem his undertaking to be of public utility, they will grant him such countenance and assistance as may enable him to prosecute it, or at least prevent such valuable Materials from being dissipated and lost.
>
> Your memorialist begs leave to observe, that he does not presume to apply to this honble House to support him in a plan which he has now first conceived, but to enable him to pursue one long since begun, & continued by him for upwards of fourteen years.

---

[17] Edna Donnell, "Portraits of Eminent Americans after Drawings by Du Simitière," *Antiques,* XXIV (1933), 17–21; *Pa. Journal,* 25 Sept. 1782.

Altho your Mem: is not unknown to several of the honble members of your house, he humbly requests that some of your honble body may be appointed to view and examine the various materials belonging to him, that the house from their information and report may have a more complete Idea of his collection and the deserts of your memorialist.[18]

Congress appointed John Dickinson, William Fleming, and William Churchill Houston to consider the memorial and report on it. They visited Du Simitière several times, inspected the museum, and came away greatly impressed. On 26 November they made their report, recommending that Congress give Du Simitière encouragement in preparing and publishing his projected history, being "fully satisfied, that a work of this nature will greatly tend to diffuse useful knowledge." To this end they recommended that he receive $2000 yearly for three years and that he be appointed historiographer of the United States.[19]

Not until 14 July 1780 did Congress act, and then only after Du Simitière had prodded its president twice. "I do not mean to ask for Sinecure Emoluments," he apologized; "my desire is to be of public service to this country in the only line in which I can think my self in some measure qualified."[20] Congress approved the committee's report, recommended Du Simitière's plan to the several states, and assured him of their assistance in making his work complete and useful; but the provision for a yearly stipend of $2000 was struck out.[21] Keenly disappointed by the decision, Du Simitière wrote an angry reply to the president of Congress.

> Sir I have to acknowledge the reception of a letter which your Excellency has honoured me with, inclosing an act of Congress of the 14th inst. relating to my work on the civil history and geography of North America.
>
> It is with concern that I observe that there is nothing in that act that answers the purposes of my memorial to Congress, and of my letters to your Excellency requesting the patronage and Support of that hon. Body. Consequently it can be of no service to me. I beg leave therefore to return it to your Excellency requesting that it may not appear in the Journals of Congress, and also presenting my apology to that hon. Body for having taken so much of their time and assuring them that I shall not presume to the same in the future and requesting their forgiveness for my intrusion.
>
> Sir, I had some reasons to entertain hopes that the Sovreign council of the united States would have granted a decent Support for the compleating of a work pronounced of the greatest utility to the people of these States, in the pursuit of which I have now spent the best years of my life but these hopes being now at an end, and it not being convenient for me to be at any further expense and loss of time, it is with great regret

---

[18] Papers of the Continental Congress, No. 41, IX, f. 84–85 (National Archives). The memorial is printed in Sifton, *Historiographer,* 15–16.
[19] *Jour. Cont. Cong.,* XV, 1316–18.
[20] Papers of the Continental Congress, No. 78, XX, 483.
[21] *Jour. Cont. Cong.,* XV, 1410, XVII, 606, 613.

I see all the works I have applied myself to for so many years buried in oblivion, and the materials of my most valuable collection (the only one of its kind in private hands) in a short time perhaps to be scattered and lost. There are many persons of the highest rank and learning who have favoured me with their friendship, having taken the trouble to view my collection and are perfectly well acquainted with its value, these may perhaps hereafter lament that nothing was done to encourage the possessor of it or at least to prevent its loss. I shall leave it to some more fortunate and better qualified than myself to undertake the arduous task, but none will ever surpass me in the zeal and the desire I had in being really useful to the people among whom I have lived for so many years and for whom I entertain a real Esteem. May I beg leave to request that the plan of my intended work which was annexed to the report of the committee on my affair may be return'd to me and if consistent with the rules of congress that I may be favoured with a copy of the original report of the said committee.[22]

The Pennsylvania Assembly, to which Du Simitière now turned for help, in 1781 voted him £200 state money "to enable him to enlarge and improve his valuable collection of scarce and useful books, manuscripts and other papers, and to prosecute his intended history of the middle states of North-America." The gesture was appreciated, but £200 in inflated currency meant nothing.[23]

No disappointments, however, could check Du Simitière's tireless search for material. He asked Colonel Lamb for a collection of pamphlets on the Stamp Act; he begged Colonel Brodhead to get him "Things in Use among the Indians," such as clothes, weapons, utensils, "maneetoe-faces," even scalps; minerals, fossil bones, shells, specimens of natural history of every sort; even an alligator, which "if not too big, might be preserved in common rum, otherwise Stuff'd and dried."[24] To Governor Clinton of New York his request was virtually a catalogue:

I shall take the liberty to mention some articles for your Excellency's information which are within the compass of my cabinet under the denomination of curiosities and may perhaps by means of this hint fall under your future notice.

It is a fact attested by the earliest historians that the first settlers in the several parts of this continent made use and wore defensive armor in their wars with the natives and others, and yet as far as my inquiries have reached nothing of the kind has been discovered lately, but it seems to me that these weapons such as helmets and breast plates being made of lasting materials must have resisted in a great measure the injuries of time and that some such piece of antiquity might still be found among some of those families who came early and have formed lasting settlements which their posterity en-

---

[22] Du Simitière, Letter Book, page 7a, quoted in Sifton, Pierre Eugene Du Simitière, 30–31, and in his *Historiographer*, 46–47. Du Simitière regretted the tone of the letter at once and asked leave to withdraw it. *Jour. Cont. Cong.*, XVII, 648.
[23] 3 *Pa. Arch.*, V, 165; Pa. Gen. Ass. *Minutes*, 5th Assembly, 4th sitting (Phila., 1781), 492.
[24] Du Simitière to Daniel Brodhead, 29 Aug. 1781. Society Coll. (HSP).

joys to this day. It is only by personal acquaintance with the local of the ancient settlements dispersed in various parts of the country that one could be able to meet with those remnants precious to antiquarians, and perhaps in the beginning of this was when every kind of old weapons were mustered up some such piece might have come to light.

Altho there were in the last century many capital engravers of prints all over Europe but especially in Flanders and Holland, yet the fashion of decorating appartments with prints, framed and glazed did not then exist, nor indeed has it become universal till very lately. The taste was then, particularly in the Netherlands to cover the walls with pictures chiefly painted in oyl, on boards in black ebony frames highly polished, of these kinds the Dutch settlers brought a great many with their other furniture, . . . I have some of those pictures myself which your Excellency may perhaps recollect. I pickt them up in New York, in garrets, where they had been confined as unfashionable when that city became modernized, and no store was any more set by them. I shall leave entirely to your Excellency's judgement when you should be able to procure any such, only adding that the good paintings were always in Ebony or Pear Tree frames highly polished, and sometimes the inner border near the picture covered with waved lines.

I have very considerably increased my collection of American Books and Papers, since your Excellency was here last, for notwithstanding that I have not traveled out of this city for this four years and a half, yet I have procured several valuable materials from abroad by means of some acquaintances in different parts of the country, but from your state I have received nothing at all, . . . which induce[s] me to mention how acceptable it would be to me [to have] such books and papers both old and new, in Dutch or English, relating to the history, geography, Politics, Indian affairs &c., of your State. I beg leave to add as a memorandum the titles of the books I have met with wrote by Dutch authors as very probably some of them might fall in your Excellency's possession; and I have none of them in my library.

. . . Of the modern political publications of your State I have little or nothing since the year 1772. I believe it might be in your Excellency's power to procure me the laws and votes of your Assembly since the revolution: they would be a valuable acquisition (when convenient should be glad also of your newspapers which I seldom see). I am favoured here with the publications of Congress, by the Secretary, with the votes and laws of our Assembly by their clerk, the Secretary of the Council gives me what is published by that Board and I have also from some of our printers, copies of what they print also. . . . Another branch of my recollection on which I lay great stress is the Indian Antiquities, it is a new subject and not touched upon by authors. I have many but I find every new specimen I get is different from the former ones, so that where there is such variety one cannot increase the number too much. Those curiosities consists [sic] of stone hatchets, pestles, tomahaws, hammers, arrow heads and points of darts, cups, bowls of pipes, idols figures cut on clam shells and many other things found in the old burying places, for which there is no name. I should not forget their earthenware of which I have as yet but small fragments brought me from the western part of this state and from Virginia.

The highlands and mountains of your State must be productive of curious fossils such as ores, minerals, agaths, chrystals, marbles, petrifactions, &c. I will only beg to add that the fossils enter into my collection and form a considerable part thereof.

Coins and medals ancient and modern I have a collection of, but now a days these are become scarce, notwithstanding I meet with some now and then.[25]

By now Du Simitière's museum had become famous, and visitors to the city asked to see it. The Marquis de Chastellux in 1780 thought it "rather small and rather paltry," owing its reputation in America to the fact that it had no rival there.[26] The Brunswick army doctor Johann David Schoepf, on the other hand, commented favorably on both the natural curiosities and "a not inconsiderable number of well-executed drawings of American birds, plants, and insects."[27] Americans, Du Simitière told his foreign visitors, probably with a foreigner's condescension, showed the greatest interest in a Hessian fusilier's cap and a pair of courier boots, which they were pleased to believe had been Charles XII's.[28] So many people wanted to see the collections that in 1782 Du Simitière established regular hours and a fixed charge for admission.[29]

Despite fame and solid recognition—the College of New Jersey had awarded him an honorary degree of master of arts in 1781[30]—Du Simitière was in an increasingly difficult financial plight. He was no business man, but gave all to art and history. Thomas Jefferson sent his daughter Martha to Du Simitière to learn to draw—the lessons would have been worth a few guineas—but the girl had no talent and Du Simitière refused to waste his time on her.[31] In 1783 and again in 1784 he appealed to the Pennsylvania Assembly for relief—all he asked was enough to pay his rent, and he promised to bequeath his collections to the Commonwealth. A committee recommended that something be done for him, but the Assembly rejected the report.[32]

The last months of his life, like the fifteen years preceding them, were devoted to the museum. He drafted a "Plan of a Work for illustrating the Revolution of America by Devices, Medals, Coins &c. that have been published on the occasion of the Revolution both in America and in Europe," a work which would include an appendix of earlier seals, including those of corporations of churches, universities and colleges, academies, and free schools.[33] He became especially interested in the remains of prehistoric beasts which had been uncovered on the Ohio, examined

[25] Quoted in Potts, "Du Simitière," *PMHB*, XIII (1889), 345–49.
[26] Chastellux, *Travels in North America* (Howard C. Rice, Jr., ed., Chapel Hill, 1963), I, 145.
[27] Johann David Schoepf, *Travels in the Confederation* (A. J. Morrison, trans., Phila., 1911), I, 85–86.
[28] Evelyn M. Acomb, trans. and ed., *The Revolutionary Journal of Baron Ludwig von Closen, 1780–83* (Chapel Hill, 1958), 118; "Diary of a French Officer, 1781," *Mag. Amer. Hist.*, IV (1880), 380.
[29] *Pa. Packet*, 18 April 1782; *Pa. Journal*, 2 July 1783.
[30] 2 *N. J. Archives*, V, 302.
[31] *Papers of Thomas Jefferson*, VI, 381, 417, 444–45, 542.
[32] Pa. Ass. *Minutes*, 7th Assembly, 2nd sitting (Phila., 1783), 822; 3rd sitting, 906; 8th Assembly, 2nd sitting, 99, 155, 167, 194.
[33] Du Simitière, Commonplace Book (Lib. Cong.).

the fossil bones in Dr. John Morgan's collection, exhibited some of those excavated by the Reverend Robert Annan near Walkill in New York state,[34] and expressed a wish to travel into the Mississippi and Missouri Valleys "to view those enormous quadrupeds who are said to be still existing there."[35] Perhaps only a sure prospect of seeing a mastodon would have taken him to the Mississippi. He was in fact permanently settled in Philadelphia. To a friend who invited him to visit in the country, he replied:

> I have not the least inclination for a country life in No America. Beside I Object to the Waggon with six horses as much as I do to Stride on a Single one. Indeed I have by long habit become So much of a Citt, that if I was to loose Sight of Christ Church Steeple I would think my Self bewildered. . . . When our Philadelphian Philosophers have brought the Air balloons to that degree of perfection as [will] enable us to navigate in the Air perhaps I might venture in that Vehicle, but hitherto we have had too many Cooks about them, and of course they Sometimes Spoil the broth.[36]

On 12 August 1784, Du Simitière attended a meeting of the American Philosophical Society. It was the last time. He died early in October, and was buried on 10 October in St. Peter's Churchyard in Philadelphia. No stone was erected on his grave.[37]

His executors, Ebenezer Hazard and Matthew Clarkson, hoped that the Philosophical Society would purchase Du Simitière's collection, and the Society did appoint a committee to examine it. They found it too disorganized to evaluate, and seem to have made no further effort to acquire it. The collection was then offered to the Commonwealth, which declined it for lack of funds.[38] Accordingly, on 10 March 1785 the contents of the museum were put up to public sale.[39] The Library Company and Matthew Clarkson, one of the administrators, purchased books, broadsides, and manuscripts.[40] Many of these latter survive, in the Library Company and the Library of Congress, and give an indication of the extent, variety, and richness of Du Simitière's museum and of the intelligence and indefatigability of its creator.

---

[34] Robert Annan, "Account of a Skeleton of a large Animal, found near Hudson's River," American Academy of Arts and Sciences, *Memoirs,* II, pt. 2 (1793), 163; Schoepf, *Travels,* I, 269; Du Simitière Papers (965.F, Lib. Co. Phila.).
[35] Du Simitière to Isaac Melcher, 17 Jan. 1784, in Sifton, *Historiographer,* 115.
[36] Du Simitière to Augustin Prevost, 29 May 1784, Du Simitière Letter Book, 1779–84 (Lib. Cong.), printed ibid., 118–19.
[37] William W. Bronson, *The Inscriptions in St. Peter's Church Yard* (Camden, N.J., 1879), 565.
[38] Pa. Ass. *Minutes,* 9th Assembly, 2nd sess., 158.
[39] Ebenezer Hazard to Jeremy Belknap, 13 Nov. 1784, Mass. Hist. Soc., *Colls.,* 5th ser., II, 406.
[40] *Pa. Packet,* 9 March 1785; *Descriptive Catalogue of the Du Simitière Papers.*
Charles Willson Peale's Accession Book, 7 Nov. 1817 (APS) mentions a portrait of Du Simitière painted, presumably at Boston, by John Singleton Copley.

ANDREW OLIVER
By John Singleton Copley.
*National Portrait Gallery,
Smithsonian Institution.*

ANDREW OLIVER (1706–1774)

AMERICAN SOCIETY (CORRESPONDING MEMBER):
1 APRIL 1768

"ANDREW OLIVER ESQR OF SALEM N.E." was elected a corresponding member of the American Society on 1 April 1768. Without further identification this might reasonably be assumed to be Andrew Oliver, Jr. (1731–1799), a resident of Salem since 1760 and author, several years later, of a treatise on comets. But in the list of members of the Society printed in the first volume of its *Transactions* in 1771 the identification is "Hon. Andrew Oliver, Lieut. Gov. Massachusetts Bay." As a kind of "official" statement this list probably should be allowed to settle the question, even though Lieutenant Governor Oliver was a resident of Boston, appears to have been little interested in "philosophical" matters, and, in view of the reputation he acquired during the Stamp Act controversy, his election to a society in which Charles Thomson, "the Sam Adams of Philadelphia," was a leading spirit, is at least curious.

At the risk of raising doubt where none needs to exist, it should be pointed out that Andrew Oliver, Jr. of Salem was a judge and an inquirer into comets, lightning, water-spouts, and other phenomena interesting to the Society. This Andrew Oliver in 1771 sent the Society a specimen of asbestos and a paper on solar shadows; in August 1772 a letter on comets from "Andrew Oliver Esquire *of Salem* [author's italics]," as the minutes record, was presented to the Society; and on 15 January 1773—again in the words of the minutes—"the Honble Andrew Oliver, *of Boston* [author's italics]" was elected.

The elder Oliver died in 1774. The name of the younger, elected in 1773, should have appeared in the "List of Members . . . elected since . . . the 18th of January, 1771" (and still living) that was printed in Volume II of the *Transactions* in 1786. In fact, his name is not on that list, although he lived until 1799 and two communications from Andrew Oliver "of Salem" are published in the volume.

One need not reach for an ingenious explanation of the confusion; plausible ones will readily occur. The secretaries probably knew little of the Olivers, not even where they lived; and Boston and Salem might have seemed indistinguishable to a Philadelphian. The Society—as no one has hitherto doubted—may very well have elected the elder Oliver in 1768 (he was commissioned lieutenant-governor in October 1770 and sworn in March 1771) and elected his son in 1773. Or—given what is known about how minutes were kept and written up—the Society may have elected the younger Oliver in 1768, discovered that he had been incorrectly identified in the 1771 membership list, and rectified the error by electing him— again—in 1773 (yet perpetuating the error by calling him "of Boston"). Thus the Society may have elected the same man twice—which would not have been the only time in the eighteenth century when that was done.

Without further evidence, however, we must accept it that both Andrew Olivers were members of the Society.

The elder Andrew Oliver, secretary of the province of Massachusetts when he was elected a member of the American Society, was born in Boston on 28 March 1706, the son of Daniel and Elizabeth (Belcher) Oliver.[1] His father was a wealthy merchant and a member of the Governor's Council. Noticeably "Sober and pious" as a boy, Andrew was sent to Harvard College, where he was graduated in 1724. He settled in Boston as a merchant, formed a partnership with his younger brother Peter, and was eventually a proprietor of the Long Wharf and built a warehouse on Oliver's Dock. The brothers did a large trade in wine and textiles, but also, like most merchants, in any commodity that promised them a profit. Opposed to inflationary laws and practices, they signed the merchant's agreement of 1734 to provide credit in the province by issuing bills backed by gold and silver and especially to

---

[1] The principal source of this sketch is Clifford K. Shipton, *Sibley's Harvard Graduates,* VII, 383–413. See also *DAB.*

refuse bills from Rhode Island.² In 1768 Andrew Oliver was one of 22 persons in Boston, including the governor, Thomas Hutchinson, John Hancock, James Bowdoin, and the doctors Gardiner, Clark, Bulfinch, and Lloyd, who kept carriages.³

Oliver was married on 20 June 1728 to Mary, daughter of Colonel Thomas Fitch. They had three children. Two died in infancy; Mary herself died on 26 November 1732, leaving Andrew, who eventually settled in Salem and was elected to the American Philosophical Society in 1773. The year after his wife's death, "lonely & inclined to travel,"⁴ Oliver went to England, where he passed his time among scholars and men of religion. But he was homesick for America. "I own at your age the charms of England were more captivating to my weaker genius," his uncle Jonathan Belcher wrote him, "than they are to the strength of your vertue, & I think you are very happy to find nothing on that side of the water that will allow old England to rival your native country."⁵ He returned home in the summer of 1734 and on 19 December married Mary, daughter of William and Grizzel (Sylvester) Sanford of Newport, Rhode Island. His wife was a sister-in-law of Thomas Hutchinson, with whom the Olivers were to have close personal and political ties for forty years. Andrew and Mary Oliver had fourteen children.

In Boston Oliver became a member of St. John's Masonic Lodge in 1740, advanced to be junior warden, but did not become master of the lodge. He is recorded as joining his neighbors in 1740 in a petition against "the practice of shooting pigeons from the tops of the houses in the town" as actions likely to cause fires and disturb the sick and elderly.⁶ But it was principally to charitable causes and public service that Oliver gave his time and energy. He was especially active in the affairs of Old South Church, Boston, serving on a score of committees ranging from setting pew rents to calling new ministers. He was treasurer and later secretary of the Society for the Propagation of the Gospel in New England for work among the Indians, and oversaw the printing of religious works in Indian languages. In 1753 he was one of the projectors of a linen manufactory to provide work for the Boston poor.⁷ Two years later he was on the committee named to aid the Acadian refugees. In 1772 he purchased from London "a Number of curious Anatomical Preparations" for the use of students of anatomy in connection with the chair endowed at Harvard College by Ezekiel Hersey.⁸

In 1737 Oliver was elected Boston town auditor; he served a year as collector of taxes, and was an overseer of the poor for eighteen years. In this latter post he

² 2 Mass. Hist. Soc., *Proc.,* XVII (1903), 204–08.
³ Ibid., I (1884), 225.
⁴ 6 Mass. Hist. Soc., *Colls.,* VI, 502–03.
⁵ Quoted in Shipton, op. cit., 384.
⁶ Mass. Hist. Soc., *Proc.,* XX (1882–83), 6.
⁷ Justin Winsor, *Memorial History of Boston* (Boston, 1880–81), II, 461.
⁸ *Boston Evening Post,* 16 Nov. 1772.

served on many committees, such as one to obtain cordwood for the poor in winter, another to manage the almshouse, a third to erect a workhouse, to which he also made a large financial gift. For sixteen years he was on the committee that visited the poorer sections of the town, and for twenty-eight years he was on the committee to inspect the schools. In 1764 he was chosen moderator of the town meeting. It was perhaps the zenith of his local popularity.

To these local commitments Oliver added positions of greater responsibility and wider influence. Elected to the House of Representatives in 1742, he served three terms and was then elected to the Council. In 1755 Governor Phips named him secretary of the Province, and he held the office until 1771, when he took office as lieutenant governor.

In 1765 the British Parliament passed the Stamp Act and Oliver, apparently without his solicitation or prior knowledge, was named stamp distributor for Boston. Although privately calling the act a "public Misfortune," he accepted the appointment, even expecting "to reap a private benefit" from it. But Oliver failed completely to anticipate the angry reaction of the citizens to the law; and their anger against him rose when he met and escorted another stamp distributor, Jared Ingersoll, to his jurisdiction of Connecticut. The result was that before daybreak on 14 August the mob hanged Oliver in effigy, razed a newly-constructed building they thought he intended for the stamp office, and then attacked his house. They trampled down the garden, broke in doors and windows, destroyed furniture, smashed china, and terrified the family. The next day Oliver sent a message that he would not act as stamp agent, at which the mob expressed gratification. But when, after a few weeks, it was rumored that Oliver had not in fact resigned but only awaited instructions from London, the mob again demanded a renunciation. He gave it to the newspapers, but it was found wanting. On the next day, 17 December, taken to the same Liberty Tree from which his effigy had hung, he was made to read an "explicit and unreserved" declaration that he had taken no action under his deputation as stamp agent and that he had not and never would, "directly or indirectly, by myself or any under me, make use of the said Deputation, or take any measure for enforcing the Stamp Act in America, which is so grievous to the People." To add to the humiliation, Oliver's declaration was attested by a local justice of the peace.[9] In 1765 Oliver had been reelected to the Council by only three or four votes; in 1766 he was dropped. The General Court eventually allowed Oliver some compensation for the damage done his house and property, but the bill was disallowed by the Privy Council.

In private letters to England Oliver expressed reactions to his own experience and observations on the "turbulent spirits" in Boston. He complained that the government was too weak to cope with them and, concerned for the King's authority,

---

[9] Oliver's renunciation is printed in facsimile in Mass. Hist. Soc., *Proc.,* XII (1871–73), facing 247.

he sought ways "to take off the original incendiaries" else "they will continue to instill their poison into the minds of the people. . . ." The governor, lieutenant governor, and secretary should have larger salaries and those salaries should be paid by the Crown—"such provision I look upon as necessary to the restoration and support of the King's authority." Some alteration in the Massachusetts charter was desirable. He opined that a small group of propertied individuals might be defined and established, from whom only councillors should be selected. As for the policy of the government at London, it was foolhardy to relax the tax laws: such actions did not win the loyalty of the citizens, but emboldened them to further demands.[10] "There was a time," Oliver wrote resignedly,

> when I thought the authority of government might have been easily restored; but while it's friends and the officers of the crown are left to an abject dependance on these very people who are *undermining it's authority;* and while these are suffered not only to go unpunished, but on the contrary meet with all kind of support and encouragement, it cannot be expected that you will ever again recover that respect which the colonies had been wont to pay the parent state.

"Under such circumstances as these," he concluded, recalling his own ordeal, "why should I wish to expose myself to popular resentment?"[11] He greeted the arrival of British regulars in Boston: "We now sleep very easy in our Beds. . . ."

Some of these sentiments were expressed in 1771–72 in a periodical called *The Censor,* formed by the friends of government in response to savage attacks upon Hutchinson in the *Massachusetts Spy.* Oliver is said to have contributed to it.[12]

Meanwhile on 19 October 1770 Oliver had been commissioned lieutenant governor of the Province, succeeding Hutchinson, who became governor; he took office in March 1771.

Some of the letters Oliver wrote to England, as well as some of Hutchinson's, by a means not yet clearly identified, came into possession of Benjamin Franklin, the Massachusetts Assembly's agent in London; and by Franklin they were forwarded to Boston, presented to the House of Representatives, and published. The sensation was immediate and overwhelming. The fury of the Sons of Liberty, though aimed principally at Hutchinson, also fell upon Oliver. His honor was impugned and the House petitioned the Crown to remove him from office. Convinced of the rectitude of his conduct, his health suffered under these buffetings; his wife died, adding to the burdens of body and spirit; and on 1 March 1774 he was "seized suddenly" with "an apoplectick fit," and died two days later.

---

[10] The Hutchinson-Oliver letters are reprinted in *Franklin Papers,* XX, 539–80; Oliver's letters are on pages 551–63.
[11] Ibid., 562, 563.
[12] Isaiah Thomas, *History of Printing in America* (Marcus A. McCorison, ed., N.Y., 1970), 284–85.

The ill will that enveloped Oliver's last months followed him to the grave, where his burial was marked by violence and indecent acts. Warned of that possibility, his brother Peter had thought it best not to attend. Nor, for other reasons, did the Council or more than a few of the House of Representatives. As the grave was closed the Sons of Liberty present cheered in triumph.[13]

Governor Hutchinson praised Oliver as a man of integrity, with a "scrupulous and sacred regard to truth," whose reputation was unjustly tarnished by "the malignant, and forever to be detested spirit of party. . . ." John Eliot, an early biographer of New England worthies, concluded that "had the politicks of the lieut. governor been different, his character would have been very respectable. The family had been greatly beloved, and his abilities were connected with indefatigable industry."[14]

All Oliver's sons except Andrew of Salem remained loyal to the Crown, left Boston, and settled in England or Canada.

JONATHAN BELCHER (1710–1776)
AMERICAN SOCIETY (CORRESPONDING MEMBER):
1 APRIL 1768

JONATHAN BELCHER, Chief Justice of Nova Scotia, was elected a corresponding member of the American Society on 1 April 1768. The choice might be thought an unlikely one. Although Belcher had some knowledge of science and was sufficiently interested in it to have given Harvard College a solar microscope, a pair of globes, and some other instruments, his political views were uncongenial to the majority of American Society members. In the years that he was a member of the Society and its successor, the American Philosophical Society, he had no occasion to visit Philadelphia nor, apparently, did he ever share his philosophical interests with the Society.

---

[13] "Diary of John Rowe," 2 Mass. Hist. Soc., *Proc.,* X (1895–96), 83; Ezra Stiles, *Literary Diary* (Franklin B. Dexter, ed., N.Y., 1901), I, 437.

[14] Thomas Hutchinson, *The History of the Colony and Province of Massachusetts-Bay* (Lawrence S. Mayo, ed., Cambridge, 1936), III, 326–27; John Eliot, *A Biographical Dictionary . . . of the First Settlers . . . in New-England* (Boston, 1809), 348–50. John Adams remarked in 1796 that the papers of the Tories, notably Hutchinson, Oliver, and Jonathan Sewall, if published, would contain "the most authentic history, or the best materials" for a history of the Revolution. James E. Cronin, "John Adams and the History of the American Revolution," *PMHB,* LXXIII (1949), 93.

JONATHAN BELCHER

By John Singleton Copley. *Beaverbrook Art Gallery, Fredericton, New Brunswick, Canada. Gift of the Canadian International Paper Company.*

Born in Boston on 23 July 1710, he was the second son of Jonathan Belcher and his first wife Mary Partridge.[1] The elder Belcher, a rich Boston merchant, who was subsequently governor of Massachusetts and New Hampshire from 1730 to 1741 and of New Jersey from 1747 to 1757, for more than a decade employed his considerable influence and knowledge of the corridors of London power to promote the career of his favorite son.

Jonathan was graduated from Harvard College in 1728, but stayed on for two years studying divinity. In 1731, having been entered at the Middle Temple on 14 March 1729/30, he went to London, "designing," a Boston newspaper reported, "a considerable Stay there by Pursuing his Studies in Accomplishing himself for the Service of his King and Country."[2] Carrying a sheaf of introductions to his father's friends and acquaintances among the great, the young man was received and promoted by Arthur Onslow, Speaker of the House of Commons, the Duke of Newcastle, the Bishop of London, Lord Townshend, and others. It was important, his father believed, that his son "be well acquainted with the King's ministers & at the public offices."[3] Belcher matriculated as a fellow commoner at Trinity College on 19 January 1732/3, and received the degree of master of arts later that year. It cost his father "at least £50—a saucy job." For a time young Jonathan entertained the hope that he might be named a Fellow of Trinity.[4] Not content with studying the common law, he also studied civil law with Francis Dickins and mathematics with Nicholas Sanderson, the Lucasian professor at Cambridge—after all, Governor Belcher reminded his son, the great Lord Chief Justice Sir Matthew Hale had recommended the study of algebra to aspiring lawyers.[5] Meanwhile, completing his legal studies, the young man was called to the English bar on 24 May 1734.

All the time he was in England Jonathan received a steady flow of advice, admonition, and encouragement from his father. The governor's letters, in fact, might have formed a manual of behavior for able and ambitious young men seeking appointment and preferment. The letters of introduction alternately praised the young man and apologized for him as one "born & bred in the wilds of America."[6] There was a flow of gifts from Boston calculated to bring Jonathan to the attention

---

[1] Clifford K. Shipton, *Sibley's Harvard Graduates,* VIII, 343–64; Ralph G. Lounsbury, "Jonathan Belcher, Junior, Chief Justice and Lieutenant Governor of Nova Scotia," *Essays in Colonial History Presented to Charles McLean Andrews by his Students* (New Haven, 1931), 169–97; *Dictionary of Canadian Biography,* IV, 50–54.
[2] E. Alfred Jones, *American Members of the Inns of Court* (London, 1924), 15–16. The quotation is from Shipton, *Sibley's Harvard Graduates,* VIII, 344.
[3] "Belcher Papers," Mass. Hist. Soc., *Colls.,* 6th ser., VI, 6, 21, 23, 24, 26–27, 36, 41, 50, 55, 92.
[4] *Alumni Cantabrigienses,* pt. 1, I, 126; Mass. Hist. Soc., *Colls.,* 6th ser., VI, 270, 490, 516–17.
[5] Ibid., VII, 142–48.
[6] Ibid., VI, 6, 237.

of those with power and influence to do him good: for the Duke of Newcastle, a tea table "made out of the knots of some of our ash trees"; for Horace Walpole, some wild geese; a cage of flying squirrels for the Princess Royal; bayberry candles for the Lord Chancellor and the Lord Chief Justice; a printed religious tract for the Queen.[7] He should cultivate the English, the father advised, and not spend too much time with his fellow Americans at the New England Coffee House. The father advised his son on matters of dress and address, on appropriate recreations, even on the hours at which he should rise and retire. Jonathan wanted to cut his hair; the older man did not approve, then advised him to have the wig made "at the Court End of the town," where, though costing more, it would be "so much more nice & genteel."[8] "Besides being a good lawyer," he assured his son, "I am fond of your being a fine gentm."[9]

The governor was pleased that Jonathan had received a master of arts degree from Cambridge, mostly for the reputation of the thing, and he hoped his son might "nick" a similar degree from Oxford. He made Jonathan his agent in London, along with his brother-in-law Richard Partridge, and the young man appeared as junior counsel in some cases before the Board of Trade and at least once argued a case before the King in Council. When the Bishop of Lincoln in 1734 encouraged Jonathan to stand for Parliament, the young man's father, although not convinced this was a good idea, nevertheless provided the necessary funds for the canvass. Jonathan narrowly lost the election.[10]

All this cost the governor—in eight years in London the young man spent £2673 16s. 3d. sterling, or £334 a year, three times what other young Americans spent; but Jonathan, resolved to live like a gentleman—he kept a servant—made no attempt to curtail his expenses.[11] His father chided him for his extravagances, demanded annual accountings, then threatened to cut off his allowance; but the threats were idle, and Jonathan knew it. "As I think I have a good son," the older man wrote, "depend you have a fond father; therefore make yourself easy & comfortable."[12] The governor might complain, even sometimes grow angry, but until 1741, when he lost his office as governor, he never failed to forward the necessary sums. But despite his expensive education, social success, and powerful contacts, Jonathan seems to have achieved no distinction at the bar, principally, he confessed

---

[7] Ibid., 78, 262–68.
[8] Ibid.
[9] Ibid., 52.
[10] Ibid., 99, 197–205, 284–86, 313–14; VII, 6–8, 10.
[11] The Belcher papers contain a great many letters from Governor Belcher to his son on all these and other matters of personal conduct. See in particular Mass. Hist. Soc., *Colls.*, 6th ser., VI, 169–71, 306; VII, 34–36, 170–73, 272–73, 293, 325–26, 353–54, 430.
[12] Ibid., VI, 78.

honestly, because of "the Number of Gentlemen of Superior Merit and Interest." His father repeatedly urged him to marry some woman of fortune, but Jonathan's inclinations in this direction, though sometimes aroused, were not often or long focused.[13] Finally, in 1741, after nine years in London, with no prospect of greater success, and his father out of favor, he went to Dublin, where his family had relatives.

There after five years he received the modest appointment of deputy secretary to the Lord Chancellor of Ireland, with a salary of £150 a year. In 1754 he and Edward Bullingbrooke published *An Abridgement of the Statutes of Ireland.* Perhaps it was for this evidence of legal scholarship as well as by the recommendation of Lord Hardwicke, chief justice of England, that in response to an appeal from the governor of Nova Scotia to the Board of Trade for the appointment of a chief justice, Belcher was named to the post. The salary was £500 a year. He was received as a member of the Council on 14 October 1754 and, with a display of considerable pomp, was installed as chief justice one week later.

The year after his arrival at Halifax Belcher visited his family in Boston and went on to New Jersey, where he saw his father, now governor of that province, and made efforts—which proved unsuccessful—to obtain the lieutenant governorship and the succession to his father as governor. He did, however, acquire a third master's degree, from the College of New Jersey. Before returning to Nova Scotia Belcher was married at King's Chapel in Boston on 8 April 1756 to Abigail, daughter of Jeremiah and Abigail (Waldo) Allen of that town. The couple had five sons and two daughters, of whom only one son and one daughter survived their father.

Belcher was the first law officer in Nova Scotia formally trained in the law. As chief justice he set about at once to establish and organize his court. The Supreme Court's jurisdiction extended to criminal cases and to those involving debts above a stated amount. It heard appeals from the lower courts of common pleas, and it had the duty of proclaiming acts of Council. Rejecting the long-standing practice of following precedents from the Massachusetts courts, Belcher introduced the forms and practices of the English courts. His portrait, in the rich scarlet gown of a high court judge, dramatically made the point. Jealous of his prerogatives, Belcher defended the rights of the judiciary, resisting any who sought to encroach upon them. In addition to strictly judicial duties, Belcher was called on for constitutional advice and services. Although he had held that the sparse and scattered population of the province justified the validity of laws promulgated by the governor and Council, when the argument was rejected by the Board of Trade, he presented a plan for a representative assembly somewhat on the plan of the English parliament. The first Assembly met in 1758, and Belcher became at that time a member of the Legislative Council. He was consulted by the Assembly in drafting laws. In this

---

[13] Ibid., 516–17.

work he favored the idea that English laws were extended to the provinces with the settlers; but the position was rejected by the Board of Trade.

In March 1761 Belcher was commissioned lieutenant governor of Nova Scotia, and, in the absence of Governor Henry Ellis, functioned as governor. A man of aristocratic temperament, unsympathetic to the Halifax merchants, who were the province's political leaders, Belcher was often in conflict with the legislature. He was in the awkward position of having to defend acts of favor, extravagance, and corruption of his predecessor. He concluded treaties with the Indians and encouraged new settlements, supported the Church of England, and sought to restrict the rum industry. But he was a poor administrator, exceeded the annual budgets, and was warned by the Board of Trade to use "the exactest economy in the application of Public Money." His enemies charged him with being "unacquainted with and unskilled in the Art of Government."

Alarmed by a French raid on Newfoundland in 1762, Belcher ordered the Acadians there to be deported to Boston, despite assurances from General Amherst that they posed no threat. When Massachusetts refused to accept them, they were sent back, to the mortification of the lieutenant governor. Belcher's unpopularity, the political problems of his administration, as well as sound constitutional principles led the Board of Trade to determine, when naming Governor Ellis' successor, that the chief justice, though he might be senior councillor, might not exercise executive powers in event of the governor's absence. Belcher was removed as lieutenant governor in September 1763, but remained as a member and president of the Council, as well as chief justice, from 1764 until his death. Two associate justices were added to the Nova Scotia Supreme Court in 1764; although Belcher dominated them and his court, their presence was at least an indication that the court was now composed of several men and minds.

Of Belcher's character and career a modern historian has written:

> Fundamentally a conservative Englishman, he was just enough an American to cause dissatisfaction and distrust when he came to hold high colonial office. Like many others among the increasing number of Americans who were entering the royal service in the colonies in the eighteenth century, he was one of that hybrid type, the pre-Revolutionary loyalist—neither native Englishman nor whole-hearted American—seldom fully understood by contemporaries in either country.[14]

After his removal from the office of lieutenant governor, Belcher lived a quiet and mainly studious life. In 1767 he published a revision and annotation of the first volume of the laws of Nova Scotia—the *Perpetual Acts of the Province of Nova Scotia to 1766*—and the next year he supervised an index of English cases acknowledged to be applicable to the colonies.

---

[14] Lounsbury, "Jonathan Belcher, Junior," loc. cit., 196.

Belcher was an active member of St. Paul's Church in Halifax, having been converted to the Church of England in 1740. As a corresponding commissioner of the Society for the Propagation of the Gospel in Nova Scotia, he interested himself in educational and missionary work among the Indians. From 1760 until his death he was Grand Master of the Grand Lodge of Masons in Nova Scotia.[15]

With the outbreak of hostilities in New England in 1775, Belcher organized a Loyalist Association in Nova Scotia. His health, however, was failing; he soon ceased attending meetings of the Council, and on 2 January 1776 he petitioned the King to resign the chief justiceship on account of age and infirmity. He died at Halifax less than two months later, on 29 March 1776, before action could be taken on his request. He left a son and a daughter, and died intestate and insolvent.

JEREMIAH DIXON (1733–1779)
AMERICAN SOCIETY (CORRESPONDING MEMBER):
1 APRIL 1768

JEREMIAH DIXON, surveyor and astronomer, was first proposed for membership in the American Society on 20 March 1767, the same day as his colleague Charles Mason. Mason and others were elected at the next meeting, but for some reason Dixon was not. A year later Dixon was proposed again, and on 1 April was chosen a corresponding member. He never attended the Society, and on 8 September 1768 departed Philadelphia for New York, passage to Falmouth, and home.

He was born on 27 July 1733 at Bishop Auckland, County Durham, England, the fifth of eight children of George and Mary (Hunter) Dixon. George Dixon, who described himself in his will as a "yeoman," owned and operated a coal mine on Cockfield Fell, prospered moderately, and died possessed of at least three houses. The Dixons belonged to the Quaker meeting at Raby, though George was not an exemplary member, for, as its minutes record and he publicly confessed, he was guilty of the "loathsome practice of Gitting too much Drink." Jeremiah's older brother George was later distinguished as a naturalist, inventor, and artist. He himself was sent to John Kipling's school at Barnard Castle, where he is said to have displayed aptitude for mathematics and astronomy. For a time young Dixon worked at his father's colliery—the "pit on Cockfield Fell," where, as he told his examiners at the Royal Military Academy at Woolwich, he learned astronomy. Ultimately

---

[15] Ronald S. Longley and Reginald V. Harris, *A Short History of Freemasonry in Nova Scotia, 1738–1966* (Halifax, 1966), 19–20.

Dixon made the acquaintance of William Emerson, the celebrated mathematician from Hurworth, County Durham, and of John Bird, mathematical instrument-maker, a native of County Durham, who had settled in London. But Cockfield offered little scope for Dixon's talents, he fell into his father's bad habits, and on 28 October 1760 was disowned by Raby Monthly Meeting "for drinking to excess."[1]

Probably the censure meant little to him for he had already left his village for London and his destiny. In 1760 the Royal Society decided that observations should be made of the Transit of Venus that was to take place the next year. They obtained the cooperation of the Lords of Admiralty and the directors of the East India Company, and on 11 September they engaged Charles Mason, assistant to Dr. James Bradley, Astronomer Royal, to head an expedition to Bencoolen in Sumatra. Dixon was then recommended as his assistant, and at the same salary of £200. Dixon replied at once on 19 September, accepting the invitation "to accompany Mr. Mason, and be under his directions in respect to taking the Observations in India (at Bencoolen) according to the Terms proposed by the Society." Dixon signed his contract with the Society at London on 23 October.[2]

The equipment was put on board on 24 November; but there were vexatious delays in fitting out the vessel and from weather. By 19 December the captain had still received no orders to sail, and Mason and Dixon were growing apprehensive lest the vessel be detained still longer. Not until 8 January—too late, as Mason and Dixon now feared, to reach Sumatra in time—did the vessel sail. Within 48 hours misfortune overtook the *Sea Horse*, as Dixon reported from Plymouth on 12 January:

> Please to acquaint the Council of the Royal Society, that on Thursday the 8th Inst: about 2 in the Afternoon we set sail, & had fair Winds and good runing [sic], till Saturday in the Morning; when we were chas'd by the L'Grand a French Ship of 34 Guns, which at 11 o Clock came up with us; ... when the Action began, which lasted about 1 hour 10 Minutes, she then leaving us, tho' all the sail possible was made to keep up with her. Our loss amounts to 11 kill'd and 37 Wounded, (a great many of which are mortal,) our Riging [sic] and Masts are very much damaged being rendered quite unfit for service, and her Hull much wounded.
>
> This being the State of the Ship after the Action ended, obliged us to make the best of our way to this place to be refitted; which will take up so much time that it will be impossible for us to reach India soon enough to make the Observations upon the

---

[1] H. W. Robinson, "Jeremiah Dixon (1733–1779)—A Biographical Note," APS *Proc.*, XCIV (1950), 272–74; Norman Penney, *My Ancestors* (privately printed, 1920), 187–93; H. P. Hollis, "Jeremiah Dixon and his Brother," *Jour. British Astronomical Assoc.*, XLIV (1933–34), 294–99; [Arthur R. Hinks], "Jeremiah Dixon's Theodolite," *Geographical Jour.*, XLVII (1916), 1–3; *DSB*.

[2] "Information concerning Bencoolen, with regard to observing the Transit of Venus there," 28 June 1760; "Memorandum of a Conversation with the Directors of the East India Company . . . ," 2 July 1760 (Royal Society, Ms. MM. 10.104, 105); Royal Society Council, Minutes, 14 July, 11, 25 Sept. 1760; Harry Woolf, *The Transit of Venus* (Princeton, 1959), 86, 87.

Transit; and therefore desire to know the Societies [sic] Pleasure in regard to our future proceedings.³

The refitting proceeded slowly. As the days rolled by, the astronomers grew increasingly impatient, then despaired of being able to discharge their obligation. On 25 January they wrote Dr. Charles Morton, secretary of the Royal Society:

> It is our Opinion, as well as those of some sagatious [sic] Friends, that 'tis absolutely impossible for us to reach any port by way of the Cape proper for making the Observation that will have East Longitude sufficient to be of any use to compare with those made at Greenwich and St. Helena. We find no place on the Globe which we can reach to be of as great consequence as one made at Scanderoon. . . .

They would gladly go there if directed by the Council, but they would "not proceed from this, to any other Place, where it is impossible for us to perform what the World in general reasonably expect from us. . . ."⁴ Similar letters went to other officers of the Society. To Thomas Birch on 27 January Mason and Dixon wrote that they were "very willing to sail to any Part of the World the Council shall think proper to command us, provided it can possibly be reach'd in time . . . [but] we shall be very sorry to proceed from this Place, to any other, where the Society (as time stands) can gain no Honour, or we any Reputation, and to go to India merely for the Premium is an Intention far from our first Design."⁵

This determination by their agents astonished the Society, which sternly reminded them in reply that they were under contract. "To prevent all possibility of Doubt concerning their Undertaking the Voyage, or omitting to go, The Councils do absolutely and expressly direct and require Mr. Mason and Mr. Dixon, to go on board and enter upon the Voyage, be the Event as it may fall out." The Council did, however, authorize the astronomers to take the captain's advice and use their own judgment about a proper location for the observatory. Mason and Dixon capitulated.⁶ On 3 February they wrote Dr. Morton again:

> . . . we are very sorry the council . . . interpreted our good Intentions (as we thought) in such a Light as they have: We shall to our best Endeavours make good the trust they have pleas'd to confer in us. We are and hope to be found their dutiful Servants.
> P.S. We hope to sail this Evening.⁷

---

3   Dixon to Thomas Birch, 12 Jan. 1761 (British Library; copy in APS).
4   Charles Mason and Dixon to Charles Morton, 25 Jan. 1761. Except as otherwise indicated, this and other letters of Mason and Dixon cited here are in "Letters and Papers relating to their observation of the Transit of Venus, 1761," in Royal Society, London, MM. 10. 104–51.
5   Charles Mason and Dixon to Thomas Birch, 27 Jan. 1761.
6   "Sketch of a Letter to Messrs. Mason and Dixon," [31 Jan. 1761].
7   Charles Mason and Dixon to [Thomas Birch], 3 Feb. 1761.

Accordingly they decided to go ashore at the Cape of Good Hope, where they remained from April until October.

> We arrived here the 27th of last Month, having had an exceeding good Passage from St. Cruz Bay, and as it is the Captain's Opinion that we can proceed no further with certainty so as to be at any Settlement in India before the 6th of June; (without allowing us any Time to adjust the Clock, build an Observatory, &c;) he has thought proper to land us at this Place, where we are making all the dispatch possible to erect our Observatory, which I hope will be ready in a Week's time after the Date of this.
> All our Instruments are in good Order, from which and a clear Sky at the time of Observation I hope we shall be able to give as good an Acct. of the Phenomena as the Situation we are in upon the Earth's Surface will permit.[8]

The observations were duly made, and on 12 October Mason and Dixon joined Nevil Maskelyne at St. Helena. They returned to Plymouth at last on 7 April 1762, and at once presented their reports to the Royal Society.[9]

The observations Mason and Dixon made at the Cape of Good Hope and with Maskelyne at St. Helena on the voyage home won them no small reputation, as well as the approbation and support of influential members of the scientific community, notably Maskelyne, who was to become Astronomer Royal in a few years. Accordingly, after the Proprietors of Pennsylvania and Maryland agreed in 1760 to settle the ancient boundary dispute between their respective provinces and recognized that the solution was not political but scientific, they looked about for qualified surveyors to do the job. The team that had worked so effectively at the Cape was recommended, and promptly engaged. Mason and Dixon lost no time in collecting their instruments, and on 15 November 1763 they reached Philadelphia, met the next day with the Pennsylvania commissioners, and so began the work that made their names synonymous with a lasting political, social, and economic boundary in the United States.

For nearly five years Dixon worked with Charles Mason on terms of perfect equality and harmony—establishing bases and testing their instruments, taking observations, making innumerable tedious calculations, hiring and supervising gangs of laborers to cut the "vistos" and place the marker stones; and then, when they had finished the boundary survey, undertaking for the Royal Society a new series of observations and measurements, with permission of Lord Baltimore and Thomas Penn, to determine the length of a degree of longitude. Only when winter came and they dismissed their crews and suspended work until spring, did the men

---

[8] Dixon to Thomas Birch, 6 May 1761 (British Library; copy in APS).
[9] Charles Mason and Dixon, "Observations made at the Cape of Good Hope," *Phil. Trans.,* LII (1762), 378–94; "Mason and Dixon's Expences &c. to the Accompt of the Royal Society."

separate. Only then does the journal of the expedition, usually so impersonal, terse, and mathematical, break out into any personal reaction. The men worked as superb professionals, they appear never to have had a falling out either with one another or with their principals, and they left America as they came—together. Several years later, perhaps reflecting on his years in Pennsylvania and Maryland, Dixon subscribed for a copy of Peter Kalm's *Travels into North America* (Warrington, 1770–71).

It is no more possible to distinguish the work of Dixon from that of Mason in the great survey of 1763–68 than to divide the Mason and Dixon line itself. The story of that memorable collaboration is told in the sketch of Charles Mason; unchanged, it might equally appropriately have appeared here.[10]

On 3 June 1769 another transit of Venus was to take place; and once again the Royal Society called on Dixon, this time to lead an expedition alone. He was sent to Hammerfest in Norway (Mason went to Ireland), where he arrived on 7 May. "After much search and travel" he found a suitable spot and erected the house and observatory. His instruments included a quadrant of one-foot radius made by Bird, a two-foot reflector with achromatic object glass and micrometer by Dolland, a four-foot transit instrument by Bird, with an achromatic object glass made by Dolland, a barometer, an astronomical clock, a journeyman clock, and an alarm clock. With William Bayley, who observed the transit at the North Cape, Dixon made "A Chart of the Sea Coast and Islands near the North Cape of Europe," which was published, with the two men's observations, in the *Philosophical Transactions*.[11]

Of Dixon's life after his return from Hammerfest little is known. He settled at Cockfield, where he lived the comfortable life of a "gentleman" and sometimes practiced his profession of surveying. In Auckland Castle, for example, is "A plan of the Park and Demesne at Auckland Castle, belonging to The Right Revd. Father in God, John Egerton Lord Bishop of Durham. Taken in 1772 by Jere. Dixon." In 1773 he was elected a Fellow of the Royal Society.

Dixon never married, but there is a curious clause in his will, by which he left his copyhold houses, garth, gardens, dye houses, and premises in the manor of Bondgate in Auckland in trust and for the benefit of one Margaret Bland, the income of the same to go to the maintenance of the two daughters of the said Margaret. Dixon died at Cockfield on 22 January 1779, and was buried in Friends ground at Staindrop.[12]

---

[10] See the sketch of Mason in this volume; also A. Hughlett Mason, transcriber, *The Journal of Charles Mason and Jeremiah Dixon* (APS *Memoirs*, LXXVI, 1969) and Hubertis M. Cummings, *The Mason and Dixon Line* (Harrisburg, Pa., 1963).
[11] Dixon, "Observations made on the Island of Hammerfest, for the Royal Society," *Phil. Trans.*, LIX (1769), 253–61. Bayley's observations are ibid., 262–72, the Chart of the Sea Coast facing p. 272.
[12] Robinson, "Jeremiah Dixon," loc. cit., 273–74.

ALPHABETICAL LIST OF MEMBERS, 1743–1768

Alexander, James, 86
Alexander "gardiner", James, 476
Alison, Francis, 149
Bard, Samuel, 373
Bartram, Isaac, 247
Bartram, John, 48
Bartram, Moses, 280
Bartram, William, 414
Belcher, Jonathan, 519
Bensel, Charles, 497
Bettle, William, 303
Biddle, Clement, 321
Biddle, Owen, 292
Bond, Phineas, 79
Bond, Thomas, 37
Bryan, George, 197
Chapman, John, 424
Chevalier, Peter, 207
Clayton, John, 166
Clymer, George, 236
Colden, Cadwallader, 110
Coleman, William, 15
Coxe, John, 103
Davis/Davies, "Mercht.", Benjamin, 306
DeLancey, James, 120
Dickinson, John, 383
Dixon, Jeremiah, 525
DuSimitière, Pierre E., 504
Eldridge, Samuel, 304
Eliot, Samuel, 468
Evans, Cadwalader, 391
Evans, David, 396
Eve, Oswell, 465
"Mr. Faries", 148
Franklin, Benjamin, 19
Franklin, William, 219
Godfrey, Thomas, 62
Harrison, Joseph, 488
Harrison, Peter, 492
Henry, William, 348
Home, Archibald, 101
Hopkins, Stephen, 481
Hopkins, William, 232

Hopkinson, Thomas, 10
Horsmanden, Daniel, 125
Howell, Joshua, 229
Jackson, Paul, 233
Jamineau, Isaac, 427
Johnson, William, 361
Lukens, John, 314
Martin, David, 105
Mason, Charles, 366
Mather, Joseph, 209
Mercer, Hugh, 447
Mifflin, Thomas, 400
Mitchell, John, 138
Morgan, John, 327
Morris, Jr., John, 411
Morris, Robert Hunter, 94
Murray, Joseph, 130
Nicholls, Richard, 107
Odell, Jonathan, 429
Oliver "of Salem", Andrew, 514
Parsons, William, 72
Paschall, Isaac, 212
Paschall, Joseph, 290
Pearson, James, 251
Physick, Edmund, 214
Powel, Samuel, 257
Rawle, Francis, 203
Rhoads, Samuel, 67
Roberts, George, 277
Robinson, Samuel, 480
Rush, Benjamin, 452
Sellers, John, 500
Smith, William, 134
Syng, Philip, 210
Tennent, John, 158
Thomson, Charles, 183
Waln, Nicholas, 308
Wells, Richard, 440
Wharton, Thomas, 270
Wister, Daniel, 275
Woolley, Stephen, 205
Zane, Isaac, 286

A cumulative name and subject index will be printed in the last volume of the work. Reflections and observations on the entire membership may also be included in the final volume.